"Pritam Singh and Asha Bhandarker's new book *In Search of Change Maestros* is by far the most profound book written by them ever. The common dimensions of Change Maestros encapsulate all of the significant elements of highly successful leaders and when embedded in the stories of seven extraordinary change agents of history, they bring out the understanding of what such leaders are about to all of us in a powerful and provocative way. Their contribution is both an inspiration and a guide to what we all aspire to do and hope to find in others."

— *Roger R. Stough*
NOVA Endowed Chair and Professor of Public Policy and
Vice President for Research and Economic Development,
George Mason University,
USA

"The most misused and least understood words in management are 'change' and 'strategy.' Very few people understand what change and strategy really mean. Although dozens of books are produced every year on these themes, hardly any of them provide meaningful insights into the complexities and nuances of crafting strategy and managing change. It is particularly true in the complex environment in which we live and, therefore, strategy cannot be practiced without relevant boundary conditions. In this context, this book, *In Search of Change Maestros*, is a unique contribution. It provides powerful and meaningful insights on change, strategy, and role of the leader. I highly recommend this book to all leaders and those aspiring to become Change Maestros."

— *Analjit Singh*
Founder and Chairman,
Max India Ltd

"During a period where change leadership is in short supply globally, the authors have provided us with an amazing book containing some outstanding examples of change leaders from India. By following a systematic scientific analysis and thorough research the authors have discussed the leadership characteristics of seven prolific leaders, their profiles, as well as the key characteristics of the organizational culture they were able to instill in their organizations, which made them role models with universal appeal. With subtle accurate movements of their baton-pen, they highlight the variations of each personality in a harmonious and well-coordinated way, so as to bring to surface the elements that make each one of them a great leader. An outstanding research and practice book, a must read for everybody involved in bringing change in an organization."

— *Gregory Prastacos*
Rector, Athens University of Economics and Business,
Greece

"*In Search of Change Maestros* reads like an odyssey in the inner spaces of leadership. The authors have woven together a constellation of seven of the brightest stars of corporate India in a narrative that is both credible and compelling. Pritam Singh and Asha Bhandarker have brought about a unique symphony of insights that will help the reader grasp finer nuances in the artistry of leaders who have brought about fundamental changes in the beliefs and practices of millions of people in India. This book celebrates our home-grown heroes without apology or inhibition! It is a telescopic vision of the vast mindscape of transformational leadership. In this, the authors are pathfinders. The dizzying array of stories, cases, and evidence-based concepts will be a part of our academic and corporate folklore for many years to come."

— *Debashis Chatterjee*
Director,
IIM Kozhikode, India

"Pritam Singh and Asha Bhandarker's selection of the cast of Change Maestros in the book *In Search of Change Maestros* is remarkable for its extensive representation: a young inheritor; an empire builder; an indomitable entrepreneur; a tenacious innovator; a righteous bureaucrat; an expansionist technocrat; and a prescient banker. It highlights the fundamentals of the game-changing moves adopted by Change Maestros to build excellent organizations through case studies of some of India's celebrated business strategists. I strongly recommend this book to all managers, corporate CEOs, future business leaders, scholars, and academia."

— *Rekha Sethi*
Director General, All India Management Association (AIMA),
New Delhi, India

"This book reflects a magnificent understanding of what leads to building great Indian corporations. It shows how outstanding Indian leaders have woven growth and people power, keeping in view cultural uniqueness, into the organizational fabric for creating outstanding and globally competing organizations. It is definitely the book you must read if you wish to seek inspiration and gain understanding of the intricacies for managing change."

— *Alfredo Behrens*
Professor of Management, FIA, University of Sao Paulo,
Brazil

"After a long time, I read a management book that is not only original and backed by solid research but also lucidly narrated. The book *In Search of Change Maestros* clearly brings out a framework that combines ancient Indian wisdom of business excellence with deep understanding of 21st century leadership requirements for managing global competition. I congratulate the authors for the painstaking and in-depth digging into the minds of iconic Change Maestros to identify the drivers of leadership, strategic thinking, and change management. This book will be an invaluable asset for every manager around the world who aspires to make a difference to society and organizations."

— *Arun K. Jain*
Professor and Chairman, Center for Accelerated Learning,
Innovation and Competitiveness,
Heilbronn, Germany

"This book is an eye opener and a treatise on India's corporate czars. It has successfully bridged the gap on meaningful awareness of towering personalities in the Indian corporate sector. The book proves the age-old point that power of the written word is what can make these leaders famous far and wide. *In Search of Change Maestros* is a serious research work presented in a lucid style. One of the many inferences which I drew from the book was that thoughtful collaboration is a superior method to combat mindless and cut-throat competition."

— *K.R. Kamath*
Chairman and Managing Director, Punjab National Bank,
India

"An excellent and mind boggling work, *In Search of Change Maestros* beautifully dovetails research with flowing narrative. Depth and scale of this book are fascinating. This scholarly work supported by rich data with rigorous analysis quenches the thirst of the practitioner as well as the serious academic. I consider *In Search of Change Maestros* an essential reading for budding managers and practicing executives dreaming to become Change Maestros."

— *R. Ravi Kumar*
Chairman and Senior Professor-OB Area,
IIM Bangalore, India

"This is the age of India and China. Both countries are net importers of natural resources. Yet, they are to and will likely remain the two fastest growing major economies in the world for the next few decades. This is as stark an evidence as any that human capital has a far stronger impact on economic and social development than is ever possible from an abundance of natural resources. Even in comparison with China, India stands out for the organizational and managerial capabilities of its corporate leaders. In terms of macroeconomic indicators, China is currently far ahead of India. However, if we look at the organizational strength of its large companies, India handily beats China. This fascinating book by Pritam Singh and Asha Bhandarker offers valuable insights into the factors that make many of India's corporate leaders Change Maestros par excellence. The corporate leaders profiled in this book are likely to emerge as highly regarded legends on the global stage over the next 10–15 years."

— *Anil K. Gupta*
INSEAD Chaired Professor of Strategy,
INSEAD, Singapore
and Co-Author of *Getting China and India Right*

"Pritam Singh and Asha Bhandarker provide in their work in-depth research and analytical and integrative skills that make this book a highly significant contribution to the literature on Indian wealth creators and innovative business leaders."

— *Pradip N. Khandwalla*
Former Director,
IIM Ahmedabad, India

"The book brings out the unique essence of leadership qualities of proven corporate leaders who could leave an indelible mark in the annals of driving change through innovation and foresight. A must book for every aspiring change leader."

— *M.D. Mallya*
Chairman and Managing Director,
Bank of Baroda, India

"The seven change maestros whose stories of leadership, quest for excellence, entrepreneurial innovation, value-driven governance and empowerment to people presented in this book are truly the icons for the new generation leaders. They represent amongst themselves a wide spectrum of corporate India, from first generation entrepreneurs to established house, from public owned private institution to public sector institution, I compliment Dr. Pritam Singh and Dr. Asha Bhandarker for this excellent work. The book not only highlights the life story of these iconic heroes of vibrant and emerging India but also their exemplary contribution to the nation. This is a must read for the middle & senior level executives, start-up entrepreneurs, administrators and even academicians to gain valuable insights."

— *M.V. Nair*
Chairman and Managing Director
Union Bank of India

"In 1982 Tom Peters wrote his all time best seller IN SEARCH OF EXCELLENCE which had a lasting impact on millions of people. Now Dr. Pritam Singh and Dr. Asha Bhandarker have come up with a brilliant book, IN SEARCH OF CHANGE MAESTROS. I am positive that this book too will bring a major change in thinking of Management Practitioners, Academia and Students."

— *Sudhir Jalan*
Industrialist, India

IN SEARCH OF CHANGE MAESTROS

IN SEARCH OF CHRIST'S STACE

IN SEARCH OF CHANGE MAESTROS

PRITAM SINGH AND ASHA BHANDARKER

Research Team
Ajay Jain
Sumita Rai

Copyright © Pritam Singh and Asha Bhandarker, 2011

All rights reserved. No part of this book may be reproduced or utilized in any form or by any means, electronic or mechanical, including photocopying, recording or by any information storage or retrieval system, without permission in writing from the publisher.

First published in 2011 by

SAGE Response
B1/I-1 Mohan Cooperative Industrial Area
Mathura Road, New Delhi 110 044, India

SAGE Publications Inc
2455 Teller Road
Thousand Oaks, California 91320, USA

SAGE Publications Ltd
1 Oliver's Yard, 55 City Road
London EC1Y 1SP, United Kingdom

SAGE Publications Asia-Pacific Pte Ltd
33 Pekin Street
#02-01 Far East Square
Singapore 048763

Published by Vivek Mehra for SAGE Publications India Pvt Ltd, typeset in 10/16 Aldine401 BT by Tantla Composition Pvt Ltd, Chandigarh and printed at Sai Print-o-Pack, New Delhi

Fourth Printing 2016

Library of Congress Cataloging-in-Publication Data

Singh, P. (Pritam)
   In search of Change Maestros/Pritam Singh, Asha Bhandarker.
      p. cm.
   Includes bibliographical references and index.
   1. Chief executive officers—India—Biography. 2. Leadership—India—Case studies. 3. Creative ability in business—India—Case studies. 4. Business ethics—India—Case studies. I. Bhandarker, Asha. II. Title.

| HD38.25.I4S564 | 388.092'254—dc22 | 2011 | 2010053794 |

ISBN: 978-81-321-0586-2 (HB)

The SAGE Team: Rekha Natarajan, Sushmita Banerjee, Rajib Chatterjee, and Deepti Saxena

To my wife Saroj Singh,
Mohit Chawla, my son-in-law, and
my dear grandchildren:
Akanksha, Vihan, Nishank, Varun, Viraj, Virat, and Anvit.
Pritam Singh

To my precious nephews: Ashish and Advik, and
my loving parents Venkatesh and Vilasini.
Asha Bhandarker

Thank you for choosing a SAGE product! If you have any comment, observation or feedback, I would like to personally hear from you. Please write to contactceo@sagepub.in

—Vivek Mehra, Managing Director and CEO,
SAGE Publications India Pvt Ltd, New Delhi

Bulk Sales

SAGE India offers special discounts for purchase of books in bulk. We also make available special imprints and excerpts from our books on demand.

For orders and enquiries, write to us at

Marketing Department
SAGE Publications India Pvt Ltd
B1/I-1, Mohan Cooperative Industrial Area
Mathura Road, Post Bag 7
New Delhi 110044, India
E-mail us at marketing@sagepub.in

Get to know more about SAGE, be invited to SAGE events, get on our mailing list. Write today to marketing@sagepub.in

This book is also available as an e-book.

CONTENTS

List of Tables ix
List of Figures xii
List of Abbreviations xiii
Foreword by Brijmohan Lall Munjal xix
Preface xxvi
Acknowledgments xxxiv

1. Change Maestros' Kaleidoscope 1
2. **KUMAR MANGALAM BIRLA:** Looking Within, Looking Around, and Looking Beyond 45
3. **MELEVEETIL DAMODARAN:** Renaissance Artiste 95
4. **SAJJAN JINDAL:** Romancing Limitless Growth 151
5. **KUNDAPUR VAMAN KAMATH:** Enfolding the Future within the Present 195
6. **SUNIL BHARTI MITTAL:** The Game Changer 249
7. **ANIL MANIBHAI NAIK:** Toward the Next Orbit 295
8. **KIRAN MAZUMDAR SHAW:** Entrepreneurial Path Breaker 355
9. **CHANGE MAESTROS:** Action Architecture and Persona 409
10. Change Maestros' Gestalt 443

References 463
Index 471
About the Authors and Research Team 479

LIST OF TABLES

1.1:	Change Maestros	34
1.2:	Sample Details—Questionnaire- and Interview-based	35
2A.1:	Accolades to K.M. Birla over the Last Decade, 1998–2009	77
2A.2:	Accolades to Aditya Birla Group over the Last Decade, 1998–2009	84
2A.3:	Perceived Organizational Culture of the Aditya Birla Group	88
2A.4:	Sales and Profit of Five Companies under the Aditya Birla Group from 2003 to 2009 (in ₹ billion)	90
2A.5:	Perceived Style of K.M. Birla as a Change Maestro	91
3A.1:	Accolades to M. Damodaran over the Last Decade, 2003–2008	138
3A.2:	Recognition and Accolades to UTI Mutual Fund during Mr Damodaran's Tenure, 2002–2006	140
3A.4:	Perceived Organizational Culture of UTI and IDBI	145
3A.5:	Perceived Style of Damodaran as a Change Maestro	147
4A.1:	Recognition and Accolades to JSW Steel Ltd, 2006–2008	187
4A.2:	Accolades to Sajjan Jindal	188
4A.3:	Perceived Organizational Culture of JSW	189
4A.4:	Sales and Profit of JSW Steel Ltd, 2003–2009 (in ₹ billion)	191
4A.5:	Perceived Style of Sajjan Jindal as a Change Maestro	192

5A.1:	Recognitions and Accolades to ICICI Bank, 2007–2008	238
5A.2:	Accolades to K.V. Kamath, 2000–2008	239
5A.3:	Perceived Organizational Culture of ICICI Bank	240
5A.4:	Revenue and Profit of ICICI Bank, 2003–2009 (in ₹ billion)	243
5A.5:	Perceived Style of K.V. Kamath as a Change Maestro	243
6A.1:	Accolades to Sunil Bharti Mittal over the Last Decade, 2000–2009	279
6A.2:	Recognition and Accolades to Bharti Airtel, 2003–2008	286
6A.3:	Perceived Organizational Culture of Bharti Airtel	288
6A.4:	Revenue and Profit of Bharti Airtel from 2003 to 2009 (in ₹ billion)	290
6A.5:	Perceived Style of Sunil Mittal as a Change Maestro	291
7A.1a:	Projects Undertaken by L&T in Major Core and Infrastructure Sectors of the Indian Industry	341
7A.1b:	Recent Recognition and Accolades for L&T	344
7A.2:	Accolades to A.M. Naik, 2008–2009	346
7A.3:	Perceived Organizational Culture of L&T	348
7A.4:	Revenue and Profit of Larsen & Toubro, 2003–2009 (in ₹ billion)	351
7A.5:	Perceived Style of A.M. Naik as a Change Maestro	351
8A.1:	Recognition and Accolades to Biocon Ltd over the Last Decade, 2000–2009	400
8A.2:	Accolades to Kiran Mazumdar Shaw over the Last Decade, 1999–2009	402
8A.3:	Perceived Organizational Culture of Biocon	403
8A.4:	Sales and Profit of Biocon Ltd, 2003–2009 (in ₹ billion)	405
8A.5:	Perceived Style of Kiran Mazumdar Shaw as a Change Maestro	405
9.1:	Means, Standard Deviations, and Ranks	412
9.2:	Comparative Picture of Organizational Culture	414

9.3:	Rank Order Coefficients of Correlation across Twenty-one Company Pairs	415
9.4:	Factors, Eigenvalues, Explained Variance, and Scale Reliability of Organizational Culture Items	417
9.5:	Overall Mean Values of Change Maestros' Profile	419
9.6:	Change Maestros' Dominant Profile	421
9.7:	Change Maestros' Self-assessment vs. Perceived Profile	422
9.8:	Rank Order Coefficients of Correlation across Twenty-one Change Maestros' Pairs	423
9.9:	Factors, Eigenvalues, Explained Variance, and Scale Reliability of Change Maestros' Profile Items	424
9.10:	Comparison of Percentage Change in Revenue and Profit across the Seven Organizations Over Time	428
9A.1a:	Rotated Component Matrix of Organizational Culture	430
9A.1b:	Rotated Component Matrix of Change Maestro Behavior	434
9A.1c:	Means, SDs, Inter-correlations among the Sub-scales of Change Maestro Behavior Inventory and Organizational Culture Inventory	438
9A.2a:	Fit Measures of the Measurement Model	439
9A.2b:	Fit Measures of the Path Model	440

LIST OF FIGURES

1.1:	Model of Change Maestros	6
5A.1:	Operations of ICICI Bank	234
8A.1:	The Innovation Matrix of Biocon	397
8A.2:	Businesses of Biocon	399
9.1:	Factors of Organizational Culture	417
9.2:	Factors of Change Maestros' Behavior	425
9.3:	Change Maestros' Impact on Organizational Culture	427
10.1:	Integration at the Self Level	454
10.2:	Integration at the Organizational Level	455
10.3:	Change Maestros—Holistic Integration at all Three Levels	456

LIST OF ABBREVIATIONS

2G	Second Generation
3G	Third Generation
AAG	Asia America Gateway
ABB	Asea Brown Boveri
ABMCPL	Aditya Birla Management Corporation Pvt Ltd
ADB	Asian Development Bank
ADR	American Depositary Receipt
AIG	American International Group Inc
AIMA	All India Management Association
APQO	Asian Pacific Quality Organizations, Inc
ARPU	Average Revenue Per User
ASSOCHAM	Associated Chambers of Commerce and Industry
AT&T	American Telephone and Telegraph Systems
B2B	Business-to-Business
BCG	Boston Consulting Group
BCZ	Bio-Chemizyme India
BFSI	Banking, Financial Services, and Insurance
BITS	Birla Institute of Technology and Science
BMA	Bombay Management Association
BNP	Banque Nationale de Paris (BNP Paribas, a French Bank)
BQIL	Biocon Quest India Limited
BRIC	Brazil, Russia, India, and China
CAG	Comptroller and Auditor General
CBI	Central Bureau of Investigation

CFO	Chief Financial Officer
CII	Confederation of Indian Industry
CIS	Commonwealth of Independent States (Formerly Russia)
CMD	Chairman and Managing Director
CMIN/DF	Normed chi-square; standardized form/degrees of freedom
CNBC	Consumer News and Business Channel
CPR	Center for Policy Research
CRC	Custom Research Company
CRISIL	Credit Rating and Information Services of India Ltd
CVC	Central Vigilance Commission
DFI	Development Financial Institution
DSL	Digital Subscriber Line
DTH	Direct-to-Home
E&Y	Ernst & Young
EADMET & PK	Absorption, Distribution, Metabolism, Excretion, and Toxicity
EASSY	Eastern Africa Submarine Cable System
EBITDA	Earnings Before Interest, Taxes, Depreciation, and Amortization
ECC	Engineering Construction & Contracts Division
ED	Executive Director
EEPC	Engineering Export Promotion Council
EFA	Exploratory Factor Analysis
EIG	Europe India Gateway
Emap	East Midland Allied Press
EMEA	Europe, Middle East, and Africa
EPC	Engineering, Procurement, and Construction
ESOP	Employee Share Option Plan
EXIM	Export–Import
FDA	Food and Drug Administration
FICCI	Federation of Indian Chambers of Commerce and Industry
FIIE	Foundation of Indian Industry and Economists
FKCCI	Federation of Karnataka Chambers of Commerce & Industry

FTE		Full-time Equivalent
GE		General Electric
GDR		Global Depositary Receipt
GFI		Goodness-of-Fit Index
GM		General Manager
GMG		Global Markets Group
GOI		Government of India
GSMA		Global System for Mobile Communications Association
GVC		Governance and Value Creation
HHL		Henning Holck-Larsen
HO		Head Office
HTM		Held to Maturity
IAS		Indian Administrative Service
IBM		International Business Machines Corporation
ICAI		Institute of Chartered Accountant of India
ICC		Indian Chemical Council
ICE		Information Communication and Entertainment
ICT		Information and Communication Technology
ICICI		Industrial Credit and Investment Corporation of India
ICRA		Internet Content Rating Association
IDBI		Industrial Development Bank of India
IDMA		Insurance Data Management Association
IDRBT		Institute for Development and Research in Banking Technology
IEI		Institution of Engineers India
IIIE		Indian Institution of Industrial Engineering
IEP		India Equity Partners
IETE		Institution of Electronics and Telecommunication Engineers
IFCI		Industrial Financial Corporation of India
IFTDO		International Federation of Training and Development Organizations
IIM		Indian Institute of Management

IMC	International Management Center
IMD	International Institute for Management Development
IMEWE	India Middle East and Western Europe
INR	Indian Rupee
INS	Indian Nuclear Society
INSEAD	Institut Européen d'Administration des Affaires—European Institute of Business Administration
INTACH	Indian National Trust for Art and Cultural Heritage
IP	Intellectual Property
IPO	Initial Public Offering
IPTV	Internet Protocol Television
IQMM	International Quality Maturity Model
ITC	Indian Tobacco Company
ITES	Information Technology-enabled Services
JIPM	Japan Institute of Plant Maintenance
JISCO	Jindal Iron and Steel Company Ltd
JPC	Joint Parliamentary Committee
JPOCL	Jindal Praxair Oxygen Company Limited
JSW	Jindal Steel Works
JUSE	Union of Japanese Scientists and Engineers
KKR	Kohlberg Kravis Roberts & Company
KPMG	Klynveld Peat Marwick Goerdeler (KPMG is a global network of professional services firms providing audit, tax, and advisory services)
L&T	Larsen & Tourbro
LBS	London School of Business
LIC	Life Insurance Corporation of India
LTP	Long-term Plan
MIS	Management Information Systems
MIT	Massachusetts Institute of Technology
MLE	Maximum Likelihood Estimation
MRA	Multiple Regression Analysis
MRPL	Mangalore Refineries and Petroleum Chemicals Ltd

LIST OF ABBREVIATIONS

mt	militons
mtpa	Million tons per annum
mw	miliwatts
NASSCOM	National Association of Software and Service Companies
NAV	Net Asset Value
NDTV	New Delhi Television Ltd
NEB	Nuclear Equipment Business
NIFTY	National Stock Exchange's Fifty
NPAs	Non-performing Assets
NYSE	New York Stock Exchange
ONGC	Oil and Natural Gas Corporation
OSD	Officer on Special Duty
PCA	Principle Component Analysis
PHCs	Primary Healthcare Centers
PHDCCI	PHD Chamber of Commerce and Industry
PMO	Project Management Office
POs	Probationary Officers
POSCO	Pohang Iron and Steel Company
ρ	Spearman Rank-Order Correlation (Rho)
RMSEA	Root Mean Square Error of Approximation
SAARC	South Asian Association for Regional Cooperation
SAS	Statistical Analysis System
SARFESI	Securitization and Reconstruction of Financial Assets and Enforcement of Security Interest
SASF	Stressed Asset Stabilization Fund
SAW	Submerged Arc Welded
SBI	State Bank of India
SBU	Strategic Business Units
SEBI	Securities and Exchange Board of India
SEC	Security and Exchange Commission of USA
SEM	Structural Equation Modeling
SISCOL	Southern Iron and Steel Company Limited
SME	Small and Medium Enterprise

STP	Short-term Plan
SUUTI	Specified Undertaking of Unit Trust of India
TCS	Tata Consultancy Services
Telcos	Telephone Companies
TERI	The Energy and Resources Institute
TPM	Total Productive Maintenance
UCE	Unique Competitive Edge
UCO	United Commercial Bank
US-64	Unit Scheme-1964
USIBC	US–India Business Council
UTI	Unit Trust of India
VRS	Voluntary Retirement Scheme
VSF	Viscose Staple Fibre
WEF	World Economic Forum

FOREWORD

It gives me immense pleasure to write the foreword of this book, *In Search of Change Maestros* by Dr Pritam Singh and Dr Asha Bhandarker, both widely known for their scholarship and academic contributions in the field of leadership.

McGregor Burns has aptly quoted the following in his book titled *Leadership*: "Leadership is one of the most observed and least understood phenomenon on earth."

The kaleidoscope of leadership has many myriads. *In Search of Change Maestros* is an attempt to understand the seven wealth creators and institution builders of contemporary India. Right from the era of illustrious thinkers like Aristotle, Chanakya, Confucius, Machiavelli, and Socrates to political leaders of acclaim, namely, Churchill, Gandhi, and Martin Luther King to leaders of academic approbation like Homi Bhabha, C.V. Raman, Vikram Sarabhai, and many others, the human quest to understand these Change Maestros continues.

This book is a multi-pedagogic work, which studies in depth the seven fountainheads of Indian businesses, who contributed to the Indian business landscape and took it to unprecedented heights, despite calamities and circumstances.

The seven Change Maestros include Kumar Mangalam Birla, Meleveetil Damodaran, Sajjan Jindal, Kundapur Vaman Kamath, Sunil Bharti Mittal, Anil Manibhai Naik, and Kiran Mazumdar Shaw. They belong to the galaxy of leaders who have made India proud through seminal contributions to building world-class organizations.

Drawing a simile from Hindu mythology where Lord Surya is seen riding a chariot drawn by seven horses, these seven Change Maestros of Indian business, as a metaphor, symbolize the celestial cosmic rays, which radiate affection, kindness, and verve. As they transcend through the skies, they pave the path toward light and remove darkness on their way through sheer determination, will, and drive!

From an academic point of view, this book is a treasure trove of a well-researched study, whereby the emphasis has not only been on the seven business personae under study, but also the empirical-backed research pinning Change Maestros' attributes: attitude, behaviour, and style that chartered them toward success. The action architecture and cultural landscape to become a change agent in the Indian context with in-depth review of literature, supplemented with extensive work with CEOs and Board Members, highlights the eight driving principles governing them:

1. **Contextual sensitivity:** An uncanny ability to understand the context, sensitivity, and intense concern for aspirations and needs of the masses.
2. **Compelling vision and purpose:** Change Maestros being powerful visionaries and dreamers with focus on larger purpose for the betterment of organization and society.
3. **Winning streak:** Change Maestros' burning ambition and desire to reach the goal faster than others.
4. **People connect and engagement:** Actualizing their vision through collaboration with stakeholders; lion-hood leadership through the power of grooming and feedback.
5. **Meaningful contribution with speed:** Obsession for larger organizational, national, and societal goals with energized speed.
6. **Creative destruction for transformation:** Born out of human unlearning and experimenting new ideas and approaches.
7. **Evolving self:** Striving to actualize their full potential; transforming the "I."
8. **Culture architecture:** Change Maestros attempt to nurture and build a robust organizational culture that is difficult to emulate.

The Change Maestros' study is unique because of the emphasis on researching CEO-level leadership, self-assessment by CEOs as well as perceptions of top team and multiple modes of data gathering.

Kumar Mangalam Birla, the first Change Maestro in this study, well portrays a leader who is "Looking Within, Looking Around, and Looking Beyond," as summed. He is the man who brought in tremendous transformational journey for the group and transitioned the company from its presence in five nations to twenty-five nations since 1997. Many milestones were achieved with growth in business, profits, customer base, ROI, market capitalization, etc. The case study revealed his key strength areas including:

- Value-driven governance internalized throughout the company.
- Global: taking india to the world with presence in twenty-five countries and global operations contributing about 60 percent of the group's revenue.
- Futuristic and forward-looking group: robust growth strategy.
- Moving toward meritocracy with personal touch.

The pre-dominant feature of his persona that contributed toward his success included humility and politeness, people centricity, visionary and strategic thinking, empowering style, intellectual power, crafting strategy architecture, and ability to harmonize opposites.

A karma yogi, a silent contributor, a great listener, a caring person, a calm and poised person, possessing a positive disposition, very driven and passionate, strategic thinker, razor sharp with quick thinking capability sums up his simplistic persona!

Renaissance artist, M. Damodaran, is the man who brought in a drastic makeover turnaround, and transformed the strategic architecture of both UTI and IDBI. He repaired the ship and fixed the problems as it sailed along, without dropping anchor at any point

The strategic action taken and the culture built by him owed to his seamless communication strategy, the ability to script a new vision like a true visionary leader, creating a culture of openness and empowerment, brought confidence and transparency amongst varied stakeholders. To top it, a clear-cut talent management plan with recognition in place, with special emphasis on promoting innovation was instituted. Ethical governance as an omnipresent driver was observed by all!

What happens when a Change Maestro's persona is compelling? His personal attributes steered the path of success through the hearts of people. A persuasive communicator, courageous, and bold, he took to the entrepreneurial path and enabled par excellence performance with a humane approach. A talent shaper with a strong ability to balance divergent forces best describes Damodaran.

Thus, he is a renaissance artist who transformed UTI and IDBI and inured to tackling missions where stakes were high. He took that leap of faith for public interest!

The great Indian poet and mystic Rabindranath Tagore, after writing 6,000 poems, was crying as he lay on his deathbed, praying for rebirth so that he could write yet another which could be his best poem! This quest of excellence is deeply visible in the case of Sajjan Jindal. He, with his entrepreneurial DNA, commenced his long journey to build JSW, actualizing it in a short span. With an impressive growth from ₹ 93 crores in 1993 to ₹ 12,700 crores in 2008, the scale of achievement was due to the robust business model with forward and backward integration.

"Romancing Limitless Growth" defines and deepens the quest for excellence that he is known for. His odyssey to deliver at a furious pace while letting the future chase the present as if there is no tomorrow is a known differentiator to be a Change Maestro.

As a Change Maestro, his rock-like resilience clubbed with limitless ambition, wealth-creating strategy, and action-centred strategy yielded toward this humungous growth. His knack of dealing with people and societal centricity, along with his ability to converge opposites are some of the unique traits of his charismatic persona.

"Enfolding the Future within the Present" is the mission carried out by K.V. Kamath who transformed ICICI from a preponderant development bank into a vibrant, dynamic financial powerhouse, through his overarching vision, foresightedness, capability to sense looming danger, risk-taking, and entrepreneurial innovation.

Continued growth velocity with the foundational mantra of growth, with a will to excel, compete, and win worked for ICICI. Thinking big with the aim of reinventing the financial sector landscape and entrepreneurial innovation facilitated the company's growth. This seamless organization was created and empowerment with accountability, associated with techno-centric work culture, worked for ICICI. The ability to build talent and leaders assisted in identifying the leadership pipeline.

Kamath's photographic and elephantine memory, his focus on continued learnability, his relentless quest for excellence, Himalayan ambition, and concord speed has equipped this crystal gazer to continuously seek to think of tomorrow today.

When David fought Goliath with sheer determination using unconventional approaches, he succeeded. This is exactly what Sunil Bharti Mittal did for Bharti Airtel. Albert Einstein once said: " ... it takes a touch of genius and a lot of courage to move in the opposite direction."

It is his entrepreneurial architecture, innovation, and mega vision with winning streak that made Airtel where it is today. The "Customer Always" approach and significant people power, with emphasis on performance for excellence helped build this mosaic culture which is so unique to Airtel. Overriding it is the emphasis on ethical governance.

Sunil, being futuristic and great at spotting opportunities, quick at converting threat into opportunities, is also blessed with an amazing sixth sense! He himself learns from moment to moment and this maketh the Czar!

Oscar Wilde's famous quote who can find his "way by moonlight, and see the dawn before the rest of the world," aptly describes the Change Maestro, A.M. Naik, who is a dreamer. He stands out as a Change Maestro who did not build a ship by herding people together to collect wood and assign them tasks; rather, taught them to long for the endless immensity of the sea!

Naik the leader, who moves "Toward the Next Orbit," believes that excellence is a journey, not a destination! He visualized a decade ago the tsunami of competition that was going to hit India. Thus arose the strategy of thinking tomorrow today with preparedness in scanning the emerging trends to map the future. The "Go Global" emphasis over a decade ago has today yielded results and to compete and excel globally has been the by-line. He transformed a "sleeping giant" into a "sprinting giant"! The thrust on value creation with focused growth strategy worked for L&T. Under his aegis, L&T flowered with the spirit of entrepreneurial and innovative culture. On customer focus, the L&T mantra is to "take care of the customer and the profits shall rise"! He acts by constantly shifting the goalpost and raising the bar like Jonathan Livingstone Seagull.

Vincent Van Gogh puts it that "great things are done by people who are not afraid to be great"! Kiran Mazumdar Shaw "traverse[d] the road less traveled..." into a domain that was seen as male monopoly. Biocon is the epitome of her vision with unbounded determination and zest to passionately pursue the same, to look for innovative approaches and solutions, and relentlessly executing her dream. She is, in the true sense, an "Entrepreneurial Path Breaker." She transitioned the company from making only enzymes to being a pharma biotech.

Kiran is seen following a dynamic growth strategy constantly creating a second curve before the first curve declines. Allowing her people to think of it as their own company, Biocon is an organization that is flatly built and non-hierarchical, thereby, facilitating quick decision-making and working toward building a friendly, trusting culture. Innovation is in the DNA of the company and its people. The philosophy that "achievement without a sense of honesty and a sense of integrity is worth nothing" governs the lives of Biocon's employees.

An empirically researched book on the topical theme of leadership and what it takes to be a "Change Maestro" and has been well-articulated through case studies of these seven business icons, which are reinforced and validated with research. The personae entwined with organizational culture and action architecture discussed in the context of these seven business personalities of eminence have indeed contributed as "Change Maestros" and toward nation building, besides creating world-class organizations.

This book unfolds in the story-telling mode as a descriptor for each of these Change Maestros and how they transformed and built great institutions and built a sense of pride amongst their employees. It also touches upon the aspects of Gestalt duality and Newtonian reductionism; thus highlighting the need to look at holistic integration of different aspects of business as well as the levers the Change Maestros use to create winning organizations. It talks about integration at the self level, at the organizational level, and the holistic integration at the self, organizational drivers, and business strategy levels. The journey continues for the corporate czars.

This book is a seminal contribution in the field of CEO-level leadership and all CEOs and CEO aspirants would immensely benefit by reading this book.

Brijmohan Lall Munjal
Chairman
Hero Honda Motors Ltd

PREFACE

The history of great nations reveals that they respect, recognize, and honor their heroes for their contributions. Needless to say, acknowledging the leaders and heroes leads to the creation of role models for posterity. Such recognition creates a sense of identity and pride among people who bask in their reflected glory.

In the words of Henry Longfellow:

> Lives of great men all remind us
> We can make our lives sublime,
> And, in departing leave behind us
> Footprints on the sands of time;

The book *In Search of Change Maestros* has been written in this spirit. It documents the contributions of seven great Indian wealth creators and institution builders of whom India is rightfully proud. They are Kumar Mangalam Birla, Meleveetil Damodaran, Sajjan Jindal, Kundapur Vaman Kamath, Sunil Bharti Mittal, Anil Manibhai Naik, and Kiran Mazumdar Shaw.

Blue Print

During our sojourn to various academic citadels and organizations across the globe—Canada, Greece, Egypt, Thailand, Russia, the US, France, and Germany—we found, to our pleasant surprise, that even today, Gandhi's luminous thoughts continue to evoke larger interests among the academicians, business czars, as well as intellectuals, decades even after he has faded away from the political scene. We were astounded to find that no intellectual or academic discussions on leadership were complete without a reference to Gandhi and his ideals. Today, we all are witness to a world that has increasingly become a competitive battleground characterized by rising intolerance, violence, division among human beings, and terrorism. Perhaps people across the world are trying to seek answers in Gandhi's political, social, economic, and moral prescriptions. His triumph against British imperialism is seen as the epitome of leadership and no less a person than Einstein once remarked about Gandhi that, "future generations will scarce believe that a man like him walked on the earth."

In the West today, special weightage is laid on Gandhi to re-examine him and re-emphasize his role as a supreme political leader of his times. The life and leadership profile of Gandhi, as depicted in Richard Attenborough's film *Gandhi*, is used today globally in many institutions for imparting training and education for leadership development. Gandhi has thus become a widely accepted leadership icon and role model. Gandhi's grand vision for humanity and concerns for those at the bottom of the pyramid, his deep respect for the customer, his capability to connect with people and mobilize the masses, his simplicity and humility, his capability to combine idealism with pragmatism, his questioning of age-old stereotypes, his learning stance and hunger for new ideas, his passion for path-breaking reforms through creative solutions, his constant experimentation and quest for self-transformation, his courage and conviction to stand up for and do what is right, and, last, his endless pursuit of the right cause are mantras frequently quoted by leaders.

In our humble attempt to present an extensively researched and comprehensive documentation on seven of India's leading corporate czars who have made a valuable contribution to the development and growth of the Indian economy, we realized that most of them, in some ways, can be compared with Gandhi on his leadership attributes as cited earlier. However, it should not be inferred that any of them has reached the towering height and stature of Gandhi—the latter being a great philosopher, educationist, political thinker, social reformer, etc. Having said this, if assessed independently, each of these business giants is indeed respected and admired more for his moral authority, business acumen, high passion, and zeal for the larger purpose.

It is with this perspective, therefore, that we dared to juxtapose the photo of Gandhi along with the photographs of the seven Change Maestros on the cover page of the book. The photograph of Gandhi has been placed at the center of the cover page to highlight Gandhi's odyssey of transformational leadership from a Lawyer to the Mahatma. Gandhi's leadership journey in some ways resounds in the leadership voyage of our seven Change Maestros.

THE PLOT

We vividly recall an interesting event which occurred when the senior author of the two was invited to address the Paris Chamber of Commerce (in 2007) on the theme of "Emerging Corporate Olympiad: Mantras to Lead." There was a barrage of questions and plenty of curiosity shown for L.N. Mittal, the steel tycoon who had taken over Arcelor, a quintessential European organization. To our dismay, we realized that there was neither adequate awareness nor enough curiosity about other Indian corporate icons—Anil Agarwal, Anu Aga, Anil Ambani, Mukesh Ambani, K.M. Birla, M. Damodaran, Adi Godrej, Sajjan Jindal, Baba Kalyani, K.V. Kamath, Sunil Bharti Mittal, Narayana Murthy, B.L. Munjal, A.M. Naik, Azim Premji, Deepak Parekh, Anji Reddy, Kiran Mazumdar Shaw, H.S. Singhania, Nandan Nilekani, E. Sreedharan, Venu Srinivasan, Ratan Tata, etc.—whose vision has made giants out of men and organization.

It was even more painful to find during our classroom interactions that Indian students and corporate executives have greater awareness about leaders like Percy Barnevik, Larry Bossidy, Warren Buffet, Bill Gates, Lou Gerstener, John Harvey, Jeff Immelt, Lafley, Steve Jobs, Sam Walton, Jack Welch, and others than about many Indian leaders who are perhaps in the same league as the mentioned international icons. We could largely attribute this ignorance about our own corporate heroes to the lack of literature and documentation on them. It is one of the most intriguing aspects of the publishing world in India that there are so few books written about the outstanding Indian corporate leaders. The awareness and popularity of Western business leaders could perhaps be a result of the plethora of literature available on such leaders and their organizations, and the corresponding paucity of documentation about Indian corporate honchos.

The vision of great heroes and leaders across the world like Churchill, Gandhi, De Gaulle, Lincoln, Martin Luther King, Mandela, Roosevelt, etc. is kept alive and it echoes through centuries because of the power of the written word. The prolonged presence of their indelible images in the collective memory has been sustained and reinforced through compelling stories about the historical role they played through the written and spoken words. They are hailed as the creators of new history.

This was the primary motivation for us to research and document the stories of the outstanding Indian Change Maestros who have played a critical role in the transformation of India into an economic power. We were certain that such a work will not only fill the yawning gap in the available literature on Indian Change Maestros, but it would create, in the Indian context, the beacons and role models with universal appeal for the budding generation of leaders. This work can also serve to remind leaders in the making to wake up the lion of leadership lying dormant within, which perhaps did not manifest itself in the absence of inspiring and appropriately documented role models. The criticality of mentors and role models for the development of leadership competencies is paramount as depicted in the following story.

Once upon a time, there was a new-born lion cub that fell off the cliff and landed amidst a passing herd of sheep below. It went along with the herd and was reared by the shepard along with the other sheep. Soon it began to walk like the sheep, ate grass like the sheep, and began to bleat like the sheep. One day a lion while hunting stood aghast at the sight of a young lion grazing peacefully with a herd of sheep. The older lion forgot all about hunting and began to chase the younger lion. As it got closer, the sheep fled. Like the sheep, the younger lion also began to bleat and run. The faster it ran the more the older lion chased it. Finally, the older lion caught up with the younger lion and began to talk to it. The younger lion was quivering with fear and begged the older lion to spare its life, and prayed, "Sir, I am a poor sheep, please don't kill me." The older lion was taken aback and tried its best to convince the younger lion that it was a lion and not a sheep. The more it tried, the more the younger lion refused to believe. Finally, when all counseling failed, the older lion took the younger one to a nearby pond and showed it their respective reflections. He said, "Now can you see, we look the same; we have the same mane, the same paws; you are indeed a lion like me!" And the older lion roared aloud. The younger lion was finally convinced and roared along with the older one and accepted its lion-hood!

This story is a powerful reminder that every human being can achieve lion-hood—leadership—through the power of grooming and feedback, which helps people become aware of their inherent potential. Although every human being is endowed with leadership potential, few have been able to actualize this. Thinkers like Assagioli, Nathaniel Branden, Erikson, Freud, Fromm, Jung, and Rogers, based on their extensive counseling and research, have concluded that the explored potential of a human being is only equivalent to the tip of the iceberg.

This book talks of the achievement and contribution of seven leadership icons of India whom we consider as Change Maestros—K.M. Birla, M. Damodaran, Sajjan Jindal, K.V. Kamath, Sunil Bharti Mittal, A.M. Naik, and Kiran Mazumdar Shaw. They belong to the galaxy of leaders who have made India proud through their seminal contributions to building world-class organizations. Case studies have been developed on each of the seven Change Maestros which form Chapters 2 to 8 of the book. The brief sketches of each of these cases[1] are presented here:

"Kumar Mangalam Birla: Looking Within, Looking Around, and Looking Beyond" is the story of the man who took over the reins of one of India's largest business empires (in tragic circumstances of the death of his father, A.V. Birla, a doyen among Indian corporate leaders) and, contrary to the expectations of most industry watchers, took the group to new heights. In the span of twelve years, the Aditya Birla Group expanded globally and prepared the traditional, conservative 100-year-old "Old Economy" group to face the corporate Mahabharata of the 21st century.

"M. Damodaran: Renaissance Artiste" is the story of the man who left a legacy of rich contributions right from his days as District Magistrate and other administrative roles at the state level in Tripura, then moving on to a posting as Joint Secretary, Department of Banking and Finance, followed by Chairmanship of UTI, IDBI, and SEBI, one after the other. He rewrote the destiny of three commercial banks—Bank of India; UCO Bank; and Indian Bank—which were on the verge of demise via liquidation. In the phoenix-like rise of UTI from its near crash, it was Mr Damodaran who created hope among all the stakeholders and crafted and executed its remarkable turnaround. His contribution to giving a new lease of life to IDBI through the creation of the "Stressed Assets Stabilization Fund" is greatly acknowledged and adopted by banking honchos. He re-architected SEBI from being a preponderantly regulatory body to a developmental institution engaged in promoting robust governance practices.

"Sajjan Jindal: Romancing Limitless Growth" highlights the movement of JSW toward Himalayan peaks of growth. It is the incredible odyssey of JSW from being a mere ₹ 93 crore company in 1993 to becoming a ₹ 12,700 crore company in 2008, with the ambition to attain a ₹ 50,000 crore turnover in 2012—a meteoric rise to the top echelons by any standard. From a tiny manufacturer of steel pipes to a conglomerate with interests in steel, cement, power, and ports, it has indeed been a breathtaking journey for the group.

"K.V. Kamath: Enfolding the Future within the Present" traces the journey of the man who redrew the Indian banking landscape. It is a stunning story of converting a traditional development bank into a vibrant, cutting edge, dynamic, and aggressive universal bank. Today, ICICI Bank is the second largest Indian bank (ranked 55th globally in terms of market capitalization) and the architect Mr K.V. Kamath is considered to be the fourth most influential corporate giant in India, according to a recent survey by *Economic Times* (2009).

"Sunil Bharti Mittal: The Game Changer" depicts the phenomenon of a young David challenging the mighty Goliaths of telecom in India. Bharti Airtel exploded many shibboleths and myths of managing telecom business profitably, by questioning and redefining many well-entrenched business models. This is the group which had the courage and gumption to move from the existing vertical integration model to the virtual model which has today become a global benchmark in the telecom sector. From two circles in Delhi and Himachal Pradesh with 0.1 million customers as recently as 1999, it moved to twenty-two circles and a 179 million customer base in April 2010, raring to touch 200 million within the next three years. With the takeover of Kuwait's Zain Telecom, Airtel has become the fifth largest mobile phone operator globally.

"A.M. Naik: Toward the Next Orbit" depicts the exciting saga of a bureaucratic multi-business conglomerate which successfully aligned its business models, strategies, structure, processes, culture, and leadership styles with the emerging future. L&T is a unique and truly public institution, owned neither by the government nor by any private business house. However, it is this very uniqueness which has made it an attractive takeover target from time to time and this has cast a perennial shadow in the minds of the management and its employees. It was under Mr A.M. Naik that the future of this conglomerate as a truly public institution was secured through a combination of business portfolio restructuring along with the creation of an Employee Trust owing 15 percent of shares. Today, L&T has become one of the most vibrant and creative groups in the Indian corporate world with continued zeal to align its business strategies with national priorities and interests and ceaselessly trying to move into the next orbit.

"Kiran Mazumdar Shaw: Entrepreneurial Path Breaker" dwells on the gripping story of the Biocon icon who has made a rare place for herself and her organization in the pharma world, poised to provide low-cost drugs to a society which is on the brink of a major health crisis—heart disease and diabetes. Today, Biocon is ranked 20th amongst global bio-pharma companies. Kiran has earned the titles of "India's Biotech Queen" and "Mother of Invention."

Trajectory of the Book

The book has been organized in ten chapters. Chapter 1 "Change Maestros' Kaleidoscope" explores the Change Maestros' profiles and extracts the distilled essence of their leadership characteristics. Chapters 2 to 8 are the detailed case studies on each of the seven Change Maestros, highlighting their styles, actions, and organizational cultures they have built (quantitative details are available in the appendices of each case chapter). Chapter 9 "Change Maestros: Action Architecture and Persona" presents the comparative study across the Change Maestros' styles and organizational cultures. Chapter 10 "Change Maestros' Gestalt" dwells on concluding thoughts and emerging models of Change Maestros' styles and competencies.

This book seeks to share the wisdom of the seven Change Maestros with both the academic audience as well as corporate audience. Although rigorous research methods have been used in data collection and data analysis, in terms of presentation, the focus has been on enhancing readability for a wider audience. Hence, research analysis and details are presented in the appendices at the end of each chapter for easy reference of researchers and academicians.

Note

1. Case studies about the Change Maestros have been presented in alphabetical order of their last names in the book. Although there is one woman in the sample, we have largely used the term "he" for ease of presentation.

ACKNOWLEDGMENTS

Many persons have inspired us to embark on this work, helped us sustain it through this exciting journey, and goaded us to complete it in time. We would like to acknowledge each one of them here. First and foremost we would like to acknowledge, with profound gratitude, the Paris Chamber of Commerce for provoking us to start this work. Elena of the MIRBIS School of Business (Moscow), Gregory Prastacos of Athens University of Economics and Business, and Jyoti Gupta of ESCP EAP, Paris, deserve special thanks for inspiring us to write about Oriental Business Leaders. We would like to extend our gratitude to the AICTE for its financial support in conducting this study. Our heartfelt thanks to Late Dr Swadesh Gupta, Advisor, AICTE, who supported us on this project because he could see the value of this work. Equally important has been the contribution of Management Development Institute (MDI), Gurgaon, which provided us support and infrastructural facilities. Thanks are due to those who patiently filled the questionnaires and shared their valuable time for the long interviews. Thanks are also due to Dr B.S. Sahay, Director, MDI, who supported us in the completion of this project. We would like to extend our special thanks to Dr Sugata Ghosh, Vice President, Commissioning—Books & Journals, SAGE Publications, for inspiring us to begin this journey. His excitement and enthusiasm and gentle style of nudging helped us complete the project.

Many others have helped us along the way at different stages of the work. Some of the names that we would like to acknowledge are Gita Bajaj, Faculty of Communication, MDI; Soumendu Biswas, Faculty of HRM, MDI; Jerome Bon, Former Director General, ESCP EAP, Paris; Anil Gupta, Chaired Professor in Strategy, INSEAD, Singapore; Arun K. Jain, Professor of Strategy, IIM

Lucknow; Nira Jain, Faculty of Communication, MDI; M.P. Jaiswal, Dean, Research, MDI; Ashok Kapoor, Dean, MDP and Consulting, MDI; Manoj Kohli, CEO, International and Joint MD, Bharti Airtel Ltd; Ram Kumar, Vice President, HR, ICICI; R. Ravi Kumar, Professor of OB, IIM Bangalore; M.D. Mallya, CMD, Bank of Baroda; B.A. Metri, Dean, Graduate Programs, MDI; Santrupt Misra, Group President, Aditya Birla Group; V.K. Nangia, Registrar, MDI; Shailendra Rai, Faculty of Finance, MDI; Reeta Raina, Faculty of Communication, MDI; Pragnya Ram, Head, Corporate Communication, Aditya Birla Group; Thothathri Raman, *Business India*; A.K. Rath, Head, Public Policy Program, MDI; Anjanee Rathore, Vice President, Bharti Airtel; S.N. Roy, President, Business Strategy and Development, L&T; Paula Sengupta, Head, Corporate Communication, Biocon; S.Y. Siddiqui, Managing Executive Officer, HR, Finance, and IT, Maruti Suzuki India Ltd; Anirudh Singh, Vice President, Group HR, JSW; Subir Verma, Faculty of OB, MDI; Valerie Wattelle, Consultant, Paris; and numerous others. We would also like to express special thanks to Ashita Goswami, Kshipra Rustogi, and Swati Singh who worked on this project with great dedication.

Last but most important, we thank our respective families. We are indebted to them for their ungrudging support and unstinted cooperation in this gigantic endeavor.

1

CHANGE MAESTROS' KALEIDOSCOPE

Every *akshara* has the power of mantra,[1] every plant has medicinal value, and, likewise, every human being has the seed within him to become a Change Maestro. While in some this seed blossoms to its best, in others, it blooms to various other degrees; however, in most, it simply lies dormant.

This chapter maps the path which people followed to reach the crescendo of leadership and became Change Maestros.[2] It also sketches the contours of the research design which has been used in this work.

PART I: RATIONALE OF THIS WORK

History has witnessed many Change Maestros who built great empires, nations, and institutions. They have played a vital role in the lives of human beings and therein lies the endless human quest for Change Maestros. Illustrious thinkers like Aristotle, Chanakya, Confucius, Machiavelli, Plato, Socrates, Lao-Tzu, and many others have pondered this issue and in the absence of definitive answers, the search continues, not only in the political and social realms, but also in economic institutions. In the business world, this search has assumed greater importance at a time when many corporate leaders turned into corporate villains, creating an unprecedented global financial crisis, damaging the lives of large numbers of individuals, ruining institutions, and denting economies.

One of our earlier studies (Singh and Verma, 2010: 414–30) clearly reveals that leadership is one of the key concerns which worry Indian corporate executives. Five of the top seven concerns expressed by them—lack of political statesmanship (rank 1 [rk 1]); crisis of leadership in all walks of life (rk 2); crisis of faith in government (rk 3); corporate governance (rk 5); and increasing corruption at all levels (rk 6)—are in the domain of leadership.

In today's political world, people are equally skeptical and cynical about leaders, barring exceptional Change Maestros like Churchill, Mahatma Gandhi, Rajiv Gandhi, Charles de Gaulle, Lincoln, Martin Luther King, Mandela, Mahatir Mohammad, Nehru, Obama, Sardar Patel, Deng Xio Peng, Lal Bahadur Shastri, Lee Kon Yew, Atal Bihari Vajpayee, etc., who are viewed favorably for their contributions to nation-building in general and society at large.

The prevalent view about the bulk of political leaders is that they are corrupt, busy in amassing wealth, dividing to rule, and misleading citizens with false promises. Many political leaders are seen to be overly focused on clinging to power at any cost and working to further their self-interest. People commonly see these leaders as devoid of integrity and character, both of which are extremely important for nation-building as well as creation of role models.

Bureaucrats worldwide are also under attack for being insensitive to the needs of the populace. They are generally perceived to be busy colluding with power groups and perpetuating their self-interest and careers for personal advancement and gains (Singh and Bhandarker, 1994).

Our observation as trainers, coaches, and consultants in the corporate world in the last thirty years have shown us that there is a paucity of Change Maestros in the Indian corporate world. Generally, most Indian corporate leaders tend to display a hierarchical mindset, show distancing and status-conscious behavior, and utilize institutional power to rule rather than for institution building, creating wealth, and meaningfully contributing to society. Barring notable exceptions like O.P. Bhat, Aditya Birla, G.D. Birla, K.M. Birla, M. Damodaran, Sajjan Jindal, Baba Kalyani, K.V. Kamath, Jagdish Khattar, V. Kurien, K. Mahindra, A. Mahindra, Sunil Bharti Mittal, Narayana Murthy, A.M. Naik, Nandan Nilekani, Deepak Parikh, Azim Premji, Kiran Mazumdar Shaw, H.S. Singhania, B.L. Munjal, J.R.D. Tata, Ratan Tata, and N. Vaghul, many top business leaders are today resented for their selfishness, self-perpetuating behavior, and high handedness.

The Indian academic community on its part has also not distinguished itself with significant achievements and contributions. One has to really search hard to find names of outstanding Change Maestros like Syed Ahmed, Homi Bhabha, Satish Dhawan, A.P.J. Abdul Kalam, Kasturirangan, Kothari, Pandit Madan Mohan Malviya, Ravi Mathai, S. Radhakrishnan, C.V. Raman, C.N.R. Rao, and Vikram Sarabhai.

Many people occupying positions of leadership do not graduate to the level of Change Maestros, perhaps because they lose connection with the followers and stakeholders, adopt unethical practices to continue in power, and above all, do not have nobility of purpose and higher level goals.

Part II: What Makes a Change Maestro?

In-depth study of the existing literature (see Avolio and Yammarino, 2002; Bennis and Thomas, 2002; Chan Teng, 2000; Dauphinais, 2000; Gardner, 1996; Hambrick et al., 1998; House et al., 2004; Jeffery, 2003; Jo Hatch et al., 2005; Judge, 1999; Kase et al., 2005; Khurana, 2002; Mayo and Nohria, 2005; Mintzberg, 2007; Mirvis et al., 2003; Pandit, 2005; Price and Ritcheske, 2001; Robert, 1999; Rosen, 2000; Singh and Bhandarker, 1989; Spencer et al., 2007; Srivastava, 2003; Tichy, 2002; Zacarro, 1996) brings out the following salient principles and action architecture to becoming a Change Maestro.

According to Burns (1978): "Leadership is one of the most observed and least understood phenomenon on earth." The present work *In Search of Change Maestros* seeks to fill this gap by studying the profiles of Change Maestros in the Indian context. In this part, the survey of literature has been dealt with around the following seven themes (see Figure 1.1 for pictorial representation) which have emerged from our extensive work with CEOs, board-level workshops as well as study of existing literature:

1. Contextual sensitivity
2. Compelling vision and purpose
3. Winning streak
4. People connect and engagement
5. Meaningful contribution with speed
6. Creative destruction for transformation

6 IN SEARCH OF CHANGE MAESTROS

Figure 1.1 Model of Change Maestros

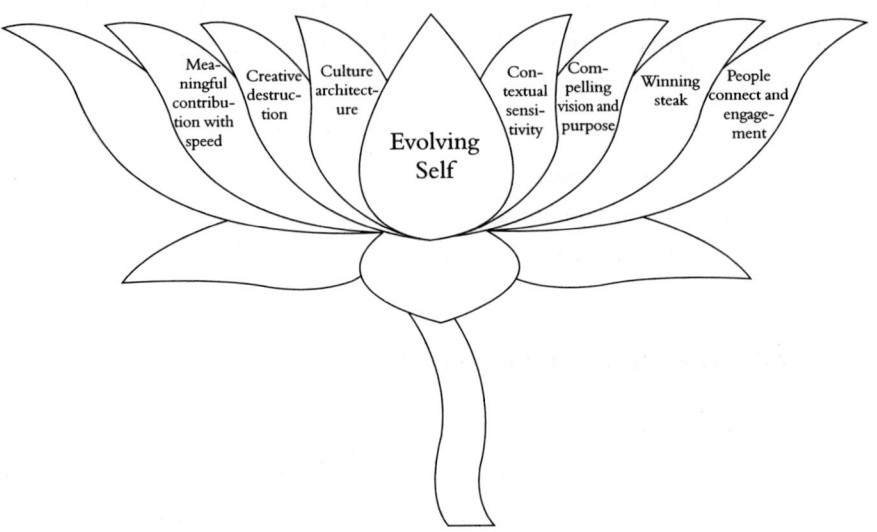

Source: Authors.

7. Evolving self
8. Culture architecture

Contextual Sensitivity

The hallmark of the style of Change Maestros like Percy Barvenik, G.D. Birla, M.K. Gandhi, Gorbachev, Abraham Lincoln, Martin Luther King, Nelson Mandela, Matsushita, J.R.D Tata, Ratan Tata, Jack Welch, and others has been their sensitivity and intense concern regarding the aspirations and needs of the masses:

> In fact they have an uncanny ability to understand the context they live in- and to spot the opportunities their times present. Entrepreneurs are often ahead of their times, not necessarily bound by the context in which they live. They frequently overcome seemingly insurmountable obstacles and challenges to persevere in finding or launching something new. Leaders confront change and identify latent potential in business that others consider stagnant,

mature, declining or moribund. Where some see failure and demise, leaders see kernels of possibility and hope. (Mayo and Nohria, 2005)

Such Change Maestros could influence and mobilize people because they built their agenda around stakeholders' needs, aspirations, and expectations of the people. In this context it is instructive to understand the thought process behind Gandhi's decision to give up Western attire and don the dress of the ordinary Indian citizen (when he returned from South Africa). When the American journalist Walker quizzed him about this change in his dress and lifestyle, Gandhi replied, "This country never cared to heed the language of kings and emperors. It always however, bowed and expressed reverence to fakirs and saints" (Singh and Bhandarker, 1989). Thus, Gandhi demonstrated sensitivity about the psyche and concerns of Indians. In response, the Indians overwhelmingly supported Gandhi's agenda of freedom from British rule.

Examination of the lives of many erstwhile kings and emperors across the world brings out one salient characteristic—they had a penchant for moving around in disguise to understand ground realities as well as the aspirations of the people. This understanding helped them build an agenda which could resonate with the needs of the people and ensure their support. Many of today's Change Maestros follow this practice when they move around their organizations unannounced, the classic example being that of Jan Carlson (CEO of SAS) who captured this beautifully in his book titled *Moments of Truth* (Carlzon, 1989).

It must be emphasized at this point that stakeholders' consent regarding Change Maestro's agenda and goals are critical to mobilizing people toward a larger purpose. In fact, without this critical component, the stakeholders' power to mobilize people is greatly diminished. He may have positional power but if he does not enjoy the consent of his constituency, he is highly disempowered.

Worldwide, many people occupy positions of power, but few enjoy the whole hearted acceptance of the constituency and, therefore, are not in a position to wield influence over the people. Those like Percy Barnevik, Aditya Birla, Larry Bossidy, Richard Branson, Churchill, Charles de Gaulle, Gandhi, Lou Gerstner, Abdul Kalam, Lincoln, Martin Luther King, Mandela, Akio Morita, Narayana Murthy, Roosevelt, Ratan Tata, Margaret Thatcher, Jack Welch, etc., became Change Maestros because they worked for their respective constituencies and were accepted by them. It is important to mention that such acceptance is a result of the match among stakeholders' expectations, contextual imperatives and Change Maestros' agenda, style, and action.

Compelling Vision and Purpose

Change Maestros are powerful visionaries and dreamers with focus on a larger purpose for the betterment of organization and society. Since their dreams are much bigger, encompassing institution, nation, and humanity, they are capable of transcending petty and narrow differences.

Gandhi's vision, like that of Nehru, Patel, and Mandela, was independence from alien rule based on the assumption of equality among all human beings. This vision is truly vast in its scope, embracing humanity across societies and races. Gandhi went a step further and worked not only for "Swaraj" (Home Rule), but also for bringing about a transformation in the social fabric of the Indian society to eradicate the crushing caste-based inequities and discrimination among people. Gandhi's declared mission was to "wipe away every tear from every eye" (Zakaria, 1989: 28). While fighting for the cause of rights of Indians in South Africa, Gandhi declared, "This struggle is a struggle for human liberty" (Fischer, 1997: 148). As Fischer put it, "he was too religious to serve one land, one race, one caste, one family, one person or even one religion. His religion was humanity" (Fischer, 1997: 162). "… Gandhi craved for his country a cultural regeneration and spiritual renaissance which would give it inner freedom and hence, inevitably outer freedom" (Fischer, 1997: 169).

Abraham Lincoln's vision emphasized equality and freedom, a fair chance for all, and elevation of the "condition of human beings." He maintained, this was the people's birthright and it should be protected and preserved for future generations (Philips, 1992: 53). In his struggle for equality across races, Martin Luther King conveyed his vision very passionately when he said, "… if we can live up to non-violence in thought and deed there will emerge an interracial society based on freedom for all" (Gardner, 1996: 207). Gorbachev had a vision "to create a society which gives equal opportunity to everybody to develop their inner potential" (Sheehy, 1990: 177).

Change Maestros like Vikram Sarabhai, Homi Bhabha, A.P.J. Abdul Kalam, and Raja Ramanna dreamt great dreams and realized India's space program as well as nuclear capabilities which created a deep sense of pride among Indians. When Abdul Kalam wrote, "a developed India by 2020 or even earlier is not a dream; it need not even be a mere aspiration in the minds of many Indians; but is a mission we can all take up and accomplish" (Kalam with Rajan, 1998: 15–16), it triggered renewed hope in people.

In case of Change Maestros operating in the corporate domain, the organization becomes the vehicle through which society is served. In the process of achieving organizational goals, the larger societal goals are also attained. G.D. Birla's vision for the nation also encompassed the vision for his companies. "Birla saw the country's economic progress firmly in terms of increasing the employment opportunities available for millions of people eking out a meagre and precarious livelihood in the vast countryside" (Ramanujan, 1993: 101). Ibuka's vision for Sony Corporation stated: "If it were possible to establish conditions where persons could become united with a firm spirit of teamwork, and exercise to their heart's desire their technical capacity, then such an organization could bring untold pleasure and untold benefits" (Morita et al., 1990: 82). A.V. Birla, in his 1994 address to his chiefs on Corporate Philosophy and Perspective, said, "Destiny beckons us that we do something, that we continue to create not just for our country but globally; not just for today, but for posterity as well" (Birla, 1994). Jack Welch of GE hoped to make GE, "the most competitive enterprise on the earth" (Tichy and Sherman, 1993: 14). Percy Barnevik of ABB was another CEO with a grand business vision. According to Gail E. Schares (1993), for Barnevik, the future contained no national boundaries and he aimed to sell power equipment to the world. The evidence lies in his acquisition of sixty companies for ABB across five continents in five years to serve customers stretching all the way from Kingston to Kuala Lumpur.

Similarly, Nandan Nilekani envisions improving the quality of public decision-making through the power of IT and access of information to people (Nilekani, 2008: 26). Katsuake Watanabe, President of Toyota Motor Corporation, has a compelling vision about building a dream car. He says:

> I don't know how many years its going to take us but I want Toyota to come up with the dream car—a vehicle that makes the air cleaner than it is; a vehicle that cannot injure people; a vehicle that prevents accidents from happening; a vehicle that makes people healthier, the longer they drive it; a vehicle that can excite, entertain and evoke the emotion of its occupants; a vehicle that can drive around the world on just one tank of fuel. That is what I dream about.... We would like to develop such a vehicle as quickly as possible. In my vision for the future, the most important themes are the environment, energy, safety and evoking emotions for comfort; these are the four key roads for the company's future and we must develop technologies for each of them.... If we accelerate our technology development we can realize the dream car. (Stewart and Raman, 2007)

John Connolly, CEO and Global Chairman of Deloitte, UK, believes that winning in these times is about leadership and the leader's ability to both conceive and deliver a vision (Connolly, 2009). The vision of Gunther Fielmann, CEO of Fielmann Optical chain, Germany's largest optical chain, has been to provide the cheapest services in the industry (Schuman, 2009). William C. Weldon, CEO, Johnson & Johnson (J&J), defined the purpose of his business in terms of serving doctors, nurses and patients, mothers, fathers, and all others who use J&J products and services (Ulrich and Smallwood, 2007). Ren Jian Xin, who began his business venture twenty-six years ago, with 10,000 Yuan, wants to develop ChemChina into a globally competitive chemical business. He has a vision to make his company into one of the top three global giants (Zhihong, 2010).

Matsushita was supremely successful in inspiring others in his company, Matsushita Electric Industrial Co. (MEI), on the strength of his vision. Matsushita's employees were convinced that they were associated with a noble and just cause and they took their company to new heights, especially in the post-war era when most industries in Japan were badly crippled. Matsushita talked about serving society by producing goods that people could afford and his company successfully realized the founder's decades-long vision (Kotter, 1997: 113). J.R.D. Tata, said of his father Jamsetji's motivation for building Tata Sons group of companies: "The acquisition of wealth was only a secondary object in life. It was always subordinate to the constant desire in his heart to improve the industrial and intellectual condition of the people of this country" (Lala, 1992: 70). H.P. Nanda, founder of Escorts Ltd (historically one of India's largest tractor manufacturers) said: "I had a rural vision, a conviction that great business potential existed in India's villages. I believed that if we improved the shadowed lives of the millions of people living in our 550,000 underdeveloped villages, we would create consumers—generators of wealth" (Nanda, 1992: 240).

Ford also had an ambitious vision (Gross and the Editors of *Forbes* Magazine, 1996: 79). In making his vision a reality, he made the car available for the masses and revolutionized private transportation. Joseph Wilson founder of Xerox Corporation (Gross and the Editors of *Forbes* Magazine, 1996: 247) started with plans to "found a ... whole new industry" and achieved it, probably on a scale which nobody, not even he, could visualize. The vision of Sony Corporation has the flavor of constant innovation. The focus of the company has been on "being at the cutting edge of technology" and serving society through innovations. As Morita said about the Sony spirit, "Sony is a pioneer, it never intends to follow others ... through progress, Sony wants to serve the whole world ... always a seeker of the unknown" (Gross and the Editors of *Forbes* Magazine, 1996: 195); "Our basic concept has been this ... to give new convenience, or new methods, or new benefits to the general public, with our technology" (Morita et al., 1990: 147). In the late 1990s Intel aimed to be the visionary leader of the entire computer industry. Andy Grove had once said that from here on Intel will create the demand in the industry (Schlender, 1992). Bill Gates envisioned the dominance of the personal computer (PC) much before others and deduced that "the software would be as important as the hardware" (Kirkpatrick, 1997). His company has successfully dominated the software market worldwide and has emerged as the undisputed leader in the industry.

Naresh Malhotra, Head of Café Coffee Day, envisioned building lifetime customers and, therefore, focused on young people who would remain in the consumer group for a long time (Gross and the Editors of *Forbes* Magazine, 1996: 336). L.N. Mittal envisioned the creation of a Global Steel Giant, while Ratan Tata envisioned the creation of affordable cars for the masses.

These instances clearly show the compelling power of vision and purpose which Change Maestros have utilized to galvanize people and take organizations to the next orbit. Not only are Change Maestros obsessed by the vision, they also have the knack of mobilizing the masses and stirring up their energies by sharing their vision vividly and powerfully. Such visions have had a profound effect on people because they have alluded to a larger cause and created a greater meaning and purpose for them. Through the communication of his vision, Lincoln stirred up in people a sense of patriotism and a consciousness of their rights. Gandhi's vision of freedom, as well as that of Mandela's, inspired the mass because they ignited self-pride and gave hope of a better life to people. Similar has been the impact of the espoused visions of corporate leaders like Aditya Birla, Akio Morita, G.D. Birla, Jack Welch, J.R.D. Tata, Lou Gerstner, L.N. Mittal, Percy Barnevik, Ratan Tata, and others on their employees.

Winning Streak

A Change Maestro's burning ambition and desire to reach the goal, to be right on the top faster than others, is the winning streak. The Change Maestro has a fire within that constantly spurs him to strive to reach higher and higher. No matter what the leader takes on, the desire is to be the best. They believe that they do not have the luxury of choosing their battles. Therefore, they have to fight each battle and win it. Change Maestros are great warriors. They never give up and keep trying again and again. In fact, they are so single-minded, obsessive, and intense that their energies get automatically channeled to work toward winning without any loss of focus or interest.

The story of Matsushita is the story of constant striving, struggling, and winning every time, by constantly setting higher goals for the self and the organization. As Kotter (1997: 13) explains, "the key to his story lies in his phenomenal drive for growth." According to Tichy, what distinguishes Jack Welch from the others is his self-confidence and drive, and an absolute desire to win. According to him, "Each success seems to increase his strength and his desire to win again" (Tichy and Sherman, 1993: 10). Stephen Green, Group CEO, HSBC (Green et al., 2003) said, "we don't look so much at what or where people have studied but rather at their drive, initiative, culture sensitivity and readiness to see the world as their oyster"—the surest way of hiring winners.

Nothing stops Change Maestros from achievements that lie on their chosen path. Adversities only seem to make them more determined. They convert every obstacle into an opportunity. In the political arena, Gandhi, Mandela, and Lincoln have, among others, displayed extraordinary grit and determination to strive till the goal is achieved. Gandhi worked untiringly for thirty-two years (1915–1946), both for India's freedom as well as social renaissance. In fact, shortly before his assassination, he expressed the wish to live longer so that he could make greater contributions to society (Fischer, 1997: 621). Mandela spent thirty long years in jail never wavering from the objective of freedom from foreign rule despite harsh treatment and extreme deprivation. He rejected the conditional offers made by the white rulers to release him from jail six times. As Mandela recounts in his autobiography: "I was prepared for the death penalty. To be truly prepared for something one must actually expect it" (Mandela, 1994: 360).

Matsushita's life story is a riveting account of a Change Maestro who overcame every obstacle before him without being defeated—he started a factory from scratch, lost it all in the World War, and re-established it after the war. His capacity to persevere was built on the foundation of being prepared for the worst. He was convinced that "adversity is good, and that it brings out the best in people" (Kotter, 1997: 102). He once said, "Truly able people do not let difficulties get the better of them. This is one of the things that a person in a position of leadership should keep in mind" (Kotter, 1997: 99).

A.G. Lafley, CEO, Procter & Gamble (P&G), said:

> … we measure our success in terms of consumer household penetration, that is the percentage of households that buy P&G brand and consumer loyalty, meaning the percentage of consumers that convert to regular users. That is how we know if we are winning with those who matter the most. We also compare P&G's performance with that of our strongest competitors to ensure that we win against the very best. (Lafley, 2009)

According to Herndon, Lincoln's law partner, his ambition, was "a little engine which knew no rest" (Philips, 1992: 108). Philips describes how Lincoln tried to make a career in several fields before he achieved success—he ran a general store, was a postmaster, a surveyor, and, eventually, a lawyer and politician. Philips described Lincoln's persistence as near compulsive (Philips, 1992: 108). Lincoln was also overambitious. He had built a remarkable ability to persevere and learn from his own failures: "No endeavor became a hindrance to his overarching goal to achieve. In fact, everything—failures and successes—became stepping stones to the presidency" (Philips, 1992: 109). As a young man, he once stated in one of his speeches, "Towering genius disdains a beaten path. It seeks regions hitherto unexplored ... it scorns to tread in the footsteps of any predecessor, however illustrious. It thirsts and burns for distinction ..." (Philips, 1992: 109), thus, clearly revealing his great aspirations.

Closer home, J.R.D. Tata averred that he was a highly-driven person (Lala, 1992: 52). The level of personal motivation of Dhirubhai Ambani, founder of the Reliance group of companies, has been rated as amazingly high, and his drive "even more insatiable than before" (Piramal, 1996: 14). In his own words: "I consider myself a pathfinder ... what excites me is achievement ..." (Piramal, 1996: 10). The desire starts in a general way and fructifies into achievements in the chosen arena of one's life. Ambani recalls: "I wanted to start earning as quickly as possible.... I wanted to make a success of whatever I did. That was the paramount thing in my life" (Piramal, 1996: 10). And again: "I had dreams of starting a company like Burmah Shell while working for Shell Company in Aden" (Piramal, 1996: 20).

Change Maestros are clear thinkers and quick decision makers. They are able to simplify complex issues and make decisions on that basis. As Andy Grove put it: "The best thing is to make the right decision. Making a wrong decision is O.K. too. The worst thing to do is to hedge. To hedge is to fail" (Gross and the Editors of *Forbes* Magazine, 1996: 247). And: "Under Grove's leadership, Intel is still paranoid in a healthy way ... like a jogger running on an accelerating treadmill. Intel has had to run faster just to maintain its position and even faster just to stay ahead of everybody else" (Gross and the Editors of *Forbes* Magazine, 1996: 264).

Sam Walton's life again reflects indefatigable perseverance, the trait of not giving up. This is reflected in his own words, "[A]fter a lifetime of swimming upstream I am convinced that one of the real secrets to Wal-Mart's phenomenal success has been that very tendency (to learn and do). Many of our best opportunities were created out of necessity" (Walton, 1993: 63); "[I]t never occurred to me that I might lose; it was almost as if I had a right to win. Thinking like that after some time seems to turn into sort of a self-fulfilling prophecy" (Walton, 1993: 18).

L.N. Mittal, the steel tycoon, emphasizes the role of hard work to win. He says: "[E]veryone experiences tough times. It is a measure of your determination and dedication how you deal with them and how you can come through them" (Thomas, 2009). Steve Jobs, the maverick IT icon, defines winning in terms of doing what the competitor cannot do. He says: "[W]e are the only company which owns ... the hardware, software and operating systems" (Lashinsky, 2009).

Change Maestros combine desire to win with perseverance and hard work. They seem to thrive on competition, almost as if competition challenges them to do more and more in their quest to win. This is illustrated in the style of leaders like Ambani, Percy Barnevik, A.V. Birla, Bill Gates, Andy Grove, Matsushita, Jack Welsh Welch, and others. Change Maestros are characterized by a tremendous sense of optimism; they are undaunted by failure and have the ability to bounce back from adversities, which only seems to make them stronger. Both Gandhi and Mandela have been great optimists and for them each day seemed to be a new opportunity to try again. "I am a born fighter who does not know failure," Gandhi once said to his audience in a prayer meeting (Fischer, 1997: 588). Mandela's conviction is visible in his statement: "I am fundamentally an optimist. There were many dark moments when my faith in humanity was sorely tested, but I would not and could not give myself up to despair. That way lay defeat and death" (Mandela, 1994: 377). Franklin Roosevelt's struggle with polio only seemed to give him greater strength to take bold steps as President of the United States of America (Collier with Horowoa, 1994: 254).

A number of examples indicate that perhaps Change Maestros set tough internal standards for themselves and usually meet them. Matsushita laid down high performance standards and they kept getting bigger (Kotter, 1997: 130). J.R.D. Tata was focused on excellence (Lala, 1992: 53); Ambani had an uncompromising commitment to quality, an obsession to be "the first in India with the finest technology the world can offer" (Piramal, 1996). Describing the need to relentlessly shift the goal post for winning and achieving, Ramadorai, CEO, TCS, said: "A dream is like a 100 metre race. If you do it in 11 seconds, the next bar is, doing it in 10 seconds. Then the next bar can go below the 10 second level" (Piramal and Netarwala, 2005: 56). Such Change Maestros are like the Olympians, with great fervor to break their own records and outdo themselves. They are never satisfied and are always restless to establish new benchmarks. Above all, they are result- and action-focused. The Gita became Gandhi's gospel because it glorifies action (Fischer, 1997: 43) and the victory of good over evil—*Satyameva Jayate.*

People Connect and Engagement

Change Maestros believe strongly in the role of people-power in actualizing their vision and creating winning organizations. They shape the context and actualize their vision of transformation through collaboration with their employees, partners, and other stakeholders. They have mastery over creating a larger support base by co-partnering with various stakeholders and synthesizing apparent contradictions among them. Herb Kelleher, CEO, South West Airlines, frequently flew in South West Airlines flights just to know his employees and customers—a huge departure from the typical office-bound CEOs. He developed close relationship with his employees who often went above and beyond the call of duty for him. "They came up with creative ideas to better serve customers and turn around planes faster." This helped them to become what *Fortune* magazine calls the most successful airline in the industry (Spreitzer, 2006).

Change Maestros follow a win–win approach and try to secure the interests of relevant parties. They are experts in engaging people, dialoging with them, and, through that, galvanizing and channelizing their energies toward organizational goals. They are good in designing and managing a collaborative process of decision-making and conflict resolution to which all stakeholders subscribe (Allio, 2009). They seem to follow the leadership maxim stated by Lao Tzu, the great Chinese philosopher—the wicked leader is he whom people despise;

the good leader is he whom people revere; and the great leader is he of whom people say "we did it together."

In his inaugural speech at the International Federation of Training and Development Organization (IFTDO) conference, New Delhi, 2004, Abdul Kalam (Kalam with Rajan, 1998) narrated an incident which occurred after the failure of the missile launch from Sriharikota, off the Bay of Bengal in India. The media, watching the failed event, rained a volley of questions on Kalam, who was the project leader. Immediately, Kalam recalled that Satish Dhawan (his superior) asked Kalam to step aside and took on the media. When the missile was successfully launched sometime later, and the media turned to Dhawan, in a rare gesture of collegial empowerment, the latter asked Kalam to deal with the media. Kalam narrated this incident to say that great leaders do not take credit for success; they make people feel that it is their success. This echoes Lao Tzu's maxim, as cited earlier.

In order to galvanize people, Change Maestros also cultivate positive connections at the workplace. They are extremely good in expressing, encouraging, and cultivating positive emotions among the followers, which in turn helps in developing stronger connections between themselves and their followers. They use the power of experience—sharing and story-telling—to reach the minds and hearts of people (Mirvis and Gunning, 2006). They believe that the original nature of soul is love, peace, happiness, mercy, tolerance, and patience; David Novak, CEO, Tricon Global Restaurants, says: "I believe that people and teams make it happen. You show me anything that's been done that has not been done by people working together" (Chan Teng, 2000: 129). According to Lou Smith, CEO, Ewing Marion Kauffman Foundation: "True leaders genuinely care about people. They feel a responsibility to create a work environment in which people are respected and recognized, and they allocate funds to ensure that their people are adequately trained" (Chan Teng, 2000: 134). According to Stan Shih, CEO, Acer Inc.: "Money is not the solution (to going global). People are the solution, and it takes time to develop people. The strategy is that while you enjoy the current returns; don't forget to invest in the future" (Chan Teng, 2000: 79).

Lives of Change Maestros like Gandhi, Mandela, and Martin Luther King show us that they were spiritual; they had great capability to powerfully connect with the masses. It is this power which enabled them to mobilize people toward the larger purpose they decided to pursue:

> Transformational leaders don't exercise power which is tyrannical, autocratic, coercive and manipulative. Use of such power in today's egalitarian and democratic societies will only alienate people. Such leaders define their journey of life in terms of connecting with self, connecting with others, connecting with the universe and connecting with God. (Mirvis and Gunning, 2006)

In order to connect with people in larger numbers, religious and godly figures like Jesus, Buddha, and Guru Gobind Singh created enablers to spread the message far and wide. Jesus groomed twelve disciples, Buddha guided five, and Guru Gobind Singh shaped five.

Meaningful Contribution with Speed

While goal obsession puts organizations on the right track to achievement, focus on contribution brings perspective, guiding the selection of the right goals, keeping both the present and future in mind. It also provides balance since obsession is not for achievement of narrow, self-related goals, but for larger organizational, national, and societal goals. When in despair, Change Maestros remind themselves about the vision and conscious agenda to be re-energized. Contribution centricity triggers them to focus on goals with the long-term impact and value, and invariably leads to efforts at arriving at new and creative solutions to vexing and unresolved problems.

Change Maestros like to facilitate exploration by others and also explore to reach the best possible solutions. In the process, as creative persons, they themselves become the biggest learners and experimenters. Gandhi's life is the perfect example of a lifetime of learning and experimentation leading to the development of his philosophy of Satyagraha—Gandhi's distinctive contribution to the world. Soichiro Honda's (Mitto, 1990) philosophy provides a unique perspective on creative contribution. He stated, "to put short term results before creative and original efforts is to court ultimate downfall." He encouraged people to follow their dreams, keep a youthful outlook and to respect theory, new ideas, and time. These broad guidelines clearly reflect focus on creative contribution rather than merely getting the job done. Honda's R&D President, Tadashi Kume, gave the following speech to reinforce the creative spirit: "The driving force in the growth of an enterprise is ideas. At the R&D centres, priority should be given to ideas over technology, since technology is the crystallization of ideas..." (Mito, 1990). This clearly brings out the contribution focus of the leader.

Change Maestros combine the desire for making creative contribution with burning obsession to speedily reach the goal. It is almost as if they have to move relentlessly in order to achieve the goal—whether it is freedom, social transformation, or becoming the path-breaking organization. It is this combination of speed and desire which helps Change Maestros reach their goals.

O.P. Bhatt, CEO of the largest Indian public sector bank, State Bank of India (SBI), has changed the bank's DNA to that of a private sector bank. SBI has over 130,000 employees, 11,500 branches, and a fairly cumbersome hierarchy. But with change initiatives like "Parivartan," he transformed SBI from a lumbering public sector bank into a nimble-footed and fast-moving organization (Srinivas, 2009).

"In all businesses, to provide value, whatever you do, you've got to do fast and with immense efficiency," said Andy Grove (Sherman, 1993). Grove has put to practice his own professed statement. It is no wonder that Intel is looked up to as the pace-setter in the microprocessor industry.

ABB chief, Percy Barnevik, insisted that ABB employees be committed to customers and respond quickly to their needs. "Speed is everything" was his favorite statement (McClenahen, 1994). In his tenure as CEO of ABB, he traveled and worked with great speed and attended meetings straight away after long transcontinental flights (Schares, 1993: 211).

In pursuit of their goal—"Never follow others"—the Sony team has been the most consistently inventive consumer electronics enterprise. Throughout its history of forty-five years, Sony has brought out highly successful products (Schlender, 1992: 76) and ensured for itself the pre-eminent position worldwide in the electronics industry. Ratan Tata made the Nano, a super-low-cost small car, a reality, something which no other car maker thought possible. He said:

> If I had conceived a million dollar super car, you would have had every reason to question whether that is a right product at the right time on the planet that we are living in. What has happened in the changing global economic situation reinforces, if nothing else, the fact that a low cost car has a place and Tata Motors has done it. (Schuman, 2009)

One of Iacocca's characteristics has been speed and he expected the same from his employees. As he put it: "I've always found that the speed of the boss is the speed of the team" (Iacocca with Novak, 1985: 100).

In India, Dhirubhai Ambani of Reliance built a reputation for quick project implementation on par with global standards (Piramal, 1996: 41). Another figure on the Indian industrial scenario has been Aditya Birla, who built seventy green field plants manufacturing core products, over a career spanning twenty-five years (Piramal, 1996: 153). His grandfather, G.D. Birla, is credited with having made landmark contributions to both Indian business and society. G.D. Birla once said: "I am an impatient man and my dreams always run ahead of me" (Ramanujan, 1993: 114). He has been described not only as a man of vision, but also one of speedy action. According to Kaiser: "... [H]e takes that vision, organizes it with a plan and translates it into tangible accomplishments ..." (Ramanujan, 1993: 103). The bedrock of G.D. Birla's action focus lay in his belief in hard work: "Hard work never killed any man—indeed only hard work can help me to live long and serve my people in my own humble way" (Ramanujan, 1993: 106). His optimistic outlook further reinforced his action focus: "A cynic doesn't accomplish anything. It takes a believer to do something. I am a born optimist.... There is no room for diffidence or despondency ..." (Ramanujan, 1993: 42). In a short span of a decade-and-a-half, L.N. Mittal built a steel colossus, the largest steel manufacturing company in the world. This was possible because of his high focus on speedy decision-making and implementation.

The story of Abraham Lincoln has been a fascinating one. During the Civil War, Lincoln could take actions with great speed because he was right at the war department's telegraph office, getting the information as soon as it came (Philips, 1992: 19). He worked through people by creating enthusiasm among followers and by demonstrating a sense of urgency toward attainment of his goals (Philips, 1992: 110).

Gorbachev unleashed a near breakdown in the USSR through his transformation efforts. His major claim to greatness has been in breaking the communist way of life and politics in the USSR with the idea of ushering in freedom and a democratic way of life. Descriptions of the man give us a glimpse of that very speed which characterizes Change Maestros: "It's as though his temperature is a little higher than normal; and he's running a little faster than anybody else" (Sheehy, 1990: 3). "You feel his tremendous energy, curiosity and restlessness—he's moving all the time" (Sheehy, 1990: 3). In fact, the pace at which he worked is reflected in his own words: "I feel like I've lived through three lifetimes in the last 5 years" (Sheehy, 1990: 4). Since 1985, he had been living not only at three times the normal pace, he had also gone through three incarnations: from disciple to reformer; from reformer to revolutionary; and from revolutionary to quasi-democratic leader (Sheehy, 1990: 275).

What enables Change Maestros to work fast is the clarity of their goals. They clearly establish long- and short-term goals and relentlessly chase them. Goal clarity facilitates quick decision-making because they are able to regularly compare where they have to reach with where they are today. This becomes an internal compass guiding the Change Maestro to achieve the goal. Change Maestros integrate the creative idea with action focus and they envision as well as enact.

Creative Destruction for Transformation

Growth, advancement, and learning are built on the human capacity to destroy old ways of doing things and supplementing them with newer approaches. In fact, creativity flowers in the fertile debris of destruction. It is born out of human unlearning and experimenting with new ideas and approaches. It is a precursor to transformation within self, organization, as well as society. The Bhagavad Gita, Song Celestial (Arnold, 2007) propounds the view that life begins from death. The old Zen parable about the importance of the empty cup in life emphasizes the need to cultivate empty cups (spaces in the mind) by destroying old habits and approaches in order to facilitate absorption of new ideas. Creative destruction is possible only when there is systematic abandonment of whatever is established, familiar, and comfortable, whether it is a product or process, a set of skills, human and social relationships, or the organization itself (Drucker, 2006). Unless creative destruction takes place there is no scope for any change much less transformation, whether in the individual, group, or organization.

One of the major deterrents to creative destruction is the human attachment to one's own creations and ideas. This keeps many leaders in the past and makes them reluctant to initiate the drastic changes which transformation demands. Studies (Amabile et al., 2004; Chen et al., 2009; Mumford and Licuanan, 2004; Pamela et al., 1999) have shown that leaders influence and encourage employees' creativity and performance. Change Maestros are able to act ruthlessly with their own creations because their focus is not on what is being lost, but on the bigger issue of what is being gained through newer approaches. Such analysis is possible because of their capacity to detach and focus on the long term. A second important factor which facilitates creative destruction is the Change Maestro's openness to new learning experiences. As Obama said: "[C]hange will not come if we wait for some other person or some other time. We are the ones we've been waiting for. We are the change that we seek" (Libert and Faulk, 2009: 13).

The story of ABB is the saga of creative destruction. Barnevik created ABB by merging the erstwhile Asea with Brown Boveri. Then "he split ABB into profit centres, slashed staff, shrunk headquarters and converted ABB into a lithe organization." He continued with many more experiments, which helped build competitiveness of the company through creative destruction mode (Hotheinz, 1993).

Jack Welch spent more than fifteen years trying to build a transformation at GE. The act of divesting businesses which were not in the top slots in their industry segment, even though they were good performers, is an apt example of creative destruction. Although people were stunned by his decision, he could stay by it amidst public reactions because of his long-term perspective for the transformation of GE. His basic philosophy has been that at every moment, change has just begun and that change never ends (Corelli and Dwyer, 1991). His approach has been to constantly anticipate and respond to dynamic changes in the environment, destroy redundant ideas and methods, and constantly evolve new approaches for transacting business. Cook, Founder of Intuit Corporation, said that "... new business ideas come from watching other people work and live normal lives ... you see something and ask why do they do that?" (Dyer et al., 2009), giving a clue that it is the "why" which leads to destruction and new creation. Understanding what makes us ask the "why" is also useful—Ray Croc, Founder of McDonald's has been adroit and perceptive in identifying popular trends. He sensed that America was a nation of people who ate out. He converted his observations into a new business model, new business processes, leading to new kind of customer service. Thus, McDonald's was born—a simple, casual, identifiable restaurant with friendly service, no waiting, and no reservations, perfect for those who eat out everyday.

Gandhi's call for Satyagraha was a call to influence the oppressor by a novel approach—that is, through passive resistance, designed to jolt the latter out of strong mindsets, and conditioned modes of response. Gandhi's work for social transformation of India—destroying old modes of perception of caste and religion through personal example—was a method to break the old ways and replace them with new ones. In fact, even though, it was not his original intention, Lincoln (Philips, 1992: 139) practically redefined the presidency while, at the same time, notably, revising the American constitutional system.

In the year 1977, when the eighty-two-year-old Matsushita found that his company was becoming complacent and beset with all the ills of a large company, he appointed one of his youngest divisional heads, Yamashita (known for his forthrightness and boldness), as President, a step contrary to prevalent norms (Kotter, 1997: 192). Yamashita then systematically shook up the organization and transformed it to become as agile and customer-focused as it was earlier.

Intel's constant quest to invent a new product—smaller and more powerful versions of the microprocessor—and introducing the product much before the market got saturated ensured that it is on a consistent growth curve. Andy Grove contributed very powerfully by having the courage to discontinue a product line while the going was strong, and moving on to another product. Grove said: "Success can trap you. The more successful we are as a microprocessor company, the more difficult it will be to become something else. To take advantage of some of the opportunities I see ahead, we are going to have to transform ourselves again ..." (Sherman, 1993). Such relentless creative destruction was essential to build corporate transformation at Intel.

In the process of creative destruction both Welch and Barnevik used the mode of communication, education, and training to prepare people mentally for the impending changes. Jack Welch's slogan of breaking boundaries and building bridges across departments was one of the messages pushing for destruction of traditional interdepartmental rivalries. When Jack Welch took over as CEO, he immediately "seized the revolutionary's three main levers of control: the police, the media and the schools" (Tichy and Sherman, 1993: 94). The schools refer to the management education center, media refers to executive speeches and publications of the company, and police refer to the strategic planning and finance staff. These levers were used by Welch to systematically recreate GE. Action workshops and open dialogue sessions were used to convey GE's new values. "The perseverance to repeat his message, day after day, year after year, may be Welch's greatest strength" (Tichy and Sherman, 1993: 168). Eight years after Welch became CEO, the "work out" program was launched—the idea being to involve people in management education in a 1,000 different places, in order to influence their attitudes and behavior.

Given the size of GE, efforts to bring the "best practices" movement was another approach in the long march to the transformation of GE. It consisted of probing the management techniques of ten other world-class companies. The findings were subsequently converted into case studies and disseminated across the organization's interdepartmental executive teams which regularly got together, mapped existing processes, and then worked to shorten them. Through this approach GE was able to break down many internal boundaries and created a boundary-less organization. Phase three of the program of "work out," called the "change acceleration" program, was designed to breed a new type of GE manager, a professional change agent, to initiate change, accelerate it, and make it stick. All the training programs and workshops were designed with the ideas and involvement of Welch. The GE experience succinctly highlights the systematic and step-by-step approach to handling destruction and creating transformation by preparing people, building skills and commitment for the future.

One of Barnevik's greatest strengths is the capacity to motivate employees to stretch themselves. Barnevik's potent weapon to influence people was to get the skeptics to see the performers in the company (Schares, 1993: 208). "He would get one factory running at peak efficiency and then bring in managers from less profitable units across the world to see it" (Schares, 1993: 208). In Barnevik's words:

> ... you have to exploit your successes to break resistance. We, human beings, are driven by habit, history and the rear view mirror. If you want to break direction you have to shake people up, not by threatening them, not by offering a bonus, but by illustrating in a similar situation what can be accomplished. (Schares, 1993: 208)

Barnevik's style was to destroy the mental barriers of employees by providing them visible evidence of what is possible.

The importance of creating the right culture to encourage organizational innovation which has to follow creative destruction in the organization has been stated by Keshub Mahindra, Chairman, Mahindra and Mahindra: "The CEO with respect to his team, will have to inculcate a culture where innovation thrives and enough delegation of authority is done to make people feel the freedom to create and innovate" (Spencer et al., 2007: 29).

Change Maestros succeed because they focus not on the past, but on the present and future. They are able to destroy what is irrelevant in their quest for transformation, so that newer modes and approaches can be introduced in the company.

Evolving Self

Life is a challenge, a discovery, an exploration, and an evolution of self. Change Maestros are constantly on the growth path, striving to actualize their full potential. They focus their energies to bring change and, in the process of dealing with outer realities, also end up transforming themselves. They are constantly experimenting, testing, pushing, learning, growing, and reinventing themselves. They actualize themselves through creation and contribution to the world. They are highly open-minded and reflective people, and this forms the basis of the ability to receive feedback, learn, and reorient themselves accordingly. The power of their vision drives them to constantly transform themselves. In this connection Obama said, "[I]t is only when you hitch your wagon to something larger than yourself that you realize your true potential" (Thomas, 2007: 279).

The life of Gandhi is a fine example of the evolution of self. The title of his autobiography, *My Experiments with Truth*, aptly describes the attitude of the man to himself and his life—always experimenting and testing, with the spirit of constant learning and improvement. To the end of his life, Gandhi attempted to master and re-make himself (Fischer, 1997: 39). "He remade himself by tapping inner resources ... using the clay that was there, he transformed himself into another person" (Fischer, 1997: 56). "His zeal and cause dissolved his timidity ..." (Fischer, 1997: 67). Fischer (1997: 157) also said:

> It helped him to realize his potential. One of the underlying factors of Gandhi's evolution was his focus on self-conquest and self-mastery, which he progressively achieved by seeking to master his needs at every level. Gandhi said about his life that it was an unending experiment. He experimented even in his 70s. There was nothing set about him.

The following statement made by Gandhi is ample testimony to his learning and growing disposition:

> At the time of writing ... I never think of what I have said before. My aim is not to be consistent with my previous statement on a given question, but to be consistent with the truth as it may present itself to me at a given moment. The result is that I have grown from truth to truth. (Fischer, 1997: 440)

Similar is the story of Confucius who said:

> ... at 15 I set my heart on learning; at 30 I had formed my character; at 40 I had no doubts; at 50 I knew the mandate of heaven; at 60 nothing disturbed me; at 70 I could follow my desires without trespassing the boundaries of right. (Fernandez, 2004)

Abraham Lincoln is a great example of a person who continuously learnt from people around him (Philips, 1992: 138). He had the desire to learn new things, and this made him innovative. He is incidentally the only American president to hold a patent for an innovation (Philips, 1992: 138). It has been said of Abraham Lincoln that "he always learnt from his mistakes, he shared responsibility for the mistakes of others and he did not hold grudges" (Coutu, 2009).

Gorbachev has been analyzed as a person who at critical stages of his life underwent "deep personal transformation," which made him a different person each time. "... [A]nd those leaps of inner psychological development ultimately became the catalyst for a transformation of the society out of which they come. It allows the path leader like Gorbachev, to perform creative actions that cause leaps of growth in human societies" (Sheehy, 1990: 25). According to Mlynar (one of the men who worked with Gorbachev), "he is open-minded, curious, has an ability to listen, learn and adapt. All this is the root of his self-confidence" (Sheehy, 1990: 76).

The life of G.D. Birla is an example of the person who continued to grow throughout his life. He started life as a broker with very little education. However, in his generation, he went on to become a colossus on the Indian business and political scenario. As a close associate of Gandhi, G.D. Birla played a very important role not only in providing monetary support for the freedom movement, but also frequently acted as a negotiator and diplomat with British leaders.

The life story of Matsushita is the odyssey of evolving self. Kotter (1997: 8) writes:

> As a young adult in his early twenties, he was nervous and sickly; yet, by the time he was thirty, he was inventing business practices that would be highlighted in the late 1970s by Tom Peters and Bob Waterman. By age forty, he had become the kind of visionary leader that has been championed recently by Warren Bennis, Noel Tichy and others. After World War II, he created an institution that adapted phenomenally well to rapid growth, increasing technological change and globalization. In the 1970s and 1980s, he took on additional careers as author, philanthropist, educator, social philosopher and statesman. Most of all, throughout his life, he demonstrated a capacity for growth and renewal that is astonishing....

"From apprentice to merchant entrepreneur, to business leader, to institution builder, to educator and philosopher, the single biggest theme, that runs throughout his life is associated with growth—as a human being, as a business person and as a leader" (Kotter, 1997: 240).

Another evolving Change Maestro has been Jack Welch. The spirit is nicely captured in the following statement: "Change doesn't scare Welch, it excites him. Throughout his career, he has benefited from his willingness to create change—not only in the organizations he has run, but in himself ... he has evolved from a demanding boss to a helpful coach" (Tichy and Sherman, 1993: 11); "[T]he cranked up ferocity of the CEO's interactions with subordinates gave way to a more wholesome attitude—an urge to respect and empower people that began to seem convincing and genuine" (Tichy and Sherman, 1993: 255); "The Jack Welch who took over GE is not the Jack Welch you see today," says Noel Tichy (Tichy and Sherman, 1993: 256).

D. Smith, CEO of Kimberly Clark, has been another example of continuous learning and evolving orientation. The statement by Abdul Kalam "... this change must bring with it new thoughts which lead to innovative actions.... I know my imagination will never let me down; neither will my dreams ..." (Kalam, 2003) is an apt example of the evolving personality. According to Mashelkar, Director General, CSIR (Council of Scientific and Industrial Research), "I believe there is no limit to human achievement and to human endurance ..." (Piramal and Netarwala, 2005) indicating the vast potential which human beings have and which has also pushed him higher and higher toward greater levels of leadership as a scientist.

What is it that impels Change Maestros to push themselves to bring inner evolution? Gardner's (1996) study of great leaders like Gandhi, Martin Luther King, Eleanor Roosevelt, Alfred Sloan, M. Thatcher, etc., provides us with useful insights on the subject. Carl Rogers' conceptualization, "on becoming a person" also provides us with some answers (Rogers, 1989). Gardner found that the leaders he studied were evolving, self-confident, experimenting, and optimistic and many of them also had the sense of being unique and different. Self-awareness has been found to be associated with profiles of transformational leaders (Sosik and Megerian, 1999). Based on his long years of counseling experience, Rogers concluded that self-esteem is the basic and essential characteristic of the evolving human being. Self-confidence and self-esteem, along with purpose, push the leader toward reflection, improvement, and self-evolution. Others like Nathaniel Branden (1989) have also emphasized the power of self-esteem for self-transformation.

Further reflection on the psychological forces impelling toward inner growth indicate that perhaps the ideal vision of self strongly beckons the person on the path to self-transformation and becomes the guiding star in the struggle to become what one can. The evolving Change Maestro uses self-talk to consciously meet tough inner challenges. Such people are the explorers who enthusiastically embrace life in its myriad hues. Another force mobilizing the Change Maestros toward internal evolution may be the challenges of life itself, where unless the perspective changes, the Change Maestro may not be able to get on top of the situation—thus, the external demands strongly push for inner evolution. Change Maestros have the curiosity to know, courage to own, and determination to change.

The evolving Change Maestro has the exciting capacity to be both a part of people as well as stand apart from them and reflect. The importance of this ability to withdraw and reflect has been aptly described in the Upanishads: "Let a man strive to purify his thoughts. What a man thinketh, that is he; this is the eternal mystery ... man becomes that which he thinks" (Watson, 1988: 173). This characteristic helps the Change Maestro balance himself, a trait which is essential both for making accurate assessments and taking appropriate actions for growth.

Culture Architecture

Researchers, scholars, and thinkers (see Denison, 1990; Hofstede, 1986; Kanter, 1983; Krefting and Frost, 1985; Marcoulides and Heck, 1993; Moos, 1979; Ouchi, 1980; Peters and Waterman, 1982) in the field of management are more or less unanimous that organizational culture is critical for achieving organizational goal, performance, and effectiveness, as well as for promoting creativity, innovation, employee commitment, and motivation. Schein (1981) defines organizational culture as a pattern of shared basic assumptions that the group learned as it solved its problems that has worked well enough to be considered valid and is passed on to new members as the correct way to perceive, think, and feel in relation to those problems. Organizational culture is normally built around the philosophy, values, and vision of the organization and, therefore, helps the organization set direction, goals, standards, and ideals. It clarifies actions which are acceptable and those which are unacceptable, thereby signaling what are desirable and undesirable behaviors.

Change Maestros like Percy Barnevik, A.G. Lafley, Aditya Birla, Larry Bossidy, Jan Carlson, Lou Gerstner, Narayana Murthy, Azim Premji, J.R.D. Tata, and Sam Walton, therefore, laid heavy emphasis on building organizational culture to create winning and high-performing organizations along with laying focus on business architecture and imperatives. It is by now an accepted truism that all levers of competitive edge—cost leadership; quality leadership; customer centricity; speedy business processes; innovation; organizational architecture; and strategy—can, in due course, be imitated by others. However, it is only organizational culture which is extremely difficult to imitate or duplicate (Fitzgerald, 1988; Barney, 1986). Thus, when it is aligned to organizational vision and goals, organizational culture has the capability to provide unique competitive edge to the firm. In order to build a sustained competitive advantage and performance excellence, Change Maestros, therefore, make special effort in building robust organizational culture and nurturing talent.

Vision and goal clarity set the direction and growth trajectory on which the organization moves. In fact, in the process of vision and goal setting, many issues like emerging industry trends and competitive scenario are clarified to organization members. Based on such scenario mapping, the growth strategy, strategy for promoting organizational excellence, and evolving instruments for competitive edge are planned accordingly. Since organization culture is built around vision and goal, it sets the tone for both value prioritization as well as performance imperatives. It leads to creation of collective mindset, collective perspective, and, therefore, channelizes collective energy toward the common goal. In fact, organizational culture is the glue which binds and bonds people together.

Research has powerfully brought out that leaders have significant impact on organizational culture. In a recent study on CEOs' values, organizational culture, and firm outcomes (Berson et al., 2008), it was found that CEOs' self-directive values were associated with innovation-oriented culture, security values were associated with bureaucratic culture, and supportive values were associated with supportive cultures. Bass (1985) demonstrated that leadership style has significant impact on culture. It has been found that leaders have a central role in shaping and controlling organizational culture both being closely intertwined (Schein, 1992). Hennessey (1998) found from his research that leadership played a major role in nurturing the appropriate culture which helped to improve the implementation of specific government reforms. Ogbonna and Harris (2000) concluded from their research that organizational culture is a mediating variable between leadership styles and organizational performance. Thus, CEOs, and more so Change Maestros, have been found to have a significant impact on creating and nurturing organizational culture and utilizing the same for building competitive edge.

The following salient conclusions emerge from the discussion in this chapter:

- Although leadership issues are extensively researched, discussed, and debated, there is no definitive leadership model and the search continues even today.
- In the contemporary world there is an unprecedented crisis of leadership in all walks of life having tremendous impact the lives of people globally.
- Research on leaders indicates the importance of contextual sensitivity, compelling vision, winning streak, people connect and engagement, meaningful contribution with speed, creative destruction, evolving self and culture architecture for becoming Change Maestros.

Part III: Contours of Research Methodology

Before dealing with the methodology in detail, we present the conceptualization about Change Maestros and Organizational Culture.

Change Maestros: Conceptualization

In addition to possessing unique mastery over competency drivers which enable a person to effectively play the role as a manager,[3] as a leader,[4] and as a change master,[5] change maestros have capabilities to effortlessly work at all three levels:

- Self level
- Business level
- Context level

Self level: Change Maestros demonstrate high degree of consistency among the purpose they pursue, the philosophy they articulate, values they espouse, attitudes they display, and behavior they adopt.

Business level: Change Maestros have mastery over harmonizing and integrating organizational vision, business strategy, structure, processes, culture, leadership styles, and skills. In addition, they are able to equally focus on multiple drivers enabling competitive advantage—cost leadership; quality leadership; customer centricity; speedy decision-making; entrepreneurial innovation; people power; and ethical governance.

Context level: Change Maestros have a finely tuned radar-like sensitivity and alertness which enables them to scan and register events and information about the social, political, economic, and global levels. This in turn is used to appropriately align the organization to take advantage of the business opportunity.

Organizational Culture: Conceptualization

It encompasses shared values and collective mindsets regarding different facets of business (customer, owners, business partners, and employees). Most importantly, it includes the do's and don'ts which guide behavior of organizational members for achieving organizational goals.

Research Design

In order to overcome the in-built limitations and biases in every type of data—structured questionnaires; interviews; autobiographical/biographical; anthropological inquiry; and secondary data—we have used an eclectic approach in this research consisting of self-assessment through structured questionnaires as well as interviews and secondary data.

- Data has been gathered regarding the Change Maestro and the organizational culture from the top and senior team using the Change Maestros' and the Organizational Culture Inventory (for details, see Appendix 1A.1);
- Change Maestros' Inventory was also used to collect Change Maestros' self-assessment;
- Interviews were also conducted with the top team directly reporting to the CEO on a one-to-one basis, ranging from one to two hours (for details, see Appendix 1A.2); and
- Financial data regarding the company performance has been gathered from secondary sources (appended at the end of each case, that is, Chapters 2 to 8).

Stage I: Identification of Change Maestros

The research team wrote to 400 Indian CEOs requesting them to identify names of those CEOs (Indian) whom they considered as Change Maestros in the last decade. The team received 143 usable responses. The top seventeen names which appeared in the survey responses are Anil Ambani, Mukesh Ambani, O.P. Bhat, K.M. Birla, M. Damodaran, Sajjan Jindal, K.V. Kamath, Jagdish Khattar, Anand Mahindra, Keshub Mahindra, Sunil Mittal, Narayana Murty, A.M. Naik, Nandan Nilekani, Deepak Parekh, Kiran Mazumdar Shaw, and Ratan Tata. The purposive sample technique was applied to select the final list of names of the Change Maestros keeping in view the requirement of a heterogeneous, cross sector sample. The names of the nine leaders finally selected on this basis are given in Table 1.1.

The authors received a positive and timely response from seven of the nine Change Maestros and, therefore, decided to reluctantly drop two Change

Table 1.1: Change Maestros

Long Established House	Ratan Tata, K.M. Birla
First-Generation Entrepreneurs	Kiran Mazumdar Shaw, Narayana Murthy, and Sunil Mittal
Second-Generation Entrepreneur	Sajjan Jindal
Publicly owned Private Institution	K.V. Kamath, A.M. Naik
Public Sector Institution	M. Damodaran

Source: Authors.

Maestros—Narayana Murty and Ratan Tata—from the research plan and carried forth the study on the other seven Change Maestros.

Stage II: Intra-company Sample and Data Collection

The research method at this stage consisted of:

1. Detailed unstructured interviews with the top team directly working with and reporting to the Change Maestros. The authors interviewed each of the members for an hour and thirty minutes (see Table 1.2).[6]
2. Responses on structured questionnaires on the style and behavior of the CEO as a Change Maestro, as well as on the Organizational Culture of the respective organizations were gathered from a sample of top and senior level that have had some exposure to the CEO, rather than having just heard about him.[7] The questionnaires used in the study were the Change Maestro Inventory and Organizational Culture Inventory.[8]
3. Family members (one or two) of the Change Maestro were interviewed for an hour to hour-and-a-half each.
4. Each Change Maestro CEO was interviewed for a duration ranging from two to five hours.
5. During the interview process, the authors asked questions to the CEO regarding their self-perceived leadership attributes and based on their responses, the Change Maestros Inventory items was ranked.

Table 1.2: Sample Details—Questionnaire- and Interview-based

Company Name	Questionnaire Sample*	Interview Sample
Aditya Birla Group	88	25
UTI and IDBI	66	21
JSW	96	18
ICICI	71	25
L&T	98	20
Biocon	38	23
Airtel	68	21
Total Sample	**525**	**153**

Source: Authors.

Note: * The average age of the respondents was 48.77 years varying from 25 to 74 years; 91 percent respondents were male; and 75 percent had postgraduate degrees.

6. Financial performance data (turnover and profit) was gathered for a five-year period for each case. This was done to examine whether the vision and actions of the Change Maestro were converted into winning performance of the organization, which is the ultimate litmus test for a Change Maestro.

To understand the Change Maestro in a holistic sense, ideally, there is a need for three levels of analysis: what a Change Maestro thinks of himself; what others think of him; and who he actually is. The present work has mapped the Change Maestros' profile at two levels: what others think of him and what he thinks of himself. This was done with a view to find out the extent of match and connect between what leaders think of themselves and what others think of them. The greater the disconnect and resulting gap between the two, the lower the CEO credibility, and vice versa. The uniqueness of this work lies in adopting multiple modes of data gathering—structured questionnaires; in-depth interviews; and anthropological inquiry. There are hardly any studies where the three criteria mentioned further have been utilized simultaneously to study Change Maestros:

1. Researching CEO-level leadership;
2. Self-assessment by CEO as well as perceptions of the top team; and

3. Multiple modes of data gathering using both questionnaire, interview technique, anthropological and secondary data sources.

Appendix 1A.1: Inventories

Change Maestro Inventory

This inventory was initially developed through focused group discussion conducted upon 175 executives with at least five years of work experience in various post-experience MBA programs conducted at MDI, Gurgaon. Based on content analysis of this data, a pool of sixty-five items was developed. Each leadership attribute was measured on a 5-point scale, 1 being "Least Visible" and 5 being "Most Visible." The Change Maestro Inventory was subsequently administered on a sample of 333 executives. The sixty-five items were then reduced to thirty-five based on factor analysis (Singh and Verma, 2010).

General Instructions
- Please answer ALL the questions.
- Please give your first and spontaneous answer—try not to dwell too long on each question.
- Work quickly through the questionnaire—it will only take you about twenty minutes to complete.
- All answers will be kept confidential and used only for the purpose of aggregation.

This section aims at mapping out the prominent leadership qualities of K.M. Birla, M. Damodaran, Sajjan Jindal, K.V. Kamath, Sunil Mittal, A.M. Naik, and Kiran Mazumdar Shaw. Given further is a list of thirty-five Change Maestro attributes—attitude, behavior, and style. Based on your experience of interacting and working with him, kindly rate each attribute on a 5-point scale, 1 being "Least Visible" and 5 being "Most Visible."

Note: While giving your rating, kindly use the full scale range, viz., 1, 2, 3, 4, and 5. This will help us to identify those attributes which uniquely describe his leadership.

Change Maestro Characteristics	1 Least Visible	2 Somewhat Visible	3 Moderately Visible	4 Highly Visible	5 Most Visible
1. Is demanding and performance-centric					
2. Is a strategic thinker					
3. Respects the dignity of others					
4. Has empowering and supporting attitude					
5. Leads from the front					
6. Makes people feel that they are valued by the organization					
7. Is an effective communicator					
8. Stands like a rock in the face of calamities					
9. Is a team builder					
10. Provides clear sense of direction					
11. Is honest and transparent					
12. Is reliable					
13. Radiates positive energy					
14. Is innovative and creative					
15. Is fair and impartial					
16. Is open to new ideas					
17. Leads by example					
18. Is result focused					

(continued)

(continued)

Change Maestro Characteristics	1 Least Visible	2 Somewhat Visible	3 Moderately Visible	4 Highly Visible	5 Most Visible
19. Has ambitious plans for the organization					
20. Grooms and develops people					
21. Has high credibility					
22. Is a man of words					
23. Has helping attitude					
24. Is a role model for others					
25. Makes people feel that they have great worth					
26. Pursues excellence in everything					
27. Has a global mind-set					
28. Fast in making critical decisions					
29. Is entrepreneurial					
30. Is a visionary					
31. Is interested in the growth of his people					
32. Recognizes and rewards performance					
33. Sensitivity					
34. Humility					
35. Business strategist (growth, mergers, and acquisitions)					

Organizational Culture Inventory

This inventory was initially developed based on an extensive survey of the research literature. The initial pool of sixty-two items was subsequently administered on a sample of 333 executives. Each item of work place characteristics was also rated on a 5-point Likert-type scale ranging from 1 being "Very Low Extent" to 5 being "Very High Extent." The sixty-two items were then reduced to thirty-three based on factor analysis (Singh and Verma, 2010).

General Instructions

- Please answer ALL the questions.
- Please give your first and spontaneous answer—try not to dwell too long on each question.
- Work quickly through the questionnaire—it will only take you about twenty minutes to complete.
- All answers will be kept confidential and used only for the purpose of aggregation.

Given ahead are certain organizational characteristics. Kindly indicate the extent to which you see each of these in your organization on the 5-point scale alongside. The scale ranges from "Very Low Extent" to "Very High Extent."

Kindly keep in mind that where you tick reflects the extent to which that particular characteristic is visible according to you, in your organization. Please respond to on all the items ahead:

Organizational Culture Characteristics	Very Low Extent	Low Extent	Moderate	High Extent	Very High Extent
1. Communication and information flow: Vertical—(a) Top-Down					
2. Vertical (b) Bottom-Up					

(continued)

(continued)

Organizational Culture Characteristics	Very Low Extent	Low Extent	Moderate	High Extent	Very High Extent
3. Communication and information flow: Horizontal (a) Within department					
4. Horizontal (b) Across departments					
5. Teamwork					
6. Role clarity					
7. Openness and transparency					
8. Performance-based promotion					
9. Culture of celebration of achievements and successes					
10. Centralization of decision-making process					
11. Cross-functional collaboration					
12. Nurturing innovation					
13. Speed of response to external demands and challenges					
14. Empowerment and delegation					
15. Tolerance of differences					
16. Support for risk taking					
17. Focus on continuous improvement					
18. Speed of response to internal demands					
19. Result orientation					
20. Performance excellence					

Organizational Culture Characteristics	Very Low Extent	Low Extent	Moderate	High Extent	Very High Extent
21. Process focused					
22. Trust					
23. Ethical governance					
24. Responsiveness to customer					
25. Outward looking					
26. People orientation					
27. Openness to new ideas					
28. Community culture					
29. Entrepreneurial					
30. Participative					
31. Nurturing talent					
32. Global perspectives					
33. Focus on building on competitiveness					

Techniques of Data Analysis

Data from questionnaires have been analyzed using basic analyses like Mean, Standard Deviation as well as advanced techniques like Factor Analysis and Structural Equation Modeling.

APPENDIX 1A.2: INTERVIEWS

Interview Questions for Top Management Team

Interview Process and Schedule: Each interview commenced by introducing the study in terms of purpose and description of the method used to identify the Change Maestros under study.

1. Each interviewee was asked to introduce himself/herself so as to understand the background and length of association with the organization;
2. They were asked to mention five adjectives which he/she would like to use to describe the organization;

3. They were asked to explain why these adjectives were used with examples to support the statement;
4. Each interviewee was asked to mention five adjectives to describe XXX as a Change Maestro and as a person;
5. They were asked to explain why these adjectives were used with examples to support the statement.

Interview Questions for Change Maestro

Interview Process and Schedule: Each interview commenced by introducing the study in terms of purpose and description of the method used to identify the Change Maestros under study:

1. Each Change Maestro was asked to mention five adjectives which he/she would like to use to describe his/her organization;
2. Each Change Maestro was asked to explain why these adjectives were used with examples to support the statement;
3. Each Change Maestro asked to mention five adjectives to describe himself/herself as a Change Maestro and as a person;
4. They were asked to describe his/her dream and vision;
5. They were asked about the people who had a deep impact on them in their younger days or whom they admired from the political and business domains;
6. They were asked to narrate the life changing experience they have undergone.

Technique of Analysis

1. Grounded Theory Method was used to arrive at the emergent model of Change Maestros' profile. Based on the concepts presented in the literature review as well as comparing conceptualized data on different levels of abstraction, an emergent model of Change Maestros profile has been developed. The interview data has been coded using three types

of coding, closely connected with one another—Open coding, Axial coding, and Selective coding (Strauss and Corbin, 1990).
2. The method of *content analysis* was also used in processing the interview data. It involved systematically identifying properties of the large amount of textual information, using the frequencies of most used keywords, thereby detecting the more important structures of the communication content. The information was then categorized for analysis, providing at the end a meaningful reading of content. It is "a systematic, replicable technique for compressing many words of text into fewer content categories based on explicit rules of coding" (Stemler, 2001).

Notes

1. Mantra is a hymn chanted as an incantation or prayer. It is believed that such chanting bestows the person with superpowers.
2. Change Maestro is a person who has mastered the art of transformational leadership, who effortlessly harmonizes diverse forces and channels them toward achieving the overarching mission and goal.
3. The managerial category consists of competencies like decision-making, problem solving, managing people, managing task, managing conflicts, building team, and communicating effectively. These competencies enable a role holder to be an effective manager.
4. The leadership category encompasses competencies like shaping talent, networking, managing boundary, mobilizing resources, making patterns by connecting dots, focusing on continuous improvement, motivating people, along with basic competencies mentioned in the manager category earlier. These together facilitate a person to effectively function as a leader.
5. The Change Master category comprises of competencies like continued quest for excellence, high learning orientation, quest for creating winning organization, harmonizing the interest of stakeholders, envisioning the future, strategizing growth architecture, renewing organizational energy, revitalizing entrepreneurial spirit, repositioning the organization to take on emerging challenges, ethical governance, enabling, and empowering people. They perform these roles with high degree of speed and contextual sensitivity and subsume the competencies mentioned under the category of leader.

6. In each organization we have interviewed most of the members of the top team, above 90 percent.
7. The questionnaires were sent to each organization in the year 2008–2009 to the top levels via email. The response rate was excellent—above 85 percent—across the seven organizations.
8. The two inventories have excellent psychometric properties (Singh and Verma, 2010).

2

2

KUMAR MANGALAM BIRLA: LOOKING WITHIN, LOOKING AROUND, AND LOOKING BEYOND

A mighty Chinese King once went to the Grandmaster (known for his rare capability to mentor great kings) seeking his help to groom his son to become the greatest King. The Grandmaster said, "Mighty King, it is a difficult task but I will attempt, provided the Prince stays in my school for five years and undergoes rigorous training.

"I will devote three years to groom him as a great warrior and ruler and another two years will be spent to instill capabilities to make him a philosopher–king."

The Grandmaster diligently spent many hours and coached the young Prince to become a great warrior and an able ruler, which, according to the Grandmaster, was not enough to make him a great and wise King. Hence, in the next phase of the mentoring he was sent to the forest for a year and on his return was asked to narrate his salient experiences, which he vividly recounted over a period of five days. He described the chirping of the birds, trumpeting of the elephants, roar of the lion, mooing of the cows, vivid colors of the forest, and startling beauty of the blue waters and white clouds. The Grandmaster heard him patiently but expressed disappointment with his progress and sent him back to the forest for another nine months.

On his return, as asked previously, the Prince had to present his experiences. This time his narration to the Grandmaster focused on his experiences with the tribal communities living in the forest—their lifestyles;

culture; rituals; beliefs; etc. He talked in-depth about how he became a part of the community and tried to help the people integrate with the world. This time he took only a day to narrate his experiences. However, the Grandmaster was still dissatisfied and sent him back to the forest for another three months, which the Prince spent in deep reflection—both within and in communion with the surroundings. He used this period to undertake the journey of self-discovery and self-reflection. In this state of silent meditation he developed heightened sensitivity both toward his inner world and outer world and helped develop the prescient capability to see the future.

This time when the Prince returned he asked only for a minute to share his experiences. In a ruminative tone, he said, "Grandmaster, during my stay in the forest I heard the sound of sunrays warming the petals of the roses; I also heard the sound of the unborn child…." A delighted Grandmaster nodded approvingly and proclaimed, "Oh Prince! You have finally succeeded in developing the deepest level of mastery, i.e., mastery over self and capability to integrate the same with the outer world; you have developed the rare capability to see beyond the obvious and anticipate the future. You are now ready to become the greatest King of all time. You will be fondly remembered by posterity for building a great kingdom where people live without fear; where there is dignity and sense of justice; where people experience care and kindness when they are in trouble; where they feel valued for their capabilities; where there is freedom to experiment … and where there is empowerment. Above all you will be able to protect this kingdom for a long time by the power of your intuition which will facilitate you to see the future. Let me tell you Prince, that such a kingdom, under your guidance, will flourish for a long time because you have mastered the art of looking within, around and beyond."

William Shakespeare has said "Be not afraid of greatness: some men are born great, some achieve greatness and some have greatness thrust upon them." We may be tempted to call Kumar Mangalam Birla a man born for greatness having been born into one of India's pre-eminent industrial houses. However, we cannot deprive him of the greatness that he has earned on his own in a short span of time. If K.M. Birla stands tall on account of his own strength among the business czars of India today, it is not only because he was lucky to be born great, but also that he achieved greatness. He has proved Drucker's well-known statement: "Effective leadership is defined by results not attributes." When he took over the conglomerate of the Aditya Birla Group, he put all his energies to build its present and future, without, at the same time, discounting the past. K.M. Birla has rightfully earned the distinction of being called one of the youngest and most dynamic businessmen in India; the Change Maestro who looks within, around, and beyond.

The case study "Kumar Mangalam Birla: Looking Within, Looking Around, and Looking Beyond"[1] has been organized into three parts: Part I provides a brief profile sketch of the Aditya Birla Group; Part II highlights the action architecture and culture landscape initiated and nurtured by K.M. Birla; and Part III discusses his profile and persona.

Part I: Brief Profile Sketch of the Aditya Birla Group

K.M. Birla (for details of the Change Maestro's profile, see Appendix 2A.1) took over the reins of the Aditya Birla Group Empire (for details of the organization's profile, see Appendix 2A.2) in 1995 under painful circumstances of having lost his father, Shri Aditya Birla, a doyen among Indian industrialists. This was a critical moment for the 28-year-old K.M. Birla as also for the group, which had a galaxy of veterans heading numerous companies, nineteen of them spread across Thailand, Philippines, Indonesia, and Egypt apart from ten key locations in India including UP, Jharkhand, Gujarat, Andhra Pradesh, Maharashtra, Kerala, Dadra and Nagar Haveli, West Bengal, Karnataka, and Orissa.

From 1997 to 2008, it has been a tremendous transformational journey for the group, having scaled many new heights in its history which dates back to the early part of the 20th century. In fact, it appears as if the group has traversed the last twelve years (since 1997 when K.M. Birla took over) in preparing the company toward becoming a global giant in the 21st century.

The company has many milestone achievements to its credit: growth in business; profits; customer base; Return on Investment (ROI); market capitalization; etc. During the regime of K.M. Birla, the Aditya Birla Group has seen impressive growth through both organic and inorganic routes. It has, in this period, tremendously expanded its global presence with operations in twenty-five countries—India, the UK, Germany, Hungary, Brazil, Italy, France, Luxembourg, Switzerland, Australia, the USA, Canada, Egypt, China, Thailand, Laos, Indonesia, the Philippines, Dubai, Singapore, Myanmar, Bangladesh, Vietnam, Malaysia, and Korea. The expansion into twenty countries took place over a short span of approximately a decade (1997 onwards). By any stretch of imagination this can be considered a monumental achievement.

Part II: Action Architecture and Culture Landscape

The interview data were content-analyzed and the seven emergent themes are as follows:

- Value-driven governance
- Global: Taking India to the world
- Futuristic and forward-looking group
- People centricity
- Robust growth strategy
- Toward meritocracy with personal touch
- Managing change with continuity

Value-driven Governance

In our experience as consultants for many Indian organizations and MNCs, we have observed a significant gap between the company's espoused values and operating values. In the Aditya Birla Group, however, it is heartening to see a high degree of congruence between the professed and practiced values.

All the twenty-one executives[2] we met narrated how difficult it was to do business in India if they tried to be scrupulously ethical. They said that India ranks high on the corruption list of the Transparency International Survey 2008, at 85 out of a total of 180 nations. They further added that considering the political and governmental pulls and pushes, sticking to certain principles and consistently living by them is a Herculean task for Indian organizations.

In this context, it was amazing to hear all the interviewees say with pride that the Aditya Birla Group is highly value driven. Twenty interviewees said that in future, ethical governance and practice will be their core differentiator for building a competitive edge. The five veterans said that the group always had such an emphasis (on values and value-based functioning); however, under K.M. Birla it received a fresh impetus and thrust.

Almost all the persons (twenty-four respondents) talked about the group's values with great passion—integrity; commitment; and ethical governance—all indicating a high degree of internalization of these values. The five relatively recent entrants to the group as CEOs (in the last ten years) said that they joined it because they were attracted by the group values, and have stayed on owing to group adherence and commitment to the stated values. One of the CEOs, who had worked in some leading global conglomerates for years and decided to return here, said: "I chose the Aditya Birla Group over another Indian organization offering me twice the salary, because of the strong value system of this group." According to him:

> Here you are not treated as a number; one is a person, one is empowered to do. We are valued for our ideas.... I am proud to say that we get different respect from the bureaucracy, because we do nothing underhand nor do we grease palms....

Most interviewees (twenty of these) highlighted that the Gandhian idea of trusteeship guides the organizational approach to wealth and wealth creation and that they consider the Aditya Birla Group a trustee of shareholders' wealth.

As many as twenty interviewees said that in this group value orientation is driven from the top. In many cases where the company could have been adversely affected because of certain decisions, the response from K.M. Birla was: "Don't worry; I would prefer to take the business hit, rather than compromise on values." Quoting the case of Mangalore Refineries and Petroleum Chemicals Ltd (MRPL), one of the interviewees said:

> Our partnership with HPCL (Hindustan Petroleum Corporation Limited) had failed. We could have easily taken the BIFR (Bureau of Industrial and Financial Reconstruction) route which would have however hurt the investors' interests. But we did not do so, because K.M. Birla said "we must think of our 1200 shareholders" (who would be affected by the decision); so we sold it to ONGC for a much lower price to ensure the shareholders' interests and value creation for them.

The well-known precept of K.M. Birla is: "In business, I consider that means are as important as ends." As many as eighteen executives expressed: "The mandate here is to abide by the law on issues like labour, environmental pollution, rural development etc. The expectation is actual compliance and not just lip service." Nine executives said "In this group, financial impropriety is almost nonexistent."

Almost all the interviews (twenty-one of them) emphasized the power of value driven governance and said that Aditya Birla Group fights the battles of competition through robust business strategy, a responsive structure facilitating speedy decisions, evolving appropriate processes and systems rather than cutting corners. Such an approach, according to them, has helped the group in building robust competitive edge without sacrificing its ethical approach.

This is the group where the Chairman personally wrote to each of the CEOs advising them not to take shortcuts with law, even if it benefits the group. Through this letter K.M. Birla clearly set the tone and pace for the group to remain adhered to the stated values.

According to five interviewed top team members:

> ... we are one of the few companies that set up an electoral trust to fund political parties. Prior to this we had many problems when we refused to pay political donations in cash. People threatened us but over the years they have stopped because they know that we will take legal recourse.

In order to ensure that the stated values of integrity, commitment, passion, seamlessness, and speed take deep roots and spreads widely across the organization, Aditya Birla Group has evolved robust processes:

- The group has evolved and widely disseminated an elaborate code of conduct.
- The values are fostered and nurtured by honoring value leaders through a series of awards given at a highly prestigious annual award ceremony. The process comprises nomination of such value leaders (that is, those who live by the values) by other colleagues and the winners are selected after an elaborate screening process by a jury.

The following views of the top executives we met further confirm the abiding concern of the Aditya Birla Group regarding value-based governance and good corporate citizenship:

- Eleven top executives said: "The group is socially sensitive and responsive corporate citizen."
- Twelve top executives mentioned: "Social issues like education, health and environment are paramount to this group. The promoter sees himself more as a trustee (of the Aditya Birla Group) than the owner."
- "In Corporate Social Responsibility (CSR), Birla family works with a Karma Yogi (one who strives for self realization by engaging in work) spirit, focusing more on making a difference through action rather than on publicizing the work they do." Fourteen top executives confirmed this. They have partnered with the government at the village level in 3,700 villages in India on implementation of schemes for polio eradication, education, and water. "The group has played a lead role in professionalizing education in schools."

In the Aditya Birla Group, seventeen respondents said that the Chairman is often heard saying "What kind of [a] world are we leaving for our own children?" indicating his deep concern for the world which perhaps leads to good citizenship behavior as mentioned earlier. Today the Aditya Birla Group spends about ₹ 200 crores per annum on CSR activities mainly in the domain of health and education. This annual spend is an expression of their deep concern for communities and society.

One of the CEOs proudly said: "[W]e have a division of CSR headed by Mrs Birla [K.M. Birla's mother] herself which runs like a business division, formulating strategies, implementing them for social development, as well as effectively monitoring various projects."

The group subscribes to the principles of the Triple Bottom Line which places emphasis on people, profit, and CSR—sixteen interviewees said this. The Aditya Birla Group has ensured that every group company discharges its CSR role.

Global: Taking India to the World

Till 1997, this group had operations only in five countries including India. Today, however, it has operations across twenty-five nations as mentioned toward the beginning of the chapter. Thus, it has become a true MNC and a transnational Goliath.

Highlighting the global thrust of the group, twenty-one interviewees said that in the Aditya Birla Group, they view the market beyond political and geographical boundaries. Twenty interviewees said that they think and link customers across the world, while nineteen said there is a burning desire within the group to become a global giant featuring somewhere among the top Fortune 200 companies.

According to nineteen respondents, today, 60 percent of the group's revenue is generated through global operations. Another dream which the group nurtures is that of becoming one of the top three players at the global level. All their businesses and strategies, structure, processes, and people are geared toward this aim as sixteen respondents mentioned. Coming from the top team, such aspirations reflect the vision, determination, and passion of the group to become a global player. According to five CEOs we met: "Today when we talk about the group, we talk about global scale, global size, global processes and best practices." Seventeen Interviewees said "We continuously do global benchmarking and find out the areas where suitable strategies and action plans are to be implemented to be a winning group in the global arena."

The group, as said by twenty interviewees, consciously seeks to develop a global mindset and cross cultural sensitivity among its key people through exposure and training in the top B-schools across the world—Kellogg, Harvard, LBS, Wharton, INSEAD, IMD, etc.

As Mr Birla says: "Just to remain competitive and in the reckoning, you have to become a global winner because our objective is to become the first three in every business. There is no point being in a business and be in a losing position."

Futuristic and Forward-looking Group

The capability of an organization to capitalize nascent opportunities is governed by its futuristic vision and forward-looking orientation. Organizations which successfully do this always move ahead to create the second curve, rather than perpetuating the past, which may not be very relevant to cope with the emerging future.

The Aditya Birla Group has, over the years, developed the distinctive capability to be forward-looking, futuristic, and intuitive. All the eighteen interviewed CEOs proudly said: "We do not miss (business) opportunities and quickly respond"; "We constantly scan the environment for new opportunities and capitalize on them by building appropriate strategies." Eighteen respondents said: "In this group, consolidation, mergers and acquisitions, and divesting business are common practices. These are continuously done keeping the bigger global landscape in mind." The group constantly strives to be in the league of top three global players in all its businesses. This vision helped them decide to take over Alcan and Novelis of Canada. In fact, Novelis is three times bigger in size than Hindalco. Today, Hindalco ranks among the top three aluminium companies in the world.

As many as sixteen interviewees gave another example of the futuristic orientation of the group by citing the acquisition of the major stake in Idea Cellular of which the group has been a partner along with the Tatas. Idea is growing at a phenomenal pace since its acquisition of majority stake and its market capitalization has touched ₹ 207.26 billion (in November 2009).

The takeover of the cement division from Larsen & Toubro (L&T) is another example. At the time of its takeover, this move was not viewed positively by the market. The deal was struck in 2004 when there was a glut in the cement market, but today, in the booming construction scenario, this decision has turned out to be a boon as confirmed by twenty interviewees. Likewise, the setting-up of the copper business in the late 1990s, without access to deposits in the country, needed a futuristic strategy. Although it was initially treated with skepticism by industry watchers, today, it is a cash cow; and this, as eleven respondents said, was achieved by backward integration through acquisition of copper mines in Australia. These acquisitions were like riding against the tide but were done because of their capability to discern the future scenario.

The Aditya Birla Group has moved from the preponderant traditional economy business to new economy businesses such as telecom, insurance, and retail at a good pace. Today, revenue from new economy business is to the tune of 30 percent in the group. These examples powerfully bring out the mastery which the group has developed in forecasting the future and preparing for the same.

People Centricity

Among the various pillars of competitiveness, the quality of people is most crucial since it plays a critical role in fostering innovation, which continuously enhances the competitiveness of the organization. When people feel empowered, recognized, and valued, they feel charged up and carry the agenda of the organization forward whole heartedly to excel and win.

The twenty-one people belonging to the Aditya Birla Group who we spoke with conveyed a sense of belonging, excitement, pride, and a sense of being valued by the organization. Twenty people said that this group has a strong people-centric focus; twenty-two people said that the group takes care of people when they have personal pains and problems; twenty people said that people here are treated with respect and dignity; the group human resource (HR) function is highly proactive and responds quickly to people's needs—this was asserted by twenty respondents; and another eighteen respondents said that there is equity, fairness, and objectivity in the group and, therefore, people feel happy to work here. Twenty people mentioned many such instances where the group went far beyond formulated rules, whether for medical issues or cases of death, showing true humanism and magnanimity. The HR policy of the Aditya Birla Group appears to be an interesting amalgamation of Western HR practices and an Indian sense of community and humanism, as said by seventeen interviewees.

Another emphasis of the group has been to build leadership talent through the use of best global HR practices like a 360 degree appraisal, assessment center, mentoring, counseling, and robust succession planning. This approach extends down the line across the group companies. In Gyanodaya—the learning center of the group—a series of distinguished lectures and workshops are organized by global gurus to provide exposure to the top team. In addition, the group also provides global exposure through training programs in the world's best business schools. One of top team members showed us the handwritten letter of appreciation he received from K.M. Birla with a great sense of pride. This reflects the relationship which K.M. Birla has cultivated with his senior team members and the effort he makes to reach out to them at a one-to-one level.

Robust Growth Strategy

According to the Group Executive President, Corporate Strategy and Business Development, the Aditya Birla Group is aiming to double its revenue to $60 billion from the current standing of $29.2 billion in the next five years. This is a clear indication of the ambitious growth strategy of the group. The group's main businesses are aluminum, cement, telecom, viscose staple fiber (VSF), chemicals, financial services, carbon black, and textiles. Out of these, metal, carbon black, fiber businesses, and chemicals have a global presence.

All the twenty-one interviewed executives said that the group uses multiple routes to growth—mergers and acquisitions; takeovers; expansion—thus combining both organic and inorganic methods. The group has identified Europe, South America, South East Asian countries, and China as its target areas for growing its business. The growth strategy of the group, as reflected by the statements made by the sixteen top executives, indicates that it focused on both domestic and international domains. Discussions on this subject reveal a burning ambition to grow.

Nineteen respondents said that the group has to be a dominant player with dominant presence both at the national and at the global levels, whereas twenty said that the group is open to multiple mechanisms to grow—Greenfield/Brownfield; merger and acquisitions; organic/inorganic. The robust growth strategy is supported by the strategy of consolidation—restructuring the group into strategic business units (SBUs), each group headed by the CEO, indicating a good symbiosis in the robust growth strategy along with a focused approach. This focused approach has helped the group in value creation and value addition, besides bringing synergy and complementarity.

Toward Meritocracy with Personal Touch

In the name of objectivity the business model of people management at the workplace, while emphasizing meritocracy, invariably leads to impersonality, which then results in anxiety, fear, tension, and stress at the individual level. In fact, the rise of humanistic psychology and large scale spread of the "T" group movement, emerged as a balancing force in response to the excessive emphasis on objectivity and impersonality at the workplace. However, the influence of such movements did not strike at the deep roots in mainstream American (corporate) consciousness, because they did not comply with the work value system, characterized by overemphasis on rational orientation at the expense of positive emotion orientation.

In this context, it has been a refreshing experience to see the Aditya Birla Group balancing meritocracy and objectivity with personal touch. All the interviewed executives said that they believe in both meritocracy and personal touch in this group; in this company the HR policies center on grooming, building, and mentoring people, along with demanding performance excellence, replied twenty executives; fifteen respondents said that there are robust performance-centric rewards through rigorous performance appraisals, followed by counseling and mentoring; and nineteen executives said that the Aditya Birla Group makes efforts to treat people not as a performance resource, but as a member of the family, showing care and concern and extending help when needed.

Most of the interviewees (twenty-two of them) said the group follows a strong culture of performance excellence; fifteen executives said that the group believes in stretched targets and in raising the bar continuously; and eighteen respondents mentioned that the group compares with global standards of performance but equally takes care of its people.

According to twenty interviewed executives, while group level performance monitoring is done centrally, performance appraisal is carried out at the individual level, which ensures performance excellence and promotes meritocracy. People stated that performance data are used to promote people and they must emphasize that this is the only basis to promote people. In this group, reward is totally linked with contribution, and is devoid of nepotism, favoritism, and other such considerations.

Managing Change with Continuity

The Aditya Birla Group has made great strides toward globalization, shifting to new economy businesses, inculcating new mindsets in line with emerging challenges and demands, and toward building collective leadership.

By any standard, the transformation of Aditya Birla Group, within a span of twelve years, from a 20th-century organization (entrenched in old economy businesses, old mindsets, and solo leadership pattern) to a 21st-century organization is mind boggling.

In our experience, wherever such large-scale transformation has taken place, normally the surgery mode has been used. Drastic measures like firing powerful people or rolling their heads or reducing them to insignificance are common strategies. However, in the Aditya Birla Group, eighteen people said "we believe in change with continuity; we believe in transformation without drastic surgery; we believe in change without hurting the people fabric of the organization." This is the basic philosophy which guided the transformational odyssey of the Aditya Birla Group: "Although some people were shuffled and given VRS (390 persons), it was done with utmost grace." According to them, K.M. Birla ensured they had a generous compensation. Most important, each person was dealt with dignity and K.M Birla spent time with many of the outgoing employees to explain the decision to them. According to fourteen top group members, structural changes such as introduction of Group MIS, Think Tank Group, ABMCPL (Aditya Birla Management Corporation Pvt Ltd), and SBU model were brought in so smoothly that people did not feel the jerks. During our visit we met some of the old guards who were given dignified roles and relevance in the group—Askaran Aggarwal and Puran Malka being two such people who were highly regarded for their contributions in their initial days. Eleven people said that in the change process, various levels were infused with new blood, most importantly in the corporate office, to create a new organization which is competitive and globally responsive.

Commenting on the pace and process of change, five of the top executives conveyed that change has been gradual and rightly so given the size of the group. "Bringing drastic and radical change is tough in a successful group and, therefore, change was introduced with utmost sensitivity to the existing situation," said seventeen respondents. Perhaps the following statement made by one of the senior-most members of the top team aptly captures the spirit of the change process: "Extra efforts have been made to maintain continuity and there has been very little destruction. A new house has been built on the same site as the old house and then the old house has been broken down."

The following quote beautifully brings out the history of change in the Aditya Birla Group: One member of the Think Tank group went to the extent of saying that "it was bloodless and slow and resulted in a transformation of the group." As he put it:

> ... the group was behind times ... in many ways and they had to catch up with others; in order to move ahead; they had to become younger; get their governance pattern right; shift mindsets, and execute cultural shifts. The transformation has been evolving over 10 years. In order to help this process the group brought in the people who can drive markets, to replace the erstwhile accountants who headed the firms preponderantly with the accounting and finance mindset. The group has successfully moved from strong manufacturing focus to a service focus.

This shift has helped the group to successfully become one of the leading global players.

ACTION ARCHITECTURE AND CULTURE LANDSCAPE OF ADITYA BIRLA GROUP: SALIENT CONTOURS

The interview and questionnaire responses (for details of questionnaire data on organizational culture, see Appendix 2A.3) bring out the following salient features about the achievements, action architecture, and culture landscape of the Aditya Birla Group:

- The six-year financial performance data (for details of financial performance of the group from 2003–2009, see Appendix 2A.4) reveals many phenomenal achievements: its income revenue has registered a growth of 261 percent. Similarly, its net income increased from 10.63 billion to 50.39 billion demonstrating a growth of 374.04 percent in this period. This spectacular and landmark performance has been widely recognized and *Hewitt-Fortune* magazine even rated the Aditya Birla Group 6th out of 150 great companies in the Asia-Pacific region in 2009.
- The Aditya Birla Group has built a strong culture characterized by ethical and value-based governance, promoting entrepreneurship and innovation, customerization, focus on building competitiveness along with result orientation and performance excellence, enhancing people power through focus on people orientation, trust, community culture, nurturing talent, people participation, and teamwork.
- The Aditya Birla Group is a company which continuously explores opportunities and develops its business operations in a borderless and global context. In fact, "global perspective" is a buzzword in this group. This also emphasizes culture characteristics which nurture entrepreneurship, speedy response to external demands and challenges, innovation, support for risk-taking behavior, and tolerance of differences.

All these factors have together enabled the Aditya Birla Group to build continued and enduring global competitiveness.

Part III: K.M. Birla—His Profile and Persona

At this stage the reader may be curious to know more about the architect and choreographer of such an outstanding group. This part is designed to address this curiosity.

The following nine emerging themes have been identified through content analysis gathered from the interview data. They have been put in the order of importance keeping in view the passion and intensity which the respondents demonstrated while speaking about K.M. Birla:

- Humility and politeness
- People centricity
- Ethical
- Visionary and strategic thinker
- Empowering style
- Intellectual power
- Crafting strategy architecture
- Style of dealing with CEOs and the top team
- Harmonizing opposites

Humility and Politeness

While describing K.M. Birla, all the twenty-one interviewees said that he is full of humility and politeness. He demonstrates respect for the dignity of others. They were heard to say: "He never gives the impression that he is the Boss and you work for him and that he is one of the richest persons in the world"; "He never throws his weight around"; "Arrogance is absolutely absent." His humility also extends to his tendency to underplay his many achievements. Everyone has mentioned that he prefers to be low key (25). Twenty people said that he is known to say "Let results speak for themselves," while eight said that "He is a karma yogi." The Novelis acquisition, as eighteen interviewees claimed, was done without any fanfare unlike the style of many other business houses. All the twenty-one interviewees mentioned that he is an unassuming and underplayed person, and that he does not like to be in the media glare. He has been described as a "Silent contributor."

The absence of brash flamboyance—displayed by some corporate leaders—seems to be admired and liked by the employees of the Aditya Birla Group as indicated by both interview data as well as questionnaire data presented subsequently. It seems that this is especially admired because given his position, K.M. Birla can well throw attitude and get away with it. This personal characteristic of K.M. Birla has a deep impact on his credibility and acceptance as a Change Maestro. All the interviewees have highlighted his politeness in the same breath as calling him humble and modest. Polite and charming, well behaved, quiet, and courteous were some words used for him.

Being humble and polite, however, does not mean that K.M. Birla is perceived as weak or soft. The following quotes give further insights on this issue: "He is a good combination of Humility and Assertiveness," said twelve executives; "He can be assertive without hurting someone's dignity," mentioned nine executives; "Even harsh messages are conveyed politely and softly by K.M. Birla," as seventeen executives said.

People Centricity

While describing K.M. Birla's disposition and behavior toward people, all the twenty-one interviewees tremendously admired his demeanour, style, and persona. People spoke at length on this aspect citing many examples and illustrations from personal experiences as well as widely-known instances. They have been grouped into the following two categories:

- Caring person with strong humanist touch, and
- Interpersonal skills

Caring Person with Strong Humanistic Touch

The twenty-one interviewees strongly affirmed that K.M. Birla is a caring person. He is particular about the way he treats people. Those who walk into his office are treated with dignity and respect; nobody is ever insulted for any reason. The Indian corporate world, especially family-owned enterprises, are witness to tremendous displays of ego and a sense of superiority by people who reach the uppermost echelons of the organization. People become abrupt, rude, sometimes even abusive, forgetting all niceties of decent human behavior. There are extreme examples of CEOs publicly humiliating senior and top personnel. Most of the interviewed executives (seventeen of them) highlighted this phenomenon and said that K.M. Birla's style is a welcome contrast to the other CEOs and, therefore, there are no unnecessary tensions and uncertainties while working in the company. Most of them (twenty executives) said that interacting with K.M. Birla is a pleasure and that this experience is productive and meaningful for the organization.

K.M. Birla demonstrates enormous concern for people and goes out of his way to help when people are in trouble like accidents, illness, hospitalization, and even death. For example, following the demise of Mr Bagrodia (one of the top executives of the group), K.M. Birla went to the cremation ground and, according to one of the Directors, "He stood there with the family members for hours and was the last person to leave." He was overheard expressing his sense of loss to Mrs Bagrodia and offering help: "Aditya Birla Group is always available to you for any help you may need." There are many instances where he used his personal money to pay medicals bills of, for example, his peon's son's kidney transplant, hospital treatment for a colleague struggling with cancer, and so on. His strong concern for people can be seen in the fact that all the interviewed persons said: "If any of us is in trouble, we will definitely get help—the family is taken care of."

His sensitivity, care, and concern for people and his humanistic touch make him a good counselor to his CEOs when they feel disheartened. Some of the CEOs we met have expressed the fact that he is able to comfort and counsel in times of trouble with the businesses.

Interpersonal Skills

Apart from his humanistic touch, people have spoken about K.M Birla's interpersonal skills and its impact on managing people. The following quotes bring out the aspects of his style which make him likeable and an acceptable Change Maestro.

Twenty people said: "Mr Birla has a soothing interpersonal style while dealing with people;" another seventeen mentioned: "He has a cool temperament no matter what the provocation"; "I have never seen him get angry"; "Not even heard from anyone that he gets angry." According to them, some of the notable adjectives used to describe him are one possessing a "calm temperament" and someone "absolutely cool with a soothing touch." Again, twenty respondents said: "Mr Birla is a highly self-controlled person never raising his voice, nor visibly demonstrating anger or agitation."

Interestingly, K.M. Birla combines his cool temperament with assertiveness when required as brought out by the following statements made by all the interviewees. According to them, even when he has to say something unpalatable he says it firmly with logic and a soft touch; he is assertive without raising his voice; he is a soft-natured man made of steel; he is very polite and unassuming said twenty executives. The listening capability further enhances K.M Birla's ability to strike a rapport with his CEOs and top team members: "He listens patiently to what people have to say even if it is trivial," as said by twenty executives; fifteen respondents said: "Great listener, does not react and does not get agitated"; and fifteen said: "He is always smiling, very positive person; he does not like negative thoughts therefore his style is very encouraging."

Ethical

All the interviewees emphatically stated that K.M. Birla is highly ethical and a man of integrity and honesty. Seventeen interviewees said that they have rarely met persons in the corporate world with such value clarity. K.M. Birla's clarity on values and priorities, therefore, gives a clear message on how he prefers the group to do business—with honor; adhering to the law of the land; keeping shareholder and national interest in mind; and considering the repercussions of decisions on the people involved as mentioned by eighteen interviewees. Most of the interviewees have highlighted that he has expressed such views several times.

In all spheres of society, especially in the corporate world, ethics, integrity, and honesty constitute the ultimate test for a Change Maestro. This earns the

Change Maestro tremendous respect from peers, government, and society. In the case of K.M. Birla this orientation is seen most powerfully in the modes and practices he emphasizes in managing the Aditya Birla Group. Some of the relevant quotes, as they feature ahead, substantiate this observation:

"As a promoter he is one of the cleanest. He expects not a penny from the projects (unlike many other promoters)," is a statement made by the interviewees. As mentioned in the part on culture, eighteen interviewees said, "for him means are as important as ends. His mandate for us is to abide by the law of the land in labor, rural development and environment."

One interviewee said, "Today 'managing' political environment is considered a done thing and accepted. There have been many cases where we alone have stood up and refused to bend rules for the company's benefit." Twelve interviewees quoted K.M. Birla and mentioned that he says: "Ethical governance and practices will be our key differentiator in the future." "He is very ethical and ensures that moral and ethical values are adhered to," as one interviewee said. This has immensely helped to build the reputation of the Aditya Birla Group," as fifteen respondents confirmed.

There is a clear mandate from K.M. Birla to not take shortcuts with the law of the land. He has, in fact, written a note to his CEOs not to take shortcuts with law in the belief that they are benefiting the company as eighteen respondents affirmed; nine interviewees said that he is concerned both about the means as well as the ends; and fifteen people said that he would not like to exploit people at any cost. K.M. Birla is a strong nationalist and believes in contributing to nation building. "Such nobility of purpose inspires us all," said twelve respondents. Another important value which is visible in K.M. Birla's statements and behavior is on the dimension of giving back. In fact he believes in the Gandhian trusteeship concept—"our group holds public money in trust and therefore we handle it responsibly," responded twelve people.

As an owner of a company, he is a unique business tycoon in India. Fifteen interviewees responded: "He never uses public money for personal benefit, something which he can easily do, as is the practice in many Indian business houses." This is very rare in India where many owners are known to book even personal expenses to company account—this never happens in the Aditya Birla Group, said twelve people.

What is striking is the extent of percolation of these values across the organization as emphatically stated by all the respondents. People highly admired this quality of K.M. Birla which they felt makes an employee's life hassle free and less complicated.

From the cited quotes and descriptions, it can be concluded that the greatest strength of K.M. Birla is his ethical orientation and value-based governance—be it in business transactions; personal dealings with people; dealing with the government; or relating with the outside world. He has a rare discerning mind—discriminating between the lesser goal and the greater goal; between first and second level of outcomes; between fair and unfair; and between personal interest and national interest.

Visionary and Strategic Thinker

All twenty-one respondents said that K.M. Birla is highly intuitive, futuristic, and has capability to visualize what is not obvious. All the interviewees said that K.M. Birla is a visionary with a fine blend of strategic orientation and goal focus. The following quotes substantiate this visionary quality of K.M. Birla.

"Visionary," "focused," "very driven and passionate"; "His focus is on macro issues and business decisions are made with focus on the long-term perspective," said fifteen people. Another fifteen people said that "He is a Visionary as well as a strategic thinker." Twenty respondents have expressed that he is an excellent strategic thinker: "Strategic thinking and planning are meticulously done by him," said fifteen people; thirteen people said that "He is extremely quick to spot emerging opportunity." The quick shift made by the group from traditional commodity business where it has been highly successful, to new economy businesses—telecom, insurance, retail, branded apparel—is indicative of K.M. Birla's capability to seize emerging business opportunity.

Not only does K.M. Birla have an opportunity-sensing mind, he has also got enormous capability to convert opportunities into strategy, business plans, and actions: twenty-two interviewees were heard saying this. The acquisitions of the Canadian firm Novelis, as also that of Indal, Ultratech, and Idea in India are powerful indicators of his farsightedness. It is this vision and strategic thinking which has helped the group move from one orbit to the next in terms of building competitive advantage and creating a cutting edge organization. In our experience, one of the most critical factors for the downfall of many Indian business houses has been the absence of an alert antenna, opportunity sensing mind, and lack of strategic thinking which we see prominently in K.M. Birla.

Empowering Style

In order to continuously maintain growth and excellence, any conglomerate with global operations and diverse businesses needs multiple leaders. This is possible only when the leader at the apex is highly envisioning, enabling, empowering, and trusting. All the twenty-one interviewed executives said that unlike many other business tycoons K.M. Birla is highly empowering in dealing with his top team. He does not dictate; he gets people to share their thinking on relevant issues like growth, business strategy, and moving the organization to the second curve, said twenty respondents. "There is no imposition of targets; it's a collective decision," said twenty-one respondents; "People said that he doesn't come to meetings with decisions to be imposed on others," as was heard from sixteen respondents. Eighteen people felt that there is plenty of freedom given to the CEOs and the approach is highly interactive, dialoging, and participative. K.M. Birla primarily focuses on issues of strategic importance to the group; eighteen interviewees responded that once there is consensus on the strategies, there is complete operational autonomy and freedom. There is considerable delegation and empowerment; there is no need to go to K.M. Birla and consult him on operational issues at all, said twenty people. Fifteen people said empowerment (however) is given by him when there is congruence between group values and business action. He is empowering and prefers to focus (only) on strategic value adding issues: this was affirmed by fourteen respondents. K.M. Birla spares time to review only a few important and new businesses. Empowerment works because it is combined with a high degree of trust as indicated by the statements given ahead.

Twenty-one people said that when lakhs and crores of payments are to be made, K.M. Birla trusts his team members and signs the papers. Eleven respondents said that "he trusts people's judgments and therefore people become doubly careful." One person said: "When I take a decision, I don't have to look over my shoulder as to what will my boss think; I know he will support and this encourages and emboldens me to get much beyond a professional manager-this encourages me to be entrepreneurial."

The empowering style is further reflected in the support given to the CEOs, even when their decisions go wrong. Many people (eighteen respondents) have cited examples of tolerance of failures and tolerance of mistakes.

As a human being, he is fantastic, smiles away small matters, said eight people. If a CEO makes mistakes, he gets time to rectify it unlike most other Indian private sector organizations where CEOs are known to be thrown out, sometimes even within an hour, said six people. Three executives were heard saying in other companies normally heads roll when mistakes are made but here calculated mistakes are treated as a part of the learning process.

Delegation and empowerment without effective monitoring can lead to abdication. However, tight monitoring can lead to centralization of power; it also kills entrepreneurial zeal. In the Aditya Birla Group, K.M. Birla has arrived at a fine balance of both. Fourteen respondents said empowerment is invariably preceded by clear consensus and ownership of decisions, followed up by rigorous reviews at various stages to keep track of the results. Sixteen respondents mentioned there is a quarterly review of numbers; followed by one or two specific business reviews around agreed plans and budgets; there are three years rolling and strategic plans along with monthly exceptional reporting, which is what his corporate cell advises him. K.M. Birla is a highly focused person and is selective about where he should invest his time, attention, and energy. He believes in concentrating on the big picture and giving a broad sense of direction on areas where he can add value, said eleven people. The following statements indicate his approach in empowering people.

Eighteeen people said that he shows overall direction and policy level focus; twenty-two people said his focus is on strategic and value adding issues; whereas sixteen responded saying business decisions based on value creation-this is his focus.

At the same time, this does not mean that he skips the details; eleven respondents said that he delves deeper into the details in cases where he feels he can make a distinctive contribution. In the areas of branding and marketing, for example, in the cases of Idea (telecom sector) and Madura (garments sector), as well as branding of the group, fourteen people said that he devotes a lot of time and goes into minute details.

Eight people said: In this group, control takes place through budgeting and review. For a conglomerate with such a huge turnover, K.M. Birla has evolved a good system (SBU model) which ensures multiple responsibility and accountability centers.

Intellectual Power

Twenty-one people mentioned K.M. Birla's razor sharp qualities, with a quick thinking capability. Nine respondents said that he has a dissecting and discerning mind, with capability to drill to the core of the problem. Twenty-one people said that he has a phenomenal memory especially for numbers and people know that he cannot be misguided on facts and figures. He can, at a glance of a powerpoint sheet, spot the flaw in the figures; such is his command over numbers, said fifteen people. There are times when people try to skirt on issues—if it is a minor matter, he does not react. The only indicator is perhaps a smile, which to the cogniscenti, said five people, is a message that says: "I know what you are trying to do." According to the top team (comprising twenty-one executives, as cited earlier), he is a keen listener. This capability is very powerfully used by him to absorb information and points of view. Twenty interviewees mentioned that he also observes people to get into their minds to understand their thinking procedures. At presentations, review meetings, and strategy meetings of the group companies, he is known to observe facial expressions and visible body language to gauge the key concerns of the group members. He uses this information to probe further by asking pinpointed questions, said nineteen people.

Twenty respondents mentioned that he is extremely open-minded (to opposing viewpoints) with a high learning capability. This enables him to get his finger on the pulse of the businesses.

Crafting Strategy Architecture

Generally speaking, it is difficult for an individual however versatile he may be, to gain expertise of all the diverse businesses in the conglomerate set up. Therefore, great Change Maestros operate through modes like brainstorming and dialoging to arrive at effective decisions. Such forums also provide opportunity to learn and appreciate business nuances which subsequently helps them decide where to focus and where to give freedom and autonomy. K.M. Birla has a style of conducting brainstorming sessions where everyone is encouraged to frankly articulate their views even if they contradict the dominant views of the group and himself. Being a good listener works to his advantage: He is known to first listen to everyone and then ask questions and clarifications, as nineteen people said.

On major issues like mergers and acquisitions and divestments, such a brainstorming approach has been used. Ten relevant people together brainstorm on a topic—as each one speaks, K.M. Birla makes notes, then he looks at each person in the eye and asks for their personal views. After the presentations and discussions, K.M. Birla expects people to take a position and express their views, rather than just agree and go with his views. If he feels he has sufficient information then he gives his view; even in such case he keeps the matter open for others to raise objections, if any. This process helps build consensus. He has, thus, modified the typical brainstorming process by this intervention which facilitates the group to move forward to build consensus. Seventeen respondents affirmed that at every stage he is open to a different view and is never in a hurry on issues of strategic importance. Nineteen people said that he conducts meetings very calmly with thorough preparation and eighteen said that he is focused and brings the discussion back on track when it goes off tangent.

He applies his command over intuition, reading body language through camera vision, scanning faces to identify who holds a contrarian view or concern, but is also unable to express owing to hierarchy, relationships, sensitivities, etc. Eighteen people said that he uses this to catch the contrary view which provides a different perspective on the issue under consideration. Whereas fourteen interviewees said during such meetings he goes round the table, and asks people who are quiet: "You look like you have something to say. You look uncomfortable." According to six persons, by doing this, that is, going round the table and asking such questions, K.M. Birla creates space for the minority view and scope for meaningful discussion.

From these quotes it is clearly evident that K.M. Birla's style is participative in a true sense. He strongly believes in the group decision-making mode which is, needless to say, essential for idea generation, consensus building, and creating ownership. He has excellent capability to synthesize divergent views which aids him in conducting brainstorming sessions. In these sessions, he always looks for different views which render a fresh perspective to the discussion. Therefore, his futuristic orientation along with intuition helps him go beyond the visible and apparent to hear the unheard sound.

Style of Dealing with CEOs and the Top Team

K.M. Birla has mastered the subtle art of dealing with the CEOs and getting the best out of them. His extreme sensitivity, observation capability, personal touch, and humility, all contribute to a style which the CEOs find respectful and empowering. His superior cognitive capabilities and sharp eye for details keep the CEOs on their toes. He is always polite to a fault in his reactions. As one of the CEOs described, "the highest visible expression in moments of extreme irritation is to say—this is not acceptable," something which is mild, to say the least.

He is an intense person; however, in terms of expression of emotion, he shows a finer range of reactions, tuning his gestures, words, and facial expressions in such a way that the intensity of communication is conveyed with minimal range of expression. Thus, eleven executives said, his every gesture and word is imbued with meaning to those who have tuned into his frequency levels. If at all there is a need to confront any CEO, it is always done by him in private and the message is firm and assertive, as nine interviewees mentioned. This is, however, done in such a way that people get the message without being hurt and humiliated, said eleven people.

K.M. Birla dislikes back-biting and people carrying tales about each other. In the event of such an occurrence, twenty executives confirmed that K.M. Birla calls the concerned parties together and asks them to sort out their differences.

This gives a strong message to people and discourages them from trying to influence him in this way. This style discourages people from back biting; as people are busy working with little time for politicking.

K.M. Birla has a soothing style full of humility and gentleness in relating with people. He can make people feel that they are valued, wanted, and have great capability to contribute to the growth of the organization. These qualities helped K.M. Birla to be seen as a great role model and powerful mentor by almost all whom we met and spoke to.

Harmonizing Opposites

As many as fifteen persons expressed great admiration for K.M. Birla's unique capability to harmonize opposites. Nine persons gave examples saying he balances change with continuity; seven said he beautifully harmonizes the past with the present and future; five said he does business with ethics; and five said he says what he means. Fourteen people said that for him means are as important as ends. Nine executives said he believes in the triple bottom-line with focus on people, profits, and CSR. Eleven persons said he believes in balancing profit with ethics. Fifteen respondents were heard saying as a person he is a soft-natured man of steel; twelve people said that he is a man of humility with assertiveness; five said he can be assertive without hurting someone's dignity; three people said he maintains a distance and yet is able to give a sense of being close ... he is able to finely balance between both. Three interviewees commented: "He manages formal informal boundaries very well" and that he appears reserved but is friendly. These statements highlight the mastery of K.M. Birla over harmonizing opposite forces without compromising either of the two, an exemplary but rare quality.

K.M. BIRLA AS A CHANGE MAESTRO: SALIENT CONTOURS

Responses on the structured questionnaires (for details of questionnaire data of K.M. Birla's Change Maestro style, see Appendix 2A.5), as well as the interview-based findings, bring out the following striking conclusions about K.M. Birla as a Change Maestro and a person:

- K.M. Birla demonstrated remarkable capability to balance change with continuity while preparing the company for the 21st century. This approach of carrying the best of the past with focus on creating a new future significantly enabled the Aditya Birla Group to grow, compete, excel, and move from one horizon to the next without much internal disturbance and turmoil. In a true sense, K.M. Birla has succeeded in continuously creating the second curve for the Aditya Birla Group.
- K.M. Birla has an immense repertoire of leadership competencies giving equal thrust to all the pillars of competitive edge—cost; quality; customerization; people power; ethical governance; and above all entrepreneurial innovation and speedy response to emerging opportunities.
- K.M. Birla has a finely-tuned head, elephantine memory, opportunity sensing mind with a visionary, global, and strategic thinking approach.
- His humility, people centricity, and value-driven governance are extraordinary and put him in the galaxy of great human beings and leaders. Such a unique combination has given K.M. Birla tremendous credibility in the eyes of the employees and he is viewed as a role model. He has a reflective temperament enabling him to hear the unheard and aided him to look within, around, and beyond.
- K.M. Birla has made monumental contributions to the nation and to the global economic order. His services have been recognized by numerous awards and honors bestowed on him, notable among them being the AIMA-JRD corporate leadership award in 2008 and Business Leader of the Year award by *The Economic Times* in 2003. He has also been ranked one among the top five Asian leaders by the CNBC-INSEAD sponsored "Asian Business Leader Award" in 2002.

K.M. Birla: Concluding Contours

K.M. Birla, the iconic Change Maestro of the Aditya Birla Group, is the embodiment of humility, which has been conceptualized by Jim Collins, as noted by one respondent, as the core characteristic of the highest level of leadership—

Level 5. He is a man with oceanic dreams and a Himalayan vision, relentlessly striving to take the Aditya Birla Group to the galaxy of great global companies. He wants to be remembered as a builder of sustainable world-class institutions strongly characterized by the fervor of integrity and ethical governance. He strongly believes that ethical governance is the basic foundation for sustaining the business over the long term and building competitive advantage.

He has the steely resolve and laser-like focus to cope with myriad business challenges which confront him. He successfully mastered the art of balancing continuity with change, a truly rare and outstanding quality for a Change Maestro. K.M. Birla is a man who has the capability to respond to and manage seemingly contradictory challenges. He is a great harmonizer and synthesizer. This quality has significantly enabled him to powerfully channelize organizational energy toward building a great institution.

He loves his work, is very passionate and ambitious about it, and enjoys every minute of it. He strongly believes in performance excellence and value creation which—in his judgment—enables the organization to become cutting edge.

K.M. Birla has a high learning orientation and never shies away from asking people to explain if he cannot understand something, thus, continuously enhancing his own knowledge base. He is a strategist and focuses more on the long-term organizational goal, rather than short-term gains. Mr Birla has a high degree of sensitivity to the employees and spends a lot of time reflecting on issues having impact on people. He is an empathetic coach and mentor and spends considerable time grooming and building members of his team.

K.M. Birla has an immense range of leadership competencies, focusing simultaneously on all the pillars of competitive edge—cost; quality; customerization; people power; ethical governance; and above all, innovation and speedy response to emerging opportunities. He has a highly reflective temperament enabling him to hear the unheard and to *look within, around, and beyond*.

K.M. Birla has successfully created a world-class organization. In his company there is a culture of freedom and empowerment and entrepreneurial innovation. The group strongly emphasizes value-based functioning and also provides dignity to their people, thus enabling them to attract top of the line global talent.

Under him, the group has become a truly Indian multinational spanning twenty-five countries. The group's performance scorecard may well be the envy of other Indian conglomerates; such has been the scale of growth achieved under his leadership.

Appendices

Appendix 2A.1: Brief Sketch of K.M. Birla

An iconic figure, Kumar Mangalam Birla is Chairman of the Aditya Birla Group, India's first truly multinational corporation with operations spanning twenty-five countries. With him, the remarkable and inspiring contribution of the House of Birlas to nation building has continued through economic independence and social regeneration. As a true inheritor of the Birla group's ethos and its commitment to the cause of the nation, he has not only transformed his company to make it an US$ 30 billion global enterprise, but also, in the process, has spearheaded efforts to make India an economic super power.

A role model and a formidable force in Indian Industry, K.M. Birla holds several key positions on various regulatory and professional boards. He serves on the Prime Minister of India's Advisory Council on Trade and Industry. He is the Chairman of the Board of Trade constituted by the Union Minister of Commerce and Industry, Chairman of the Ministry of Company Affairs' Advisory Committee, and Director of the Central Board of Directors of the Reserve Bank of India. On the academic front, K.M. Birla is the Chancellor of BITS, Pilani; Director of the G.D. Birla Medical Research and Education Foundation; and member of the Asian Regional Advisory Board of the London Business School.

Several accolades have been showered on K.M. Birla such as Bombay Management Association's "Entrepreneur of the Decade Award— 2009," "JRD Tata Corporate Leadership Award—2008," AIMA, "The Business Leader of the Year" (2003) by *The Economic Times*, "Business Man of the Year" (2003) by *Business India* and Ernst & Young, "Entrepreneur of the Year" (2005), and "Lakshmipat Singhania—IIM, Lucknow National Leadership Award" (2006), and "The Outstanding Business Man of the Year" by the National HRD Network.

Table 2A.1: *Accolades to K.M. Birla over the Last Decade, 1998–2009*

Year	
2009	• "Entrepreneur of the Decade" Award by Bombay Management Association.
2008	• The AIMA "JRD Tata Corporate Leadership Award." • "The Corporate Role Model Award" by Amity International Business School.
2007	• Honored with the Asia-Pacific Global HR Excellence "Exemplary Leader" Award. • Named "Global Indian Leader of the Year" by NDTV Profit in their Business Leader Awards category. • "The Most Socially Responsible Leader" by *Outlook*.
2006	• Represented India at the Ernst & Young World Entrepreneur Award in Monte Carlo, Monaco in June 2006, where he was inducted as a member of the Ernst & Young World Entrepreneur of the Year Academy.
2005	• Awarded "The Ernst & Young Entrepreneur of the Year—India." • Named "Young Super Performer in the CEO Category" by *Business Today*. • PHD Chamber of Commerce and Industry—Udyog Ratna.
2004	• In recognition of his exemplary contribution to Indian business, the Banaras Hindu University awarded him the D.Litt. (*Honoris Causa*) degree.
2003	• Named "The Business Leader of the Year" by *The Economic Times* Awards for Corporate Excellence 2002–2003. He was selected *Business India*'s "Business Man of the Year—2003."
2002	• Ranked among the first five Asian business leaders for the CNBC/INSEAD sponsored "Asian Business Leader Award 2002."
2001	• The Rajiv Gandhi Award for "Business Excellence and His Contribution to the Country" by the Mumbai Pradesh Youth Congress.
2000	• The Bombay Management Association honored K.M. Birla as "The Management Man of the Year 1999–2000."
1999	• The Lions Clubs International's "The Achiever of the Millennium." • The Rotary Club of Ahmedabad's "The Legend of the Corporate World."

(continued)

(continued)

1998	• K.M. Birla was the first and only industrialist to have been appointed as a public nominee on the governing board of the Securities and Exchange Board of India (SEBI) by the Finance Ministry. • Recipient of the Rotary Club's "Award for Vocational Excellence."

Source: Company data.

Note: In the eleven years that K.M. Birla has been at the helm of the Aditya Birla Group, he has won recognition for his contribution to the industry and to professionalizing management. An indicative list has been given prior to the table in Appendix 2A.1.

The transformation of the Aditya Birla Group within a span of just twelve years to become a global Indian multinational is truly phenomenal and K.M. Birla, by his own right, has emerged as a great role model and powerful mentor of business leadership of India. If his great grandfather G.D. Birla played a crucial role in liberating his country from alien rule, K.M. Birla has added his might to making the free nation an economic super power.

Appendix 2A.2: The Aditya Birla Group—A Value-based Indian Multinational

Birla is a name almost synonymous with the industrial history of the country from the days of British rule in India to date. The name means many things to many people and for the nationalist who were fighting the Raj, it spelt courage; for the post-war industrial India, it meant promise; for the fast globalizing India, it signified a group that has already done it all; for the millions whose lives it touched through untiring development work, it was sheer hope; and for the youth, it meant a constantly changing and expanding universe where there are extremely promising careers to be made.

The US$29.2 billion Aditya Birla Group employs over 130,000 people drawn from thirty different nationalities and cultures and earns more than half of its revenues from overseas operations. K.M. Birla, while barely in his mid-20s, had to take over the management of one of the most extraordinary industrial groups of India rooted in history and economic prosperity of the land both in the pre-Independence and post-Independence era, after the demise of his father Aditya Vikram Birla in 1995, who was barely in his 50s. The story of the Aditya Birla Group is all about the tumultuous years between 1995 and 2009 which saw the young industrialist inheritor Kumar Mangalam mature into a leader of extraordinary capabilities with a deep sense of ethical values. It is only natural that under his leadership the Aditya Birla Group also experienced a meteoric rise to become one of India's truly home-grown multinationals of great value and power. It is no wonder that in the transformational journey the country itself underwent changes by adopting economic reforms to emerge as an economic superpower, the man and his company played no small role. The fact that SEBI, the financial sector watchdog, chose K.M. Birla as the chairman of the expert group that set standards for corporate governance for the Indian companies, should speak volumes about the trust and confidence the nation had reposed on this industrialist leader.

Aditya Birla Group: Its Historical Landscape

The charismatic Ghanshyam Das Birla, the founder of the Birla group saw no contradiction in building an industrial conglomerate under an alien rule, but also supporting the nationalist movement opposed to the British led by his friend Mohandas Karamchand Gandhi. This required extraordinary moral courage and sense of sacrifice, an underlying ethos that runs through the group till date. The "Birla House," the headquarters of the flourishing business enterprise, naturally became the beehive of nationalist activity and the Father of the Nation, Mahatma Gandhi, breathed his last here after being slain by an assassin's bullet.

Once freedom was won, the Birla group continued to build its enterprises and also help the nation add to its industrial fortunes with unmitigated zeal. Being a visionary with a strong sense of purpose Mr G.D. Birla could sense opportunities in textiles, aluminum prospecting and processing, chemicals, cement, and numerous other businesses which were needed to make India a strong industrial nation. His own grandson Aditya Vikram Birla, father of the present chairman and the Birla inheritor, Kumar Mangalam, realized its true potential by not only building on its already established fortunes, but breaking into new markets overseas, something that required a vision of seeing the world as borderless to practice business in.

Such a global perspective has pushed the company to embrace international best practices, processes, and strategies. The result is that the group's footprint today extends to twenty-five countries with as many as fifty-odd enterprises, some of which are of global scale. The group has several distinctions as well which include owning the world's largest aluminum rolling company, leadership in VSF industry, the tenth largest cement producer of the world, fourth largest producer of carbon black and insulators in the world among other things.

The Inheritors

- The Aditya Birla Group, India's first multinational corporation, traces its origins back to the tiny village of Pilani in the Rajasthan desert, where Seth Shiv Narayan Birla started cotton trading operations in 1857. Pilani incidentally is the spot the group chose to start its educational endeavor in 1964 and today, the Birla Institute of Technology and Science (BITS) Pilani has spread wings to Goa and Hyderabad; Dubai is its first international destination.
- Starting with its roots in cotton business, G.D. Birla—the grandson of the original founding father of Birla clan, Shiv Narayan—entered the manufacturing sector in 1919 by setting up a jute mill. G.D. Birla, a close confidant of Mahatma Gandhi, remained a powerful institution builder, making a fortune by dealing in textiles and chemicals along with prospecting and extracting aluminum. He was also famous for setting up Hindustan Motors, the manufacturer of the legendary Ambassador cars.
- Aditya Vikram Birla, who then took over the reins, had an industrial degree in Chemical Engineering from MIT; being an untiring and hardworking leader with an uncanny vision for building a global enerprise, he could push the group to untested waters of South Asian and near East markets. Even though he died young at the age of 52 following a brief illness, he laid the foundations of the highly diversified, truly Indian multinational that Aditya Birla Group has become today.
- When India became independent in 1947, Grasim, the flagship company of the group today, took shape as a small rayon weaving unit in Gwalior.

Hindalco, the aluminum heavyweight, was born in 1958 and its Renukoot complex started production in 1962. This was followed by Eastern Spinning Mills & Industries Ltd which was set up in 1965 by the young Aditya Birla. The Birla group had by then built enough financial strength to bid for Indian Rayon Corporation in 1966.

- In 1969, Aditya Birla set up Indo-Thai Synthetics Company Ltd, the group's first overseas company. This was followed by the setting up the first Birla Company in Indonesia, P.T. Elegant, a spun yarn manufacturing plant. The group then set up a viscose rayon stable fiber manufacturing plant in Thailand in 1974 and a joint venture spun yarn firm in Philippines, Indo Phil Group, followed suit in 1975. By then the appetite for acquisitions, both in India and abroad and setting up of overseas ventures, had become routine in the Birla group. In quick succession, Pan Century Edible Oils in Malaysia and Thai Carbon Black in Thailand followed suit in 1977 and 1978, respectively. The Malaysian venture went on to become the world's largest single-location palm oil refinery. The next overseas venture took place four years later with P.T. Indo Bharat Rayon, the first producer of VSF in Indonesia. Two years later in 1984 Thai Polyphosphates and Chemicals commenced production of sodium phosphates.

- After a massive appetite for overseas venture, it was time for looking at India afresh for investments. Indo Gulf, India's first gas-based fertilizer plant in the private sector was established at Jagdishpur, Uttar Pradesh, in 1985. The financial services business took roots with the setting up of the Birla Growth Fund in 1986. In the following year, Indian Rayon was renamed as Indian Rayon and Industries Limited (IRIL).

- By then, Birla group had grown massively in strength and diversity, giving it enough muscle to enter the energy sector in a joint venture with Hindustan Petroleum Corporation Ltd to set up a 3 million tonnes refinery, Mangalore Refineries and Petrochemicals Ltd (MRPL), at Mangalore, Karnataka. A series of overseas ventures, Thai Acrylic Fibre, Thai Peroxide Pan Century Oleo chemicals Malaysia, Thai Epoxy, and Allied Products followed in quick succession. The period also saw K.M. Birla returning from his studies to actively take part in the group's operations from 1990. The next pit stop was in 1994 when the first Egyptian venture, Alexandria Carbon Black took shape. The group's vision was evident: it saw an opportunity in 1995 in telecommunications when it went ahead to set up a joint venture with AT&T (USA). The group had by then grown to be a ₹ 8,000 crore global enterprise, with assets of over ₹ 9,000 crores, comprising of fifty-five benchmark quality plants, an employee strength of 75,000, and a shareholder community of 600,000.

Behind the Rising Sun

In the fateful year of 1995, after Aditya Birla passed away, the burden of running this Indian multinational group, fell on K.M. Birla who had just then returned with an MBA degree from the London Business School (LBS) and a Chartered Accountants certificate under his belt. The young inheritor trained by not one but by three grandmasters, Ghanshyamdas Birla—the great grandfather—B.K. Birla—the grandfather—and his own father A.V. Birla, saw no difficulty in plunging straight into business. He went about it with meticulous care and planning. Tracking the breathtaking history of the group unravels the fact that success was imprinted in every move the group made while it built its fortune bit by bit at every turn of history. Courage and conviction has been the hallmark of the group from its founding days to date. Kumar Mangalam's own personal style has been to think big, aggressively expand, and acquire existing companies if necessary whether in India or abroad and keep consolidating and restructuring in order to make the next big leap.

- The first task was to launch a new corporate logo—Aditya, the rising sun—followed by a total consolidation of all the group companies under the umbrella of Aditya Birla Group. Also, the first thing the young inheritor did was to start PT Indo Liberty in Indonesia and formed a 50:50 joint venture company with Tembec Inc. of Canada, called A.V. Cell Inc., to supply pulp for the Group's VSF operations in the year 1997. In the same year, Grasim acquired Dharani Cement and Shree Dig Vijay Cement to consolidate the group's leadership position in cement. The business acumen of K.M. Birla was evident when he made a move to acquire the cement business of L&T.

The group, earlier, also went for restructuring of the cement businesses of Indian Rayon and Grasim which became the biggest such operation done in corporate India. The group also moved to copper business with the commissioning of Indo Gulf's copper smelter—the largest of its kind in India. Elsewhere, the Thai Organic Chemicals began commercial operations of Chlor-Alkali and Epichlorohydrin. The same year, three of the group companies won the Federation of Indian Chambers of Commerce and Industry (FICCI) annual award for their rural development work and a third Hindalco got the CFO award for excellence in financial management.

- The next year saw Indian Rayon being re-christened as Aditya Birla Nuvo and the group announced the setting up of a world-class aluminium project in Orissa. Awards and accolades followed even as the group companies made stronger ties with global players. Hindalco signed a joint venture with Almex USA Inc. and one of the Birla companies, TransWorks Information Services, acquired Minacs Worldwide, while Grasim Industries Limited, India, Thai Rayon Public Company Limited, Thailand, and P.T. Indo Bharat Rayon, Indonesia together formed a joint venture with Hubei Jing Wei Chemical Fibre Company, China, for VSF marking a breakthrough for the group in entering the Chinese market. Emphasis of large size and also continuous re-visiting and restructuring businesses was the strategy the young Birla adopted which paid results. The year 1998 saw the financial service business being consolidated after a tie-up being signed with the Canadian financial services giant, Sunlife. Closely following this, the telecom businesses were restructured with the Birla AT&T and Tata Cellular being merged.
- The young Birla built a combined industrial enterprise based on value-driven governance and a global outlook toward business which won him "the Best Employer in India and among the top 20 in Asia" awarded by the Hewitt–*Economic Times* and *Wall Street Journal* Study 2007. It is also one of the handful of business groups of India earning over half of its revenue purely from overseas options having offices in the UK, Germany, Hungary, Brazil, Italy, France, Luxembourg, Switzerland, Australia, the USA, Canada, Egypt, China, Thailand, Laos, Indonesia, the Philippines, Dubai, Singapore, Myanmar, Bangladesh, Vietnam, Malaysia, and Korea. The international business space

is expanding for the group with in-roads being made into newer markets and strengthening of its influence in the Asia-Pacific region.
- The success of the Aditya Birla Group and of its Chairman, Kumar Mangalam Birla, is grounded in the group's emphasis on personal ethics and value-based governance, high degree of customer support, and clear adherence to performance excellence seen by way of quality and cost and, above everything, a total endorsement of people power.
- The string of awards followed in the year 2009. Idea Cellular won *The Economic Times'* "Emerging Company of the Year Award for 2009." Vikram Cement and Aditya Cement won the Federation of Indian Mineral and Industries' "Social Awareness Award for the year 2008–2009," and the Rajiv Gandhi Award for Eminence in Social Field, 2009 was conferred on Mrs Rajashree Birla (Kumar Mangalam Birla's mother) for her path-breaking work among the poor carried out through the Aditya Birla Center for Community Initiatives and Rural Development.

Table 2A.2: *Accolades to Aditya Birla Group over the Last Decade, 1998–2009*

2009	- The Hewitt–*Fortune* magazine study of "Top Companies for Leaders" has ranked the Aditya Birla Group 6th in their recent study of over 150 companies in the Asia-Pacific region.
- Idea was adjudged the "Emerging Company of the Year 2009" by *The Economic Times*.
- Birla Sun Life Mutual Fund has been named "The Asset Management Company of the Year, India," by the Hong Kong based magazine, *The Asset*, in the country awards category of their "Triple A Investment Performance Awards 2009."
- Vikram Cement and Aditya Cement have also won the Federation of Indian Mineral and Industries "Social Awareness Award for the year 2008–2009."
- Hindalco Renusagar's power division bagged the Golden Peacock Environment Management Award during the Global Convention on Climate Security.

	• "The Best Labor Relations and Welfare Award, 2009" was conferred on Indo-Thai Synthetic Company Limited. ***Grasim*** • Grasim's plants, Vikram Cement (Khor, Madhya Pradesh) and Aditya Cement (Sambhupura, Rajasthan), were recognized with the TERI CSR Award for their sterling work in thirty-seven villages among 12,550 families in the area of healthcare. • Asian Corporate Social Responsibility Award was presented to Grasim (Staple Fibre Division) for its "Healthcare" programs in 2009. This division had won the Asian Corporate Social Responsibility Award earlier in 2005 for its "Education and Empowerment Programme." ***Novelis*** • Gold Award from Bombardier Recreational Products for quality and service. • Prime Minister's Industry Excellence Award from the Government of Malaysia. • Environmental Leadership Award from General Electric. • Product Excellence Award from the Government of Malaysia.
2008	• Hindalco was awarded the Greentech Safety Gold Award 2008 for outstanding achievement in Safety Management in the coal-based power sector. • PT Indo Bharat Rayon received the coveted IMC Ramkrishna Bajaj National Quality Award 2008. ***Novelis*** • Bronze Award for Supplier Excellence from Rexam plc. South Korea's Presidential Commendation for labor-management relations. • Top Supplier Rating from Malaysia's Kian Joo Group. Supplier of the Year. • Most Innovative Supplier and Best Quality awards from Alcoa Architectural Products. • Supplier of the Year Award from Plus Pack in Europe.

(continued)

(continued)

2007	- The Aditya Birla Group was adjudged "The Best Employer in India and among the top 20 in Asia" by the Hewitt–*Economic Times* and *Wall Street Journal* Study 2007. - *Forbes* magazine ranked Grasim among the fabulous fifty companies in Asia. - Indo Liberty Textile—APQO's International Asia Pacific Quality Award. ***Hindalco*** - The Golden Peacock Award 2007 by the World Environment Foundation. - The Safety Innovation Award 2007 for excellence in the field of occupational health, presented by The Institute of Engineers India. - The CII National Award for Excellence in Water Management (Beyond the Fence) 2007, for its land and water management projects in neighboring villages. - The IMC Ramkrishna Bajaj National Quality Award. - Renusagar—Special Award for Excellent Performance in the Service category.
2006	- Thai Carbon Black was one of the only three companies to have been selected as the Best Performance Management Company by the Stock Exchange of Thailand. - PT Elegant—"Best in its Class" award in the Big Industries category from the Asia-Pacific Quality Award Organization in 2006. - PT Indo Liberty Textile—IMC Ramkrishna Bajaj National Quality Award in 2006, awarded the "Zero Accident Award" for achieving 12.6 million accident-free man-hours from the President of the Republic of Indonesia from 2002 to 2006.
2005	- Indo-Thai Synthetics—Best Labor Relations award by Thai Prime Minister from 2002 to 2005.

	• Thai Carbon Black—TPM Consistency Award and the TPM Special Award from JIPM, Japan. • PT Elegant—The coveted IMC Ramkrishna Bajaj National Quality Award 2005. • Indo Liberty Textile—CII-EXIM Bank Commendation Award for Strong Commitment to Excel in 2005
2004	• Grasim—The 2004 Stockholm Industry Water Award presented to Staple Fibre Division, Nagda. • PT Elegant was recognized with the Quality Benchmark in the International Category by Qimpro Standards, India for implementing International Quality Maturity Model (IQMM). • PT Indo Liberty Textile—The Golden Peacock Global Quality Award. • The Asian Corporate Social Responsibility Award from Asian Institute of Management, Manila was awarded to Hindalco for its Rural Poverty Alleviation Project.
2003	• Grasim—The IMC Ramkrishna Bajaj National Quality Award presented to Birla Cellulosic, Kharach. • Indo-Thai Synthetics—Best Employer in Thailand award from Hewitt Associates. ***Thai Carbon Black*** • Adjudged the Best Employer in Thailand and ranked the 5th Best Employer in Asia by Hewitt associates in 2003. • The Prime Minister of Thailand has bestowed the Thailand's "Quality Class Award." • TPM Consistency Award and the TPM Special Award from JIPM, Japan.
2002	• Thai Carbon Black—The Prime Minister of Thailand has bestowed the Thailand's "Quality Class Award."
2001	• Thai Acrylic Fibre—The Deming Prize from the Union of Japanese Scientists and Engineers (JUSE).

Source: Company data.

Appendix 2A.3: Organizational Culture of Aditya Birla Group—Analysis of Questionnaire Data

Table 2A.3: Perceived Organizational Culture of the Aditya Birla Group

N = 88

S. No.	Organizational Culture	Mean	SD	Ranks
1.	Ethical governance	4.61	0.58	1
2.	Result orientation	4.33	0.73	2
3.	Global perspectives	4.31	0.79	3
4.	People orientation	4.23	0.71	4
5.	Performance excellence	4.22	0.78	5
6.	Focus on building competitiveness	4.21	0.78	6
7.	Focus on continuous improvement	4.2	0.79	7
8.	Trust	4.18	0.88	8
9.	Community culture	4.17	0.75	9
10.	Performance-based promotion	4.15	0.71	10.5
11.	Openness to new ideas	4.15	0.86	10.5
12.	Nurturing talent	4.12	0.8	12
13.	Participative	4.11	0.72	13
14.	Teamwork	4.1	0.7	14
15.	Responsiveness to the customer	4.07	0.79	15
16.	Outward looking	3.99	0.81	16
17.	Empowerment and delegation	3.94	0.81	17
18.	Role clarity	3.93	0.75	18
19.	Communication and information flow: Vertical (a) Top-down	3.92	0.84	19.5
20.	Communication and information flow: Horizontal (a) Within the department	3.92	0.83	19.5
21.	Entrepreneurial	3.89	0.86	21
22.	Culture of celebration of achievements and successes	3.87	0.89	22.5
23.	Speed of response to external demands and challenges	3.87	0.94	22.5

S. No.	Organizational Culture	Mean	SD	Ranks
24.	Openness and transparency	3.86	0.81	24.5
25.	Process focused	3.86	0.84	24.5
26.	Nurturing innovation	3.74	0.87	26.5
27.	Support for risk-taking	3.74	0.83	26.5
28.	Speed of response to internal demands	3.71	0.83	28
29.	Tolerance of differences	3.59	0.76	29
30.	Communication and information flow: Vertical (b) Bottom-up	3.57	0.91	30
31.	Cross functional collaboration	3.46	0.81	31
32.	Communication and information flow: Horizontal (b) Across the departments	3.34	0.82	32
33.	Centralized decision-making process	3.09	0.9	33

Source: Authors.

Perusal of Table 2A.3 brings out the following salient features of the perceived organizational culture:

- The mean scores of the Aditya Birla Group's organizational culture range from a minimum of 3.09 to a maximum of 4.61, indicating that the results are above average on all the organizational culture parameters.
- There is tremendous homogeneity in the responses as indicated by the low (≤ 1.00) standard deviations (SD) across the culture attributes. Further analysis of the table indicates that task-centric parameters such as result orientation, performance excellence, building competitiveness, continuous improvement, and performance-based promotions, are rated between 4.15 and 4.61 on a 5-point scale. This finding strongly brings out the high focus of the group on result orientation, performance excellence, and building competitiveness.
- Another visible feature is the emphasis on building people power as indicated by the high scores on attributes like people orientation, trust, community culture, nurturing talent, people participation, and teamwork. These two clusters of attributes together clearly indicate the powerful focus of the Aditya Birla Group on both high quality results and people power.

- The other important attributes which emerge strongly from the findings is global perspective, indicating the tendency to view the world as a borderless business arena when the group thinks and plans the business operations. Such a global perspective might have pushed the company to embrace global best practices, processes, and strategies.
- The group emphasizes both customerization and customerness, which are supported by outward-looking orientation.
- The most exciting finding, however, is the top most rating—ethical governance. This finding stands out in the current context of the ethical crisis, the greed, dishonesty, and self serving mindset of organizational community which is engulfing the current global corporate landscape.

Appendix 2A.4: Financial Performance of the Aditya Birla Group at a Glance

Table 2A.4: Sales and Profit of Five Companies under the Aditya Birla Group* from 2003 to 2009 (in ₹ billion)

Year	Income Revenue	Net Profit
2003	126.23	10.63
2004	174.91	17.97
2005	228.69	23.58
2006	268.17	29.62
2007	387.12	51.41
2008	431.1	64
2009	455.73	50.39
% Change over 2003	261.03	374.04

Source: Prowess website.

Notes: Values of revenue and profit for Aditya Birla UltraTech have been added 2004 onwards.

*Note that these figures refer to the financial performance of the main companies of the group which operate in various industrial sectors through subsidiaries, Joint Ventures (JV's); Aditya Birla Chemicals Ltd, Grasim Industries, Hindalco Industries, AB Nuvo Ltd, and UltraTech Cement.

Appendix 2A.5: K.M. Birla as a Change Maestro—Analysis of Questionnaire Data

Table 2A.5: Perceived Style of K.M. Birla as a Change Maestro

N = 88

S. No.	Change Maestro Attributes	Mean	SD	Ranks
1.	Respects the dignity of others	4.94	0.28	1
2.	Has a global mindset	4.91	0.29	2
3.	Has high credibility	4.9	0.46	3
4.	Humility	4.89	0.38	4
5.	Is honest and transparent	4.88	0.37	5
6.	Has ambitious plans for the organization	4.84	0.43	6
7.	Is reliable	4.8	0.51	7
8.	Is a man of words	4.79	0.53	8
9.	Has empowering and supporting attitude	4.77	0.47	9.5
10.	Business strategist	4.77	0.52	9.5
11.	Is a role model	4.72	0.62	11
12.	Is a strategic thinker	4.7	0.57	13
13.	Has helping attitude	4.7	0.59	13
14.	Is a visionary	4.7	0.65	13
15.	Makes people feel that they are valued by the organization	4.69	0.54	15
16.	Is fair and impartial	4.68	0.62	17
17.	Is open to new ideas	4.68	0.54	17
18.	Makes people feel that they have great worth	4.68	0.6	17
19.	Radiates positive energy	4.66	0.64	19
20.	Sensitivity	4.65	0.61	20
21.	Is interested in growth of his people	4.59	0.69	21
22.	Is entrepreneurial	4.58	0.71	22
23.	Pursues excellence in everything	4.52	0.71	23
24.	Recognizes and rewards performance	4.51	0.73	24
25.	Is an effective communicator	4.49	0.68	25
26.	Stands like a rock in the face of calamities	4.46	0.8	26
27.	Provides a sense of clear direction	4.45	0.73	27

(continued)

(continued)

S. No.	Change Maestro Attributes	Mean	SD	Ranks
28.	Leads by example	4.4	0.74	28
29.	Is a team builder	4.38	0.84	29
30.	Is result focused	4.34	0.79	30
31.	Grooms and develops people	4.3	0.92	31
32.	Is innovative and creative	4.28	0.77	32
33.	Fast in making critical decisions	4	0.87	33
34.	Leads from the front	3.95	0.92	34
35.	Is demanding and performance centric	3.88	0.83	35

Source: Authors.

Financial performance of the group has been extraordinarily impressive, having leap-frogged from a turnover of $2,655.9 million (in 2003) to $10,772 million (in 2008) registering a stupendous 305 percent growth. During this period, net profits jumped from $223.5 million to $1,599 million, registering a growth of 615 percent.

Perusal of Table 2A.5 brings out the following salient features of the style of K.M. Birla as a Change Maestro:

- For the purpose of analysis, the mean values of the thirty-five items have been broadly grouped into three categories: *(a)* Most Visible (4.5 and above); *(b)* Highly Visible (3.5 to 4.5); and *(c)* Visible (less than 3.5).
- On a 5-point scale, all items describing the qualities of K.M. Birla as a Change Maestro are rated more than 3.88. The mean values range from 3.88 to 4.89 indicating that the rating of all items is either Highly Visible or Most Visible. Of the thirty-five items in the inventory of Change Maestro's style, twenty-four fall in the Most Visible category. The remaining twelve items feature in the Highly Visible category.
- There is significant homogeneity of perception about the style of K.M. Birla as a Change Maestro, as indicated by the low standard deviation (≤ 1.00).

- The items in the Most Visible group are broadly classified into four broad categories: *(a)* People; *(b)* Character; *(c)* Business; and *(d)* Path-breaker. The number of items in each being 9, 6, 7, and 2, respectively.
- Items in the "People" category are respects the dignity of others, humility, empowering attitude, helping attitude, makes people feel they are valued, makes people feel they have great worth. People-centric style of the Change Maestro has a significant impact on the employees' morale, motivation, commitment, sense of excitement, and passion to win and excel. It makes them feel connected with the leader; it generates trust and commitment among them, develops a sense of ownership, and, would, in turn, unleash people power.
- There are six attributes in the "Character" cluster: high credibility, reliable, man of words, role model, honesty, and transparency, fair, and impartial. These character-linked items heighten the influencing power of the Change Maestro.
- The "Business" focus category constitutes seven items which indicates that K.M. Birla has ambitious plans for the group. He has a global vision and is strategic thinker with high focus on performance excellence.
- In the "Path-breaker" category there are two items: open to new ideas and entrepreneurial. This cluster indicates K.M. Birla's capability to listen to and absorb new ideas, take risks, think differently, and embrace transformation and change.

Notes

1. The authors gratefully acknowledge and appreciate the intellectual contributions and emotional support they received from Santrupt Misra, Group Director, Human Resources, Aditya Birla Group, in the course of this work. He spent many hours with the authors in conceptualizing the framework and providing focused directions to the case. However, for the conclusions and views expressed in this case study of the Aditya Birla Group and K.M. Birla as a Change Maestro, the authors own entire responsibility.

2. The respondents are out of twenty-one top team members interviewed by the authors. The number of respondents varies since the interviewing method was largely unstructured. We recorded what they said, giving greater priority to what came out of top-of-the-mind in response to our broad questions, rather than getting them to respond to a set of questions.

3

MELEVEETIL DAMODARAN: RENAISSANCE ARTISTE

3

This story is set in a small European village—a few hundred years ago—when the church played a crucial role in the social life of the village community. The church, being referred to, was very old, and one day it partly collapsed, making it dangerous for further religious and social congregations. People were asked not to visit the church for prayers and religious ceremonies. This also, by the way, brought an end to the regular social and religious activities of the village. As a consequence, the village experienced a serious breakdown in terms of social behavior and erosion of moral values leaving the villagers uncomfortable and disturbed. One day, the village elders got together and discussed these problems at length. They concluded that the only way to repair the social fabric was by building a new church and for this purpose the village elders made the following resolutions:

- *Since the church played a significant role in their lives, they decided they must build a new church. They were sure that this would arrest the breakdown of moral and ethical values and protect the community;*
- *The village elders debated regarding the likely location for building the new church and after long discussions, they decided that it must be built in place of the old church, as the place has been held sacred and evoked a sense of divinity; and*
- *The third resolution, "the new church must be built without destroying the old church" was the trickiest one.*

The third resolution beautifully describes the human dilemma of the want to do something new without letting go of the past: the human need for creation without destruction. The story also illustrates the human predilection for analysis–paralysis. Very few individuals are capable of stepping out of this dilemma, constructively break away from the past and move toward the future. It needs exceptional capability of managing change with continuity, appropriately balancing yesterday with tomorrow, and integrating seemingly contradictory forces. Mr Damodaran is a renaissance artiste who has demonstrated this difficult feat throughout his career.

But Damodaran is the optimist (who) sees opportunity in every problem rather than focusing on the problems in every opportunity. With this spirit, he reenergized the future of two giant companies—UTI and IDBI. Damodaran, the frame bender, shut out the past except that which helped him weather tomorrows. Damodaran, the architect of change, brought back the lost glory of these two crown jewels of the pre-liberalized Indian financial sector and restored the trust of the people in them.

The case study "M. Damodaran: Renaissance Artiste"[1] has been organized into the following three parts: Part I provides brief profile sketches of UTI and IDBI; Part II highlights the action architecture and culture landscape; and Part III discusses M. Damodaran's profile and persona.

Part I: Brief Profile Sketches of UTI and IDBI

M. Damodaran (for details of his profile, see Appendix 3A.1) belongs to the elite service of India—the Indian Administrative Service (IAS). His career started in the Tripura cadre (in 1971) and culminated in the Chairmanship of Securities and Exchange Board of India (SEBI) (in 2008). In Tripura, he rose to become the chief secretary of that state; he has also served as joint secretary in the banking division of the Ministry of Finance, Government of India. This was followed by an assignment with the Reserve Bank of India (RBI, India's central bank), where he earned reputation for scripting the turnaround of three banks—Union Bank of India; Indian Bank; and UCO Bank—which were in a perilous state.

He was then appointed by the government as Chairman of UTI (for details of the organization's profile, see Appendix 3A.2), which was suddenly swamped by scandals and heading toward a national calamity in the financial sector. While chairing UTI, he was also appointed CMD of IDBI (for details of the organization's profile, see Appendix 3A.3) which was fast losing relevance as a development bank. The transformations scripted and executed by him both at UTI and IDBI were followed-up with the assignment of setting a new direction for SEBI.

Although Damodaran's career and achievements have such a wide span, the focus in the present study has been preponderantly on his turnaround of UTI and IDBI. In order to help the reader understand the contextual constraints and challenges in which Damodaran had to operate, brief sketches of UTI and IDBI have been presented further.

UTI: A Brief Sketch*

UTI has been one of the crown jewels among the organizations in the Indian financial sector in the pre-liberalized economic scenario. It was once described as a proxy for the Indian financial sector. It continued this way into the late 1990s, in newly liberalized India, as one of the most trusted government organization. UTI was, at that time, the most trusted brand where the Indian middle class invested its hard-earned savings.

In 2001, however, UTI was besieged by a series of debacles. The nub of the problem lay in the board-level decision to close the exit option of their Number One product—the US-64 (Unit Scheme-64). The majority of the investors (65–70 percent) in this unit consisted of small account holders who thought they had safely stashed away some of their hard-earned money. Suddenly they were dismayed when UTI, which they trusted so blindly, changed its stance and announced that "there will be no sale and purchase [of US-64] for the next six months." This notification sent panic signals through the market. The stock market plummeted and the share value dipped. The announcement of the (lower) Net Asset Value (NAV) price further reinforced the fears of the public that they were losing money. One-and-a-half crores of investors and thousands

---

*This section is based on interviews.

of intermediaries felt cheated by UTI's decision. There was shock and disbelief among all because UTI had been a trusted brand for 38 years! The biggest fear was that UTI would shrink from a 60,000 crore company to a 13,000 crore company if all unit holders withdrew their money in the ensuing panic caused by the falling NAV.

The episode resulted in a national-level calamity since the media took up cudgels on behalf of the ordinary investor and it became a highly emotional issue with political dimensions. Questions were asked in the Lok Sabha for a week and it was like Draupadi's *chirharan* (literally the act of trying to disrobe someone, making them naked in public with the intention to humiliate as was done to the mythological character Queen Draupadi [wife of Pandavas] in the Mahabharata—the great epic). The first person who stressed the need to save UTI was Dr Manmohan Singh (who was the then leader of the Opposition). Attributions of corruption were being made against the UTI top brass and, in a bid to mollify public sentiment, the government sacked the chairman of UTI. (CBI arrested him a week later in connection with an investigation of some dubious investments.) Two executive directors (EDs) were also arrested; one of them died of a heart attack as soon as he was released. In fact, for two weeks all work at UTI came to a standstill. One of the EDs was holding charge but the overall situation was full of uncertainty and ambiguity and there was a threat of job loss and a fear of prosecution.

Based on the interviews with the UTI sample of ten personnel, the following picture has been drawn to highlight the UTI scenario when Damodaran took over as the CEO.

There was utter confusion at that time; it was a fluid situation and no one knew the depth of the problem. There was suspicion among employees, doubts regarding the management, and fingers were pointed at people even at the level of the then prime minister. Employees felt scared to face the public because they had no answers to their curious questions. It was a strange feeling for them because, for years, UTI maintained a good image and suddenly the public looked at them with suspicion and even hostility. There was no doubt that things were being mismanaged in UTI, but unfortunately aspersions about corruption were being cast on the company and its people. People were totally shaken up by the media blitz on UTI. Clearly the morale of the employees of this once reputed organization went down. People were insecure and uncertain about their future and that of the organization. Even the families of the officers became uncertain, thanks to the whispers of corruption and arrest of the chairman and two EDs.

Not only did the employees suffer uncertainty, the investors and, likewise, the UTI agents, who used to sell the products, also suffered. Owing to the extensive media coverage matters reached a stage where the Parliament also got involved. Although all the facts supported the decision of UTI (to stop the sale and repurchase of US-64 units), the reactions created a slur, which was difficult (for employees) to live down.

This fluid situation continued for two weeks until Damodaran, who was, at that time, officer on special duty (OSD) with the RBI, was appointed by the government as chairman of UTI.

At the time of his appointment, Damodaran was relatively unknown in the financial sector. People were skeptical about the joining of an IAS officer and thought that he was coming to wind up the show. It was a situation where emotions ranged from fear to suspicion and anxiety.

When he took charge as the chairman of UTI, he was besieged with multiple problems on all fronts. He was viewed with emotions ranging from skepticism to hostility by different stakeholders.

Damodaran himself was aware that people were quite apprehensive about his taking over and, in fact, speculated that selection of an officer handling inter alia the vigilance function of the banking division would definitely raise doubts on his intentions and that of the Government of India.

"I knew that in order to gain acceptance, I had to show that I was my own man and not the ministry's man," he said. Nobody even imagined that the new incumbent had a positive agenda for revitalizing UTI. His first few days in UTI were watched with a huge amount of trepidation. Along with appointing Damodaran as the chairman, the government also decided to hand over the case for investigation to the Joint Parliamentary Committee (JPC) which helped to cool down the media, but significantly added to his workload.

Damodaran (who was suddenly informed by the Finance Minister about his appointment as the chairman of UTI) had to rush to Mumbai with barely a day's notice; such was the urgency in the situation. He reached his office in Mumbai at 4 pm on a Sunday and immediately presided over his first board meeting as Chairman, UTI. Even before UTI employees had met Damodaran, a major decision was taken at the hurriedly convened board meeting chaired by him to open the repurchase window on US-64, the sore point which triggered much of the public outcry in the first place. The window for sale of units was, however, opened only to those small investors below ₹ 3,000. A scheme was floated by which they would get a higher repurchase price every subsequent month, thus, those who could hold out would be tempted to keep the units rather than withdrawing the money.

The first few months were very difficult (post June when the US-64 episode happened) because of a series of events which led to fall in the stock markets. Within three months of this episode 9/11 happened; then there was an attack on the Indian Parliament and to top it all the Indian government exploded a nuclear device. These events created many ripples in the financial sector; it caused a lot of pain to the investors and most importantly there was no money available to meet redemption needs. The UTI appointed spokesperson in that situation narrated his harrowing experience to us, "I had direct meetings with the investors in several cities across India. I saw the wrath, all sorts of abuses they would hurl at me. That was the level of anger they carried at that time, because their investments were at stake."

IDBI: A Brief Sketch**

While UTI was embroiled in scandal, public outcry, and media glare, IDBI was on the verge of collapse as a Development Financial Institution (DFI). In 2003 business had come to a standstill, morale was at its lowest ebb, and it was a hopeless situation, everyone knew the company was going down. In fact as early as 1992 they wanted to take steps to shift from the DFI mode to the robust banking mode (which was incidentally adopted by ICICI in the mid-1990s), but could not do so because of opposition from various quarters and lack of strong will of the management. The need for changing the direction for IDBI was known, but the issues that arose were who would do it and how would it get done. There were discussions on the subject and committees were appointed to decide on a course of action. However, there was a need for someone courageous enough to push through things and get the government support. IDBI needed to reinvent itself as a universal bank as that was the only route to survival.

In such circumstances, IDBI was filled with a sense of doom, poor morale, and helplessness at the inevitable slowing down and likely slippage of the

---

**This section is based on interviews.

organization into sickness. In its heydays, IDBI ruled the roost as the premium DFI disbursed as much as 50 percent of the loans in the market; however, when capital markets took off in India the days of monopoly were gone.

IDBI was in deep trouble. Profitability was hit since the cost of capital was more than the cost of lending; operations were in dire difficulties owing to high levels of Non-performing Assets or NPAs (10–12 percent) and to top it all, their ratings (as a premier financial institution) came down. The money, which they were getting from the government (for lending), was also withdrawn. IDBI had the highest lending rates at 12.5 percent (compared to the prevailing market rates of 10.25 percent and 10.05 percent offered by SBI and ICICI, respectively). Therefore, triple A clients simply walked away and borrowings drastically came down. Matters reached a stage where IDBI started showing profits not through operations, but through sale of assets, which was a sure sign of a company in crisis.

It was in this troubled context that Damodaran was asked to take over as the chairman of IDBI while he was also heading UTI (September 2003–March 2005) because of the dramatic transformation he achieved at the latter place. Damodaran had achieved a reputation as a turnaround master and people looked in anticipation for him to repeat this feat at IDBI.

The UTI of 2003 was a place filled with suspicion and anxiety while by 2005 it became a place where people regained their confidence, esteem, and pride. Reinventing IDBI has been another stellar contribution made by Damodaran. As a DFI organization, IDBI was weighed down by heavy NPAs. It was fast losing its relevance and was floundering in a directionless manner. This is because of factors like high cost of funds, poor asset quality, and the flight of good customers. Taking IDBI from this dead end situation and reinventing it has been Damodaran's contribution in giving it a new lease of life.

Part II: Action Architecture and Culture Landscape

Organizations going for a drastic makeover, turnaround, and transformation need to evolve a powerful strategic architecture. This is because coherence among the organizational structure, processes, turnaround tactics, and action plans can take place only when there is such a clear and well defined strategic architecture. In the absence of such architecture, change related actions will be temporal; the organization will not be able to lift itself out of its inertia and move in the desired direction, and organizational energies would be misdirected and dissipated. Transformational leaders, therefore, make efforts to build the strategy, articulate the same and vigorously pursue it. Damodaran took multiple steps to address the issues and build confidence among different stakeholders of UTI and IDBI, which included the government, media, investors, employees, and society. As Damodaran vividly described it, "the ship had to be repaired as it sailed along; there was no chance of dropping anchor, fixing the problems and then sailing again." In this section an attempt is made to highlight the key strategic actions which were taken to transform UTI and IDBI.

All the ten interviewees from UTI spelt out the key actions taken by Damodaran which are enlisted ahead. Initially the strategy was to calm down the stakeholders and reduce their anxieties and fears. Parallelly, efforts were made to build confidence among the investors, shareholders, and employees, as mentioned earlier. Subsequently, Damodaran chalked out the following plan of action:

- Erstwhile UTI was bifurcated with the pure mutual fund schemes being transferred into UTI Asset Management company. The assured return/capital protection schemes were parked in a new vehicle called the SUUTI (Specified Undertaking of UTI);
- The need to protect UTI because systemic importance was communicated to the government with the clear indication that if UTI (which was perceived to be government-owned and promoted) was allowed to fail, there could be a run on the weaker public sector banks. On the strength of this argument, the government was persuaded to guarantee the bonds to be issued by SUUTI in order to meet the commitment to the investors;
- Banks were also persuaded to provide liquidity in case of emergency requirement. To persuade the banks, meetings were held with respective CEOs. These meetings created a positive public perception that they were backing UTI;

- In order to persuade investors of US-64 not to immediately redeem the units by offering them a 10 paise monthly increase in the repurchase price from August 2001 to May 2003;
- A performance-centric reward system was brought in by introducing performance linked pay. The scheme was devised by an external agency and operated by the UTI Institute of Capital Markets to provide objectivity to the scheme;
- Three top performers identified partly through peer evaluation were invited to lunch with the Board;
- In order to make UTI youthful, vibrant, competitive, and savvy, Damodaran introduced a Voluntary Retirement Scheme (VRS). Around 50 percent of the employees took advantage of this and, in the process, UTI was relieved of a lot of deadwood, thus, making way for younger talent to occupy senior positions;
- Damodaran himself conducted all exit interviews as part of a learning process;
- Damodaran influenced the board to reduce the retirement age from 60 to 58 years in order to get rid of a few senior-level officers who had become irrelevant and could not be seen as part of the solution at UTI;
- 6.75 percent tax free bonds (for a five-year duration) were created and offered in place of US-64, to avoid sale of UTI's holdings at depressed prices to meet redemption needs;
- At a later date, UTI also took over Infrastructure Leasing and Financial Services (IL&FS) asset management fund to scotch rumors about UTI's lack of robustness and to convey that it was not a takeover target, but an acquirer; and
- In the aftermath of the scandal, the then chairman of UTI had been removed from the board of the India Growth Fund,[2] by the other directors operating outside India. In a few months, Damodaran, as the new chairman, re-established credibility to such an extent that he was re-invited to join the board, from where his predecessor was sacked.

The interviewees also said that the task of turning around UTI was stupendous and that only someone like Damodaran could have even dared to initiate this: "It is mind boggling ... when we think back it seems unbelievable."

All the ten interviewees in IDBI never thought that such a transformation will take place in IDBI and that the following will occur:

- IDBI will become a commercial bank (this changeover was done on October 1, 2004);
- Such a creative solution would emerge to the problem of NPAs through formation of the Stressed Asset Stabilization Fund (SASF) (for details, see Appendix 3A.2) which in turn cleaned the balance sheet and helped in getting triple A rating from financial rating agencies;
- IDBI Bank would be merged with IDBI; they got access to more than 100 branches for retail banking overnight and also reduce the cost of deposits; and
- VRS[3] would be implemented in a place like IDBI where, in the past, unions had been dictating and obstructing management actions.

Among other key actions taken by Damodaran (both in UTI and IDBI) the following are the most prominent:

- Focused efforts were made to reposition the organization in the public domain by creating a new logo and introducing new colors. In the case of UTI this exercise was conducted within a year while in IDBI the exercise was done within the first six months;
- In both organizations consultants were involved. In a tongue-in-cheek fashion Damodaran confessed that this was done more for branding than for getting ideas and solutions, which according to him can only come from within the organization;
- Training was used as a device to change mindsets of people in both UTI and IDBI; and
- Front offices of these organizations were transformed to change the feel of the organization from a typical public sector office to a private sector firm, thus enhancing both employee and customer experience.

The interviews conducted with the top team members of UTI (comprising ten executives) and top team members of IDBI (again comprising ten executives) have been content-analyzed to identify the strategic actions taken and culture built by Damodaran when he entered UTI and subsequently IDBI. These are presented here as eleven dominant themes:

- Seamless communication
- Scripting a new vision
- Openness
- Empowerment
- Talent management
- Recognition
- Ethical governance
- Promoting innovation
- Speedy decision-making
- Performance orientation
- Restructuring and role clarification

Seamless Communication

Just as the human body suffers myriad problems when the free flow of blood is affected, blockage of communication in the organization leads to several organizational problems. In the absence of free flow of communication, members of the organization experience directionlessness; they experience anxiety and fear, and feel disconnected. All these problems result in destruction of collective spirit, collective energy, and collective perspective. While communication is perennially important in organizations, it becomes exceedingly critical in the context of organization turnaround and transformation.

UTI: The Initial Steps

All the interviewees affirmed that Damodaran opened multiple channels of communication, reaching out to all stakeholders. The day Damodaran took charge, ten interviewees said, he walked into the emergency board meeting where everyone was anxiously waiting for him to discuss the issues and arrive at critical decisions.[4] Soon after, he addressed a press meet and articulated his plan of action for damage control, as mentioned by nine respondents. Another ten respondents said that within two days of taking charge, he assembled the staff in the dining hall and addressed them. He connected well with the people, established rapport, and sought to calm them down. He clearly conveyed two things—he was there to take charge of the situation and bring back the former glory of UTI, as gathered from nine responses. Eight persons said that he expressed this with a caring attitude. The people at UTI got the feeling that he had not come to conduct an inquisition, but to take care of the organization. In the employees' meeting, nine respondents said that he generated optimism, hope, and reassurance about their future.

The next step was to call meetings with employees, individually and in small groups. The purpose of these meetings was to closely interact and listen to people speak. According to nine interviewees, in all the meetings, he communicated the need to stay together, struggle together, and fight together to overcome the problems besieging UTI. With the seniors, he initially conducted such meetings daily, and after a while staggered them to weekly meetings. With the staff, he conducted such meetings first weekly, then fortnightly, and then monthly. In these meetings, he repeated that the organization has tremendous faith in "you," said six interviewees; and "don't lose your sleep and start working for the unit holders who have such strong faith in us," as five interviewees said. Such meetings not only provided a morale boost to the staff but also enabled Damodaran to understand the issues and concerns from the employees' perspective.

Parallelly, focus was also brought to manage the media by using an extensive communication strategy. Damodaran addressed the media and said "there have been questionable investments. We have failed in making investments which may not have been prudent and in the interest of the investors." According to seven interviewees, he was not defensive; he owned the responsibility on behalf of UTI although he was not the incumbent chairman when the scandal broke out. He sought to calm down the media and told them "don't worry we will find a solution … we will work out packages by which investor's interest will be protected," said nine interviewees. In a bid to reassure various stakeholders, ten interviewees said that he traveled all over India for two to three months and held frequent meetings with investors, chartered accountants, tax consultants, and SEBI.

Ten interviewees said that he made bold and reassuring statements to all, indicating that he was in charge, and that solutions will be found in the interest of all those involved.

Damodaran was acutely sensitive to the fact that he had to show some early wins to build confidence, both internally and externally. He was also conscious of the need to show that something was happening and that things were changing. As he put it: "You have to prove yourself quickly. Nobody will give you benefit of doubt in that kind of situation." With this in view, Damodaran addressed an open letter to the investors in the newspaper on January 1, 2003 saying: "As an organization we have mis-conducted ourselves but now we are getting things right." Further, Damodaran shared with the authors: "I passionately believe that the more difficult the times, the more the necessity for the CEO to communicate extensively and continuously." Media was invited to even small events so that they could report things shaping well in UTI, thus keeping UTI in the news all the time.

IDBI

In the turnaround and transformation of IDBI, similar communication strategy was adopted. All the interviewed employees said that after assuming charge as the chairman of IDBI, Mr Damodaran initiated extensive communication with various stakeholders (as he had done in UTI). The first step was an internal communication blitz where he met people one-to-one, in small groups as well as in large assembly of employees. Ten interviewees claimed that one round of meetings with groups of investors was completed within three months for which he traveled extensively throughout the country. His meetings with the internal people enabled him to understand the functioning of every department of IDBI, the time taken to clear proposals, the number of signatures needed before the file reached him, and so on. Communication meetings were used to paint the present and future scenario of IDBI and the options before IDBI, all the time pressing the need for change without which the future was seen to be bleak, said nine interviewees.

This strategy made people realize that either they move forward as an organization or they perish. This helped people to accept the idea of IDBI converting from a DFI into a retail bank. In the communication meetings, it was repeatedly emphasized (according to the interviewees) that "if we have to save IDBI, we have to become a retail bank. We have a difficult path to tread but if we all work together towards the goal, we will succeed."

All the interviewees mentioned that the communication strategy was used by Damodaran to "connect with people," "galvanize them," and "build confidence, hope and optimism." He also extensively met customers and addressed them at every opportunity, thus reassuring them of the bank's capability. In these meetings, eight interviewees said, he addressed young employees and boosted their morale by saying "you guys know your jobs, you can beat the competition if you pull yourself together."

Scripting a New Vision

An organization without vision stumbles along groping in the dark. In other words, it has a poor sense of what it wants, where it wants to go, and how to reach there. Therefore, for organizations to endure and grow, clarity of vision is *sine qua non*. This becomes vital in the case of organizations like UTI and IDBI which had virtually derailed and where employees experienced anxiety, powerlessness, helplessness, and directionlessness.

In UTI, after extensive interactions with stakeholders, Damodaran moved on to stemming the downfall of UTI and then scripting a new vision to rebuild the bank. According to ten interviewees, he had fifteen to twenty brainstorming meetings with thirty best brains of the company. The technique was to list five problems—typically around how to stop bleeding of the resources of UTI and how to create investor confidence. People used to debate and discuss these points and then arrive at solutions. A similar brainstorming approach was adopted with bankers and investors, said ten interviewees. Such a strategy adopted by Damodaran helped in developing collective consensus on the appropriate course of action to be adopted by UTI, which, as per nine interviewees, it also boosted the morale of various stakeholders and reassured them that UTI will be saved. This also enabled the company to shift the collective mindset from anxiety and fear to hope and excitement.

In IDBI, nine respondents said, formal vision-building exercises were undertaken in Leadership Renewal workshops designed for the top team. Senior and top level people (from both UTI and IDBI banks) participated in these workshops. Issues regarding the post-merger scenario were shared and sorted out and subsequently, Vision/Mission statements for IDBI (the integrated entity born out of the merger) were crafted. Based on these recommendations, the final Vision/Mission statement was developed and disseminated across the organization thus helping in creation of collective mindset and expectations.

All twenty interviewees across UTI and IDBI highlighted that by scripting the Vision/Mission, Damodaran succeeded in creating a sense of ownership among people, and set a clear-cut direction to move ahead. These helped in renewing positive energy, sense of excitement, and challenge which generated a renewed vigor among employees.

Openness

Organizational openness is quite critical for creating a transparent organization and also building a sense of ownership among people. This leads to dialog and sharing of ideas which enable the organization to build synergy, develop an innovative organizational culture, and make the organization creative. This becomes more vital in those organizations which are beset by problems like decay, inertia, and threat of extinction. Invariably, in such situations, people become insecure and tend to politicize, become suspicious and make wild attributions against each other, thus, ruining the social and emotional fabric of the organization. The organizational climate is polluted and without fresh inputs, people can get asphyxiated. The only way to reduce such pollution is by creating openness, sharing forums for speaking out, and unloading.

All the interviewees said that Damodaran joined both UTI and IDBI with the clear agenda of saving these institutions and setting them right. Damodaran made it clear that what one said was more important than who said it. He also made it clear that the organizational agenda was above any other considerations. He personally conveyed that he enjoyed the contrarian viewpoint and was known to say: "This is my view; I now want you to challenge it." As discussed earlier, his mode was to organize a series of brainstorming meetings that included discussions, dialogs, and debates.

As a chairman unlike most others, Damodaran became the champion of openness and accessibility by being available in person whenever needed, either in his office or over the phone or through SMSes when he was away. In fact, eighteen people said that he was one person who almost always replied with an SMS if he could not take a call. In addition, he encouraged other senior colleagues to be available to their peers and juniors. All the interviewees highlighted that as a result, politics went down, suspicion reduced, and collaboration and teamwork were heightened enormously.

Empowerment

In the contemporary workplace, the most hated lingua is "Bureaucracy," which is characterized by hierarchy, centralization, and a lack of empowerment which negatively affects workplace performance. The credo of the 21st century organizations, therefore, is to democratize, decentralize, and empower. Leaders and organizations across the world have realized and accepted the potent power of democratization for releasing people power and creating winning organization.

Twenty interviewees from both UTI and IDBI unequivocally shared that in the past both the institutions were highly hierarchical, bureaucratic, and non-empowering. In UTI, it was well known that decisions to buy or sell units were taken only at the level of the chairman, whereas in IDBI, the number of signatures needed before a decision could be arrived at was eight to ten. Therefore, decision-making was slow and, consequently, they lost many business opportunities. In financial institutions, speedy decision-making is critical to capitalize business opportunities. Unfortunately, most of the people in UTI and IDBI were file pushers. This attitude led to the situation of non-accountability, lack of ownership, and distancing from top and senior executives.

When Damodaran took charge, one of the first things he did was to break hierarchical barriers. He started calling relevant people down the line to his office for discussions. He did not bother about the status and level of the person; he was more concerned about the insight or ideas a person had. He built close rapport with the fund managers, the key talent of UTI. Many younger people (eight interviewees) who did not get a chance to be noticed earlier said that they got the chance to meet the chairman and were asked to share their ideas. Thus, a greater sense of involvement and participation started to take place. In IDBI, the interviewees said that many officers at the junior-most grades (A, B, and C) were invited at random to the twenty-fourth floor of the office building to meet the chairman in his office, which was something unprecedented in the history of the organization.

After experiencing these behaviors, people in UTI and IDBI started feeling that this chairman was different. Nine interviewees said: "Damodaran's style was not only to seek ideas and views from us but also to share his own ideas." A culture of dialoging and discussion started taking place. Eighteen people said: "We felt valued and recognized." In this process, the hierarchy was dismantled. Damodaran had his own way of knowing who was doing valuable work; he would call up performing officers giving the signal that he values contribution, not position. People said that "many times, he would just pick up the phone and talk to us straightaway," something unheard of in IDBI and UTI. Ten interviewees mentioned a lot of people saying "he called me, I feel proud about it;" they would say "this is the first time I am meeting the Chairman." They said that Damodaran has the knack of making people feel they are important, their ideas are valuable, they are special people, and they are the people who can change the organization.

All twenty interviewees said that Damodaran brought in a highly empowering and supporting mode of functioning in UTI as well as in IDBI. In UTI, all interviewees were heard saying that "huge empowerment was given to fund managers ... he had the great ability to delegate." They also said that "UTI was a huge organization and even in 2003, after the crisis, we were sitting on 58,000 crores of assets and he delegated decision making to fund managers, which till then was with the Chairman." This turned out to be the most effective way of managing the company. His action demonstrated tremendous respect for the fund managers. Five interviewees said that Damodaran would say: "I would love to chat with your fund managers over tea" or "I will meet them when they have the time" or he would call up and say "whenever you are free, please come over and have some tea." The earlier chairman was so centralized that even buying or selling decisions had to be cleared by him. Damodaran, however, gave this power to those who dealt with the buying or selling day in and day out. Fund managers had a lot of freedom to make decisions who got delegation through norms set by the Board. In UTI, fund managers are the critical decision makers in the chain, and, therefore, empowering them by cutting the layers above them was the biggest shift introduced by Damodaran. This helped UTI make faster and better decisions. Empowerment by Damodaran was, however, not abdication since, said ten respondents, a system of checks and balances and feedback was put in place.

All the interviewees at IDBI echoed similar views regarding decentralization and empowerment. The empowerment by Damodaran was not random. He did his homework in depth and knew who was doing what. One of the interviewees said: "I sacked one of the unethical officers (of course, after doing a thorough check)." The matter even went up to the Board level and Damodaran supported this stance all the way. One interviewee recalled that Damodaran used to say: "I don't mind you making mistakes; I am there to support you. I am only concerned that whatever decision you take, is in the interest of IDBI." Another interviewee narrated an interesting episode: "The empowerment he gave me, it's fantastic...." Quoting Mr Damodaran he said that he told him two three times: "You are in a very difficult area because any of your decisions could be questioned at any point, so whatever you are going to do, don't worry about it; I am there to protect you. You take your decision but document why you are taking the decision." He gave moral support to all especially to those who were carrying out the tough task of follow-up and recovery of the stressed assets. This created so much confidence that the recoveries took off with great speed and between 2004 and 2008, 400 (out of 634) cases were settled and ₹ 3,000 crores (out of the ₹ 6,000 crores settlement amount) were collected. "He is the person who gave me the confidence to go ahead and take decisions. I conveyed this to the staff and told them, I have the support of the Chairman," said one interviewee. Another person highlighted that when he informed the chairman about one of the difficult decisions he was about to take, Damodaran said, "do you think it's in the interest of the company?" When the employee answered, "Yes sir," he said: "Go ahead you have my full support." One interviewee was heard saying that this support was extended by Damodaran even at the board level.

People began to experience tremendous amount of empowerment in decision-making after Damodaran took over the company; they found support for their decisions even if he did not personally agree (with the decisions). Three interviewees said that he supported others' decisions as long as the other person had a sound logic to bear them out.

Talent Management

Great institutions are built through the power of talent; therefore, such organizations assign high priority to attracting, retaining, and growing high quality talent. This factor becomes even more critical in times of turnaround especially when competing organizations are able to attract better quality talent based on their paying power and image.

When Damodaran took charge of UTI and IDBI, he put high emphasis on building people power through effective talent management, as said all the interviewed employees.

As mentioned earlier by ten interviewees, Damodaran had a powerful balance sheet of strengths and weaknesses and potential of people which he assessed and identified through a series of meetings, group discussions, and personal chats with a large number of people in the respective organizations. Fifteen interviewees said that "he knew who could do what," whereas sixteen said that "he knew who were the smart and talented people in the organization." According to all the interviewed people, Damodaran showed great focus on the following four key aspects of talent management:

- Establishing linkage between talent and assignments, giving clear a message that important assignments would not be seniority centric, but talent centric;
- Recognition, reward, and promotion linked with talent and contributions;
- Attracting people from outside to fill in the gaps (in terms of talent availability); and

- Allowing a graceful exit option to those who could not cope with the new challenges.

According to all the interviewees Damodaran clearly signaled that people would be valued for their performance and contribution to organization building and not for any other reason. Strong signals on performance and organization orientation were given by making a couple of exemplary punishments. He made it clear that the only way out of the mess (in UTI and IDBI) would be through performance excellence, hard work, and ethical behavior.

Recognition

Damodaran demonstrated that recognition was important to ensure sustained performance excellence. Seventeen interviewees said that high performers were encouraged and motivated to give their best. All the interviewees in UTI said that he praised performers in public and made heroes out of them. Ten people said this was done even on small matters amidst all the difficulties. He identified the right people and gave them sustained support. He introduced a trusting culture. He praised and appreciated UTI employees during his personal meetings. In an unprecedented move, photos of UTI managers were even featured as part of their advertisements. He started recognizing people at a personal level by sending a small note or card to employees for their achievements and performance. He also bought them some small gifts now and then.

Ten interviewees at IDBI said that morale building took place through meetings and interactions. This was one way of signaling to people that they are valued, important, and would be consulted, and that they are capable of making worthwhile contributions. By involving people tremendous pride and energy was created in the organization. As in UTI, interviewees at IDBI said that he was keen to learn of others' special abilities. People realized that the only way they can grow, be recognized, valued, and rewarded was through performance. This approach led to a reduction in politicking and jockeying for power and increased focus on working for the organization.

Damodaran realized that UTI was needed to be prepared for the future with the right kind of talent. With this in mind, he began to actively pitch at top business schools in order to attract bright talent to join UTI. Seven interviewees said that Damodaran picked the right person for the right job.

As mentioned earlier he introduced VRS in UTI with a view to create space for upward mobility of talented people and induct fresh blood to revitalize the organization. This scheme was quite generous. Adequate communication was made about the future of UTI and the need for change following which around 50 percent of the employees availed of the VRS and left. The entire process took six to seven months in which Damodaran was personally involved in educating and persuading people to take VRS. Seven interviewees said that this helped UTI in reducing its manpower from 2,400 to 1,300.

He demonstrated strong faith in the importance of talent. He was known to say "procedures are incidental; I will hire talent wherever it is available." He started looking at the rest of the market and if he met talented persons, five interviewees claimed, he would immediately negotiate and bring them to the company. When he brought in people, eight interviewees said that he started communicating with the organization: "[W]e have a competitive market and to compete effectively we need talented people; we should not shy away from this." In a sense he redid the entire organization.

He brought competent people to the company, he changed the salary structure, brought the variable component (of the salary), therefore, preparing the organization for the future. Younger and competent people got the chance to rise in the hierarchy. According to Damodaran, "They were not bad guys but it was clear that they would not be able to drive the needed change in UTI." Ten interviewees from IDBI echoed similar views as their UTI counterparts and informed that there was high focus on talent management along with some focus on VRS. In both UTI and IDBI, Damodaran emphasized the need for re-skilling people to prepare them to meet the new challenges and demands of the financial sector. Twenty interviewees said that mass scale training programs were initiated in both UTI and IDBI.

Ethical Governance

Ethical governance is the backbone for sustainability of any institution. The recent meltdown and collapse of many institutions like Lehman Brothers, AIG,

Satyam, among others has decidedly established the connection among ethical governance, performance excellence, growth, and continued sustainability. Ethical governance assumes greater importance in the financial sector where companies handle public funds.

When Damodaran took over at UTI, the real issue was to restore its lost credibility. As mentioned in an earlier section, UTI employees were viewed with suspicion. One of the early steps taken by the new chairman was to clearly signal that corruption was unacceptable. This he did by exemplary punishment—seven interviewees said he threw out those who were found operating against the interest of UTI. He strongly backed men of high integrity.

All the twenty interviewees said that "Damodaran is a man of integrity," "he is an out-and-out organization man," and "he would not tolerate anything which hurt the organization." At the board level, as per two responses, he initiated many good practices passing the litmus test of good governance.

Promoting Innovation

"Innovate or perish" has been Damodaran's mantra. His other powerful mantras are: "Can we do it differently?" and "Can we find out ways and means to surmount the problems blocking the unfettered performance of the organization?" He has been heard saying, "are we [being] stopped from doing? If we are not stopped from doing something, why not try?"

In UTI, introduction of variable pay, hiring talented people, and fixing their salaries closer to private sector norms, while in IDBI, creation of Stressed Assets Stabilization Fund (SASF) are some of the examples of Damodaran's unconventional initiatives in the public sector context.

All the interviewees said that Damodaran always emphasized on out-of-the-box thinking and lateral approach to solve problems. He has been preponderantly outcome centric. He focused more on the purpose and, according to eleven interviewees, has been heard saying, "what can be the appropriate means to achieve that purpose?" Nine respondents said: "He used to ask people to re-examine process and if there is need to change, he encouraged them to come out with alternatives." To promote innovation he encouraged dissenting voices. He relished listening to contrarian views and in fact had greater interactions with people with such views. His empowering approach and encouragement of risk-taking was another step to make people feel that they are the owners and will have to be entrepreneurial in their approach. Fifteen interviewees, both in UTI and IDBI, highlighted that they had the great opportunity to question, dissent, and explore different alternatives under his leadership.

Speedy Decision-making

Most of the companies have more or less similar strategies and approaches to excel, win, and grow. What differentiates the winners from the others is the speed and velocity with which they are able to execute these strategies and approaches. Needless to say, the velocity and speed of decision making, moving forward, and executing actions become even more critical in companies undergoing crises like those at UTI and IDBI. All the twenty interviewees said that Damodaran introduced the risk-taking approach and timely decision-making. They said that it was amazing to see a leader who talked about speed, risk-taking, determination, and the language of being bold in public sector organizations, characterized by hierarchy, fear of the Central Vigilance Commission (CVC), Central Bureau of Investigation (CBI), and Comptroller and Auditor General (CAG). It must be emphasized that in UTI, owing to the dynamic nature of fund management, speed of decision-making becomes key to making—and losing—crores of rupees. In such a situation, centralized decision-making can be preposterous, to say the least. In UTI, Damodaran empowered the fund managers for decision-making regarding the buying and selling of units. He reversed the culture of the upward delegation in both UTI, according to eight interviewees and in IDBI, according to nine interviewees. In IDBI, he was known to say "if you want to compete with commercial banks you have to change your working style.... You will have to be fast. This is the only way you can compete with commercial banks." Speedy decision-making took root because it was supported by empowerment, decentralization, and restructuring.

Performance Orientation

Ultimately, an organization is judged by its performance. Performance is essential for its survival and growth. Without it, organizations dwindle and eventually die. Striving for performance is a very important requirement for ensuring good organizational health.

According to all the interviewees, Damodaran laid heavy emphasis on performance. Strong signals on performance were given by taking action against those found working against the organization, as also mentioned earlier in this chapter. In some extreme cases, people were thrown out of the company; others were transferred to dead-end jobs, while some were given no work at all, to give the signal to them as well as to others in the organization that they were no more relevant to the organization. The direction of moving toward high performance was clearly charted out and people were influenced to move in this direction by giving them a clear picture that unless they worked hard, things would get difficult.

In UTI, variable pay was introduced through performance-based incentives at par with the industry, which conveyed that performance was highly valued in this organization. In a bid to give a boost to high performers through promotions, the retirement age was reduced from 60 to 58, so that younger people got a chance to occupy important positions. Better role definitions were made and technological solutions were also introduced to aid speedy decision-making.

Similar steps were taken in IDBI, as indicated by the views shared by the ten interviewees. Non-performance and lack of decision-making were strongly discouraged; this was a big shift from the years of public sector functioning where not taking decisions was the best route to survival. The emphasis was on taking decisions and delivering speedy performance, as nine interviewees mentioned. The typical fears were allayed because of the culture of empowerment which was created and, said ten respondents, people could focus on making decisions knowing they will be supported in case things went wrong. The high performers and people with good ideas were recognized. As in UTI, the ten interviewees claimed, VRS was introduced and in various meetings the message that was given was that IDBI is going to change (from a DFI to a commercial bank) and those who could not re-skill themselves would get a generous VRS.

Restructuring and Role Clarification

Building role focus is a core requirement to make organizations sharply focused and become effective vis-à-vis the customers they serve. Without clear focus, organizations lose a sense of priority which thereby affects the allocation of resources and decision-making.

Interviews with the twenty executives of these organizations brought out that clarity was built into the expectations. In UTI, the fund manager was treated as an important figure who was given empowerment, so as to take speedy decisions, although he occupied a lower position in the hierarchy. Besides, at UTI, work flow was restructured. The fund manager was the decision maker regarding what to buy, what to sell, and at what price. The dealing department was separated. Additionally, Chinese walls were created between fund managers and brokers, between fund managers and dealers, and between dealers and the back office. So research came first, followed by the fund manager, dealers, back office for calculations, fund accounting provision, etc., and, last, introduction of concurrent audit.

Likewise, in IDBI the shift from a DFI to a commercial bank went hand in hand with extensive training in commercial banking so that people could switch to their new roles to serve retail customers rather than sanction loans to large corporates—a big change in mindset. The expansion of the branch network through merger and takeover helped in kick starting the new entity—IDBI Bank. In IDBI, "process changes were brought in to ensure speed of decision making."

The best technology and processes for data management were introduced in UTI, which was a major shift from maintaining the manual record and file system. Needless to say, this immensely changed the efficiency levels along with maintaining confidentiality of sensitive information.

ACTION ARCHITECTURE OF UTI AND IDBI: SALIENT CONTOURS

The findings from both the questionnaire (for details of questionnaire data of organizational culture of UTI and IDBI, see Appendix 3A.4) and interview responses reveals that Damodaran gave a strong thrust to activate multiple culture attributes—ethical governance; performance excellence; customer centricity; extensive communication to all stakeholders; empowerment; talent shaping; recognition; external orientation; and teamwork—for scripting the renaissance of UTI and IDBI. Some of these are enlisted here:

- In order to restore credibility and quickly move from the situation of scandals in UTI, Damodaran put heavy accent on ethical governance.
- Performance was one of the important mantras emphasized by Damodaran to shift people from gossip and politicization to performance focus both in UTI and IDBI.
- Attention in both UTI and IDBI was shifted from being myopic and inward-looking institutions to outward-looking institutions.
- Mammoth efforts were made to instill a collective mindset of competing and excelling among the employees of UTI and IDBI.
- UTI could successfully come out of the shroud of suspicion to regain its earlier place as a most trusted Indian mutual fund (although today it has been reborn in the form of UTI AMC and SUUTI. It is no wonder that both UTI and IDBI quickly bounced back. Today, IDBI is a renewed organization, having shed its crushing burden of stressed assets from its balance sheet and becoming a retail bank, firmly set on a positive and high growth trajectory.
- In the period of 2003–2005, UTI was honored with many awards for its performance, transparency, and outward-looking behavior. Two UTI products—TI Bond Fund and UTI, Liquid Cash Plan—were bestowed with the CNBC TV-18–CRISIL awards in 2006. UTI mutual fund was awarded the Awaaz consumer award as the most preferred mutual fund (in 2005).

PART III: M. DAMODARAN—HIS PROFILE AND PERSONA

This part of the chapter brings out the findings about M. Damodaran as a Change Maestro, based on content analysis of the interviews conducted on twenty people across UTI and IDBI. The following twelve themes have emerged from the content analysis of the interview material:

- Visionary strategist
- Courageous and bold
- Persuasive communicator
- Entrepreneurial path breaker
- People centric
- Humane
- Interpersonal connectedness
- Enabler par excellence
- Positivity
- Credibility
- Talent shaper
- Balancing divergent forces

Visionary Strategist

Damodaran is an outstanding visionary as well as a strategist according to the ten interviewees we met each in UTI and IDBI. This capability has been described by them in words such as: "He was a visionary, he had a vision"; "A visionary to the core"; "He saw tomorrow today and was years ahead of his age and time, he could foresee what could happen"; "He has been highly visionary in his thinking. He would not look at the organization today; he would look at it 5 years and 10 years ahead." This long-term perspective played an important role in all his decisions and actions. One person explained: "I say visionary because what Damodaran did here [in IDBI] in 2003 is what they are doing in the US now with regard to management of stressed assets and NPAs." Ten interviewees said:

> In IDBI we needed someone with a vision and he provided that vision. He could really anticipate the issues bank would face in the short term and long term and prepared the organization to face both. He has the agility of mind to see the future....

Commenting on the contributions of Damodaran as chairman in UTI and IDBI, one of the leading global consultants said:

> ... it was remarkable; a great achievement the way he handled UTI. He had a positive agenda for UTI; had a vision to make it succeed, he created a structure around that and he managed the whole process. Although he came new to the business, he grasped what was required pretty quickly created a plan which he sold to the government and got its support...; in IDBI, NPAs were going to kill it—he brought ₹ 9,000 crores from the government and once the company sort of stabilized, he recognized that the DFI model would not last long and moved to change IDBI into a commercial bank. Though I have worked with many leaders, I have not seen someone like Damodaran.

Further, all the twenty interviewees said that Damodaran has possesses the remarkable quality to sell his vision by engaging, discussing, and having dialogs with people. He masters the capability to paint the future scenario, contrast it with the present, and mobilize people to consent to his vision strategy and action as he did in UTI and IDBI.

The interviewees further said that his approach was initiated to capture the imagination of the people by highlighting both the gloomy scenario (if nothing was done) and the bright scenario (if the proposed steps were taken). In fact one of the interviewees said that Damodaran had mastered the powerful visualization technique of what the future is going to be like and used it to galvanize people in the proposed direction.

All interviewees confirmed that Damodaran has the great capability to convert his vision into action, thus, enabling smooth execution. Damodaran has versatility to work out multiple plans to actualize his vision. According to twelve people: "We used to discuss these scenarios, threadbare. Dissent was highly encouraged by him to arrive at the optimum solution."

Courageous and Bold

Damodaran has been seen by all interviewees as extremely bold, taking ownership of his decisions, and standing by them. He is the man who leads from the front and who does not fear controversy choosing to make decisions in organizational interest. He is tenacious and perseverant to achieve the planned goals.

Some of the descriptions and examples of this aspect of Damodaran's profile are given ahead:

> He has innate confidence in himself, the way he speaks, the ease with which he handles issues;
>
> He has great guts and boldness. He was extremely bold in the most difficult situations which he faced in UTI and IDBI;
>
> He took the bull by the horns in IDBI which required a lot of guts and self-confidence;
>
> He is never taken aback by any problems. He can take a problem head-on and deal with it without any fear or uneasiness; no hesitation in taking tough decisions, bold decisions.

During the fact finding sessions of JPC regarding the UTI case, some said, "although he took colleagues along, he himself answered all the questions despite having been in the organization only for a few days, such was his self-confidence."

In IDBI, nine interviewees mentioned that he:

> ... directly reduced the PLR which enabled the bank to move forward. If he was convinced about the need to do something in the interest of the organization, he would go ahead and not bother much about disagreement. In fact he was a fearless person and did not bother about controversies.

According to two former CEOs of public sector banks, "he is a completely goal oriented man, he pursues his goals come what may and he can demolish any obstacles that come in the way." One of the former CEOs from the banking sector said that "Mr Damodaran is a man of independent thinking, he had courage of convictions and that's why he never succumbed to any pressure, nobody can bully him, whether politician or boss."

Persuasive Communicator

All the interviewees unequivocally said that Damodaran has an enviable command over languages; he is a polyglot and chooses to speak in a language which the other person would understand and favorably respond to. He is known to speak extempore; all respondents said they have never seen him use a scrap of paper as an aid. Even when he had to suddenly speak at the last minute, he would do the same with a command not only over the language, but speak with ease and at the same time capture the spirit of the occasion. According to fifteen interviewees, Damodaran has "the gift of the gab," "he is very eloquent," "expresses himself beautifully," and "he is so articulate that whatever he speaks, people would listen to him with rapt attention."

As one person put it eloquently:

> His communication ability is unmatched. You would never see someone speak so effectively using few words; even in writing, his remarks would express what is apt, no more, no less. His remarks were precise, written as well as spoken, very articulate, along with a very good sense of humor. He is a very good storyteller. It is one thing to experience lot of things in life, but to recollect and tell them in the right manner at the right time and place is very important. He has got so any anecdotes that he keeps sharing.

Another person remarked that he is a:

> ... great communicator! And through that communication, he used to motivate, he used to reach out to people.... All other leaders, I find this problem [of poor communication despite good intentions] there is mis-signaling or mixed signaling. He was very focused and clear about what he wants to communicate.

While another interviewee said that he is "a very powerful communicator.... He can convince you that whatever he said is the ultimate truth and absolute truth."

Another interviewee said: "He has informal ways of communicating with you ... he makes you feel that you are very important to him, he puts so much faith in you.... That is what makes him a leader and not an administrator."

Through his communication, Damodaran was able to convey empowerment because he says "You can do it" and that encourages a person to do his best. He was also able to persuade and sell his point of view.

Fifteen interviewees said that he is a reservoir of information, extremely well-read right from science and technology to literature. He has a highly analytical mind and marshals his arguments in a very cogent and coherent fashion.

His power of communication, however, went far beyond language; it was so powerful because of his skill at speaking from his heart (using the power of emotion) along with rendering sensitivity to the occasion. In UTI, he communicated to allay fears of all the stakeholders; in IDBI, his communication was focused on preparing people to shift from a DFI to being a commercial bank; and in SEBI, he was tough in his statements regarding maintaining ethics of working, again a response to the context in which he was operating.

According to eleven interviewees, Damodaran mixes a lot of humor with business and this helped to keep his perspective in place. Even in the JPC, seven interviewees claim, he used this many times and it works wonderfully well in the most serious of situations.

In Damodaran's words:

> I passionately believed that the more difficult the times are the more necessary it is for the CEO to be the communicator and not put some PR (public relations executive) on the chopping block to take the questions; because in times of difficulty if CEO remains hidden in the board rooms or meetings and don't go out and tell people that, they don't even tell the employees and all communication suffers.

Entrepreneurial Path Breaker

As many as eight interviewees (who worked very closely with Damodaran) said that Damodaran's life is full of endless horizons because: "He believes in moving from best to next"; "He always look to the next orbit"; "He is highly ambitious, has a big dream and looks for new challenges"; "He thrives on challenges"; "He does not readily accept conventional wisdom"; "He looks for out of the box solutions"; "He is fearless and a risk-taker"; and "He believes in treading the untrodden path." In Tripura, in particular, he was known for doing many radical things, whether it was dealing with political parties, immigrants from Bangladesh, managing tribal angst, or initiating many projects for social development.

His scripting of the turnaround of the three banks—UCO; Indian Bank; and United Bank—flew against the face of conventional thinking of merging these banks. Many examples of his path-breaking turnaround strategies in the case of UTI and IDBI bear testimony to his spirit as an entrepreneurial path breaker.

Fifteen people said: "His focus is always on the possibilities which the future brings rather than the problems of the present"; "He takes controversial issues head-on and seeks to solve them through unconventional means." Twelve people said "there is always novelty in his approach and creativity in his solution."

People Centric

The predominant quality which people see in Damodaran is his people orientation. He is concerned about people and likes to relate with them. This emerged very strongly in all the twenty interviews with people who knew him in UTI and IDBI. He remembers the people by their names and the promises he makes to them.

His humane orientation is visible in his interpersonal behavior and it has touched a lot of people as indicated by the following quotes:

> The way he relates to people ... the way he is able to bring out the best in people, an approach that makes you comfortable, he never makes you uncomfortable....
>
> Extremely people oriented person; Praising, recognizing, appreciating is an important part of his style.... He had the ability of making us feel wanted and trusted.
>
> He was very good with staff. They all liked him. He was helpful to people. He is a very sensitive human being. Though he may not show that but he is very sensitive about others.

According to a senior partner of a reputed consulting firm:

> ... for a very senior bureaucrat, he is I would say ... almost respectful of ideas. So he doesn't care whether you are senior or junior, he doesn't care where the idea is coming from. As a result, he treats people with a lot of respect. He had the ability to get a team's trust ... it is his personal qualities that make him acceptable as a leader.

According to the CEO of a leading multinational bank: "I have observed that even in hostile meetings and difficult situations, he didn't lose personal courtesies—the mutual disagreements were never personal disagreements, they were due to principles. He would greet extremely politely with a personal touch and warmth."

He seems to have bonded with different people in different ways—with some it was love of football. Three interviewees said one thing which got them very close was his love for football which they discussed occasionally. With eleven others it was by inquiring about their families and also sharing about his family. In fact he would know family details of many of his officers, the names of their children, their educational qualifications, achievements, and so on. Another level at which he bonded with people was by always being available. Yet another way was by helping those who needed help.

Most importantly, Damodaran had the ability to develop rapport with young people at junior levels, who are routinely undervalued by large public sector organizations which focus more on hierarchy. All the persons whom we met made this observation and expressed the following: "He has the ability to energize younger people and make them feel important and get the work done;" "Young officers are dedicated to him probably because he cuts across hierarchy. It is an unusual experience. You develop a rapport that way"; "Through his communication he used to enthuse and energize people"; "Great motivator, can bring even a dead person alive"; or that he "reaches out to people."

Humane

All the interviewees strongly stated that Damodaran is a great humanist. He makes all possible efforts to help people when they are in trouble. His humane orientation is reflected by the following quotes:

> When my mother passed away, Damodaran happened to be at a meeting somewhere else and I don't know who told him this news, but I received his phone call saying, "I am sorry, I'm not able to come. I would have liked to come and pay my condolences." He was very soft, very gentle.
>
> If you have a personal problem, he will always be with you.
>
> I was in Agartala and my brother had died so he organized a ticket for me immediately to go home. When I said: "Sir I did not apply for leave," he said "Who has asked you to apply for leave? Relax, complete all the things and then come back."
>
> My father was not well. That morning, I panicked and I wanted some contacts to help, so I called him up. I was surprised at the way he helped out. He was very spontaneous, helpful and very responsive.

Eighteen people from UTI and IDBI combined said that Damodaran has been very compassionate. They gave the example of the VRS package where he made all efforts to give a generous deal to those who were leaving the organization. He did whatever he could to help people. People commented that he is an "extremely humane person.... I can personally vouch for it, he went all out to help his officers in trouble. There are many untold stories out there"; "he is magnanimous at heart"; and "he is very generous with the staff."

The true testimony of this is the fact that people who worked with him thirty years ago—cooks or drivers—approach him and get help from him even today.

Interpersonal Connectedness

Damodaran's capability to connect with people, build a rapport with them, and make them feel valued and important has been of a very high order, so said all the interviewees. He is extremely non-hierarchical in his dealing with people. He is well known for directly speaking to people, no matter which level they belonged to.

Damodaran is admired for being highly accessible to anybody who wished to meet him. Fifteen respondents were heard saying: "We were encouraged to call him directly, he quickly responded to SMSes which we sent to him."

All employees in UTI said that "he is the first Chairman and Director in UTI who broke the hierarchy and freely reached out to people." Nine of them said: "We feel connected with him because his style was of patient and respectful listening, deep understanding of our issues and problems and being supporting and helping in resolving them." Seven employees said: "We all felt that he would not belittle us or reprimand us if we made mistakes. In fact he would go out of his way to support us." Again, seven employees were heard saying: "We haven't seen a leader who can so easily connect with youngsters. He never gave us a feeling that he was a big man."

Enabler Par Excellence

All interviewees emphasized that along with envisioning and enacting, Damodaran has been a great enabler as indicated by the following quotes:

> He gives high degree of freedom and empowerment to people down the line to enable them to perform their jobs to their best capability, without being hampered by bureaucratic delays which is the bane of public sector organizations.
>
> He gave us lot of freedom. Of course, along with freedom, there was accountability.
>
> He wanted people to perform and to do their best, at the same time, he knew what they were doing and what problems they were experiencing.

As many as eight persons said: "Many times, we got help from him without demanding it. He used to be fully aware—who is doing what." Again, eight interviewees said: "Damodaran has been a great delegator, in UTI, he empowered his fund managers, delegated decision-making to them."

Fifteen people said: "Damodaran has been a highly trusting boss. He lays utmost trust in people and supports them to the hilt." Fifteen employees said that the enabling style of Damodaran helped people to take initiative, take speedy decisions and take risks when needed, knowing fully well that they would be supported for omissions and commissions. He was so trusting ... we all tried to live up to his trust. Nine employees felt that his trusting style was reciprocated by them.

Positivity

Damodaran's positivity has been mentioned by all the interviewees. People said that even in the most difficult circumstances in UTI as also in IDBI. Damodaran focused on the future, rather than the past; through his optimism, he built new hope among the people. Twenty people claimed that he used to say "things will change and can be changed; the future for all of us will be different"; nine people said Damodaran believed "every problem has a solution"; and nine people said that "he gave hope to people when we were all feeling bleak in UTI." Others said: "The great thing about Mr Damodaran is that he sends positive signals to you. You may be in any mood, but he can excite you, give you meaningful role and space. He emits a lot of positive energy. His positivity is infectious." Ten people said he would convey a lot of hope and optimism to people, that the future can be much better than the present and if they believed in this future and moved toward it, their lives would be different and that together they would build a great IDBI.

Credibility

All the interviewees said that Damodaran is a man of high integrity. Fifteen interviewees said that he is a man with clarity of purpose. Seventeen of them said that he possesses strong convictions and beliefs. For him, according to twenty interviewees, organizational interest is paramount. Twenty interviewees said that he is uncompromising on values. On many occasions he stood his ground rather than being swept away by public opinion or fear of politicians, as confirmed by fifteen respondents. Five people said that he is a visionary strategist and is clear in his dealings, whereas seventeen said he is a man of firm convictions. At the same time, he is not a rigid person. If you explain to him through profound logic, he would change his stance, one interviewee mentioned. Five interviewees said that he will not give an inch to a politician if he is convinced that the politician's stand is irregular and illegal. Damodaran is a man of humility. There is no arrogance in him whatsoever, said fifteen people. He will get into the matter, will enter into discussions with open mindedness, with a sense of listening and appreciating others point of view. Fifteen people said that many times he changed his opinion and stance, and would say in the end, as mentioned earlier in this chapter, "go ahead, you have my support."

Fifteen people said that they were prepared to do anything for him because he is a man they could trust. As many as twelve interviewees said that he never allows his personal likes and dislikes or personal interests to cloud his judgment regarding the right decision for the organization. When UTI needed a lot of liquidity, many bankers supported Damodaran because they confided in him, knowing that he was working in the interest of UTI, affirmed five interviewees.

His listening and learning capabilities have also been talked about extensively; everyone said that Damodaran's listening capability is immense. All the interviewees said that he demonstrates tremendous perseverance, listens to others' ideas, howsoever contrarian they may be. His ability to learn—and open-mindedness—has been viewed as phenomenal along with his willingness to explore new ideas. As someone put it eloquently, "in every new situation, he has the beginner's mind, listening, absorbing and quickly going up the learning curve."

Talent Shaper

Damodaran is known to spot talent and attract, retain, and shape the new recruits—identify talent and employ them in the right positions—so said all the interviewees. He has the ability to get extraordinary results from ordinary people. He has great people skills. He believes in Jim Collins' dictum to get the right people, give the right seats, and get the bus to move.

Three people said he used to tell them that:

> ... to be a leader, you need not know the nuts and bolts; what you require is to get the right people in the right slots. You must focus on the big picture. You must coach and mentor your subordinates, groom them and build them. This is the only way you get time to focus on the bigger picture.

He actively engaged in interacting with people on a personal basis. This enabled him to know what are the talents and capabilities of different people. In fact in UTI, when he realized that the EDs and GMs did not have much idea about fund management, he empowered the fund managers and groomed them into great investment bankers.

Damodaran's favorite mantra has been the following:

> God has not made everyone alike, each one has his own unique strengths. As a leader it is my job to bring out the best of what God has given them. I cannot change the basic characteristics of the people, what I can do is to bring out the best in them.

Through the process of decentralization, empowerment, and delegation, Mr Damodaran provided people ample opportunities and mentoring to develop and grow. He used training as an important tool to develop people by expanding their knowledge base and preparing them for higher positions: "Dialoging with Mr Damodaran used to make us feel that we are great guys and that we can do many great things. This inspired us to live up to his expectations."

Balancing Divergent Forces

There was unanimity of opinion among all the twenty interviewees that Damodaran has the rare capability of creating a mosaic through the power of balancing divergent forces. He has the amicable style of engaging with diverse forces and viewpoints without getting swept away by any of them. His style has always been one of interacting and debating rather than arguing and imposing his viewpoint. No doubt he has his own views on the issues but his unique style is to listen, appreciate, absorb, discuss, and resolve. Damodaran has the habit of raising the level of debate to a higher level, while bringing a holistic picture to the discussion, enabling people to work in the larger interest.

In fact one of his key strengths in allowing divergent forces to co-exist is his understanding of the big picture. Everyone said that Damodaran is highly objective and does not take sides and directs people's attention to the issue at stake.

Despite all the problems at UTI from multiple sources, he could smile and act with great confidence thus making people feel secure, while he himself bore the burden of showing results at UTI, as ten interviewees confirmed. He could run the ship and repair it without dropping anchor, said five people, which is an obvious reference to both turning around UTI as well as fixing its myriad immediate problems. His skill at multitasking on at least three to four tasks simultaneously is legendary, eighteen people confirmed. Ten people said that he is a master at balancing divergent forces in the interest of the organization. While he is extremely polite in dealing with people, nine people said he is a man of firm determination and will fiercely protect organizational interest. He is a man both of high self-confidence as well as high listening and learning, said fifteen people; fifteen respondents also said he is a man who pursues both vision and action. Three people who knew him from his long tenure in Tripura also admiringly spoke about his unique ability to balance multiple political parties and still be seen as a neutral person.

M. Damodaran as a Change Maestro: Salient Contours

The following holistic perspectives about Damodaran as a Change Maestro emerges from a study of both the interview data as well as questionnaire responses (for details of questionnaire data of M. Damodaran's Change Maestro style, see Appendix 3A.5):

- Damodaran has tremendous capability to connect, touch, reach, influence, and motivate people, which is one of the most essential requirements for being a Change Maestro.
- His admirable communication capability goes hand in hand with his overwhelming credibility, which is undoubtedly another important cornerstone of leadership.
- He demonstrated tremendous sensitivity to the issues and problems of all stakeholders. He has been extremely media savvy and effectively used the media for rebuilding the image of UTI and IDBI as well as communicating with various stakeholders.
- Damodaran galvanized his followers through the power of his vision, strategic thinking, and ambitious agenda for the organization along with his fine skills at naturally connecting with people.
- He instilled tremendous confidence among the people through the power of his optimism and capability to radiate positive energy.

- He has been highly performance centric and entrepreneurial.
- He not only encouraged new ideas but also actively promoted out-of-the-box thinking and solutions.
- In a holistic sense it can be said that Damodaran used all the gears for achieving corporate turnaround and transformation in UTI and IDBI.
- Damodaran was honored as the Policy Change Agent of the year, in the Indian financial sector by *The Economic Times* for 2006–2007. He has also been honored by AIMA for Public Service in 2010.

M. Damodaran: Concluding Contours

M. Damodaran, the Renaissance Artiste who transformed UTI and IDBI, is a man inured to tackling missions where the stakes are high. Throughout his checkered career, he has risen admirably to the occasions and tackled situations fraught with risk and challenges. Damodaran is a leader with a strong sense of justice and fair-play. He has a reputation for being upright, outspoken, bold, and courageous. Damodaran believes in keeping his ears and eyes open and is always ready to learn from people around him.

His decision-making has always been for the greater good. Therefore, he viewed rules as guidelines through the lens of outcomes and impact rather than mindlessly following them. Damodaran, thus, has the capability to look for solutions without being limited by the framework. This has enabled him to come up with solutions having far-reaching impact on organizations.

He has been a master at taking risks and plunges because that is the best course of action in public interest.

Damodaran has immense faith in god, believing that to every problem god has created a solution and it is up to the individual to find it. He is extremely fearless having undergone many difficult and life-threatening experiences which only seem to have made him much stronger, more resilient, and more determined to tackle tough situations.

As a strongly optimistic and positive person, he has always chosen to look at the strength of an organization and work to take it ahead. He believes that this is a better way to deal with troubled organizations rather than being overwhelmed by weaknesses. Thus, he prefers to move ahead rather than being trapped by the past.

He has an uncanny sense of people's expectations in troubled situations and admirably gears himself up to respond to the same. Through the power of his communication and credibility he reduces skepticism, demonstrates quick wins, bolster the confidence of the employees, and enlists their wholehearted support for turnaround and transformation. Through intense listening, he conveys to people that they are worthy both to him and the company. Even in the most difficult situations he keeps a bold front to allay fears and build confidence of the team.

Damodaran's major contribution—among many other things—has been to invest in people, and, as a CEO, create an enabling and empowering environment. Damodaran is well known for winning people over through his oratorical magic. He is a great mentor and uses the same for building talent and harnessing people power. He has used his by now legendary communication capabilities in effectively handling the media, government, and other stakeholders. He has immense capability of balancing multiple stakeholders' interests.

It is no wonder, therefore, that with this repertoire of Change Maestro capabilities and personal qualities, Damodaran could successfully put two organizations on the right track. In both UTI and IDBI, he could convert despair into hope, enlisted the support and goodwill of the employees, government, and other stakeholders. His greatest strength has been that he is an out and out people's man. He encouraged talented people to rise and contribute to rebuilding the organization, a seemingly impossible feat in the difficult circumstances experienced in UTI and IDBI.

APPENDICES

Appendix 3A.1: Brief Sketch of M. Damodaran

In the annals of Indian bureaucracy, Meleveetil Damodaran's name would be permanently etched as a true corporate leader. Working within the maze of red-tape that typically afflicts the government system, he not only succeeded in transforming the entire financial sector, but also made it the engine of growth and the crucial lynchpin of India's emergence as the global economic superpower. In a career spanning nearly four decades, this IAS officer's ability to create institutions has been legendry. His restoring UTI to health and strength and his restructuring of Industrial Development Bank of India (IDBI) in an innovative manner are two of the most evocative turnaround stories in the Indian financial sector. As Chairman SEBI, he brought improved practices to India's securities market.

He has been conferred with several honors and accolades. As one of the foremost advocates of corporate governance in India, Damodaran is on the boards of various committees and advises them on improving boardroom performance. He is an Advisor on Strategy and Corporate Affairs at ING Group of the Netherlands, Independent Director on the Boards of GMR Group and GMR Varalakshmi Foundation, Hero Honda, Tech Mahindra and Mahindra, Satyam, Chairman of Srei Sahaj e-Village Ltd, and Member of Committees at INTACH, Experian Credit Information Co. of India, KPMG, and Bessemer Venture Partners. He is also a part of the Development Evaluation Planning

Table 3A.1: Accolades to M. Damodaran over the Last Decade, 2003–2008

2008	• Rotary International District 3050—Rotary Award for Professional Excellence.
2007	• *The Economic Times* Award for Policy Change Agent of the year 2006–2007.
2006	• Featured 47 in the list of the most influential business people in Asia-Pacific—*Asiamoney*. • CNBC Award for outstanding contribution to Indian business. • Rotary district 3140 award for Vocational Excellence.
2005	• Priyadarshini National Award 2002–2004 for Public Service. • Centenarian Award for Professional Excellence. • Finance Man of the Year 2004 conferred by the Bombay Management Association and six other Apex Bodies.
2003	• Institute of Directors Golden Peacock Award for Leadership in Corporate Transformation.

Source: From company details.

Committee of the Planning Commission and the Chairman of the Taskforce on Corporate Governance constituted by FICCI.

Appendix 3A.2: Brief Profile Sketch of UTI

Recognizing the need for a strong organization with nationwide presence to mobilize the savings of small investors and to apply it to productive purposes, the Government of India set up the Unit Trust of India (UTI) in 1963. UTI was promoted, at the instance of the Government of India, by a number of financial institutions and banks with the IDBI being the major promoter. In 1964, UTI launched its first scheme known as Unit Scheme-1964 (US-64) with an administered sale and repurchase price for its units. Since it was the only scheme of its kind which continuously offered higher returns than commercial banks, it became, over time, the preferred investment option for millions of Indians in different income groups. The fact that it was set up under an Act of Parliament led to the belief that it was a government-owned institution which could not fail. The scheme soon grew to a size which made it the prime mover in India's securities market. In the late 1980s, on account of a change in the Income Tax Act, corporates with significant cash balances found it more productive to bring their surplus funds for short purpose in US-64. This led to increasing volatility in a scheme which was originally intended for retail investors. UTI's importance had reached a level when it was described as a proxy for India's financial sector. A free conceivable industrial enterprise in India had UTI as one of its major investors. In effect it had the unique role of mobilizing vast amounts of savings of a very large number of investors and channelizing the same for productive purposes.

The fundamental weakness of US-64 was that the sale and purchase price was not based on the intrinsic value of the unit. None in the capital funds industry has net asset value (NAV). Over time, the gap between the sale and repurchase price and the NAV reached such levels as to undermine the solvency of the scheme. In addition to the problems which were bound to surface sooner or later in US-64, UTI also had in the mid-1990s reintroduced monthly incompliance which assured capital protection and in some cases a pre-determined rate of return with the markets on tenure throughout. It became extremely difficult for

UTI to honor those commitments incurred, ensure return on capital as well as make payments of an assured return, and by early 2001 the difference between the amount required to honor the commitments and the value of the holdings of the scheme exceeded ₹ 10,000 crores. By the middle of 2001, the power of UTI taken together was on a negative net worth in excess of ₹ 16,000 crores. Thus, the organization which was set up to mobilize the investable surpluses of the average and to put them to protective use was not in a position to keep its basic commitments of safety of capital, liquidity of the investment, and the reasonable return on the investment. Also, in an industry which had become competitive with an increasing number of profitable affairs, UTI was over-staffed and the skill sets of much of its senior workforce were not relevant to a competitive sphere. As a media commentator put it, these were persons from an era in which units were bought, not sold. Now they had to go out and compete in marketplace unlike in the past when investors came to them.

The transformers of UTI required a new management to address the present concerns of investor confidence, availability of funds to meet commitments on a daily basis, with such commitments increasing as negative reports started getting out in the media. Most importantly, the re-engineering of the human capital in terms of size, skill sets, moral and motive, and compensation needed to be addressed on a war footing.

Table 3A.2: Recognition and Accolades to UTI Mutual Fund during Mr Damodaran's Tenure, 2002–2006

2006	• UTI Mutual Fund received two CNBC-TV-18–CRISIL Mutual Fund of the Year Award, 2006 for two its of schemes, namely, UTI Bond Fund and UTI Liquid Cash Plan.
	▪ UTI Bond Fund has been ranked by CRISIL Fund Services among the two Best Performing Income Funds for the Year 2005 based on its performance in the CRISIL~CPR.
	▪ UTI Liquid Cash Plan has been ranked by CRISIL Fund Services among the two Best Performing Liquid Funds for the Year 2005 based on its performance in the CRISIL~CPR.

| 2005 | • UTI Mutual Fund has been awarded the Awaaz Consumer Award 2005 in the "Mutual Fund" Category as the most preferred mutual fund.
• UTI G-Sec Short Term Plan has been ranked ICRA-MFR1 by ICRA/ICRA Online and has been awarded the Gold Award for "Best Performance" in the category of "Open Ended Gilt Scheme—Short Term" for one year period ending December 31, 2005. The award for UTI G-Sec Short Term Plan indicates the Best Performance within the stated category, which had a total of fourteen similar schemes, including this scheme.
• UTI Bond Fund has been ranked ICRA-MFR1 by ICRA/ICRA online and has been awarded the Gold Award for "Best Performance" in the category of "Open Ended Debt Scheme—Long Term" for one year period ending December 31, 2005. The award for UTI Bond Fund indicates the Best Performance within the stated category, which had a total of twenty-three similar schemes, including this scheme.
• UTI Bond Fund has also been ranked ICRA-MFR1 by ICRA/ICRA online and has been awarded the Gold Award for "Best Performance" in the category of "Open Ended Debt Scheme—Long Term" for three year period ending December 31, 2005. The award for UTI Bond Fund indicates the Best Performance within the stated category, which had a total of twenty-six similar schemes, including this scheme.
• UTI Nifty Index Fund has been ranked ICRA-MFR1 by ICRA/ICRA online and has been awarded the Gold Award for "Best Performance" in the category of "Open Ended Index Scheme" for one year period ending December 31, 2005. The award for UTI Nifty Index Fund indicates the Best Performance within the stated category, which had a total of thirteen similar schemes, including this scheme.
• UTI Master Index Fund has been ranked ICRA-MFR1 by ICRA/ICRA online and has been awarded the Gold Award for "Best Performance" in the category of "Open Ended Index Scheme" for three year period ending December 31, 2005. The award for UTI Master Index Fund indicates the Best Performance within the stated category, which had a total of nine similar schemes, including this scheme. |
|---|---|

(continued)

(continued)

	• UTI MIS Advantage Fund has been ranked ICRA-MFR1 by ICRA/ICRA online and has been awarded the Silver Award for "Second Best Performance" in the category of "Open Ended Marginal Equity Scheme" for one year period ending December 31, 2005. The award for UTI MIS Advantage Fund indicates Second Best Performance within the stated category, which had a total of thirty-two similar schemes, including this scheme. • UTI Gilt Advantage Fund LTP has been ranked ICRA-MFR1 by ICRA/ICRA online and has been awarded the Silver Award for "Second Best Performance" in the category of "Open Ended Gilt Scheme—Long Term" for three year period ending December 31, 2005. The award for UTI Gilt Advantage Fund LTP indicates Second Best Performance within the stated category, which had a total of nineteen similar schemes, including this scheme. • UTI Floating Rate Fund-STP has been ranked ICRA-MFR1 by ICRA/ICRA online and has been awarded the Silver Award for "Second Best Performance" in the category of "Open Ended Floating Rate Fund" for one year period ending December 31, 2005. The award for UTI Floating Rate Fund STP indicates Second Best Performance within the stated category, which had a total of twenty-four similar schemes, including this scheme.
2004	• UTI Growth and Value Fund has been ranked among the three Best Performing Open-ended Diversified Equity Funds for the year 2004 by CRISIL FundServices based on its performance in the CRISIL-CPR. On the basis of this ranking the scheme won the CNBC TV18–CRISIL Mutual Fund of the Year Award in the Open-ended Diversified Equity Funds Category. • UTI Nifty Index Fund has been ranked ICRA-MFR1 by ICRA online indicating the "Best Performance" in the category of "Open Ended Index Schemes—Nifty" for one year period ending December 31, 2004 and wins a Gold Award at the ICRA Online Mutual Fund Awards 2005.

	• UTI Dynamic Equity Fund has also been ranked ICRA-MFR1 by ICRA Online, indicating performance among the top 10 percent in the category of "Open Ended Diversified Equity Schemes—Aggressive" for one year period ending December 31, 2004 and wins a Silver Award at the ICRA Online Mutual Fund Awards 2005. • CNBC-TV18–BNP Paribas Mutual Fund of the Year Award, Year 2004 has been awarded to UTI G-Sec Fund (Growth) as the Best Performing Open ended Gilt Fund (one year).
2003	• CNBC India Mutual Fund of the year Award 2003 UTI Unit Scheme 1995 (Growth) has been ranked by Moody's Investor Service as the Best Performing open-ended balanced fund—three year category. • UTI NIFTY INDEX FUND has been ranked MFR1 by ICRA Online for the best performance in the category Open-ended Index Schemes (Nifty) for a one year period ending December 31, 2003.

Source: From company details.

Appendix 3A.3: Brief Profile Sketch of IDBI

IDBI was the second Development Financial Institution (DFI) set up by the Government of India, the first being the Delhi-based Industrial Financial Corporation of India (IFCI). Over the years, IDBI became India's leading DFI and, along with ICICI, met the term finance requirements of a large number of India's corporates. In the initial years, commercial banks in India confined themselves to meeting the working capital requirements of their borrowers and leaving it to the DFIs to meet the term finance requirements. With the passage of years, commercial banks in India began to develop the skill sets and expertise required for project appraisal and for providing term finance and with their branch network and the low cost deposits that they were able to raise, the commercial banks now became a more cost effective option for the borrowing community. The DFI model with its lack of access to low cost funds began to go out of fashion. With several industries getting hit by cyclical downturns, the health of the lending institutions also suffered. ICICI responded to this challenge by a reverse merger with their commercial bank, namely, ICICI Bank which it had promoted. IDBI contemplated a similar route, but met with a considerable resistance from different quarters including the Government of India which was and continues to be the majority shareholder. The workforce also felt that a merger on the lines of what ICICI had done could over the years lead to privatization and, hence, resisted any possibility of merger of IDBI with its bank. In due course the asset quality of IDBI deteriorated considerably with non-performing assets reaching unacceptably high levels. The extent of provisioning required increased every year, obviously affecting the earnings of the organization. Since the lending rates were no longer competitive, the better customers moved to banks where cheaper credit and the complete range of services were available. Concurrently, there was also the exit of a number of persons with project appraisal experience. To ensure that it remained profitable, the IDBI continuously sold its holdings of equity in the companies which it assisted over the years. The pressure of showing profits on a quarterly basis compounded by the lack of a viable business model ensured that the organization was heeding toward problems of both liquidity and solvency. The obvious solution was the merger of IDBI with the IDBI Bank. The workforce and the work culture in both these organizations were materially different. IDBI was unwilling to reduce its majority shareholding in IDBI Bank and at the same time did not have the funds required to infuse capital into IDBI Bank. So we had the spectacle of a DFI that was rapidly moving to a disastrous situation and a small bank that could not grow for want of capital. Merger of these two institutions while retaining government's majority shareholding and in the light of continuing resistance was a merger challenge. A complete integration at the time of merger was ruled out given the different skill sets, the different compensation levels, and the resistance encountered from different quarters. The model that was implemented was a legal merger with different SBUs dealing with commercial banks and developmental banking. The integration team with equal representation from both the organizations was set up to address the impediments in the way of total integration and the preparation of a roadmap for the purpose.

Since the poor asset quality of IDBI was identified as a major hurdle, it was necessary to put in place a solution that was both unique to the needs of the organization and did not involve any immediate cash outgo from the Government of India, the majority shareholders. For this purpose the SASF was devised as a Government of India owned entity. This was necessary in order to avoid consolidation of accounts. The Government of India was to issue twenty-year interest-free bonds amounting to ₹ 9,000 crores to the SASF, which would use those bonds as consideration for the non-performing assets held in IDBI's books. This unique arrangement ensured that IDBI did not lose in regard to the value of assets at the time of the transfer since the value in its books was received by it as consideration. At the same time the bonds were declared as non-transferable by IDBI. It was deemed to be "Held to Maturity" (HTM) and, therefore, no discounting was required to be made in IDBI's books. As a result, IDBI had no loss at either stage of the transaction while taking out of its books non-performing assets to the extent of ₹ 9,000 crores. For the Government of India, it was unlike the bank recapitalization scheme, an intervention that did not require annual payout by way of interest on the bonds. The scheme was based on the assumption that some, if not most, of the assets would, over the years, become performing assets with an improvement in the fortunes of the sector to which they belonged. This hope has been realized and with improvement in the sectors such as cement and steel, the SASF has recovered more than half of the value of the assets in around four years with sixteen years left to realize the remaining value. Simultaneously, the bonds to the extent of the value realized have been extinguished, thus reducing the Government of India's liability if any at the end of twenty years.

Though IDBI's workforce was in the region of 2,800, it was found necessary to take out those that were not directly relatable to the business it was transacting. This was accomplished by a VRS which accounted for about 440 persons.

Appendix 3A.4: Organizational Culture of UTI and IDBI—Analysis of Questionnaire Data

Table 3A.4: Perceived Organizational Culture of UTI and IDBI

N = 66

S. No.	Organizational Culture	Mean	SD	Ranks
1.	Ethical governance	4.46	0.60	1
2.	Outward looking	4.24	0.78	2
3.	Result orientation	4.2	0.72	3.5
4.	Focus on building competitiveness	4.2	0.86	3.5
5.	Performance excellence	4.17	0.73	5

(continued)

(continued)

S. No.	Organizational Culture	Mean	SD	Ranks
6.	Responsiveness to the customer	4.16	0.87	6
7.	Communication and information flow: Horizontal (a) Within the department	4.15	0.75	7.5
8.	Process focused	4.15	0.72	7.5
9.	Openness and transparency	4.14	0.76	9
10.	Teamwork	4.12	0.68	10.5
11.	Role clarity	4.12	0.67	10.5
12.	Empowerment and delegation	4.11	0.73	12.5
13.	Openness to new ideas	4.11	0.85	12.5
14.	Global perspectives	4.1	0.92	14
15.	Focus on continuous improvement	4.09	0.79	15
16.	Trust	4.08	0.59	16
17.	Performance-based promotion	4.05	0.98	17
18.	Speed of response to external demands and challenges	3.99	0.78	18
19.	People orientation	3.97	0.70	19
20.	Support for risk-taking	3.9	1.03	20
21.	Participative	3.88	0.67	21
22.	Nurturing talent	3.85	0.86	22
23.	Communication and information flow: Vertical (b) Bottom-up	3.83	0.93	23
24.	Nurturing innovation	3.81	1.04	24
25.	Tolerance of differences	3.8	0.74	25
26.	Speed of response to internal demands	3.79	0.93	26
27.	Community culture	3.74	0.80	27.5
28.	Entrepreneurial	3.74	1.19	27.5
29.	Cross functional collaboration	3.7	0.87	29
30.	Culture of celebration of achievements and successes	3.64	0.88	30
31.	Communication and information flow: Horizontal (b) Across the departments	3.56	1.06	31
32.	Communication and information flow: Vertical (a) Top-down	3.39	0.69	32
33.	Centralized design-making process	3.05	0.75	33

Source: Author.

Table 3A.4 brings out the following salient features of the work culture which Damodaran promoted in both the organizations:

- All the mean values of the organizational culture parameters are more than average, ranging from 3.05 to 4.46.
- There is significant homogeneity in the perceptions of the work culture in the case of twenty-eight items, the standard deviations being less than 1.00.
- Out of the thirty-three culture parameters, seventeen are in the Highly Visible category, with mean values greater than 4.00.
- It is possible to conclude from the findings that great emphasis was laid on creating a culture of ethical governance along with a result-oriented culture as well as a culture of performance excellence. Organizational culture was shifted from its inward centric focus to the outward focus with global perspective. A culture of competitiveness essential for the organizations to survive, excel, and grow was also developed in UTI and IDBI.
- Empowerment and delegation, responsiveness to customer, communication flow (within department), process focus, openness and transparency, teamwork (within department), role clarity, empowerment and delegation, openness to new ideas, focus on continuous improvement, trust, and performance-based promotion have also been given a thrust in UTI and IDBI.

Appendix 3A.5: M. Damodaran as a Change Maestro—Analysis of Questionnaire Data

Table 3A.5: Perceived Style of Damodaran as a Change Maestro

N = 66

S. No.	Change Maestro Attributes	Mean	SD	Ranks
1.	Is a strategic thinker	4.94	0.35	1.5
2.	Is an effective communicator	4.94	0.24	1.5
3.	Has high credibility	4.88	0.37	3
4.	Stands like a rock in the face of calamities	4.83	0.38	4.5
5.	Fast in making critical decisions	4.83	0.38	4.5

(continued)

(continued)

S. No.	Change Maestro Attributes	Mean	SD	Ranks
6.	Is a visionary	4.82	0.43	6
7.	Has ambitious plans for the organization	4.79	0.48	7
8.	Is honest and transparent	4.76	0.5	8.5
9.	Radiates positive energy	4.76	0.43	8.5
10.	Provides a sense of clear direction	4.73	0.48	10
11.	Has empowering and supporting attitude	4.71	0.52	11.5
12.	Is reliable	4.71	0.46	11.5
13.	Leads from the front	4.7	0.5	13.5
14.	Recognizes and rewards performance	4.7	0.55	13.5
15.	Has a global mindset	4.65	0.69	15
16.	Is open to new ideas	4.62	0.52	16
17.	Makes people feel that they are valued by the organization	4.59	0.55	17
18.	Is innovative and creative	4.58	0.61	18
19.	Leads by example	4.56	0.56	19
20.	Is a man of words	4.55	0.68	20
21.	Is a role model	4.52	0.66	21
22.	Respects the dignity of others	4.49	0.56	23
23.	Pursues excellence in everything	4.49	0.66	23
24.	Is interested in growth of his people	4.49	0.64	23
25.	Grooms and develops people	4.47	0.61	25
26.	Is a team builder	4.44	0.61	27
27.	Is result focused	4.44	0.77	27
28.	Business strategist	4.44	0.88	27
29.	Is fair and impartial	4.41	0.72	29
30.	Is entrepreneurial	4.39	0.82	30
31.	Makes people feel that they have great worth	4.33	0.71	31
32.	Has helping attitude	4.32	0.68	32
33.	Is demanding and performance centric	4.27	0.89	33
34.	Sensitivity	4.14	0.70	34.5
35.	Humility	4.14	1.01	34.5

Source: Author.

Table 3A.5 brings out the following striking features of Damodaran's leadership profile:

- All the leadership attributes have extremely high average scores, that is, above 4.14 on a 5-point scale.
- There are twenty-one attributes which feature in the Most Visible category, the mean values being 4.50 and above. The other fourteen attributes are in the Highly Visible category with mean values ranging from 4.14 to 4.49.
- There is perceptual homogeneity regarding Damodaran's perceived style as a Change Maestro, indicated by the low SD (less than 1.00), except that for humility being 1.01. In other words people have more or less similar views about Damodaran's style as a Change Maestro. In fact in the case of the top five items—strategic thinking; effective communication; credibility; standing like a rock in the face of calamities; and speedy decision-making—there is more or less unanimity of views.
- Further perusal of the top ten items featuring in the Most Visible category brings out that Damodaran's top most Change Maestro quality is his ability to communicate powerfully. He is also seen as a leader who is seen as a visionary and strategic thinker, with ambitious plans for the organization. Damodaran is also viewed by his team as honest and transparent, who stands like a rock in the face of calamities, and as a person with high credibility. He is perceived to be decisive and as a leader who radiates positive energy. Damodaran is also viewed as a person who provides clear sense of direction.

Notes

1. Authors gratefully acknowledge and appreciate the intellectual contributions and emotional support they received from all the interviewees who gave their precious time and helped us understand the organization and the leader. However, for the conclusions and views expressed in this case study of M. Damodaran as a Change Maestro, the authors own entire responsibility.

2. The only country fund of India listed on the New York Stock Exchange (NYSE) and regulated by the Security and Exchange Commission (SEC) of USA, and in operation since 1986.
3. Incidentally 440 persons who were in the non-core functions took the VRS.
4. Twenty-one top team members were interviewed by the authors. The number of respondents varies since the interviewing method was largely unstructured; we recorded what they said, giving greater priority to what came out of top-of-the-mind in response to our broad questions, rather than getting them to respond to a set of questions.

4

4
SAJJAN JINDAL: ROMANCING LIMITLESS GROWTH

This is the story of a young man going on a pilgrimage to Mecca. He always dreamt to go to the holy land in search of Truth and God. He was passionate about his quest and impatient to realize his dream.

On his way he met Khoja, a great scholar and philosopher who, at that time, was chopping wood by the roadside. The young man asked him: "Sir, how much time would it take me to reach Mecca?" Khoja did not respond to the young man's inquiry and continued with his chore. The young man repeated the question a second time, this time speaking loudly. When he received no response again, the young man thought Khoja was deaf and rather than wasting time started running toward Mecca with great zeal and determination.

Seeing the speed, energy, and enthusiasm of the young man, the philosopher smiled to himself and called out: "Young man, wait a minute! It will take exactly 45 minutes for you to reach Mecca!" Flabbergasted, the young man stopped and asked Khoja, "Why then did you not speak when I asked you twice?" The philosopher replied, "Young man, I was sure about your dream and desire to reach Mecca. I could see the fervor and passion in your eyes. However, I was not quite sure about your speed and resolve. Now that I am sure of this, I can answer your question—it will take you precisely 45 minutes."

The reality of life is that many of us dream big, but do not have enough speed and passion to race to the goal. We dream great dreams and although we are capable of running, we decide to simply walk and still dream of reaching our ambitious goals.

Gibbon, the great historian, spent thirty years of his life on his pet creative project—writing world history. He romanced the project, living and breathing his great dream for thirty-three years. The great Indian poet and mystic Rabindranath Tagore after writing 6,000 poems, cried as he lay on his deathbed, praying for rebirth so that he could write yet another poem. An old friend sitting at his bedside asked him, "Why are you crying? You have written 6,000 songs! Shelley [one of the greatest English poets] has written only 2,000. You have defeated him 3 times over.... You should be happy and content." Tagore opened his tearful eyes and said, "I am not satisfied yet.... I have written 6,000 poems but you don't know my inner longing. I wanted to sing my best one; I tried again and again 6,000 times and failed. All those are efforts which I am not satisfied with. My best poem is still unwritten!"

In a similar vein is the episode of Gandhi after his visit to Noakhali. When reporters asked him, "What next?" he answered, " I am going to Karachi!" That was the day he was killed. "Life is a journey not a destination" has been the life story of all those who made the difference. Sajjan Jindal embodies the speed and desire of the young man in the story who dreamt of going to Mecca, the romance of Gibbon, and Rabindranath Tagore's quest for excellence. Jindal romances the idea of limitless growth of his company, JSW, who is never satisfied with what he has and aims to reach the next goal post.

He would never let his quest remain static for very long. He began his odyssey at a furious pace, letting the future chase the present as if there were no tomorrow. The unbelievable yet true story of Sajjan Jindal sends us the message to constantly expand the size of our dreams. Richard Bach said: "Here is a test to find out whether your mission in life is complete. If you are alive, it isn't." In the words of Bernard Shaw, Sajjan Jindal "wants to be thoroughly used up when I die-for the harder I work, the more I live." But it is not an ordinary living that Sajjan Jindal lives: he paints a masterpiece daily and autographs his work with excellence.

SAJJAN JINDAL

The case study "Sajjan Jindal: Romancing Limitless Growth"[1] has been organized into three parts: Part I provides a brief profile sketch of JSW Group; Part II highlights the action architecture and culture landscape; and Part III discusses Sajjan Jindal's profile and persona.

PART I: BRIEF PROFILE SKETCH OF JSW GROUP

The history of JSW (for details of the organization's profile, see Appendix 4A.1) can be traced back to 1992 when Jindal Group acquired Piramal Steel Ltd, a mini steel plant at Tarapur in Maharashtra. This plant was then renamed Jindal Iron and Steel Company Ltd (JISCO). At age of twenty-three, fresh out of college, Sajjan Jindal (for details of the Change Maestro's profile, see Appendix 4A.2) commenced his long journey to build JSW, actualizing his dream in a short span. On multiple fronts, this group has shown impressive growth—from a ₹ 93 crore company in 1993 to a ₹ 12,700 crore company in 2008 with a plan to become a ₹ 50,000 crore company in 2012, along with expansion, revenues, community development, and CSR. The striking factor is not only the scale of the achievements in institution-building and wealth creation; it is also about the relatively short time in which these achievements were registered especially considering from what level the group first commenced its journey from. Above all, this group has a robust business model where forward and backward integration has been ensured. Additionally, they have created shareholder wealth and development in undeveloped areas of India, against all odds.

PART II: ACTION ARCHITECTURE AND CULTURE LANDSCAPE

The interview data were content analyzed and the ten emergent themes are presented here:

- Mega growth vision
- Entrepreneurial DNA
- Toward the next milestone
- Empowerment with accountability

- Quest for excellence
- High performance recognition
- People focus
- Ethical governance
- Beyond profit—social concerns
- Shaping talent

Mega Growth Vision

In organizational life, great achievements are built on a mega vision. It is vision which sets the strategic direction for the organization. In fact the destiny of the organization is written in the stated organizational vision and mission. The scale of this vision determines the pace, agility, and amount of energy expended in striving toward its achievement.

JSW's mega vision can be seen in its pace of growth within a decade in terms of turnover as well as steel tonnage, as confirmed by the eighteen people who were interviewed.[2] Five people said that right from 1992, Sajjan Jindal was clear that "we cannot continue as re-rollers; we need to go for backward integration and have control on the resources."

Today, JSW Steel has a market capital of ₹ 3.8 billion and the JSW Group is planning to reach the ₹ 60 billion mark by 2020, as sixteen interviewees confirmed. JSW's ambition is to be among the top ten global companies and one of the top five in India in the steel sector. In the aluminum business, the company plans to invest ₹ 4,000 crores by 2012 of a capacity of 1.6 million tonnes of aluminum. In cement, according to nine interviewees, JSW plans to achieve a 5 mt capacity by 2012. Fifteen people at JSW were heard saying in this company, they wish to do what the Tatas did in 100 years in ten years. Twelve respondents said it is an exciting time for JSW to be in India for it to capture the abundant scope for growth.

Entrepreneurial DNA

History of great organizations reveals that they are highly entrepreneurial, adaptive, and proactive. They sense and anticipate change earlier than others. They are willing to chase the opportunity to create wealth even if it means following the unbeaten track. These organizations are highly risk-taking and experimental in nature and are not afraid of failure; they are alert, agile, and nimble footed, the very antithesis of the Dinosaurian syndrome. In other words, the entrepreneurial spirit is in the DNA of high performing and fast-growing organizations.

JSW encourages the entrepreneurial style of functioning, according to fifteen interviewees, whereas sixteen of them said that there is plenty of freedom to work. Twelve people said those up to the level of the manager can make decisions and take action. The company is considered by many of the interviewees as "highly risk taking and fast moving"; perhaps sometimes moving too fast. All the interviewees said that there is high speed of decision-making in JSW. At the same time, there is tolerance for mistakes; people are never treated harshly and are not blamed for making mistakes. At the most, as all interviewees asserted, people are asked not to repeat the mistakes.

The company is entrepreneurial and nothing "stops here" because of problems or lack of funds as solutions are always handy, said fifteen of the interviewed employees. Exploration and search for new projects is a part of the JSW culture, confimed fourteen interviewees. There is total freedom at work across the levels in JSW. Twelve interviewees said that people are allowed to think differently. Even if they exceed their authority they are supported, said nine of them. In this company, there is complete empowerment and, therefore, there are no alibis for non-performance—all interviewees adhered to this. They also said that the expectations here are very clear: one has to perform. According to the five CEOs of the group companies: "CEOs have elbow room to work independently." Ten interviewees said: "The empowered culture of JSW gives us a great opportunity to use all our capabilities and skills."

All interviewees said that JSW treads the path which others hesitate to take. They gave the example of JSW moving to Houston, Mozambique, Chile as well as their plans for Australia. Many people gave the example of moving to cement, power, ports as indicating the group's robust sensing capability and taking advantage of opportunities, and said that these moves were made with tremendous speed. In addition, nine people also mentioned that there are weekly informal meetings at the corporate office where the top team sits over tea and discusses new ideas for an hour. This creates an open culture leading to sharing good ideas. Fifteen of the interviewees said that the entrepreneurial DNA of JSW has resulted in risk-taking, speaking out, exploration of innovative solutions, and excitement at the workplace besides creating a sense of ownership.

Toward the Next Milestone

In the contemporary world, where business is equivalent to war, agility is the rule of the business game for survival and winning. Unless organizations move faster, others will overtake and win. This is the key differentiator between the leaders and the laggards. Crunching time deadlines enables organizations to become trendsetters and fast movers. Further, they are able to capture the market, take advantage of emerging trends, and reap the benefits of being the first mover. These are visible in the strategy and processes of winning and growing organizations.

In JSW, growth takes place at jet speed, said eighteen people. In fact three people said that they were afraid of the high speed, fearing that they may go wrong and said that growth and consolidation should go together.

JSW growth has been 30 percent per annum, the highest in the steel business in India: such growth is unheard of, said all the interviewees. One person said: "Achieving such growth requires a brave and bold spirit to keep doing it." All the interviewees talked of JSW's growth at a breathtaking speed: "JSW is a fast growing company ... we have grown from 3 mt to 7 mt and now we are aiming for 11 mt by 2012." Five people said that JSW is aggressively moving toward the next goal post. Eleven said: "JSW never sleeps; people are highly obsessed with deadlines and achievements." One interviewee said: "We always look for something different and something big." "In JSW we say that time is money," said nine interviewees. Again, nine interviewees said that "there is no procrastination here." Eight interviewees said that there is no postponement culture in JSW, while fifteen said: "There is a great obsession with execution."

Nine respondents said: "This is an aggressive group; there is extra momentum given to growth. Speed of project implementation is phenomenal—targets are constantly squeezed—for example if the stated deadline is 10 months it is further brought down to 6–7 months." Fourteen interviewees said: "JSW is an organization in a hurry ... it's a tough and demanding culture here." Nine of them said:

> ... all (capacity) targets are based on more than 100 percent; just 100 percent is not acceptable. No limits are accepted here. Since there are no stated capacities for metallurgical plants; it all depends on the quality of the inputs, therefore how much can be targeted is limitless.

Again, one interviewee mentioned: "The aim is to be the best in the world and hence there is no question of cutting corners. In fact we compare ourselves with POSCO." This view has been echoed by most of the people we interviewed.

Empowerment with Accountability

Entrepreneurial organizations successfully work fast by creating entrepreneurial ownership. This is inculcated by putting the right person on the right job, trusting the person as well as giving him full freedom to function and experiment with accountability. The downfall of many family-owned organizations in India can be attributed—among many other things—to the lack of trust and empowerment of the key team. Poor empowerment may deliver results to some extent in small organizations; however, organizations with mega vision and plans will have to build the culture of delegation and empowerment in order to succeed. It is worth noting that success of a behemoth like the Tata Group is based on the foundations of high empowerment, trust, and delegation.

JSW has a high performance obsession, as confirmed by the eighteen interviewees. Contribution, result orientation, and performance reward are a part of the genetic code of JSW. Nine interviewees said: "Neither JSW relaxes, nor do the people. All are constantly on the run, chasing targets and out beating them." Thirteen people said: "In JSW resource availability, delegation, and empowerment are around performance and performance alone." Sixteen of the total interviewees confirmed: "The top team's slogan is to keep trying till you achieve." Again, sixteen responded saying: "Here empowerment is significantly linked to performance accountability." They all said, in JSW, they get plenty of freedom, autonomy, and abundance of resources. All interviewees confirmed that "the only question asked here is about performance." Six of them said: "Since there is freedom and empowerment it is difficult to justify non-performance." "This culture puts enormous pressure for performance," said nine interviewees. Sixteen responded saying: "The good part is that there is no punishment for mistakes." Finally, one respondent said: "In the last so many years, I have not seen any senior person losing his job because of mistakes made or wrong decisions taken, something quite common in many Indian organizations."

Quest for Excellence

Organizations seeking excellence relentlessly benchmark their strategies, structure, processes, and culture with the best of the best, in order to attain a higher benchmark of excellence. They continuously raise the bar of excellence; once they reach the top, they start competing with themselves to improve their own standards of excellence. Winning, excelling, growing, and competing are vital components of the DNA of such organizations.

The basic DNA of JSW has been to continuously raise the bar of excellence, as confirmed by all the eighteen people interviewed. Eighteen have said: "If you see the scale of expansion we have done from 3 mt to 7 mt to 12 mt to 16 mt, you can see that we are continuously shifting the goal post of achievement." Similar has been the story in the cement, power, and ports segments where the level of achievement has been continuously increased. All eighteen respondents affirmed that they have crunched the project management timelines from thirty-six months to twenty-four months and, today, are talking of only sixteen months. Eighteen respondents said whenever JSW thinks of managerial processes, strategies, and systems, the aim rests in being in the top league at the global level. Such thinking to achieve excellence has helped JSW to continuously do things differently and improving the way things are done, said sixteen interviewees. Ten of them said: "There is empowerment, delegation, and support for doing things differently. Here people are allowed to innovate, experiment, and take risks and for that they are rewarded and recognized." In JSW, as five people confirmed, "we have succeeded in creating the culture of entrepreneurial ownership, enabling us to think big, move fast, and follow the unbeaten track."

High Performance Recognition

In any organization, the quantum of what people get is not as important as what they get as compared to performing and non-performing peers. Nothing can be more demotivating for high performers than finding poor performers (at the peer level) receiving equal or higher recognition than them. Performance-based recognition and rewards are viewed as a matter of equity, justice, and fairness; when this is met with, it creates tremendous excitement and positive motivation. Great organizations seek to generously recognize and reward their high performers, clearly signaling to the organization the type of behavior which is considered desirable in the organization.

According to fifteen interviewees, JSW has a robust performance management system. Seventeen interviewees said: "Performance milestones are clearly stated and targets are set around that. Once this target is set, there is close monitoring." Fifteen of the total interviewees said "we have a good performance appraisal system" and nine said "the KRA [Key Result Areas] system is well developed here." Nine other respondents said that people work hard to better their performance. The performance mantra works very well here because performance is generously rewarded, said seventeen respondents. Twelve interviewees mentioned: "In this company performance is the basis for getting rewards. It is truly professional in this sense"; twelve people also said that "we have ESOPs [Employee Stock Ownership Plans] scheme here. Not only the top team gets ESOPs, but 30 percent of the high performers in the junior management category also get ESOPs." In JSW, 20 percent of the cost to company (CTC) is through variable performance pay. Performance rewards are not only in terms of monetary benefits. High performers are honored and recognized at annual events and gatherings.

People Focus

There is tremendous respect for people in this company, according to the Head, HR. Twelve people confirmed this by saying: "People are well taken care of in this group." Ten interviewees said that Mr Jindal believes in sharing the wealth. "The company provides high quality township and state of the art entertainment facilities for the employees at their plant sites, some of them [plant sites] being located in the middle of nowhere"—this was confirmed by all the eighteen interviewees. Eleven interviewees said: "This organization does not view people as commodities." Again, all interviewees confirmed to the following: "The Company not only cares for direct employees but also displays concern for contract employees; the quality of township and school provided to them is of the same standard as that provided to the regular employees."

According to sixteen interviewees, in this organization, success is celebrated; high performers are recognized and rewarded for good work; the appraisal system is taken very seriously and focus is kept on timely rewards. A family atmosphere thus prevails. At the plants and the head office, various festivals are celebrated where the premises are decorated. On Vishwakarma Day, a puja is performed on the shop floor followed by a community lunch for all employees.

According to the Head, HR: "There is a lot of emphasis placed on children going to school in Vijaynagar, including children of outsourced labor. Further, parents are encouraged to send every girl child to school. Free education for the girl child is provided at school and professional levels."

Concern for people is also clearly visible in the manner in which employees were treated when the chips were down, from 1997 to 2001, during the downturn in the metals sector. Not a single person was thrown out; increments were given in this period to match inflation and salaries were not delayed even by a day. The concern for its employees is seen not only reflective in the manner of management of employees and contract labor, but also in the case of people involved in land acquisition for construction of new plants. For example, in their land acquisition in Bengal they made the landowners into shareholders in the company, as eleven people confirmed. When JSW acquired Southern Iron and Steel Company Ltd (SISCOL), the people orientation resulted in dissolution of the union by the employees. This happened because of the high trust evoked owing to the management's gesture in making all employees as shareholders in the company, said five interviewed people.

Ethical Governance

"Truth ultimately triumphs" is a perennial Indian wisdom and all great societies subscribe to it. The Enron debacle and that of many others in the recent past have shown that those who do not follow the principles of truth and ethical governance are bound to collapse. Value-based ethical governance plays a key role in enhancing organizational longevity and heightening organizational credibility. The path of entrepreneurial credibility is based on a longer-term perspective, with little scope for shortcuts with an eye on quick returns. Those who have adopted this path have reaped benefits.

All interviewees unequivocally said that JSW has a strong focus on ethical governance practices. Twelve people said: "We have performance centric reward systems." Other eleven interviewees said: "There is equity, justice and fairness in promotion, placement and recognition here. In other words, JSW believes in using high performance as the key differentiating factor for rewarding people." Again, eleven respondents mentioned: "It is a company which does not believe in caste, community, region and religion in attracting and rewarding people." Six employees confirmed: "All the independent directors are distinguished people of high achievement." Unlike many other family-owned organizations, JSW has a truly independent board where family members are not on the board (except Sajjan Jindal's mother), as two interviewees clarified.

JSW follows ethical means to reach the top; fifteen interviewees said it does not use unethical practices and short cuts to grow fast. Three interviewees said: "In the board meetings there is a spirit of questioning and healthy debate." Another three believe JSW does not indulge in tax evasions for making profits, a practice seen in many business houses. It believes in paying its taxes as well as other dues to various government bodies. Majority of the interviewees (fifteen of them) said that there is virtually no politics in JSW; no clique formation, pulling each other down, or back biting. People here face the issue and sort it out; the dreaded *chamcha* culture has not taken root in JSW since everyone is too busy with their work. Besides, since everyone has equal access to Sajjan Jindal, the scope for miscommunication and distortion of facts is minimized, as twelve interviewees confirmed.

Beyond Profit—Social Concerns

Enlightened organizations see their roles beyond profits, in terms of serving the interest of all stakeholders—shareholders; customers; employees; suppliers;

vendors; and community. They truly follow the Gandhian trusteeship model and believe that they are the custodians of public money and, therefore, use it for the benefit of community and society.

Globally, most organizations started focusing unduly on profit, forgetting their role and responsibilities to other stakeholders and had to thus face doom in 2008. No wonder, therefore, there is a hue and cry today about the need for organizations to become more socially and environmentally conscious. Enlightened organizations also see themselves as social citizens; hence play their roles beyond profit-making and contribute to community and societal development.

JSW gives great importance to its role in community development, believing that "if one's neighbor is unhappy or angry, it is difficult to prosper," said fifteen interviewees. There are robust CSR schemes in JSW. Most of the interviewees (sixteen of them) said that JSW runs schools, contributes to mid-day meal schemes (in schools), and provides access to the surrounding community to the medical and other facilities available in the colony. Young and educated women from surrounding villages are hired to work at the data center at the Vijaynagar plant, as fifteen interviewees mentioned. JSW makes no distinction between full-time and part-time employees and contract workers, providing them the same kind of facilities—housing; medical; schools for the children; etc.—something unique in the Indian industry, as informed by twelve interviewees.

JSW believes in preserving the environment and has effluent treatment plants to take care of toxic waste. In addition, JSW buys technology which reduces environmental pollution. It has gone for mammoth tree plantations and anyone who visits the Vijaynagar steel plant can see that environmentally it is one of the best plant sites in India, according to fifteen interviewees. Four persons said with great pride:

> If you compare our work [CSR work] with the Birlas, you will see that we have done substantial work in a short time span, while they have had the advantage of a legacy. Despite the large amount of work done, JSW does not publicize it.

JSW has also made a significant contribution to preserving the rich cultural heritage of Hampi town, located close to the Vijaynagar steel plant.

Shaping Talent

Great organizations believe strongly in grooming and building their leaders. They understand that it is talent through which organizations can fight their wars. This phenomenon has been part of the ethos of great organizations like GE, DuPont, ABB, Tatas, and Birlas among others. They are always on the lookout for high quality talent and make efforts to nurture and retain them.

All interviewees made the following observations about the culture of shaping talent in JSW: It provides people plenty of exposure to best practices so that people can learn, change their thinking, and do things differently. They do have formal training, but more than that it is the way the company works which shapes the talent. Nine interviewees said: "This company believes that every person will give their best in the right [work] environment." Also, fifteen interviewees said: "JSW believes in selecting the right talent—people with drive—and give them the opportunity to prove themselves."

Organizational culture of JSW is free; people are open in expression, hierarchy is not tall; genuine mistakes in the process of speedy decision-making are tolerated. Above all, people are highly rewarded and recognized for their achievements. There is hope, enthusiasm, and a sense of being a part of something very big, namely, contributing to nation-building. The amount of opportunity available as well as the freedom to take bold decisions for benefiting the organization, even if it means making some mistakes, is one of the biggest talent shaping factors, building learning orientation, result orientation, and solution centricity among the people.

Fifteen persons said that JSW has a robust performance appraisal system, good linkage of performance with reward, career planning, and identification of fast trackers. JSW has recently introduced a 360 degree appraisal for the top and senior levels. According to the Head, HR, "this organization is very generous in sending people for training programs to top business schools globally; this is one organization where we have organized workshops at the board level." As mentioned earlier, JSW has introduced ESOPs scheme for retaining talent at both senior and junior levels.

Action Architecture and Culture Landscape of JSW Group: Salient Contours

Weaving together the responses from both interviews and structured questionnaires (for details of questionnaire data of organizational culture of JSW Group, see Appendix 4A.3) brings out the following features about the achievements, action architecture, and culture landscape of JSW:

- JSW has shown remarkable financial performance during 2003–2009 (for details of financial performance of JSW Group from 2003–2009, see Appendix 4A.4). Its revenue has grown from ₹ 27.86 billion to ₹ 140.01 billion, registering a growth of 403 percent. Similarly, its net profit has increased from ₹ 1.11 billion to ₹ 4.59 billion, indicating a growth of 513.51 percent. This outstanding performance has earned JSW many awards, notably the Golden Peacock Award for Corporate Social Responsibility, as confirmed by nine interviewees, the National Energy Management Award, as said eight interviewees, TERI CSR Award, as seven interviewees said, CII Award for Business Excellence, as informed by six interviewees, among others.
- JSW demonstrates a deep appetite for mega growth.
- The organization lays heavy emphasis on promoting result orientation while linking performance with rewards, thereby promoting contribution centric meritocracy.
- The organization is extremely agile and responds quickly to external challenges, demands, and opportunities.
- The organization actively encourages and looks for new ideas and promotes entrepreneurial innovation.
- JSW is outward-looking and responsive to customer demands with the belief to begin with the end in mind.
- JSW has a highly people centric work culture which promotes trust, teamwork, and community culture, thereby harnessing people power.

- JSW culture demonstrates great concern for building competitiveness to thrive and excel.
- JSW strongly emphasizes a highly ethical and value based culture of corporate governance.
- In a nutshell, it can be said that JSW fires on all the cylinders—entrepreneurial innovation; performance excellence; customerization; global perspective; people power; and ethical governance—to build competitive edge and for achieving limitless growth.

Part III: Sajjan Jindal—His Profile and Persona

The following themes have emerged from content analysis of the interview data:

- Limitless ambition
- Rock-like resilience
- Courageous and optimistic
- Wealth creating strategist
- Action-centric strategist
- Deep appetite for excellence
- People centricity
- Societal centricity
- Networker and boundary manager
- Converging opposites

Limitless Ambition

Ambition is the engine which drives human energy in a purposive direction. Those who have made a difference have done so based on the power of their burning ambition and drive. In fact some of the greatest mega scale contributions which have transformed human societies have sprung from this compelling force.

All the interviewees unequivocally said that Sajjan Jindal is a human dynamo; a man in a hurry to actualize his bold and grand dreams. His ambition is fueled by deep passion which supports and helps him achieve his aspirations.

The views expressed by the interviewees supporting his limitless ambition are given in the subsequent paragraph.

"Over the years you will see only five steel giant industries and Jindal wants to be one of them says Sajjan Jindal," according to all those who were interviewed. The way he has pushed a ₹ 93 crores company in 1993, to ₹ 12,700 crores in less than two decades, with further ambition to push it to ₹ 50,000 crores in 2012 shows his vision and ambition, mentioned fifteen interviewees. People also said the same thing about his vision in the power sector. He began with 260 mw and today has about 1,000 mw which will increase to 3,140 mw by March 2011 and to 11,390 mw by 2015. One person exclaimed, "Can you imagine! He is talking of a ten fold growth? And we have actually done it.... We did not believe that it was possible." The story in cement is also similar to the one in the steel and power sector: "In cement we started with small volumes and today we are talking about 5 million tonnes," as ten interviewees said. The experience in the ports sector was no different either. There, they started with two berths of 4–5 million tonnes capacity and they are talking about increasing the capacity to 7 million tonnes in Goa and 10 million tonnes in Ratnagiri by 2010, as five interviewees informed us.

"He is a dreamer; his dreams are very big," said seventeen interviewees. "He is a very dynamic entrepreneur; there is a lot of hunger in the belly to go ahead with expansion and projects. He always keeps thinking and never stops anywhere and if there is a hitch, he finds another route; he will not stop"—this was said by fourteen interviewees. Twelve interviewees said that "JSW has grown so fast because of his passion and ambition to be on the top [among the top five global steel giants]." One person mentioned:

> I see great passion and ambition in him, as if he is born with it. That passion I have seen in his eyes all the time, since I first met him (15 years ago) as if he is in a hurry to do so many things in a short time. Once he takes up challenges he will pursue it.

Sajjan Jindal is passionate, and a man who is always in a hurry, said ten interviewees. "His growth plans are beyond our imagination—he keeps pushing the target," affirmed twelve respondents. As many as fifteen interviewees said that Sajjan Jindal's ambitions are boundariless and global and cited the business activities of JSW in Chile, Mozambique, and the USA, and the company's plans in Australia to support their view.

According to as many as fifteen interviewees, Sajjan Jindal is a good visionary, a great entrepreneur, and an outstanding leader; his ambition is to build another Tata House.

Rock-like Resilience

In our experience we have come across three kinds of people—those who do not start difficult projects because they fear failure; those who gather courage and start but then give up at the first sign of resistance; and those who take up something and do not give up till they achieve the goal, no matter what the hardships they encounter on the way. It is this resilient spirit which characterizes Change Maestros who have made the difference by surmounting the toughest challenges and overcoming them.

All the interviewees clearly asserted that Sajjan Jindal is a tough person with enormous resilience to bounce back from difficult situations. They gave examples of his handling of the initial hiccups in the use of Corex technology[3] at the Vijaynagar steel plant which acts as the most powerful indicator of his rock-like resilience. According to them, this happened at an extremely critical juncture when they had already invested thousands of crores of rupees in building the plant over a period of five years. Finally on the day when the furnace was made operational, due to severe rain and wet raw materials the furnace froze and did not respond (the cause became known later when the case of the furnace not lightening up was being investigated). Everyone, including the financiers, vendors, and contractors became skeptical; some even deserted him. Even key top team members from the plant handed in their resignations accepting their failure. Although the threat of insolvency was looming large, it was Sajjan Jindal's toughness, refusal to give up, along with his cool-minded pragmatism which stopped him from breaking down and accepting failure; twelve people asserted this point. According to his wife, he was very badly affected by the all-round lack of confidence and support, but was soon able to come out of the mode of despair because of his steely resolve.

The second important example given by eighteen people, again surrounding Corex technology, was regarding the risk taken in going ahead and using the Corex gas (by-product) for running the power plant. The joint venture partner was apprehensive regarding the use of Corex gas which could cause devastation and loss of lives. Therefore, over three months since inception of the use of Corex, JSW had just wasted the gas—one of the by-products—rather than using it. Sajjan Jindal decided to go ahead despite the objections or reservations of the joint venture partners. According to the interviewees, he had done a thorough study and knew that Corex gas was working elsewhere as fuel to power plant, and said that if it works elsewhere, it should work in JSW too. One day he said, "Enough is enough; I'll come to the power plant today. Start firing it [Corex gas] in my presence, if there are any poisonous leaks, I will be the first one to be affected." Early use of this gas as an input for the power plant (in place of coal) resulted in huge savings to JSW. In fact, this became one of the strong foundations of the organization. Sajjan Jindal's resilience has been described by the interviewed people in the following words:

"He is a very, very brave person; knows how to keep smiling through difficulties," said eighteen people. "He is very tough and realistic; he is a man in a hurry and therefore [highly] demanding," mentioned fifteen people. All interviewees said that "he is bold and fearless." "He is tough work-wise and does not appreciate a lethargic approach," confirmed one person, while five persons said that "he is aggressive to the core and does not buckle under pressure."

Courageous and Optimistic

All Change Maestros have followed the unbeaten track and gone against the wind and shaken the existing order. In fact, this is *sine qua non* with change and transformation. Change Maestros courageously take on seemingly impossible challenges and boldly pursue and struggle in their transformation journey, against all odds. This was possible for Change Maestros because they believe in the cause and are daring and courageous in the face of all opposition and calamities. Drucker described this beautifully when he said: "Wherever you see a successful business, someone once made a bold and courageous decision?"

Lives of Change Maestros like Gandhi and Mandela also illustrate boundless optimism and faith along with courage. They had the overarching faith that things are inherently good and that outcomes of events will be positive. They were not afraid of the darkness, since they knew it would be followed by dawn. Optimists have a positive disposition to people, to the world, and to themselves. They have a high degree of self esteem and sense of well-being. Such positivism and faith drives them to relentlessly try, experiment, and explore without getting disheartened by failures that come their way. They believe that in the long journey toward transformation, taking that first step is critical to start the movement.

All the interviewees said that Sajjan Jindal is fearless, a challenge seeker, bold, daring, and a man of strong determination once he makes up his mind to do something. In fact, everyone said that he loves to do what others dare not do.

Everyone spoke of his high self-confidence no matter how difficult the situation is: "The great thing about him is that even in the toughest situations, he does not lose confidence"—this confidence is infectious and creates a winning spirit in the entire organization. According to sixteen interviewees his confidence helped the company to come out of the most difficult situations which could have cracked any other entrepreneur. JSW could overcome the initial problems because Sajjan Jindal convinced the bankers that he will be able to revive the group. He did this by putting his own shares to help raise money for JSW; this convinced the financiers and bankers to support JSW, according to sixteen interviewees.

"He always looks at the positive side of things and when things are down he looks for the opportunities in the problems. When the steel industry was down yet all decisions regarding expansion at Vijaynagar were made in this period without any compromise," said nine interviewees. Others said when we they doing badly—and there was a downturn in the steel industry—Jindal was thinking of expansion. Although the employees were quite apprehensive, he was very optimistic. Five people recall him saying: "If business goes down other companies will be out and we will get the business because of low cost; if things turn good then we will do well anyway."

According to eleven people, JSW had many problems at the steel plant in the first five years, but this did not break Sajjan Jindal's confidence. According to them, there were problems between the contractors and shareholders, followed by technical problems, and to top it all, there was a downturn in the industry. There was no money to pay the lenders. They were not able to do the debt servicing and went for corporate debt restructuring (CDR). One person informed:

> We were in very bad shape during the first four years. Any promoter would have got frustrated and collapsed.... People thought at that time that Mr Jindal may decide these projects are not viable and wind up. Amazingly none of these problems dampened Sajjan Jindal's enthusiasm. He was in fact planning new activities. At a time when most of the persons would be depressed in such circumstances, only a courageous man like Sajjan Jindal could do it.

He also seems to love challenges. When one of his top team members mentioned that going to Bengal to set up a steel plant would involve problems, his reply said it all: "That's why we should go there." Of course this does not mean that the decision was based on a sense of challenge alone—six interviewees said that the site selected by them had adequate mineral deposits to give them a cost advantage. One person said: "He is a challenge seeker; loves to do what others dare not; he is adventurous." Sixteen others said that he is flexible, does not stop because of problems, and finds solutions to these problems; he is a terrific risk taker who does some quick analysis and then decides.

All the interviewees highlighted Sajjan Jindal's optimism in the face of dire difficulties. Eighteen of them said that he is "always optimistic." Fourteen interviewees said that "everything was going wrong but he never showed any fear; he was thinking of the next step to be taken." Five persons said: "When we went to him in those difficult times, he would ask us ok, what should we do next?" Others said:

> He could find solutions. At that point he did not get discouraged himself, nor did he allow us to get discouraged. He would always say keep on working, keep on achieving all those targets [in terms of volume quantity, quality]. He would say the "downturn will not remain forever"; it is cyclical.

Nine people said even in the days of the downturn, they thought of expanding capacities. Mr Jindal is a realist, but, at the same time, he is an optimist.

Wealth Creating Strategist

Wealth creating strategists looks at the world through a different lens and has the unique ability to see beyond the obvious. They believe that opportunities are in plenty and that "opportunities do not cease to exist because they are ignored." They see opportunities in problems and go about converting opportunities into business strategy.

All the interviewees spoke about Sajjan Jindal's powerful wealth-creating and opportunity-sensing capability.

His opportunity-sensing mindset is clearly evident in his decision to set up the plant in Bellary, a place which was no doubt mineral rich, but was poorly connected by rail and road. It was Indira Gandhi's dream to set up a plant in this region and initially public sector companies were sounded for the same. They, however, saw only the obvious problems in the region and could not sense the opportunity of being located so close to steel-intensive factories, which received their steel supplies from distant parts of India, said five interviewees. He saw this opportunity of the customers being located so close to the factories which made him decide going ahead with the plan.

The decision to diversify into cement business was born out of the opportunity he sensed in using the slag—the by-product of steel-making—as an input to make cement, as all interviewees confirmed. Their venture into the information technology (IT) segment is another example of opportunity sensing considering that the entire Jindal group itself has huge needs—worth ₹ 10 billion, as seven interviewees confirmed. His favorite statement, as six people said, is, "If we can't do it now then someone else will do it—the opportunity in India is now."

Twelve people cited the example of how they stumbled into the power business indicating the capability to explore and catch the opportunities. Initially, JSW did not think of going into the power business, but now it is bigger than just steel business. JSW has not only done related diversification (power, cement, and ports), it has also gone into unrelated diversification, for example, getting into aluminium business. All the interviewees said that this exploration of possibilities, conversion into business strategy, and diversification came from Sajjan Jindal's opportunity sensing and wealth creating mind.

Seventeen people said: "He thinks differently from the technologist; his mind works in different ways. He is able to see the opportunity more than the risk." Five interviewees said: "Even if he sees there is high risk he focuses more on the possible returns as is evident in his recent decision to buy up the iron ore mines in Chile which today has already become a money earner for the group." One person said: "As an entrepreneur, he is gutsy and full of perseverance and self confidence. He has strong business sense and makes quick decisions. After some thought he either decides for it or drops it; no decisions are put off for months." His pragmatic approach is seen in the way he handled the initial failure of Corex technology—he told the internal team, as fifteen members recalled, "we have to find the cause and solve it." "He thinks creatively and solves the problem. For example, his view that the best period for modernization is during recession indicates how he converts a difficult business situation into an opportunity," said ten respondents. Five of them said: "Although he is a technocrat, he thinks like a business strategist and is very good at cost benefit analysis."

He is able to sense opportunity because of the way he frames the problem as indicated by the following quotes:

> His perceptions and interpretations of situations are unique and this has helped him to make business decisions which others would hesitate to make, said five interviewees.
>
> Before moving into development of the port he made the statement, "steel business is not about steel, it is about logistics," said nine interviewees.
>
> Few other interviewees said while making the decision to takeover an ailing steel plant in Houston (which was making steel plates and pipes used in oil rigs) he viewed it as entering into the oil business where there was a lucrative opportunity.

Sajjan Jindal has a strong sense of business. He has been clear to do business in areas with huge opportunity to create wealth. Thus, when he first commenced work in his small ₹ 100 crores factory in Vasind, he quickly realized that merely being in the business of making steel pipes is not enough. Hence, as a young entrepreneur with a few years of experience, he realized that he should go on to the core activity of steel-making if he has to not only make big bucks, but also to survive in the long term.

Action-centric Architect

"Great ideas need landing gear as well as wings." This quote illustrates the wisdom of connecting thought with action. When the vision is not actionized, it remains a mere dream. In other words, dreams remain mere dreams in the absence of robust action architecture implemented with speed. Action architecture brings the required power to implement ideas with sharp focus like a laser beam. Change Maestros do not suffer from the analysis/paralysis syndrome. They have the unique distinction of not only being dreamers and visionaries, but also being quick action initiators.

Sajjan Jindal has been described by all the interviewees as a dreamer who is also a speedy action strategist. All the interviewees spoke about his laser-like focus on execution, having a strong grip on the pulse of the business, and relentless pursuit to actualize things. Twelve interviewees said that "he focuses on the big things; wants to know more about the trends, holistic picture, as well as execution strategies," while ten interviewees said that "he is continuously moving forward; keeps developing new agenda; at the same time he has the time for each business big or small." He keeps track of what is happening at the ground level—he moves around; makes visits; and, if needed, he takes feedback from those at the front line, as nine interviewees mentioned. Though the group has grown phenomenally in the last few years, he has statistics about the businesses on his fingertips, as seventeen interviewees mentioned.

Since the dreams are big, converting them into action happens at great speed. All the interviewees said that in JSW execution is done at a fast pace. Sajjan Jindal is a man who believes in speedy execution, confirmed all interviewees. They also said: "He wants to achieve his vision of being a global top company in a short span of time." Eighteen interviewees said: "Mr Jindal is a man in a hurry."

Eleven of them said: "Any papers put up to him are immediately answered; no time is wasted at all." One person said: "What the Tatas did in a 100 years he wants to do in 10 years.... He is known for not keeping decisions pending. No papers wait for his consent/signatures."

Jindal has been viewed by all the interviewed persons as a quick decision maker, which is an important requirement for ensuring quick actions. However, in the process of quick decision-making, nine people said that he is not rigid and close-minded. "His decision-making is very fast, but if he is not clear about something, he does not hesitate to ask questions and understand," said twelve people. Eleven people said: "He is a quick decision maker but is willing to change his own decision. He does not stick to a decision if it does not give the result."

He is able to actionize his ideas with speed because of his close monitoring. According to all the interviewees every quarter there is a project review, keeping track of progress made, resources which were allocated, budgets, and so on. In fact twenty-one interviewees highlighted that project management capabilities of JSW are excellent, the proof of this being the pace at which they have executed the expansion of their steel projects.

Fifteen interviewees said:

> He is ruthless in execution. If the original project schedule is December, in the next visit he'll say it has to be by September. And he'll follow it like anything morning, evening, everyday. Not only does he ask the head of the unit, he takes feedback from the project in charge, the civil in charge, the electrical in charge, the maintenance in charge.

Deep Appetite for Excellence

Aristotle said that excellence is not an act but a habit born out of what we repeatedly do. This wisdom brings out that excellence is an ongoing journey, not a single-point destination. Change Maestros demonstrate that they are never satisfied with what they achieve; they continuously shift their own performance goalposts, they ceaselessly reexamine their strategies and actions with a view to dynamically realign them with their new goalposts. In this process they learn, experiment, and explore.

All the interviewees overwhelmingly emphasized that Sajjan Jindal is in the habit of continuously raising the bar of performance and crunching time deadlines.

Sajjan Jindal has visited all great steel plants of the world. He always compares JSW's performance with the global best and continuously pushes us to do better than before, said fifteen interviewees. Being a technocrat he understands emerging technologies and, therefore, encourages the use of state-of-the-art technology which continuously brings improvement in the operational processes and improves productivity and cuts costs. He keeps his focus on emerging global business trends enabling him to keep track of latest developments in the business they are in.

According to all the interviewees, he is a great learner, he has an alert antenna, and he extensively and regularly interacts with people to understand what is happening in the organization. He is known to communicate with people at all levels to get feedback especially from the shop-floor levels. He discusses benchmarking issues with people within and outside the organization. He keeps track of what his competitors are doing. All this is done to continuously raise the levels of operational efficiency. One of the interviewees narrated an episode where Sajjan Jindal and team visited A.M. Naik, Chairman and Managing Director of L&T. After the hour-long meeting with him, Sajjan Jindal asked his team members, "what did we learn from L&T and how can we use it in JSW for bringing further improvements?"

Performance benchmarking and learning from others form a way of life in JSW according to ten interviewees. This benchmarking has enabled JSW to be a continuously innovating organization in whatever they do. Innovate, excel, and be the best is the oft repeated mantra of Sajjan Jindal, said fifteen interviewees. Eighteen people said that he is never satisfied with his own achievements. Raising the bar of expectations and good performance is hardwired in him.

People Centricity

Before deciding to return to Greece after many conquests in Asia, Alexander the Great is known to have said: I don't mind that my men are thirsty, that my men are tired; but now I see that my men have lost the zeal to win. This famous saying brings out the fact that wars are fought and won through the power of people and their passion to struggle, fight, win, and enjoy the rewards. Change Maestros strongly believe in people power and know how to activate and mobilize the same for creating winning, excelling, and thriving organizations. They are cognizant of the fact that while dealing with people they are also dealing with creatures of emotion, and not just logic alone.

All the interviewees said that Sajjan Jindal is a peoples' man who establishes personal connect with his people and leads from the front in difficult situations. He is generous and large hearted and shares prosperity with all employees. He has been described as simple, down to earth, accessible, modest, and hard working by seventeen people we interviewed. They said that this helped him to connect very well with people. All eighteen interviewees said that he has a humanitarian approach—he is there with people in their difficult moments. Eighteen people said:

> He takes care of people; knows about their family situation and problems; asks now and then about members of the family especially if they are unwell—this gives a very big feeling of being part of the family; that we are partners in growth and prosperity of JSW.

Again, all interviewees said that Sajjan Jindal believes in helping employees in case of sickness and in cases where money is needed beyond the insured amount through the JSW foundation. He believes in sharing the prosperity of JSW with the employees—production incentive has been almost doubled, said fifteen interviewees. Nine people said: "Mr Jindal is a good human being; he doesn't bother about petty things"; eleven interviewees responded that; eleven interviewees said that he respects people—he does not use abusive language nor does he raise his voice. Fifteen interviewees also said that he is a great communicator and is capable of exciting and inspiring people. They also said: "As a human being he is genuine and upfront." One person said "he is humane and caring. It's a basic touch that Mr Jindal brings to the table, that everybody is a part of the family." One other interviewee commented: "He goes out of his way to take care of people when they are in trouble." Again, one interviewee said: "I was in a meeting with him when I got the news about my father's death. He immediately stopped the discussions and after speaking to me for a few minutes, he arranged for his own plane to take me to my village." One person also said: "Treats his junior colleagues very well especially in meetings outside JSW and while traveling."

Fourteen interviewees said that Jindal has ensured that employees are well looked after; there is a proactive response to people's and a good quality of life for all employees.

Eleven people gave the example of the SISCOL takeover where company shares were distributed to all the workers. Six of them said that "the workers trust him because they say he wants the organization and people to grow together." In the process of land acquisition in Bengal, he made the farmers shareholders in the proposed factory, one of the first such innovative people-related experiments. Many other business barons got into trouble in Bengal on this sensitive issue, but not JSW, as five interviewees informed us. Sixteen people in the company feel good that the organization is taking good care of them. According to eleven persons, in 2001, when JSW had cash flow problems, Jindal said: "[W]e cannot touch the salaries of the people at any cost, don't even think of doing this; find out ways and means to solve the problem." Here no employees' benefits are ever touched, no matter what problems are faced by the company, said some interviewees. Nine people said: "Sometimes he does surprise checks at the canteen such is his concern that people should get the best facilities." Sixteen interviewees said: "In fact the infrastructure and facilities at Vijaynagar are world class; the place [situated in such a dry part of the country] is aesthetic, green with access to the best entertainment facilities." One person was heard saying "He is a *Sajjan*—a good man."

Another important aspect is the effort made to celebrate all major festivals in full vigor along with competitions in all locations including the corporate office. Celebration is a way of life. Sports and extracurricular activities are also given lot of impetus and Sajjan Jindal personally participates in such events.

Societal Centricity

All Change Maestros believe in giving back to society because they consider this to be their responsibility and duty. In the Indian context, to contribute to societal well-being and upliftment is considered to be a sacred Dharma and duty. Gandhi, one of the greatest Change Maestros of the 20th century, said that freedom can never be complete without wiping out tears from every eye. In fact, enlightened organizations have pursued this goal along with their business goals. Everyone mentioned that Sajjan Jindal is very particular about cleanliness, environment, and welfare at all the company locations. Perhaps there is no clearer statement of his concern for community and society than the statement recalled by seventeen of the total interviewees: "What we take from society we should return in double measure."

Sajjan Jindal has made enormous contributions to the development of surrounding communities and society wherever JSW's plants are located. The CSR budgets of JSW are high at ₹ 45 crores. According to all the interviewees, Sajjan Jindal and Sangita Jindal have been the force behind setting up the data center at Vijay Nagar, a business process outsourcing (BPO) organization for non-voice data entry which provides employment to young women matriculates from the surrounding villages, in a remote part of India in the middle of nowhere. This act has now set a new trend in the industry.

There are many examples of his concern, generosity, and compassion for less fortunate people in the surrounding communities and efforts are made to ensure their welfare. Five interviewees have said: "He has high concern for workers' families ... he wants to ensure that all kids go to school.... Data on such information is kept at his desk." Fifteen interviewees said that he takes good care of people especially those at lower levels and is concerned about their families; he likes to inquire about the welfare of their children, encourages all the children to go the English-medium township school. One interviewee said that all employees, regular or on contract, have been insured for ₹ 1,000,000 in case of accidents.

Jindal's concern for the environment is very strong and this has been demonstrated time and again from the start of his career, as two interviewees informed us. Even in the early years in his then small factory, he was clear that the effluents are not to be emptied into any of the water sources. That was the era when other factories routinely polluted canals and rivers. Even then, his statement to his plant in-charge was revealing of his concern: "This should not be done. Remember these guys would take it away and dump the effluents at a far away water source—people and environment would be damaged. Let us set up an effluent treatment plant." This incident occurred in 1992 when JSW was a tiny ₹ 60 crores turnover company and savings of even a few lakhs would have been valuable, said two interviewees.

Concern for society and environment is also reflected in the choice of technology to minimize discharge of effluents, smoke, sulphur, and polluting gases, which in turn helps protect the health and well being of people at large. The latest power plant technology acquired by JSW in Vijaynagar "is practically free of recycled gases." Fifteen interviewees mentioned the greening of Vijaynagar project site in 1996. The arid and dry land of the Vijaynagar project site was covered with 5,000 saplings planted within a single day in 1996 while the factory became operational only in 1997. When he goes to the factory, he spots those places which are messy and, hence, it is the duty of the local management to maintain all areas of the township, said nine interviewees.

Networker and Boundary Manager

Change Maestros have the capability to go beyond constraints of any kind. They have no barriers in their thinking when it comes to mobilizing resources. They seamlessly cut across apparent boundaries of organization, government, and nationalities. Such seamless thinking facilitates Change Maestros to overcome all obstacles and mobilize resources. They develop a vast network of contacts and relationships cutting across socio–political–cultural and economic boundaries. They use this to learn, size up new opportunities, and use information and learning to establish new milestones of performance for this organization.

Seventeen interviewees said that Sajjan Jindal is a great business manager; he freely connects with industrialists, policy makers, academia, and various industry bodies like ASSOCHAM, CII, FICCI, and so on. Through such industry bodies, he takes on the role as their spokesperson and represents industry interests with the government and tries to influence policy making. He has until recently been the president of ASSOCHAM. Sajjan Jindal has enormous capability to connect with shareholders and investors, suppliers, dealers, and customers. Because of this capability JSW has a different kind of goodwill and credibility among all its stakeholders, as mentioned by nine interviewees.

Converging Opposites

Sajjan Jindal has been viewed as a person who takes on and integrates multiple challenges, said fifteen interviewees. He is looked up to by all for putting his personal wealth at risk while at the same time seeking to protect the organization and stimulate growth. According to fourteen interviewees, he is known to smoothly combine vision and action with speed and excellence. Even in the worst situation, twelve interviewees claimed, he has been optimistic, managing his fears, putting up a bold front, and working to manage the growth of JSW. He is known to be a warm hearted and friendly person combined with steely determination, said fifteen people. Eleven interviewees said that he is seen to combine resilience and toughness with soft heartedness and generosity.

Sajjan Jindal as a Change Maestro: Salient Contours

Both the interview responses as well as questionnaire data (for details of questionnaire data of Sajjan Jindal's Change Maestro style, see Appendix 4A.5) together direct to the following conclusions about Sajjan Jindal as a Change Maestro and as a person:

- Sajjan Jindal powerfully demonstrates strong qualities of business leadership like ambitious plans for the organization, global mindset, visionary approach, and strategic thinking.
- He displays strong entrepreneurial qualities, characterized by openness to new ideas, fast decision-making with innovative and creative approach.
- He is highly result-focused and pursues excellence in everything and believes in continuously raising the bar of excellence.
- Sajjan Jindal is a bold and courageous leader who "leads from the front, leads by example, and stands like a rock in the face of calamities."
- Not only is he a business leader and an entrepreneur, Jindal also demonstrates tremendous people centric leadership qualities like radiating positive energy, high credibility, role modeling, reliability and dependability, honesty, and transparency along with empowering and supportive attitude.

- Sajjan is a warm hearted, generous, highly optimistic, and patriotic person with a never say die attitude, demonstrating a relentless struggle and perseverance to achieve the goal. He has a natural flair to reach out to people and connect with them.
- Though Sajjan Jindal uses all the Change Maestro competencies, the most dominant among them are his great ambition, entrepreneurial approach along with strategic thinking in a global perspective
- Like other Change Maestros, he demonstrates large bandwidth and uses multiple levers of competitive edge to achieve limitless growth.
- In recognition of his monumental contributions, he was awarded the 19th Wily Corp/Ken Averson Steel Vision Award in 2009. He was also named Entrepreneur of the Year by E&Y in 2009.

Sajjan Jindal: Concluding Contours

Sajjan Jindal, the man who romances limitless growth is fueled by a bold and grand dream. He clearly views JSW as the vehicle to fulfill the dream to be one of the architects of 21st century India while playing an important role in nation building. The forays into building steel, cement, aluminum, and nuclear power plants, railways and electricity generation, transmission, and distribution reflect his vast ambition. This grand vision compels him and the group to be aggressive, bold, and quick in decision-making. He firmly believes that JSW could be one of the twenty–thirty leading companies in taking this country forward.

Sajjan Jindal's determination to realize his grand dream was solidified by the time he was thirty years old. Interestingly he was convinced that he was the right person to build a large world class integrated steel plant.

He is a brave, infectiously optimistic, and self-confident person. The experiences of initial failure in using Corex technology became a turning point in his life. The subsequent success at rebuilding the venture convinced him that if things are done with honesty and determination results will surely follow.

Jindal is a passionate workaholic and an extrovert who enjoys meeting and relating with people whether in the board room or on the shop floor. He is ambitious, intuitive, a big picture man, and never gives up until he meets with success.

He places a lot of value on travel as the route to opening the mind, enhancing learning, improving performance, and pursuing excellence. He has himself traveled extensively and visited many of the top global organizations. Jindal is a man of tremendous self belief, perseverance, determination, and goal commitment with honesty of purpose to achieve success.

He believes that one must have ambition and that one must follow his dream, however, difficult it may be. He seems to have accepted adversities as a way of life and believes that it is only out of such experiences that real leaders emerge from the crowd.

Sajjan Jindal has been deeply impacted by closely watching his father, who has been passionate, patriotic, bold, perseverant, visionary, and an impact creator. In fact, the idea of impacting society has grown over the years to become a top value for him and he has taken many initiatives to facilitate social development.

The quick growth of this group within the short span of a decade (achieving what Tata Steel did in 100 years) could not have happened without creating a culture and work environment of complete freedom, innovation, empowerment, ethical governance, generous rewards, result focus, and global standards, and this is what he has done so admirably. All this was driven by the power of Sajjan Jindal's unending romance with limitless growth.

Appendices

Appendix 4A.1: JSW Group—Profile Contours

It is one thing to inherit some property and a legacy of hard work and social consciousness from your father, but it is completely another thing for someone fresh out of college and barely into his 20s to take on the challenge of business and build for himself a multibillion dollar conglomerate leaving footprints in many countries of the world including the US and UK in just about fifteen years! Sajjan Jindal, the soft-spoken sophisticated head of JSW Group proved that being passionate, hardworking with clarity of vision for the future, and a supersonic speed in doing things along with a deep commitment for the society can achieve spectacular results whatever be the situation in the external environment.

Jindal started out with a small inheritance from his father and today the ₹ 12,700 crores JSW group has under its umbrella JSW Energy, JSW Steel Limited, JSW Port, Jindal Praxair Oxygen Company Limited (JPOCL), JSoft, an IT and information technology enabled services (ITES) arm and other investment companies.

Sajjan Jindal is one of the inheritors of the legacy of the legendary Shri Om Prakash Jindal who built a fortune in steel in his lifetime coming from a farming family in a sleepy northern Indian village. Starting out as a trader in steel pipes, he went on to establish a manufacturing plant near Kolkata in 1952, producing steel pipes, bends, and sockets. Jindal Group has grown to be a leading steel producer, with interests spanning across the spectrum, from mining iron ore, to manufacturing value-added steel products.

The elder Jindal is credited with an attitude of seeing a door where there is a wall and walking in to seek an opportunity to do business. Where the walls had been formidable he has been seen to tear these down to make way with his exceptional skills and vision. Sajjan Jindal, who inherited a re-rolling mill as his share of father's property in 1992, brought the same iconic leadership and determination of his father and could see an opportunity where others see none. With the native grit and determination and the professional edge acquired through education and exposure to form his own enterprise, Sajjan was able to build JSW.

Leader with the Spirit of a Tiger

The group's strength lies in the leadership of Sajjan along with his carefully hand-picked team of professionals who have been with him from the start. This strength is reflected in the way individual companies spanning from steel to ports are run as part of the JSW Group. Rated as the fourth largest company measured by way of asset value, JSW Group is a company to watch out for and an industrial group to emulate while India blazes new trials to emerge a global economic super power. The journey of JSW has been arduous and quite eventful from the time it started in 1992 when Sajjan inherited a small re-rolling mill in Tarapur in Maharashtra while his three siblings went on to develop businesses of their own. Prithviraj developed Jindal SAW Pipes, Ratan took charge of Jindal Stainless Ltd, while Naveen was at the helm of affairs at Jindal Steel &

Power Ltd. Sajjan, who launched the JSW Group, was clear from the start that he would not continue to remain in the steel re-rollers business, but would go for backward integration and value-added products and businesses. True to his vision, JSW grew from a tiny steel re-rolling mill to its massive size in a short period. JSW Steel is the second largest steel company in the country today; it has the most modern, eco-friendly steel plants with the latest technologies for both upstream and downstream processes. JSW Steel Ltd has also received all the three quality, environment, and occupational health certificates.

Sajjan's ambition is take his group to be one of the top ten global companies and one of the top five in India in the steel sector. This he intends to do by expanding the operations of JSW's various business enterprises over the next decade. For instance, the investment in aluminum business will touch ₹ 4,000 crores by 2012 to create 1.6 million tonnes of alumina. The cement capacity will increase to 5 million tonnes by 2012. In the power business starting with 360 mw, the company has already achieved 1,000 mw which will increase to 11,390 mw by 2015. The bulk cargo includes import of coal for the power plant and export of bauxite and ash from the power plant. JSW Aluminum Ltd set up in 2005 in Andhra Pradesh has a 1.4 mtpa alumina refinery and 0.25 mtpa aluminum smelter.

All the verticals of the group, while being independent are also integrated through a support system of JSW through its managed services, project management office (PMO), and quality units, whose focus is to deliver world-class support, maintain high standards of quality and maintenance services across various service layers.

JSW is also known for its CSR of a very high order. JSW Foundation, an integral part of the Group, is the CSR wing, with a vision to create socioeconomic difference in the fields of education, health and sports, community relationship/ propagation as well as art, culture, and heritage. In an unprecedented gesture that also shows the commitment of JSW, the group has committed 1.5 percent of its after tax profits for CSR work.

JSW believes in preserving the environment and has effluent treatment plants to take care of toxic waste. In addition, JSW buys technology which reduces environmental pollution. It bagged the Silver Award in Metal and Mining Sector for Outstanding Achievement in Safety Management awarded by Green-tech Foundation.

Table 4A.1: *Recognition and Accolades to JSW Steel Ltd, 2006–2008*

2008	• "Golden Peacock Award for Corporate Social Responsibility for the year 2008" in February 2009. • JSW Steel, Vijayanagar Works bagged National Energy Management Award 2008 instituted by CII during August 2008.
2007	• CII-Exim Bank Award: Commendation Certificate for Significant Achievement towards Business Excellence awarded on November 1, 2007, at Bangalore. • TERI Corporate Social Responsibility Award: Certificate of Appreciation in Recognition of Corporate Leadership for Good Corporate Citizenship and Sustainable Initiatives amongst Corporations with a turnover of above ₹ 500 crore. • IMC Ramkrishna Bajaj National Quality Award: Special Award for Performance Excellence in the Manufacturing Category awarded on March 21, 2008, at Mumbai. • Gold Award in Metal and Mining Sector 2007 for Outstanding Achievement in Safety Management by Greentech Foundation.
2006	• National Sustainability Award: Second Prize amongst the Integrated Steel Plants Category by Indian Institute of Metals. • CII Award for Business Excellence: Commendation Certificate for Significant Achievement towards Business Excellence. • India Manufacturing Excellence Award: Corporate Gold Award in Metals Category by Frost & Sullivan. • Gold Award in Metal and Mining Sector for Outstanding Achievement in Environment Management by Greentech Foundation. • JSW Steel has won the "CIO 100—Giant 100 Honouree 2006" (IT Award). • The Athyunnatha Suraksha Puraskara of National Safety Council—Karnataka Chapter for the year 2005. • DMA Erehwan HR Innovative Awards: Second Place. • IMC Ramkrishna Bajaj National Quality Award: Commendation Certificate.

(continued)

(continued)

- Silver Award in Metal and Mining Sector: for Outstanding Achievement in Safety Management by Greentech Foundation.
- JSW Steel presented maximum number of papers (thirty) in the NMD—ATM 2006 and won the following:
  - 1st Prize in Oral Presentation in Mineral Section;
  - 1st Prize in Oral Presentation in Processes Section;
  - 2nd Prize in Metallography; and
  - 2nd Prize in Poster Competition.

Source: JSW report, 2010.

Appendix 4A.2: Brief Sketch of Sajjan Jindal

An aggressive innovator and an acknowledged people's manager, Sajjan Jindal, chairman of JSW Steel, achieved the impossible by transforming the small factory which he inherited into a global conglomerate leaving footprints in several countries. In the process, he rewrote the history of the steel industry in India. His belief in inclusive growth that benefits all sections of the society while being in harmony with nature not only made JSW a big, successful business, but one with a heart that engages itself with a number of rural development and transformational projects around the country.

In a fitting tribute, he was named "Ernst & Young Entrepreneur of the Year" in 2007 in the "Manufacturing Category." He was also awarded the prestigious

Table 4A.2: Accolades to Sajjan Jindal

2009	• Awarded the prestigious 19th Willy Korf/Ken Iverson Steel Vision Award at the Steel Survival Strategies XXIV Conference for bringing JSW Steel amongst the selected few global steel producers. • Awarded the Steel World Dynamics Award.
2007	• Named the "Ernst & Young Entrepreneur of the Year" in the "Manufacturing Category."

Source: JSW report, 2010.

19th Willy Korf/Ken Iverson Steel Vision Award in 2009 at the Steel Survival Strategies XXIV Conference for elevating JSW Steel to the level of a selected few global steel producers.

Mr Jindal is on the Boards of Airports Authority of India, India Council for Sustainable Development, and CII National Council. He is also a member of the Advisory Committee of TERI School of Management and a council member of Indian Institute of Metals.

Appendix 4A.3: Organizational Culture of JSW Group—Analysis of Questionnaire Data

Table 4A.3: Perceived Organizational Culture of JSW

N = 96

S. No.	Organizational Culture	Mean	SD	Rank
1.	Result orientation	4.38	0.67	1
2.	Entrepreneurial	4.34	0.68	2
3.	Performance excellence	4.28	0.63	3
4.	Teamwork	4.25	0.65	4
5.	Global perspectives	4.24	0.74	5
6.	Focus on continuous improvement	4.22	0.75	6.5
7.	Openness to new ideas	4.22	0.75	6.5
8.	Trust	4.17	0.77	8
9.	Ethical governance	4.15	0.8	9.5
10.	Focus on building competitiveness	4.15	0.72	9.5
11.	Speed of response to external demands and challenges	4.14	0.72	11
12.	Outward looking	4.13	0.71	12
13.	Responsiveness to the customer	4.11	0.77	13
14.	Openness and transparency	4.09	0.82	14
15.	Community culture	4.05	0.81	15
16.	Performance-based promotion	4.04	0.72	16
17.	Role clarity	4.03	0.79	17
18.	Nurturing innovation	4.02	0.84	18.5

(continued)

(continued)

S. No.	Organizational Culture	Mean	SD	Rank
19.	People orientation	4.02	0.87	18.5
20.	Participative	3.98	0.73	20
21.	Support for risk-taking	3.96	0.67	21.5
22.	Speed of response to internal demands	3.96	0.81	21.5
23.	Communication and information flow: Horizontal (a) Within the department	3.95	0.71	23.5
24.	Nurturing talent	3.95	0.83	23.5
25.	Process focused	3.92	0.85	25
26.	Empowerment and delegation	3.91	0.93	26
27.	Communication and information flow: Vertical (a) Top-down	3.8	0.88	27
28.	Culture of celebration of achievements and successes	3.7	0.96	28
29.	Cross-functional collaboration	3.68	0.82	29
30.	Tolerance of differences	3.6	0.82	30
31.	Communication and information flow: Vertical (b) Bottom-up	3.48	0.93	31
32.	Communication and information flow: Horizontal (b) Across the departments	3.46	0.77	32
33.	Centralized decision-making process	3.41	0.97	33

Source: Authors.

Table 4A.3 presents the mean, SD, and ranks, of the organizational culture attributes of JSW:

- A perusal of Table 4A.3 brings out that the mean values on all the culture attributes are more than 3.41, the maximum being 4.38. This indicates that all the work culture attributes are perceived to be above average. However, of these thirty-three items, nineteen are with mean value greater 4.00, ten have mean values above 3.50—between 3.60 and 3.98—and only three have mean values below 3.50;

- There is significant perceptual homogeneity about the cultural dimensions in JSW, the SD being less than 1 across the thirty-three items; and
- Further analysis of this table brings out the following dominant features of the organizational culture:

    - JSW puts heavy emphasis on promoting result orientation with a quest to continuously raise the bar of performance. This is one place where performance is linked with rewards, thereby promoting contribution-centric meritocracy;
    - In JSW, there is nurturance of entrepreneurial innovation. This is a company where there is a continuous search for new ideas;
    - JSW views the globe as the business arena. Its culture is outward looking and responsive to customer demands. It visualizes emerging environmental demands and challenges and business opportunities. It is agile and responds quickly to external challenges and demands;
    - JSW has a highly people centric work culture which promotes trust, team work, brings role clarity, and community culture, thereby harnessing people power;
    - JSW culture demonstrates great concern for building competitiveness to stay in the business, excel and thrive; and
    - JSW culture is highly ethical and value based.

Appendix 4A.4: Financial Performance of JSW Group at a Glance

Table 4A.4: Sales and Profit of JSW Steel Ltd, 2003–2009 (in ₹ billion)

Year	Income Revenue	Net Profit
2003	27.86	−1.11
2004	35.9	5.29
2005	70.36	8.7
2006	62.16	8.57
2007	85.54	12.92
2008	114.2	17.28
2009	140.01	4.59
% Change over 2003	402.55	513.51

Source: JSW Highlights, *2010 Annual Report*, p. 6.

Appendix 4A.5: Sajjan Jindal as a Change Maestro—Analysis of Questionnaire Data

Table 4A.5: Perceived Style of Sajjan Jindal as a Change Maestro

N = 96

S. No.	Change Maestro Attributes	Mean	SD	Ranks
1.	Is a visionary	5.17	0.13	1
2.	Leads by example	5.11	0.22	2
3.	Business strategist	4.92	0.31	3
4.	Has ambitious plans for the organization	4.91	0.32	4
5.	Is entrepreneurial	4.84	0.43	5
6.	Is result focused	4.77	0.45	6
7.	Leads from the front	4.75	0.55	7.5
8.	Has a global mindset	4.75	0.54	7.5
9.	Radiates positive energy	4.74	0.46	9
10.	Is open to new ideas	4.70	0.53	10
11.	Stands like a rock in the face of calamities	4.68	0.59	11.5
12.	Pursues excellence in everything	4.68	0.49	11.5
13.	Fast in making critical decisions	4.67	0.56	13
14.	Is innovative and creative	4.66	0.58	14.5
15.	Has high credibility	4.66	0.50	14.5
16.	Is a role model	4.63	0.57	16
17.	Is a strategic thinker	4.62	0.57	17.5
18.	Is reliable	4.62	0.53	17.5
19.	Is honest and transparent	4.55	0.60	19
20.	Has empowering and supporting attitude	4.54	0.56	20
21.	Is a man of words	4.48	0.73	21
22.	Respects the dignity of others	4.46	0.73	22
23.	Is demanding and performance centric	4.43	0.77	24
24.	Is an effective communicator	4.43	0.65	24
25.	Provides a sense of clear direction	4.43	0.67	24
26.	Makes people feel that they are valued by the organization	4.42	0.68	26

S. No.	Change Maestro Attributes	Mean	SD	Ranks
27.	Has helping attitude	4.41	0.70	27
28.	Is a team builder	4.36	0.72	28
29.	Is fair and impartial	4.35	0.73	29
30.	Is interested in growth of his people	4.34	0.68	30
31.	Grooms and develops people	4.29	0.65	31.5
32.	Humility	4.29	0.85	31.5
33.	Makes people feel that they have great worth	4.2	0.79	33
34.	Recognizes and rewards performance	4.19	0.74	34
35.	Sensitivity	4.09	0.86	35

Source: Authors.

Perusal of Table 4A.5 portrays the profile of Sajjan Jindal as a Change Maestro. The thirty-five leadership attributes have been classified into three broad categories for convenience of analysis: "Most Visible" with mean values ranging from 4.50 to 4.91; "Highly Visible" with mean values ranging from 4.00 to 4.49; and "Visible" with mean values ranging below 3.99.

All the items describing the Change Maestro qualities of Sajjan Jindal belong to the first two categories—"Most Visible" and "Highly Visible." In other words, his leadership attributes are clearly discernable by the people.

SDs are all below 1.00 indicating perceptual homogeneity about the Change Maestro attributes of Sajjan Jindal. This phenomenon indicates that there is consistency and transparency in the style of Sajjan Jindal, both being critical for building credibility.

Given further is a profile sketch as well as attributes which people perceived in Jindal as a person and as a Change Maestro:

- There are five items which highlight Sajjan Jindal as a Change Maestro: ambitious plans for the organization; global mindset; visionary approach; strategic thinker; and business strategist.
- Sajjan Jindal is also seen as entrepreneurial, characterized by openness to new ideas, fast decision-making, and innovative and creative approach.

- Along with being highly ambitious and entrepreneurial, Sajjan Jindal is seen as a leader who is highly result focused, with a pursuit of excellence in everything.
- As a Change Maestro, Sajjan is perceived as a bold person who "leads from the front, leads by example, stands like a rock."
- Jindal combines qualities of business leadership along with people centric leadership qualities like radiating positive energy, high credibility, role modeling, reliability, honesty and transparency, and empowering and supportive attitude.
- The "Highly Visible" category comprises of items like man of words, respects the dignity of others, provides a clear sense of direction, effective communicator, demanding and performance centric, makes people feel they are valued, helping attitude, team builder, fair and impartial, taking interest in the growth of people; humility, grooming and developing people, making people feel they have great worth, and recognizing and rewarding performance and sensitivity.

Notes

1. Authors gratefully acknowledge and appreciate the intellectual contributions and emotional support they received from Mr Anirudh Singh, Head, Human Resources, JSW, in the course of this work. He spent many hours with authors in conceptualizing the framework and providing focused directions to the case. However, for the conclusions and views expressed in this case study of JSW and Mr Sajjan Jindal as a Change Maestro, the authors own entire responsibility.
2. Eighteen top team members were interviewed by the authors. The number of respondents varies since the interviewing method was largely unstructured; we recorded what they said, giving greater priority to what came out of top-of-the-mind in response to our broad questions, rather than getting them to respond to a set of questions.
3. JSW has been the third steel plant globally to introduce Corex technology.

5

KUNDAPUR VAMAN KAMATH: ENFOLDING THE FUTURE WITHIN THE PRESENT

5

If you do not know where you are going, any road will get you there …

Lewis Carroll

… when and how long that can take, no one can guess![1]

This is the story of a King in Ujjain who was known for his valor, magnanimity, and patronage of arts and culture as well as his stately conduct and behavior. Under his rule, the kingdom prospered, agriculture thrived, trade flourished, and the land attracted poets, philosophers, and artists. The kingdom was known for its gold, splendid silks, and indigo. Kings came from far and wide to his court for his counsel and advice. People led a life with dignity and honor; the streets were safe and women were secure and free to move around freely.

This kingdom attracted the envy of neighboring kings who were looking for an opportunity to attack and conquer the territories. Attempts were made a number of times but they were foiled in time through the king's foresightedness and military intelligence.

The king had three sons whom he was grooming and training to find a suitable successor. Of the three, the youngest was like him and showed his future focus, broad vision, valor, and concern for the well-being of the people. The other two sons grew up to be the anti-thesis of the father and did not take his wise words seriously. The king wanted to forestall succession battles among the brothers and, therefore, decided to divide the kingdom into three parts, one for each son. Soon, he gave up the throne, handed over the kingdoms, and went away to the forest for meditation. The youngest followed his father's advice, fortified his kingdom, and maintained round the clock vigil and armed guards. He also ruled the kingdom like his father did and was loved by his subjects. No matter who attacked the kingdom, he was able to protect it. The other two sons, however, began to enjoy the riches of their respective kingdoms. They were too busy in the pleasures of the palace to pay attention to fortify and protect their lands and people. They felt their father had exaggerated the dangers and left the administration to their ministers. There were intrusions made by the adjoining kings and satraps. Soon, the people began to feel unsafe, streets were deserted, and the coffers began emptying. There were concerted attacks on these two unprotected lands and, one fine day, both Princes woke up to horror on their streets. There was much bloodshed; their armies being ill-equipped were easily defeated and the enemy reached the palaces and took both the Princes hostage.

It was indeed a sad day when the once vibrant, rich, happy parts of the erstwhile kingdom were razed to the ground. In contrast, the kingdom of the youngest son flourished and, in time, he attained the stature and respect which his father had once enjoyed. He defeated many kings who attacked his kingdom and in due course, expanded his kingdom and it soon became the largest empire of that era. This he could achieve by following his father's advice to be a visionary, futuristic, and strategist. He groomed many commanders and generals, but also paid attention to the administration of the kingdom. His futuristic and visionary approach, his alertness, his sensing of information of happening in and around the far reaches of the kingdom, and his canny diplomatic wisdom, helped him develop masterstroke strategies to ward off enemies and build a great empire, where people felt secure, happy, and lived a productive and prosperous life.

The contemporary corporate world is in many ways the arena where many business battles are fought. There are mergers, takeovers, and onslaughts by the competition. The race is getting so hot that the battles are reaching David–

Goliath like proportions. Today, even small companies have the audacity to take over large and established firms. In such a fierce corporate battle field, only the ones with foresight, who continuously have a 360 degree vision and take action in anticipation, and can enfold the tomorrow into the today survive. This is the story of one such leader, K.V. Kamath, who transformed ICICI from a preponderant development bank into a vibrant, dynamic financial powerhouse, through his overarching vision, foresightedness, capability to sense looming danger, risk-taking, and entrepreneurial innovation. John F. Kennedy had rightly said: "The problems of this world cannot possibly be solved by skeptics or cynics.... We need men who can dream of things that never were." Transformation in ICICI was possible owing to Kamath's telescopic visioning capability to view the emerging future and enfold it into the present. To quote Ayn Rand, "throughout the centuries, there were men who took first steps down new roads, armed with nothing but their own vision." It is such persons who made the difference in world history. This chapter presents the story of K.V. Kamath.

The case study "K.V. Kamath: Enfolding the Future into the Present"[2] has been organized into the following three parts: Part I provides a brief profile sketch of ICICI Bank; Part II highlights the action architecture and culture landscape of ICICI Bank; and Part III discusses K.V. Kamath's profile and persona.

Part I: Brief Profile Sketch of ICICI Bank

ICICI was formed in 1955 at the initiative of the World Bank, the Government of India, and representatives of the Indian industry. The principal objective was to create a DFI for providing medium-term and long-term project financing to Indian businesses. In the 1990s, ICICI transformed its business from a DFI offering only project finance to a diversified financial services group offering a wide variety of products and services, both directly and through a number of subsidiaries and affiliates like ICICI Bank (for details of organization's profile, see Appendix 5A.1). K.V. Kamath (for details of Change Maestro's profile, see Appendix 5A.2) took over the reins of ICICI in 1996. He had come fresh from his experience of eight years at the Asian Development Bank (ADB), Manila and an Indonesian business house and completely transformed ICICI on a scale which nobody could have even imagined at that point in time! In 1999, ICICI became the first Indian company and the first bank or financial institution from non-Japan Asia to be listed on the NYSE.

Part II: Action Architecture and Culture Landscape

The ten emergent patterns from the content analyses of interview data are conceptualized and presented as follows:

- Continued growth velocity
- Re-inventing the financial sector landscape
- Entrepreneurial ownership
- Thinking big
- Execution centric
- Seamless organization
- Empowerment with accountability
- Techno-centric work culture
- Contribution-centric meritocracy
- Shaping talent/building leaders

Continued Growth Velocity

The history of great organizations brings out the foundational mantra to grow, excel, compete, and win. In fact, organizational growth leads to its longevity, while organizational stagnation leads to death. All strategies and actions of great organizations, thus, center on this core reality. Among the many factors enabling organizational growth, the most critical is its future focus and opportunity sensing capability which help the organization spot and use new possibilities lying dormant in the business context.

All the twenty-five interviewees[3] unequivocally said that ICICI is extremely high on sensing opportunities and is focused on the future which has enormously helped in creating continued growth velocity. Twenty interviewees said: "ICICI takes the initiative if there is a big opportunity and quickly converts the same into a growth trajectory ahead of other companies." Fourteen interviewees said: "ICICI spots opportunities before others." Interviewees gave the example of the moves made by ICICI in setting up CRISIL, Housing Finance, and International Business as examples of their fast-paced growth orientation. Fourteen interviewees said: "ICICI could enter into blue ocean territories because of the ability to spot opportunities, believe in them and have the first mover advantage."

ICICI strongly believes that their business growth lies with the customer. ICICI moves quickly to capitalize on this much before others. Twenty interviewees informed: "We were sent abroad to different markets; consultants were brought in to advice about emerging opportunities locally and globally." This approach helped ICICI spot new opportunities in retail and chalk out its growth strategy. Fifteen people said that:

> ... our growth strategy is linked with capitalizing emerging opportunities. While in pre 1996, we were in project financing (a single niche area which was moving downhill); 1996–1999 we moved on to corporate lending to de-risk the business; in 1998–1999 we took over two non-bank finance companies—ITC Classic and Anagram—to grow our size and reach; in 1999–2000 we set up the ICICI Home Finance company. We raised money to fund our impending growth plans through a GDR issue and through this we raised $220 million; we also had an ADR issue in 1999 (becoming the first Indian bank to do so).

Twenty-three interviewees said, "we set up 2,000 ATMs which gave us a huge edge over others; in 2002 we set up our international business and today we are in nineteen countries," to which nine interviewees responded: "This we did because we realized that Indian companies were going global." Six of them said with pride, "we used to provide our office space to Indian companies for their meetings while in London, in order to be close to the customer and establish abiding relationships with them"; Six other interviewees said that "today 85% global deals made by Indian companies are through ICICI." "It is interesting that what ICICI has achieved in the last five years internationally has not been matched by any Indian bank that went abroad many years before us," said four interviewees. Today, of the $35 billion annual remittances made by non-resident Indians (NRIs), 25 percent is made through ICICI.

In ICICI, the definition of growth has morphed from time to time; there has never been a fixation with a predetermined definition. The macroeconomic indicators and the emerging opportunities that have been sighted early have always decided the definition. Sometimes it has been the white spaces in the market, at other times it has been the size of the balance sheet, while at a different time it has been the profitability. But at all times growth has been the lifeline and basic mantra of this institution.

Re-inventing the Financial Sector Landscape

Success, growth, and survival of a business organization depend on its ability to continuously align itself with the changing business scenario. Ambitious and growing organizations, therefore, swiftly contextualize their business strategies depending upon the emerging regulatory framework, changing customer profile, and geographical business boundaries. In the 1990s, the Indian business scene witnessed a dramatic shift in the regulatory framework of India, globalization of business, and change in the aspirations and needs of Indian customers. While most of the Indian banks could sense the changing context, only a few like ICICI decided to redraw their business strategies. This enabled the bank to not only survive, but to also achieve robust growth and become the second largest Indian bank.

In 1997, when ICICI decided to move into retail banking and taking on the might of the public sector banks, seventeen interviewees said "we used to be laughed at by other banks." Nine interviewees informed us, "when we got into retail banking, our speed of operation and customer service as well as marketing approach brought in a sea-change in retail banking from the way it used to be handled by other banks." According to eight interviewees, in the mid-1990s, NPAs constituted a significant percentage of the balance sheet. To handle this issue, ICICI lobbied with the government and succeeded in creating the Securitization and Reconstruction of Financial Assets and Enforcement of Security Interest (SARFAESI) Act. Eight interviewees claimed ICICI has been a pioneer in creating a Stressed Asset Management Group. Fifteen people responded that it was ICICI which took the lead in creating the online tax accounting system, introducing 8 am to 8 pm branch banking, as well as drop boxes for cash and bills. Nine people said "when we made the move to aggressively launch ATMs, the general reaction from other bankers was to ridicule us. People were skeptical because in those days the Indian customer was viewed as preferring to interact with a banker rather than use technology." This dominant view in the banking sector resulted in mammoth branch expansion paying little attention to launch ATMs. ICICI successfully exploded this myth about the Indian customer; soon other banks followed suit and introduced ATMs.

Most persons (twenty-two of the total interviewees) spoke with pride about the franchising and outsourcing model introduced by ICICI which was subsequently imitated by many other banks. They considered this to be an example of ICICI being the pioneer and first mover in introducing one of the new concepts of doing banking in India. Fourteen people said we were one of the first few that pursued the concept of mobile and Internet banking despite the prevailing wisdom against it, and now this has become a way of life for the elite segment of the population. Seventeen of the interviewees cited examples of ICICI's move to provide the new customer with the complete kit including passbook, account numbers, Internet banking facility, while opening the account which many banks are now trying to imitate.

From the foregoing presentation, one can conclude that ICICI has been a pioneering institution in evolving many new business models, introducing many world-class banking processes and practices, exploding many widely held assumptions about Indian customers, and setting new standards for boundary management and influencing government policies. Many of their strategies, processes, and systems were adapted and imitated by other Indian banks. Through their pioneering approach, ICICI redrew the landscape of the Indian financial sector.

In Mr Kamath's words:

> ... agility has now become critical part of longevity of organization. It could be as simple as looking into the future would lead you taking steps well in advance of what people around you are taking to secure the future and keep on moving without saying I am in a state of equilibrium.

Entrepreneurial Ownership

The culture of entrepreneurial ownership plays a critical role in fostering risk-taking and innovation in organizations. Entrepreneurial ownership leads to not only a sense of belonging to the organization, but goes beyond to owning the organization and, therefore, employees take the initiative as if they are the owners. It enables organizations to grab opportunities with speed and convert them into organizational growth strategies. In other words, the zeal of entrepreneurial ownership propels organizations toward fast growth by sensing new opportunities and territories. In the absence of such entrepreneurial passion and spirit, organizations normally tend to stagnate and, eventually, decay.

All the interviewees said that in ICICI entrepreneurial ownership is a way of life. According to the core top team of ICICI consisting of ten members, few people said: "In ICICI innovation is largely driven by constraints; we convert constraints and problems into opportunities." Fifteen interviewees said:

> ... when we entered into retail banking, the framework followed by other banks would not have worked effectively for us. We had to use different routes to make an entry and make our presence felt in the crowded marketplace. Over a decade the country had only 200 ATMs but ICICI activated 1,700 in one go.

"In ICICI we have developed skills to convert constraints into opportunities," mentioned five interviewees. Fifteen persons said that ICICI had limitations in the number of branches because they had a late start in retail banking, hence, they took a bet on technology. Twenty people gave the example of ICICI forming half a dozen new businesses in the post-1990s deregulated economic era when a lot of opportunities were thrown up and discontinuous changes started taking place. The entrepreneurial orientation of ICICI has been well captured by the following remarks made by various interviewees: five interviewees said: "ICICI vigorously engaged itself into positioning, repositioning and reinventing itself to stay relevant in the marketplace. We believe in the power of agility, which is critical to the longevity of the organization." Six interviewees mentioned:

"In ICICI we don't feel comfortable with a state of equilibrium and we actively seek new avenues and create continued disequilibrium for continued change." Eleven people said: "The company believes that looking into the future is critical for us to gain the first mover advantage and we have been successfully doing this for the many years." Eight interviewees claimed: "ICICI believes that a single product strategy is not enough to build sustained competitive edge and therefore we developed many differentiated products—insurance; car loan; auto loan; credit card; life insurance; general insurance; mortgage; etc." Nine interviewees mentioned ICICI quickly realized the need to jump on to businesses which provide a new growth curve. For example, when the project finance business was dying, it moved to retail banking and then to international banking; the next horizon is rural India where 600 million people live in 600,000 villages. It then launched mobile banking, viewing the high tele-density across the country. In ICICI two things are driving agility—rapid technological change and changing customer and consumer profiles.

All the interviewees said that "the key drivers of innovation in this organization are the audacious even irrational goals. The tried and tested ways we believe, can only give incremental results. It is the irrationality of objectives along with empowerment that leads to innovation." Nineteen people mentioned that they have the 80–20 rule where 20 percent mistakes in decision-making are tolerated provided they were committed while working in the organizational interest. Of course those who make mistakes are reprimanded but there is no killing, said six interviewees. Ten people said: "We have the ability to react quickly to changes because there is no bureaucracy. All five levels get together and make the needed change. This is possible because we are a non-hierarchical organization."

From the discussion the following conclusions are arrived at:

- ICICI integrates binocular vision with magnifying lens that is converts opportunities into strategies;
- Entrepreneurial ownership is a way of life in ICICI;
- ICICI is agile in spotting opportunity and swiftly grabbing it;
- In ICICI there is empowerment for decision-making and tolerance of mistakes;

- ICICI has amply demonstrated capability to find opportunities in constraints and problems;
- In ICICI there is a continuous move to the second curve of growth in ICICI;
- ICICI is non-hierarchical and non-bureaucratic; and
- All these points together foster a high degree of entrepreneurial ownership.

As Mr Kamath puts it: "Our experience indicates that entrepreneurship is a sustainable, individual quality which can be owned. For organization to truly succeed you need a large number of players who can think innovatively."

Thinking Big

Psychotherapists and psychologists like Freud, Jung, Rogers, Branden, and many others have emphasized that a significant part of human potential lies dormant and unused. Freud used the iceberg analogy to convey that only one-tenth of the human personality (potential and capability) operates at the conscious level while nine-tenth exists at the subconscious levels and, therefore, much of the potential lies unused. In fact, evolving human beings get in touch with their potential and utilize it by thinking and dreaming big and setting higher goals which they strive to reach.

Organizations, like human beings, also tend to not use a substantial portion of their potential and energy. Wherever organizations have unleashed collective potential, it has been done through the power of setting inspiring visions, larger purpose, and stretched goals. In other words, great organizations utilize their full potential by daring to dream big and making it happen through stretched goals. A study of the lives of both great leaders (like Gandhi, Lincoln, Martin Luther King, Nelson Mandela, Charles De Gaulle, and Gorbachev) as well as great organizations (like GE, ABB, DuPont, Microsoft, Infosys, IBM, Wipro, and Tatas) shows that in both cases, there is the prominent feature of thinking big with inspiring vision, larger purpose, and stretched goals.

All the interviewees said that ICICI believes in thinking big and has a global vision. Fourteen interviewees said:

In the early 1990s ICICI had only six offices, 1,000 employees and 3,000 customers. Today we have 1,400 branches; we have become the second largest bank in India. This was possible because even though we were small, we dreamt big; we had tremendous self belief that we can become a leading player. It needed a lot of self belief because the current reality of the business (at that time) was small and what we were imagining (for the future) was very big.

"We had burning ambition to become something and this lead us to take unconventional steps in a highly regulated and conservative segment like banking. The self belief grew brighter and brighter as we experienced success and this further fueled our self confidence," said thirteen interviewees. Few others said:

We don't like to be marginal players—we like to be the leaders in our domain. We have the ability to think big. This was possible because we have changed the game on every aspect of retail. ICICI companies have created entire markets in retail and insurance. We have thought big and changed the game.

One person said: "In 2003 our global ranking was 123 and yet our dream was to be one of the top banks of the world. Today in 2008 we are ranked 40th in the world having attained this in a relatively short time span."

In sum, it is clear that ICICI reaching the Number 2 position in India within a decade and Number 40 globally, have been possible because of the ability to think big, bring global perspective in its vision, and its ability to set audacious and stretched goals.

Execution Centric

Today's business world, characterized by fierce competition and ruthlessness, is witnessing the Darwinian doctrine of the survival of the fittest. It is the rule of the jungle where the Tiger and the Gazelle wake up every morning determined to outrun each other, each for its own survival. If the Tiger does not run faster than the Gazelle, it can die of hunger; if the Gazelle does not run faster than the Tiger, it can be killed. This in fact is today's business scenario, where it is not only about running fast; rather it is about running faster than the others. Those organizations which have grown and succeeded have adopted this approach.

All the interviewees said that in ICICI, "there is a bias for action and focus on speedy execution." One person mentioned that "we have the ability to change in response to changes in the marketplace, like the car driver behind a power steering, which enables him to deftly move the car according to the movement of the traffic on the road." Another person said that "we are extremely result oriented. Once we decide on the objective, we bring unparalleled speed, energy, focus, and execute the project." According to as many as fifteen interviewees, ICICI's forte is high execution focus and rapid time to market.

ICICI believes in Speed Capital which according to eighteen interviewees is "the 90-day rule, which requires that, anything new and different has to be put into practice within ninety days." Nine people said that in ICICI, "deadlines are sacred, they are deeply negotiated and crunched to enable quick time to market." Twelve people cited the following instance: "For example when we were planning to list on the NYSE the team was given ninety days for execution; the consultants who came in said it is an impossible target but we ended up achieving as per plan in eighty-eight days."

Six interviewees said the following:

> We have to be quick and innovative because our products can be easily imitated by others. Look at all our initiatives, today they are imitated by most banks. Imagine when we opened 2,000 ATMs, it shocked the banking community; today when a public sector bank opens 1,000 ATMs on a single day, no one bats an eyelid.

Nine people affirmed: "In ICICI the need for speedy execution focus to win is always emphasized."

In ICICI speedy execution is relentlessly driven and monitored. If anyone at any level faces a problem during a speedy execution, they can go to the Process Approving Committee and ask for process modification, as said by ten interviewees.

Perusal of the opinions expressed by the interviewees powerfully brings out that in ICICI, speed and flexibility are key mantras for execution and service delivery. These mantras have enabled ICICI to race ahead of its competitors.

Seamless Organization

Organizations are structured in such a way that they experience problems of horizontal coordination. This phenomenon is further aggravated since work flows horizontally, but authorial relationships are vertically structured. Therefore, there is silo functioning across divisions and departments along with highly tunneled vision among the organizational role holders. Eventually, the larger vision gets diluted and the goal focus becomes narrow and, finally, the left hand is ignorant of the actions of the right hand, so to speak. There is a tendency to pursue departmental or divisional goals, at the cost of larger organizational goals. In the extreme case, such silo functioning leads to empire building, struggle for power, and in-fighting. Great organizations are keenly aware of the problems and limitations of silo functioning and lack of larger vision. They strive to overcome these inadequacies by creating a seamless culture, systems, and processes.

Twenty-three interviewees we met said with a great sense of pride that ICICI is a seamless organization. Fifteen of them said: "There are no watertight compartments here." Eighteen interviewees said that "efforts are made to develop and remind people about the larger vision." In ICICI this has been done in many ways, said eleven people: people are not allowed to settle down in a particular role or function for long; there is frequent job rotation and people are moved across products and organizations under the ICICI umbrella. Nine interviewees claim that "there are many opportunities for groups working here." Ten people said that "there are many cross functional teams here working on many projects and issues." Members of the top team meet over lunch everyday, and there is extensive sharing of information and discussions where Kamath actively participates; "there are many forums where people working across products and companies have the opportunity to meet and discuss issues," said twenty-one interviewees. Twenty-four interviewees said there is free flow of communication in ICICI. Fourteen respondents said: "There is faster decision-making and execution; many bottlenecks are overcome because of frequent meetings and discussions."

Empowerment with Accountability

During our work as consultants in more than 100 organizations, we have come to the conclusion that nothing saps individual enthusiasm, excitement, and initiative more than the lack of empowerment and delegation. In fact, empowerment and delegation lead to the flowering of entrepreneurial ownership, initiative, risk-taking, creativity, and innovation. Needless to say, these are the basic levers for achieving competitive edge and propelling growth.

All the interviewees said that in ICICI "we experience plenty of delegation and empowerment. This is of course coupled with high accountability." Thirteen interviewees said: "The ICICI approach has been to spot the right talent and give them total responsibility and authority; the only expectation is that they should keep the superior informed about the plan of action and outcomes." Twenty-one interviewees responded that "here decision-making is left completely to the person." "Deliverables are clearly defined—in terms of shape, size, and market share. Kamath is always available for discussion; there is no follow up or micro management," said nine interviewees. Ten people said: "Since there is huge empowerment; people are able to perform far beyond their level." Thirteen interviewees were heard saying: "In ICICI people are allowed to take as much responsibility as they want." According to seventeen interviewees, the ecosystem of performance is good in ICICI—"it unleashes the potential of people and we function like entrepreneurs as if we own this place; they give needed support and then demand performance."

Techno-centric Work Culture

Technology has always played a significant role in differentiating winners from losers. It enables organizations to create differentiated products, processes, and systems along with the speed of response. Therefore, all great organizations take advantage of the power of technology to build competitive edge.

All the interviewees articulated that in ICICI, "We have been the pioneers in using technology in the banking sector." Fourteen interviewees stated that technology has provided ICICI the biggest support in achieving speed of execution as well as providing innovative products to customers. Twenty people said that technology has substantially helped ICICI in reducing the cost of delivery. In ICICI, today, 85 percent of the total transactions take place outside the bank branch, while 40 percent take place over the Internet, informed twenty-two interviewees. "Not only do we have the technology [in ICICI] but we also use it powerfully unlike many other competitors who imitate the technology but are unable to leverage it efficiently," said eleven interviewees. The power and utility of technology is demonstrated by the following quote:

> In 1996 ICICI had 5,000 customers with 100 branches and today [2008] we have 30 million customers with 1,400 branches. This was possible only through the introduction of technology and making operations technocentric. They gave examples of the introduction of Internet banking, Internet transactions, online trading, drop-box for cash, drop-box for bills, 33 (regional) processing centers, movement from passbook to bank statements, stated many of the interviewees.

This discussion brings out the fact that ICICI has significantly used technological power to bring in speed of response to the customer, efficiency in functioning, and creating differentiated products, thus, enabling creation of a cutting-edge organization.

Contribution-centric Meritocracy

One of the biggest challenges for business organizations is to establish the link between contribution and reward. People generally desire contribution-based equity and justice in the absence of which there is a feeling of disenchantment, de-motivation, and lack of ownership and commitment to the organization. Even globally, very few organizations have succeeded in creating a significant link between contribution and rewards. Those organizations which have achieved this have succeeded in creating the workforce full of excitement and commitment with a willingness to stretch for organizational goals. In fact, one of the biggest criticisms of Indian organizations is the perceived inequity, fairness, and justice because rewards are based on factors other than contribution and merit—such as nepotism; regionalism; favoritism; caste; class; and religion.

ICICI has, over the years, established a powerful reputation as that of a contribution-centric meritocracy. There is no place in this organization for the free floaters, mentioned twenty-two interviewees. Eleven people said "in the earlier days mediocrity was tolerated," but this changed once Kamath entered. Today those who do not deliver up to the expected levels have no place at ICICI. Therefore, in the late 1990s there were two rounds of VRS to deal with sub-optimal performers.

Over the years those who rose to occupy top positions have been the top performers—there have been no other bias in operation, neither age, religion, gender, nor region or educational background. Seventeen interviewees confirmed that "this approach has helped ICICI throw up leaders of high quality." Whoever proved themselves got to move forward. "There is no hesitation to give responsibility to young people—it is a meritocracy here. Both reward and penalization are based on one's performance," said fifteen interviewees.

Twenty-two people cited a number of examples where individuals were assigned roles based on their ability to deliver rather than any other consideration: Kalpana Morparia, a lawyer by profession, was asked to head treasury; Sandeep Bakshi, a project financer, was given insurance business to handle, which he turned into a highly successful business; and Madhabi Buch, a maths graduate with an MBA degree, was asked to head half the technology of the bank. In ICICI, meritocracy has been processised by institutionalizing a transparent process of assessment—a 360 degree feedback; rigorous performance appraisal; and counseling and competence-based assignments.

The foregoing analysis reveals that ICICI has succeeded in creating entrepreneurial ownership, sense of excitement, and motivation among its people through introduction of contribution-centric meritocracy. Such an approach enabled ICICI to be perceived as a place where there is a sense of justice, fairness, and equity, where merit is rewarded and valued in assigning roles and positions.

Shaping Talent/Building Leaders

Great organizations believe that their unique competitive edge (UCE) lies in the talent of their people, which, however, few organizations are able to harness satisfactorily. Although people are viewed as a great asset, when their talent and potential are not harnessed, they can become a great liability for the organization. It is in this perspective that winning organizations continuously seek to evolve systems which can help shape talent and build leaders.

"ICICI has a record of fine leaders at the top right from Nadkarni's (one of the erstwhile highly respected heads of ICICI) days," informed twelve people. Twenty interviewees claimed that ICICI always believed in picking up the best and brightest students from top educational institutions. It has created a fertile soil for leadership development over the years. In ICICI, there is a system of competency mapping for different positional roles and all developmental plans are evolved around inculcating these competencies. These competencies are known as the basic DNA of ICICI consisting of ten anchors, namely, Strategic Agility, Managing Change, Organizational Capability, Nurturing Talent, Collaboration, Sensitivity, Customer First, Compliance with Conscience, Dynamism, and Passion.

This DNA is kept in mind while recruiting to ensure a culture fit, confirmed eleven interviewees. Six people claimed:

> In ICICI we believe that knowledge can be imparted but not passion which ICICI considers the heart and soul of leadership and therefore when we recruit people it is done using passion as the threshold requirement. Along with passion we assess networking capability, risk appetite, and assertiveness rather than being hierarchy conscious.

"If someone is merely looking for a job we don't take them; our motto is you bring an attitude we give you knowledge," said nine people. Four interviewees mentioned: "If you are not visible beyond your domain, you are not a leader." Nine interviewees responded that "we select you for your strength, not reject you for your weakness," and sixteen said "we in ICICI consider selection as the key for talent acquisition and talent shaping."

ICICI has robust systems for leadership development: "We have created 2,000 internal trainers who undergo 'train the trainers' program. We select the best ones out of this pool as honorary professors and they give 10-man days to training every year," said four interviewees. Three people mentioned: "In ICICI Kamath gives 8–10 half days a year to interact with participants in the leadership workshop." "Here leadership assessment is done and accordingly talent is put into different categories—from readiness (as a leader) to nascent. This assessment is put to business heads, which are further discussed, finalized and used to give appropriate role assignments," mentioned four interviewees. At ICICI leadership is not defined by knowledge and domain skills, it is about "having a view, stating a view, and shaping an agenda."

The cornerstone of the leadership talent development at ICICI has followed the pattern of people getting picked for their unique strengths who are not cloned against any ideal god-like template. A combination of clarity in how leaders differ from managers, strong investment in talent scouting, committed senior management which personally invests in assessment and nurturance, and finally an annual celebration and showcasing of the 100 exemplars across all levels of management on the Founding Day, serve as the blocks which when glued together with the spirit of valuing plurality take the shape of a robust leadership architecture.

In order to shape talent and build leaders, ICICI has introduced leadership awards on the articulated DNA traits. People have to be endorsed by 360 degree DNA characteristic inputs from at least thirty (seniors, peers, and subordinates) following which a committee scans the list and selects the names. Communication meetings are held to highlight their success behaviors. Finally, ten persons are given awards every year at a high profile ceremony for embodying the leadership values.

ACTION ARCHITECTURE AND CULTURE LANDSCAPE OF ICICI BANK: SALIENT CONTOURS

Both the interview and questionnaire responses (for details of questionnaire data of organizational culture of ICICI Bank, see Appendix 5A.3) bring out the following landmark features regarding the achievements, action architecture, and culture topography of ICICI:

- In the last six years (2003–2009), revenue and profits have grown 219 percent and 212 percent, respectively (for details of financial performance of ICICI Bank from 2003 to 2009, see Appendix 5A.4). Its income revenue shot up to ₹ 399.75 billion from ₹ 125.33 billion; likewise the net income touched the figure of ₹ 37.58 billion from ₹ 12.06 billion. By any standard, these figures reflect phenomenal growth in the financial sector. ICICI's achievements and contributions have been recognized by conferring many awards, notable among them being the Euro-week Award for most improved market profile, as eight interviewees recollected, Global Financial Award for "Best Trade Finance Bank and Provider in India," as mentioned by eight interviewees. It also bagged the best Bank in Asia award in 2007.
- ICICI underwent a metamorphosis from being a tiny DFI to being India's second largest financial powerhouse, a feat which was achieved in one short decade.
- ICICI work culture is significantly geared toward result orientation and performance excellence, while continuously raising the performance bar and moving from the best to the next.
- ICICI culture is outward looking, global focused, and futuristic, and this has significantly helped ICICI to spot emerging opportunities and incorporate the same into their business architecture.
- Entrepreneurial ownership and risk-taking is in the basic DNA of ICICI culture enabling ICICI to promote continued innovation, creativity, and bold decision-making.
- ICICI organizational culture also lays significant emphasis on ethical governance, transparency, and openness.
- Building people talent and capability is a core value of the ICICI work culture.
- All these culture levers—performance orientation; receptivity and openness to new ideas; entrepreneurial ownership; value-based governance; and building people capability—significantly helped ICICI become a cutting-edge organization, and a financial powerhouse.

Part III: K.V. Kamath: His Profile and Persona

The following eleven emergent themes have been identified through content analysis of the interview data. They have been presented below in order of importance keeping in view the priority attached by the interviewees while describing Kamath as a Change Maestro and as a person:

- Crystal gazer: Thinks of tomorrow today
- Himalayan ambition
- Entrepreneurial strategist
- Talent architect
- Concorde speed
- Quest for connecting horizon with ground
- Relentless quest for performance excellence
- Photographic and elephantine memory
- Continued learnability
- Statesman
- Connecting and creating the dots

Crystal Gazer: Thinks of Tomorrow Today

In order to prepare the organization for the future, the capability to predict the likely future contours is critical. It is almost like a crystal gazer who is able to see what others cannot. It is this prescience which helps organizations anticipate and take advantage of emerging opportunities and incorporate the same into their business plans.

All the interviewees said Kamath is a man of "binocular vision," he has an "opportunity-sensing mind with alert antenna," he can very clearly "see tomorrow today," and he is a "template creator." The following quotes clearly bring out this crystal-gazing capability possessed by Kamath.

> Fifteen interviewees said: "He is able to predict when the next inflexion point is going to come."

> Eleven interviewees remarked: "We have seen him as the most insightful leader as compared to many others."

Seven people said: "We don't know how he connects the dots, how he does it … but what he says [about trends] actually takes place."

Thirteen interviewees mentioned: "Mr Kamath is capable of predicting future based on some data which make no sense to us maybe he has intuitive power."

Fifteen people said: "Mr Kamath's mind constantly scans the environment, analyses information and constructs patterns."

"He is extremely high on curiosity, he picks up all the time from the environment," said twelve interviewees.

"He observes all emerging opportunities like a sponge, he absorbs knowledge from every industry," nineteen interviewees mentioned this point.

"His mind operates like a radar system, continuously processing information and events," said seven people.

Ten people said: "He does not miss the opportunity of attending global summits like WEF and other annual CEO forums where global thought leaders participate [so that he keeps up with the latest thinking]."

While twenty-three interviewees said: "His bandwidth is very high."

Himalayan Ambition

Ambition is the powerful engine that propels the struggle for achievement in cases of both individuals and organizations. The larger the ambition, the greater the energy unleashed, thereby resulting in greater growth and achievements. Kamath's ambition needs to be seen in this perspective. It has been labeled "Himalayan" because of the scale and scope of his ambition.

All the twenty-five interviewees highlighted the vastness and intensity of his ambition and passion and described this in the following words:

"We are living the ICICI dream [world class, global, one of the largest Indian banks] right now, which was articulated, by Kamath about 10 years ago."

"Kamath is a man who thinks big.… He was not happy for ICICI to be a marginal player.… He used to say that whatever we do, we should have a big presence in terms of size, scale, and excellence," stated three of the interviewees.

"His singular impact on the group has been to think big," said twenty-two interviewees.

Nine interviewees said: "We have internalized that without scale and excellence, we can never be a dominant player."

Fourteen people said that Kamath would never be satisfied to be a "big fish in a small pond."

His most famous statement to his team, as twelve interviewees recalled is "If Asian tigers can do it, why not India?"

Twenty-three interviewees mentioned that Kamath set the pace for the intense efforts of the team and this helped ICICI grow from a small development bank to a giant financial powerhouse. In Mr Kamath's words: "Nothing is impossible."

Kamath demonstrated his ambition not only for changing the business contours of ICICI, but also for changing the Indian banking landscape. One of the interviewees went to the extent of saying that "Mr Kamath is the man who not only changed the destiny of ICICI but also of the country by changing the banking landscape." Another interviewee said that "he rewrote the rules of the banking industry in India." "Mr Kamath's ambition is not confined merely to the scalability of ICICI, it is a holistic ambition encompassing of speed, excellence, quality and delivery. This is an all pervasive ambition," said twenty-two interviewees.

Entrepreneurial Strategist

Entrepreneurial strategists demonstrate boldness, risk-taking capability, and growth focus. They have tremendous convictions about their vision and dreams, which enable them to boldly tread the unbeaten track. It also gives them the courage to walk alone (with their vision). Many times, they are the lone travelers on their chosen path, yet they persevere because they see something ahead which others cannot. They are capable of going much beyond the obvious and with this determination build and grow their organizations.

All the interviewed people said that the moves made by Kamath have been strategic in nature, whether it was moving from development banking to retail banking, going global or using the power of ATMs.

Eighteen interviewees said: "Had we made the conventional moves like other Indian banks, we would not have grown as fast as we have done." Fourteen responded by saying: "Mr Kamath has tremendous foresightedness. He can see what looms ahead on the business horizon." "He is able to see patterns in ambiguity," said fourteen interviewees. Fifteen interviewees said: "We have seen many leaders but have not seen anyone with such outstanding qualities." And fifteen interviewees also said: "He is always futuristic with global visions and continuously prepares ICICI to take advantage of the opportunities."

The globe is the business arena for Kamath. He has been taking ICICI into new domains, new lines of business, and new areas as indicated by the following statements made by the interviewed top team members:

"All the steps taken by Mr Kamath from 1996 to 2007 clearly bring out he is both entrepreneurial and a strategist par excellence," asserted fifteen interviewees.

"He saw the demise of development financial institutions much before others and transformed ICICI from a development bank to a total financial powerhouse," said eighteen interviewees.

Twenty-one members said: "He was quite clear about scalability as an instrument to compete and, therefore, continuously increased the size of the bank through expansion and mergers and acquisitions."

"Mr Kamath is a highly intuitive man, he is a blink kind of a person," said twelve people.

Again, twelve people said: "Mr Kamath's mind works on several levels, whether it is observing, interacting, or opportunity-sensing."

Eighteen people said: "His eyes and ears are always open, he intuitively thinks of the next opportunity."

"The biggest strength of Mr Kamath as an entrepreneur is his optimistic thinking, no matter what the situation, he doesn't get perturbed," said twenty interviewees.

"We all call him Entrepreneurial because in business, to be able to an entrepreneur, you need to have stomach and guts which Mr Kamath has got in plenty.... One must have the courage to accept both profit and loss and in ICICI, Mr Kamath demonstrates that," claimed twenty interviewees.

Kamath views organization structure as the vehicle for delivering strategy. Hence, to him structures are fluid and not visualized as boxes, names, or job descriptions. He sees them as business networks where information, people's abilities, and decisions are leveraged, which is very similar to the way start-up organizations function. He strives to keep large organizations entrepreneurial by designing and keeping the organizational structure aligned to emerging opportunities.

Talent Architect

Change Maestros transform the world through the power of enablers and messengers. Buddha created five enablers through whom his message was widely disseminated; Jesus had twelve and conquered the hearts of a large part of the world through the message of Christianity; Guru Gobind Singh developed five commanders who protected Sikhism against the onslaught of Islam. The corporate world is also replete with many such examples, whether we talk of J.R.D. Tata, G.D. Birla, Narayana Murthy, Jack Welch, or others. Such an approach powerfully helps build sustainability and continuity of growth and performance excellence of the organization. Many organizations have collapsed in the absence of leadership architecting at multiple levels, since it is they who are the enablers and executors of the CEO's vision, values, philosophy, and strategy.

All twenty-five interviewees said that Kamath has succeeded in grooming many leaders at multiple levels. They gave the example of Lalita Gupte, Kalpana Morparia, Chanda Kochhar, Shikha Sharma, Nachiket Mor, Sandeep Bhakshi, Vaidyanathan, Madhabi, Ramkumar, Vishaka Mulye, Kannan, Bhargav Dasgupta, Sonjoy Chatterjee, and many such leaders. All the interviewees also said that in ICICI, both consolidation and growth could concurrently take place because of such a high focus on creating leaders at different levels.

In the early days before assigning a new responsibility, Kamath personally coached and mentored the incumbents (something which he continued for many years). His famous dictum to new incumbents in leadership roles was "You have been a hands-on leaders, now you have to become hands-off," referring to the need to bring in the strategy component into their thinking and style. Fifteen interviewees commented: "Kamath had clarity about the needed competencies at different levels and used to coach new incumbents about this and advised other leaders to coach leaders reporting to them."

According to fifteen interviewees, Kamath used to educate people about team composition emphasizing the importance of complementary skills in team members—teams need all types of profiles like intellectuals, street smart guys, wheeler-dealers, analysts, and so on. He used to exhort team members to work together and learn from each other with a view to create synergy.

Another strategy he adopted for talent development was to coach the leaders to develop their subordinates rather than compete with them. He made it very clear that their growth would depend upon having competent subordinates to replace them. His famous slogan, as mentioned by eighteen interviewees, was: "If I don't have a candidate to replace you, your own growth is gone."

Kamath has been highly transformational in his approach to leadership development: "He is responsible for the transformation of many individuals, we never thought we could do all that we have done," said twelve respondents. "Mr Kamath has the knack of spotting the right talent and putting the person on the right job, this is a rare quality, the capability to pick up the right person for the right job," mentioned twelve interviewees.

All the interviewees said Kamath is a great delegator. He believes in empowering people with sharply defined accountability. According to five of them,

> he inspires people by saying, "You are the CEOs of whatever you are doing, you are the owner and you are the entrepreneur; I will give you some resources and after that, you are pretty much on your own." The person gets the feeling I am the boss, the owner, let me go and make a difference....

"Kamath is always available to us. When there is some crisis, he is there physically. He does not run away from problems. We hardly see any panic in him while facing difficult situations," said twelve interviewees. Ten people said:

Mr Kamath is highly empowering and Pygmalion in his approach. High achievers are appreciated and acknowledged and praised in public and this becomes a big motivator. However, he doesn't hesitate to pull up poor performers in public because he believes that this will serve as a deterrent to others.

In his own words, Kamath believes the following: "Nurturing talent is a way you move others in a particular position, where you interact with them, you see what they do ... only then you can mentor them and can test them."

This style of Kamath has developed self belief among people of ICICI.

Eighteen interviewees said: "Kamath uses a range of styles to grow and develop people—sometimes, it is challenging, sometimes, it could be by provoking, sometimes, by delegating, and sometimes it could be though supporting, praising, and recognizing people." Five people said "we consider him the Kabir Khan of *Chak De!*"

All twenty-five interviewees said that while the task and results are very important for Kamath, he also has a strong humane side to him. Nine respondents said: "Mr Kamath is very observant and notices body language and if someone looks unwell, he notices and asks about it." According to many of the interviewees, at times Kamath has gone out of his way to take interest in the personal problems of his team and tried to help whether it has been—a medical emergency; transfer-related; family matters; or schooling of executives' children. Fifteen interviewees said: "When we meet him one on one, not only does Mr Kamath enquire about work but also about the family and kids." People compared him with a coconut and said: "He has a ruthless exterior but is very kind-hearted," sixteen people said this. Or, his social concerns are also high where nine interviewees commented: "On his initiative we in ICICI have set aside up to 1 percent of profits for altruistic causes."

Concorde Speed

Speed is the essence required to be both a pace-setter and a trendsetter. Speedy organizations always race ahead of the competition and benefit from the available opportunities. All the levers of competitive edge—cost; quality;

customerization; innovation; and ethical governance—may not necessarily create a winning organization. It is the ability of the organization to adopt these levers faster than the others which provides them the competitive advantage. This applies both to organizations as well as to leaders.

All the interviewees said that Kamath is a man of speed. He believes in racing ahead of others to build competitive advantage for his organization; he also reminds that without speed and audacious goals, ICICI cannot be a winner. He is also personally time-conscious and deadline-focused and brings a time frame to all actions. He probably is the only person who refers to speed as a type of capital. To him, flexible and fluid structures are vehicles of speed and, hence, a source of competitive advantage.

Quest for Connecting Horizon with Ground

While horizon refers to ideas and opportunities which leaders are able to spot at the stratospheric level, ground connotes execution of these ideas. Great leaders not only focus on ideas imminent on the horizon, they also draw strategies and connect them to the ground by creating new products, processes, or services. Increasingly, management literature has begun to emphasize that although today, on the idea level companies are more or less on the same platform, however, to bet on ideas and convert them for organizational benefit is a rare capability. Needless to say, this capability distinguishes the leaders from the laggards.

All the interviewees also indicated that Kamath is a man who connects horizon with ground:

> "He is a very interesting combination of a big picture guy who understands nitty-gritty details," said twelve interviewees.
>
> "I have seen Mr Kamath operate at 40,000 feet and then dive down and hover one inch above the ground," mentioned ten interviewees.
>
> "In my view, he connects sky and earth," three people said this.
>
> Five people believe he has the "capability to integrate big picture thinking and minute detail focus."

> Three people said: "He does not lose the bigger picture. His ability to map out the bigger picture, yet at the same time, track what is happening at the ground level is very impressive."
>
> Oner person said: "He is able to soar high like an eagle and look below. He views the business from a much higher altitude, peeps into the future and can also zoom down a couple floors underground. This capability is just amazing."

According to fifteen of them Kamath has the big vision which he then converts into execution. Nine people remarked: "He is amazing being both a visionary and a very very operationally focused person."

Kamath possesses the capability to connect with the ground because of his strong execution focus, his being pragmatic and realistic. He truly embodies the wisdom of 'head in the clouds with feet on the ground' according to most (20) of the interviewees.

Relentless Quest for Performance Excellence

One of the most striking feature common to all Change Maestros is their passion to continuously raise the bar of performance excellence. They believe in moving from best to next, time after time, as mentioned earlier. They continuously create the new curve of performance excellence, achievement, and contribution. It is also observed that even after they reach the pinnacle of performance, they are not satisfied because they tend to compete with themselves and, thus, put themselves on a track of continuously raising the performance bar. This is a psychological state where like the Olympians there is continued urge to break their own performance records,

All the interviewees vociferously said that Kamath is well known for his performance standards and benchmarks. He demonstrates insatiable appetite to set stretched targets and continuously raise the bar. All of them said that he is highly demanding, excellence-focused, and extremely impatient with mediocrity. His well-known mantra is to advice people to "continuously raise the bar," as eighteen interviewees mentioned. "His expectations know no bounds," said fifteen interviewees. Describing his style, fifteen interviewees explained how the push for stretched targets takes place—even when a 100 percent growth plan is presented, he is known to say "I know you can do better than this, let us triple the number this year!" "He is also persuasive, provocative, and Pygmalion in his style that on many occasions, we have crunched one year timelines to three months. Not only is he demanding from others, he is equally demanding from himself and sets seemingly audacious targets," said seven interviewees. According to nine interviewees, Kamath is known to be hard driving and uncompromising. He relentlessly pursues his goal of excellence and also pursuades people to raise their respective bar of performance excellence: "You have come back tenth time with a lower target than Kamath's expectation but he comes back the eleventh time, thereby putting the ball in your court and finally your target reaches close to his expectation," as one interviewee remarked.

Photographic and Elephantine Memory

Memory is fundamental to one's sense of self, to reflect, recall, process stimuli, and respond speedily and appropriately to important events. It contains the accumulated knowledge, experiences, and wisdom from which springs intuition and action plans. Without memory, one leads life moment to moment without a sense of past, present, or future. In short, memory is a core aspect for effective human functioning. One of the characteristics of great leaders has been strong memory—the capability to remember names, faces, facts, figures, which helps them in pattern-making, responding to events fast, networking and connecting with people, establishing rapport, and so on.

All the interviewees said that Kamath has an amazing photographic memory as indicated in the following quotes:

> Eleven interviewees said: "Mr Kamath demonstrates superior intellectual capabilities compared with many leaders we have worked with."
>
> "He has a sharp memory," as twenty-two interviewees remarked.
>
> Seventeen interviewees said: "He recalls numbers with ease and tremendous speed."

Twenty-one of them said: "He has razor-sharp intelligence."

Sixteen interviewees mentioned: "He even remembers data presented two years back and [most importantly] is able to recall at the right time.... This helps him in close monitoring."

"He has the ability to see things not visible to others," said nine respondents.

"During presentations, mistakes seldom miss his gaze, therefore, we become very alert while making presentations before him," informed twenty-two people.

Twenty-three people said: "Every meeting, every interaction, every word spoken, every action taken is recorded in his mind."

Twenty-three people also said that he has the great ability to piece together different bits of information from different people and use it to take decisions. To this twelve people were heard saying: "He has the ability to connect the dots of the big picture as well as details" and twenty-one people said: "He is quick at back of the envelope calculations."

Continued Learnability

Great leaders are great learners. They constantly evolve and reinvent themselves because of their high learnability. In fact, learning is a sign of growth and development. The learning orientation of Kamath has been viewed in this perspective.

People have described Kamath's behavior which reflects his high learning orientation:

Twenty-five people agreed that "Mr Kamath is a great learner and picks up knowledge, information, ideas from anywhere and everywhere."

"He will, for example, visit an auto manufacturer, learn something there and apply to his business," said twelve interviewees.

One person said: "He meets a film producer and even applies insights from there into his business."

Five interviewees mentioned: "His ability to learn from diverse sources, connect and find relevant insights for the business is amazing."

Nine people said that his learning orientation has immensely helped him in changing business strategies, models, and processes.

Twenty-two interviewees remarked: "Mr Kamath is an avid reader. Even today, he keeps track of all the happenings around the world."

"Mr Kamath is a good listener and keen observer; he listens, observes, and absorbs," recorded all the twenty-five interviewees.

The agility of ICICI and its swift response to emerging trends is closely linked to Kamath's high learning orientation.

Statesman

There are very few corporate leaders who have achieved the stature of a statesman. This is so because most of them are narrowly focused on economic and business considerations of the organizations they lead. Those who enhance their roles by encompassing larger issues and concerns like shaping society, shaping national policy, and representing the country at the global level, become role models, icons, and statesmen.

All the interviewees said that Kamath is a statesman:

Eleven of them said: "He is somebody who creates impact."

Ten interviewees said: "He is someone who can see the macro picture."

Twelve responded by saying: "He is someone who is capable of integrating diverse roles."

"He demonstrates tremendous self belief," said fifteen interviewees.

Five interviewees said: "He is capable of selling his ideas in an extremely convincing way."

Twenty interviewees claimed: "He is a mentor for many of us."

"He has a larger than life persona which creates awe in our minds," affirmed fifteen respondents.

Seven of them said: "He is not only tall physically but also as a person and a professional."

"Today he is the ambassador of the country to the world in many ways. When he speaks, people pay attention," nine interviewees asserted.

Ten interviewees mentioned: "He is both young in spirit and a wise old man."

"People feel like meeting him when they have problems," said eleven people.

Twenty-one interviewees said: "He counsels and mentors people."

All twenty-five interviewees said: "He is a very dignified man."

They also said: "He knows how to respect value and make people feel they are important."

Twenty-two respondents remarked: "He is somebody you can look up to."

These statements reveal that Kamath is an iconic personality, a role model, and someone whom people look up to in admiration in ICICI. In the Indian corporate firmament, he strides like a colossus. No wonder, therefore, he has been ranked the 4th most influential person in India by *The Economic Times* in 2009.

Connecting and Creating the Dots

Kamath has been seen by as many as nineteen interviewees as a man who works simultaneously works at many levels of complexities. Ten people said that he effortlessly connects the sky with the earth and the horizon with the ground. As five interviewees described it, he is able to make the switch from looking at the big picture to pointing his gaze two inches above the ground with great speed. He is extremely tough and demanding, yet can be very humane when someone is in trouble, claimed nineteen interviewees. While he operates with great speed in connecting the dots and creating the pattern, he is equally speedy in execution, as twelve interviewees confirmed. He is highly assertive yet open to new ideas, said nine people. It can be concluded from all these views that Kamath successfully straddles extremes with ease and effortlessly combines these forces.

K.V. Kamath as a Change Maestro: Salient Contours

Both the interview responses as well as questionnaire data (for details of questionnaire data of K.V. Kamath's Change Maestro style, see Appendix 5A.5) together form the following conclusions about K.V. Kamath as a Change Maestro and as a person:

- Kamath is the man with a Himalayan vision who possesses crystal-gazing capability. He successfully reinvented the Indian financial sector landscape.
- He created a giant sized ICICI powered by continued big dream, growth velocity, and entrepreneurial innovation.
- In ICICI he inculcated the culture of seamless functioning across the organization, empowerment with accountability, execution and contribution-centric meritocracy, besides shaping talent and building leaders.
- He has a photographic and elephantine memory with continued learnability which enabled him to be an evolving Change Maestro.
- He has the capability to connect the dots and create patterns which helped him to create a new future for ICICI.
- K.V. Kamath has a large competency bandwidth and effortlessly uses all the gears of Change Maestro competencies to make ICICI grow, compete, and excel.
- K.V. Kamath is highly idealistic and value centric as a person. He is highly patriotic and has passion to build India as a global superpower. He is generous and large-hearted along with being ruthlessly demanding on performance. He is courageous, bold, and entrepreneurial.
- He has a razor sharp and seminal mind which can cut to the heart of the matter. He is an intense observer, listener, and learner. He has a sense of positive disquiet always looking ahead impatiently for the next horizon.
- Along with a towering public persona, Kamath is also an intensely private person.
- All these qualities together have made him the colossus of the Indian financial sector and it is no wonder that people call him a true statesman.
- K.V. Kamath has been decorated with a plethora of awards, notable among them being the Padma Bhushan, as said eight interviewees, The NDTV Profit Business Leadership Award, as eight interviewees recalled, Business Leader of the Year Award by *The Economic Times*, as six people mentioned, etc.

K.V. Kamath: Concluding Contours

K.V. Kamath is the man best known for reinventing the Indian banking landscape. His name is synonymous with the growth of ICICI into India's largest private sector bank and a truly global financial powerhouse. In 2009, he was adjudged the 4th most influential Indian corporate icon by *The Economic Times*.

K.V. Kamath has uniquely combined the power of strategy crafting and strategy execution enabling him to connect horizon with ground reality. His intuition about the future has helped him enfold the future into the present, equipping the organization to get the advantage of being the first mover. Mr Kamath's context sensitivity and sharp powers of observation are enviable. He has trained these formidable capabilities on to understanding customers and their lives in depth which he then powerfully uses to build ICICI's growth strategy, processes, and systems. He, thus, put the customer at the center stage and did backward integration of the systems, processes, and strategies of ICICI accordingly.

Mr Kamath is a keen observer, a voracious reader, and, therefore, there are very few events, information, and happenings around which miss his attention. He is an extremely demanding leader, sets stretch targets, relentlessly raises the bar of performance, pushes people beyond their comfort zone, and gets them to perform beyond their own expectations. Kamath is a highly attentive listener, absorbing everything which is conveyed, a powerful learner who uses every bit of information in terms of its relevance for ICICI's business. By being such an attentive listener as well as a patient observer, Kamath conveys to the person before him that he is valued and appreciated. Mr Kamath is highly Pygmalion in demanding performance excellence, making people feel that they have greater capabilities, thus leading them to perform to his expectations. He is highly appreciative and handsomely rewards high performers. He has been an outstanding mentor and coach and has shaped many great business leaders. Mr Kamath is a person who does not compromise on excellence and continuously makes the organization and people move to the next best option. He has used all the levers of excellence for building ICICI as a great organization.

Mr Kamath is highly patriotic, value based leader, courageous, bold, innovative and speedy decision maker with granite will power. He is the symbol of objectivity in dealing with people and issues putting the organizational goal above everything else.

The ICICI culture which he built is characterized by ethical governance, entrepreneurial freedom, value for individuals, quick growth, and recognition for high performers and global perspective which enabled such a phenomenal performance. It is scarcely surprising that under Kamath, ICICI made rapid strides in its transformation from a small DFI to India's largest private sector bank.

Appendices

Appendix 5A.1: ICICI Bank—Pushing beyond Limits

As a bank, ICICI has the reputation for constantly pushing the limits. It is the best service organization you can get, having honed the skill of a 24/7 hospitality industry and the service quality of the airline industry. It is also the iconic representation of a diversified multinational with footprints in eighteen other countries. The acronym of ICICI could aptly be "I see I care!" which best sums up what the Indian mega bank ICICI is all about.

Everything about ICICI Bank is related to pushing the limits of performance and innovation to stay on top. In this truly Indian Asian bank, constant growth is a way of life where the bar of performance excellence is relentlessly raised. The bank today is India's largest private sector bank and the second largest bank in the country with consolidated total assets of about US$ 95 billion as of March 31, 2009. ICICI Bank's subsidiaries include India's leading private sector insurance companies and among its largest securities brokerage firms, mutual funds, and private equity firms.

How did such a powerful banking and financial services company emerge? It is best explained by the bank's own statement of vision. The bank states:

> ICICI Bank's vision is to become the leading player in Indian financial markets and grow our overseas presence. The Global Markets Group [GMG], the Bank's client-centric treasury, endeavors to partner its customers in ensuring they use financial markets to optimize their risk profile and enhance value to

their stakeholders. The group seeks to do this by becoming the risk solutions provider of choice, offering quality treasury products and being the leader in product innovation.

The shareholding of Industrial Credit and Investment Corporation of India (ICICI) in ICICI Bank was quickly reduced to 46 percent through a public offering of shares in fiscal year (FY) 1998, barely within four years of its formation, which is an achievement by itself. This was followed by offer of equity capital in the form of American Depositary Receipt (ADR) listed on the NYSE in FY 2000. The bank also made bold move to acquire Bank of Madura Limited in an all-stock amalgamation in FY 2001, and its secondary market sales by ICICI to institutional investors in FY 2001 and fiscal 2002 which brought a large reserve of capital to the bank for providing liquidity in its lending operations.

The parent company, ICICI, by then had transformed its business from a DFI offering only project finance to a diversified financial services group offering a wide variety of products and services, both directly and through a number of subsidiaries and affiliates like ICICI Bank. In 1999, ICICI become the first Indian company and the first bank or financial institution from non-Japan Asia to be listed on the NYSE. All these aspects had helped ICICI Bank when ICICI reverse merged with the bank in 2002 and became India's second largest commercial bank in terms of asset size. The ICICI merger also came with two of its subsidiaries ICICI Personal Financial Services Limited and ICICI Capital Services Limited, businesses which gave the bank a greater leeway to experiment with a portfolio of services that could be offered to its customers.

Even before the ICICI merger, the bank had changed its original vision to focus attention on every Indian through:

- Retail
- Finance
- Car loans
- House
- Consumer durables loans

This brought ICICI much closer to its customer than any bank could ever do at that time. With the financial muscle and sheer size that it acquired after the 2002 merger ICICI Bank could pull out all stops to grow into a major global bank and through its innovative practices also enter into related areas like:

- Insurance
- Asset management
- Financial services
- Portfolio management
- Investment banking
- Personal banking
- Consortium lending
- Forex treasury operations
- Home financing

The roller-coaster ride continued until the global economic setback occurred in early 2009 after the crash of the financial markets in the wake of a series of economic crises starting with sub-prime crisis in the US, followed by a runway increase in oil prices, and finally ending with a near total crash of the financial system with one of the major investment companies, Lehman Brothers, going belly up. Though the bank, like most other financial services industries also faced the aftershocks and needed a short-term infusion of government funding, it could weather the crises easily and bounce bank, owing to the underlying robustness of its operations.

The Structure

The banking conglomerate has divided itself into four broad business areas (see Figure 5A.1). Chiefly, it is commercial banking which includes its Indian and international operations; second, financial services business which included the ICICI asset management and venture capital operations along with home financing and retail banking operations; third, technology banking as a backbone to all its services; and, finally, insurance, a business which ICICI started as a joint venture with Prudential Plc of London (started in the 18th century

Figure 5A.1 *Operations of ICICI Bank*

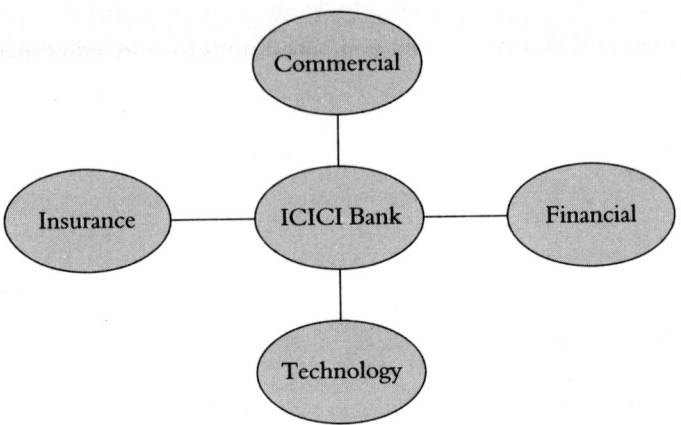

England) and Lombard General Insurance company of Canada (a subsidiary of the Canada-based $26 billion Fairfax Financial Holdings Limited).

Most of the operations are run by independent companies held by ICICI as a wholly owned subsidiary or through joint ventures with its overseas partner. But collectively, all the operations of every ICICI arm are based on the common code of ethics and the accepted practices of business and ethos of the ICICI Bank. It is no surprise that accolades are showered upon the various ICICI subsidiaries and its own core banking team for their professional services. Barely within six months of the 2009 calendar year, the bank had won three different global awards for its operations with its mobile banking operations bagging the "Best Bank Award for Initiatives in Mobile Payments and Banking" awarded by IDRBT, its business-to-business (B2B) branch, free banking being adjudged the "Best E-Banking Project Implementation Award 2008" by *The Asian Banker* magazine, and the bank being awarded by Dun & Bradstreet as the "Best Bank in SME Financing (Private Sector)." The ICICI Bank NRI services won the "Excellence in Business Model Innovation Award" in the 8th Asian Banker Excellence in Retail Financial Services Awards Program. These are merely sample of recognition being accorded to ICICI highlighting the strong impact a bank is making on the broad consumer environment in which it operates.

It Is All about Leadership

ICICI is all about people and leadership. It started with the uncanny vision of the celebrated banker, N. Vagul who gave shape and structure to the bank. This was continued by K.V. Kamath who was singularly responsible for taking the bank to new heights by the power of his sheer vision and continuity of its original founders. Kamath has left an indelible mark on the bank through his uncanny instinct for business development, and his ability to keep his flock together and add to talent at every stage, which the bank passed through to emerge as a highly diversified global banking and financial services company. When he stepped down as chairman of the bank, he was ably succeeded by the present Managing Director and Chief Executive Officer Chanda Kochhar who was picked up and personally groomed by Kamath. This speaks volumes about the ethos of continuity and change for which ICICI stands out as a stellar example. In fact, the induction of Chanda Kochhar (and other outstanding women bankers) is a unique achievement in itself, in an industry usually dominated by male bankers especially at the leadership level.

Talent Ecosystem

One of the apparent aspects of an ICICI Bank branch is that it is manned by one of the youngest and highly efficient pool of talent. The reason for this is not only the relative vintage of the bank, but also a conscious talent management policy which has developed an ecosystem of its own, attracting the best and the brightest youngsters. It should be appreciated that the rapid spread of the bank in India posed its special challenges owing to lack of qualified personnel in the rural and semi-urban branches. The bank resolved the manpower crisis by developing a talent ecosystem which would develop ready-to-use talent at two levels. Level one was to develop a close relationship with target group of universities and colleges to help improve the quality of their curriculum and inculcate practical appreciation of business realities in the academic offering of these colleges. The ecosystem could create industry ready talent pool. The program focused on:

1. Faculty development, bridging the knowledge gap in faculty members with respect to financial sector;
2. Content creation, case studies, and reading material; and
3. Learning infrastructure development through making available nearly 1,000 hours of e-content.

These initiatives covered nearly 1,000 universities and colleges.

For the managerial talent the bank adopted a more direct approach by recruiting and training its executive manpower pool with the help of leading universities.

The bank has shown an uncanny ability to envision and come up with solutions for the pressing problems of the nation which begins with providing employment opportunities for its youth. Under the "Talent Ethos" approach the bank decided to make talent and not buy it and intervene at both the ecosystem level and institutional levels, to build talent using the best of technologies available. ICICI Group probationary officers program is one such ecosystem intervention schemes which have proved to be a big hit among the youth.

Leadership development became more focused with a two-pronged approach to internally develop high level talent through mentoring and exposing such talent to leading universities and thought leaders; and through a concerted program of intellectual partnership with 100 colleges and universities. The flagship probationary officers' program is run with one of India's largest private sector university, T.A. Pai University. The objective of this initiative is to groom students drawn from smaller towns in India for the first level managerial roles through a one-year residential program providing specialized banking or insurance knowledge and skills. The program was such a big hit that in the very first year over one lakh applications were received for 1,000 posts of probationary officers (POs). This is also part of an inclusive employment initiative that does not sacrifice meritocracy. All the selected POs come from households with an income less than ₹ 3 lakhs per annum. The selection process does not insist on English language skills. It looks for compatibility with ICICI DNA and intellect that would have landed any of these talented applicants in any of the top thirty B-schools (which is beyond their reach due to socioeconomic condition of affordability of fees and a selection system anchored on English language skills which excludes them). The children of cooks, watchman, and farmers, as their parents, realize their dreams by coming through an uncompromising meritocracy.

Following is the list of milestones achieved by ICICI Bank:

- ICICI Bank is formed in 1994.
- Reverse merger with promoter group ICICI in 2002.
- Bank creates markets and defines products by stoking customer aspirations.
- ATM on wheels and mobile banking.
- 8 to 8 banking.
- Floating rate for home loans.
- Free for life credit cards.
- Home Shoppe, the first ever permanent aggregation and display of housing projects in the country.
- Technology bank.
- Multichannel, multiproduct strategy.
- Phone banking, Internet banking.
- Differentiated employee vendor performance to offer value to customers.
- Speed and agility as main levers.
- International banking business as key focus.
- Rural customer is next focus.
- Technology-based solutions, innovations, and multiple delivery channels for rural customers.
- Sustainable growth in India combining social, human development goals with economic prosperity for most Indians.
- ICICI Foundation for inclusive growth.
- ICICI Prudential becomes the largest private sector life insurance company.
- General insurance ICICI Lombard.
- ICICI Prudential Asset Management Company.
- ICICI Venture Funds Management Company.
- ICICI Securities.
- Financial Performance.

Financial performance of ICICI in the last five years has been path-breaking. Its revenue growth has been to the tune of 216.06 percent during this time. Profit growth has been 244.78 percent in the same period for year-wise profit and industry growth.

Table 5A.1: Recognitions and Accolades to ICICI Bank, 2007–2008

2008	• EuroWeek Award for "Most Improved Market Profile." • The award is designed to recognize the institution that has been most successful in building its own niche in Asia's competitive syndicated loan market. • The Asset Triple A Transaction Banking Awards, 2008 awarded by *The Asset*. • Best Trade Finance Bank in India. • Best Transaction Bank in India. • Best Cash Management Bank in India. • Best Domestic Custodian in India. • Global Finance Award for best "Trade Finance Bank and Provider" in India.
2007	• ICICI Bank wins the Gold Shield for "Excellence in Financial Reporting" by Institute of Chartered Accountant of India (ICAI) for the year ended March 31, 2007. • ICICI Bank won the "Most Customer Responsive Company" award in the Banking and Financial Services vertical at *The Economic Times–Avaya Global Connect Customer Responsiveness Awards 2007*. • ICICI Bank won "The Bankers Award" for the Bank of the year (India). • ICICI has won the Euromoney Award for the "Best Bank in Asia" and "Best Bank in India."

Source: Company data.

Appendix 5A.2: Brief Sketch of K.V. Kamath

In the contemporary history of the Indian banking industry, K.V. Kamath's name will be written in golden letters. For, it was under his leadership, as the MD & CEO from

1996 to 2009, that ICICI Bank emerged as the second largest bank in the country next only to State Bank of India. The magnitude of his achievement can be gauged from the fact that unlike the State Bank of India, which had a legacy of over a hundred years and state support all through its existence, ICICI was built for the times as a highly technology-driven customer focused banking conglomerate. Kamath's biggest achievement is in not only building ICICI as a truly global Indian bank, but also as an institution which permanently impacted on the way of working of the banking industry, a feat that brought highest civilian laurels, the Padma Bhushan. The Benares Hindu University also conferred on him an honorary doctorate award.

As a visionary thought leader and Change Maestro, Kamath is on the boards of various decision-making bodies of not only the corporate world, but also of academia. He was the president of the CII for the year 2008–2009. He has been a co-chair of the World Economic Forum's Annual Meeting in Davos. He is a member of the board of the Institute of International Finance, Indian Institute of Management, Ahmedabad, director on the board of Infosys Technologies, and a member of advisory councils of NYSE and Visa Inc.

Table 5A.2: Accolades to K.V. Kamath, 2000–2008

2008	• Received the Lifetime Achievement Award at the NDTV Profit Business Leadership Awards 2008. • Awarded the "Padma Bhushan." • Received the UK Trade and Investment Award in 2008, in recognition of the significant contribution made toward India–UK trade relationship and visionary leadership.
2007	• Won "The Asian Banker Leadership Achievement Award" for the Asia Pacific and Gulf Region 2007. • Received the award of Forbes Asia businessman of the year for 2007. • Won the lifetime achievement award at the 7th Annual Teacher's Achievement Awards.
2006	• Received Business Leader Award of the Year awarded by *The Economic Times*. • Received Outstanding Business Leader of the Year awarded by CNBC TV-18.

(continued)

(continued)	
2005	• Awarded Businessman of the Year awarded by *Business India*.
2001	• Received Asian Business Leader of the Year awarded by CNBC Asia.
2000	• Finance Man of the Year award awarded by The Mumbai Management Association. • Awarded Best CEO for Innovative HR practices awarded by World HRD Congress in November 2000.

Source: Company data.

Appendix 5A.3: Organizational Culture of ICICI Bank—Analysis of Questionnaire Data

Table 5A.3: Perceived Organizational Culture of ICICI Bank

$N = 71$

S. No.	Organizational Culture	Mean	SD	Ranks
1.	Result orientation	4.65	0.54	1
2.	Entrepreneurial	4.49	0.61	2
3.	Ethical governance	4.42	0.67	3
4.	Openness to new ideas	4.41	0.58	4
5.	Performance excellence	4.39	0.73	5
6.	Speed of response to external demands and challenges	4.37	0.78	6
7.	Nurturing talent	4.28	0.74	7
8.	Performance-based promotion	4.27	0.63	8.5
9.	Empowerment and delegation	4.27	0.72	8.5
10.	Nurturing innovation	4.25	0.82	10
11.	Focus on continuous improvement	4.21	0.77	11
12.	Global perspectives	4.20	0.86	12.5
13.	Focus on building competitiveness	4.20	0.86	12.5
14.	Support for risk-taking	4.14	0.85	14
15.	Teamwork	4.07	0.72	15.5
16.	Openness and transparency	4.07	0.62	15.5
17.	Role clarity	4.03	0.70	17.5

S. No.	Organizational Culture	Mean	SD	Ranks
18.	Outward looking	4.03	0.79	17.5
19.	Responsiveness to the customer	3.99	0.85	19
20.	Participative	3.93	0.72	20
21.	Trust	3.89	0.85	21
22.	People orientation	3.83	0.74	22
23.	Communication and information flow: Vertical (a) Top-down	3.80	0.77	23.5
24.	Culture of celebration of achievements and successes	3.80	0.95	23.5
25.	Speed of response to internal demands	3.78	0.90	25
26.	Communication and information flow: Horizontal (a) Within the department	3.75	0.73	26
27.	Tolerance of differences	3.62	0.95	27
28.	Process focused	3.59	0.82	28
29.	Cross-functional collaboration	3.55	0.82	29
30.	Centralized design-making process	3.42	0.91	30
31.	Communication and information flow: Horizontal (b) Across the departments	3.38	0.85	31
32.	Community culture	3.32	0.95	32
33.	Communication and information flow: Vertical (b) Bottom-up	3.21	0.81	33

Source: Authors.

Table 5A.3 presents the ICICI organizational culture as perceived by the sample of top seventy-one ICICIans. For the purpose of analysis, the thirty-three questionnaire items have been grouped into three broad categories based on the responses on the 5-point scale alongside each statement: "Most Visible" with 4.00 and above mean value; "Highly Visible" with 3.70 to 3.99 mean value; and "Visible" with 3.21 to 3.69 mean value.

- Perusal of Table 5A.3 reveals that the scores on the work culture attributes range from 3.21 to 4.65, all being in the above average zone;

- This table also brings out that eighteen out of the thirty-three items are in the "Most Visible" range, eight items in the "Highly Visible" range, and seven in the "Visible" range; and
- There is significant homogeneity regarding the perceived work culture in ICICI as indicated by the standard deviation being less than 1.00 in the case of all the items. This shows that the ICICI work culture is viewed by respondents in a similar way, whether they are executive directors, senior general managers, general managers, or senior managers.

Further analysis of this table brings out the following salient features:

- Five broad clusters of organizational culture attributes prominently feature in the "Most Visible" category and are discussed ahead:
  - Performance orientation consists of items like result orientation, performance excellence, performance-based promotion, and focus on continuous improvement. This indicates that in ICICI, the performance bar is continuously raised; there is a credo for doing things better than before and there is a culture of contribution-centric meritocracy;
  - Receptivity and openness to new ideas consists of openness to new ideas, global perspectives, outward looking, and speed of response to external demands and challenges. Thus, the work culture of ICICI is reflective and prepared to process and absorb ideas both from within and outside;
  - Entrepreneurial ownership comprises of entrepreneurial, empowerment and delegation, and support for risk-taking;
  - Value-based governance includes ethical governance and openness and transparency;
  - Building people capability constitutes nurturing talent, teamwork, and role clarity.
- Items featuring in the "Highly Visible" category of culture contours are responsiveness to the customers, participative, trust, people orientation, communication and information flow—top-down, culture of celebration of achievement and success, speed of response to internal demands, communication and information flow—within department.

- The third work culture category that is "Visible" includes the following six items: tolerance of differences; process-focused; cross-functional collaboration; centralized the marketing process; communication and information flow—across departments; community culture; and communication and information flow—bottom-up.

Appendix 5A.4: Financial Performance of ICICI Bank at a Glance

Table 5A.4: Revenue and Profit of ICICI Bank, 2003–2009 (in ₹ billion)

Year	Income Revenue	Net Profit
2003	125.33	12.06
2004	119.59	16.37
2005	128.26	20.05
2006	187.68	25.4
2007	289.23	31.1
2008	395.99	41.58
2009	399.75	37.58
% Change over 2003	218.96	211.61

Source: Prowess database.

Anyone who watched the bank evolve would have no doubt that ICICI is here not just to stay and sustain itself, but grow and flourish beyond limits. It strives and creates to remain a leader not through sheer size but through its power to innovate.

Appendix 5A.5: K.V. Kamath as a Change Maestro—Analysis of Questionnaire Data

Table 5A.5: Perceived Style of K.V. Kamath as a Change Maestro

N = 71

S. No.	Change Maestro Attributes	Mean	SD	Ranks
1.	Has ambitious plans for the organization	4.97	0.17	1.5
2.	Is a visionary	4.97	0.17	1.5

(continued)

(continued)

S. No.	Change Maestro Attributes	Mean	SD	Ranks
3.	Is result focused	4.96	0.20	3
4.	Has a global mindset	4.93	0.31	4.5
5.	Is entrepreneurial	4.93	0.26	4.5
6.	Has high credibility	4.92	0.28	6
7.	Is a strategic thinker	4.86	0.35	7.5
8.	Is a role model	4.86	0.35	7.5
9.	Radiates positive energy	4.85	0.40	9
10.	Is demanding and performance centric	4.83	0.38	11
11.	Pursues excellence in everything	4.83	0.38	11
12.	Fast in making critical decisions	4.83	0.38	11
13.	Recognizes and rewards performance	4.8	0.44	13
14.	Provides a sense of clear direction	4.76	0.55	14
15.	Is reliable	4.65	0.72	15.5
16.	Business strategist	4.65	0.56	15.5
17.	Stands like a rock in the face of calamities	4.61	0.67	17
18.	Is innovative and creative	4.58	0.71	18
19.	Is interested in growth of his people	4.54	0.60	19
20.	Is open to new ideas	4.52	0.73	20
21.	Has empowering and supporting attitude	4.49	0.65	21
22.	Is honest and transparent	4.48	0.91	22
23.	Is a team builder	4.38	0.9	23
24.	Leads by example	4.31	0.89	24.5
25.	Grooms and develops people	4.31	1.04	24.5
26.	Is a man of words	4.3	0.96	26
27.	Leads from the front	4.24	0.98	27.5
28.	Is an effective communicator	4.24	0.96	27.5
29.	Makes people feel that they have great worth	4.21	0.83	29
30.	Is fair and impartial	4.16	0.84	30
31.	Respects the dignity of others	4.14	0.85	31
32.	Makes people feel that they are valued by the organization	4.09	0.92	32

S. No.	Change Maestro Attributes	Mean	SD	Ranks
33.	Has helping attitude	4	0.94	33
34.	Humility	3.96	1.09	34
35.	Sensitivity	3.9	0.98	35

Source: Authors.

Table 5A.5 presents the attributes of K.V. Kamath as a Change Maestro which have been broadly grouped into three categories: "Most Visible"—4.50 and above on a 5-point scale; "Highly Visible"—4.00 to 4.49 on a 5-point scale; and "Visible"—less than 4.00 on a 5-point scale:

- Twenty characteristics of K.V. Kamath feature in the "Most Visible" category, the mean values ranging from 4.52 to 4.97; thirteen leadership characteristics are in the "Highly Visible" category, the mean values ranging from 4.00 to 4.49; and only two items fall in the "Visible" category, the range being from 3.9 to 3.96.
- It is worthwhile to mention that out of the thirty-five items, thirty-three have a mean value of 4.00 and above which indicate a high degree of visibility of these qualities in the behavior K.V. Kamath.
- Perusal of the twenty items in the "Most Visible" category brings out that six of them have a strong futuristic and global orientation—visionary; ambitious plan; global mindset; strategic thinking; and business strategist.
  - Four of the competencies of K.V. Kamath in the first cluster (4.52 and above) bring out his focus on performance excellence—result-focused; pursues excellence; demanding and performance centric; and recognizes and rewards performance.
  - Further examination of the items in the "Most Visible" category indicates K.V. Kamath's entrepreneurial orientation, the items being entrepreneurial, speed in making critical decisions, openness to new ideas, and innovative and creative.
  - The remaining five qualities which feature in the "Most Visible" category are high credibility, role model, radiating positive energy, reliability, and

stands like a rock in the face of calamities. One people-related item in this cluster is interest in the growth of people. From this analysis, it is evident that K.V. Kamath has a versatile leadership style with a wide repertoire of leadership capabilities. K.V. Kamath is capable of operating simultaneously on multiple competencies like being futuristic, entrepreneurial, excellence-seeker, and people architect. Along with this, his other qualities (as presented earlier) make him inspirational, a role model, and a charismatic person with a heroic image.

- Thirteen qualities feature in the "Highly Visible" category are: empowering and supportive attributes; honesty and transparency and team builder; leads by examples; grooms and develops people; is a man of his word; leads from the front; effective communicator; fair and impartial; makes people feel that they have great worth; respects the dignity of others; makes people feel they are valued by the organization; and helping attitude. It is worth reiterating that although compared to items in the "Most Visible" cluster, these items (in the "Highly Visible" category) feature slightly on the lower side, however, it may be noted that they have high mean values, ranging from 4.00 to 4.40 on a 5-point scale. In other words, these leadership attributes are also clearly visible in K.V. Kamath's style and behavior.

Two items—humility and sensitivity—feature in the "Visible" category, both with mean values ranging from 3.9 to 3.96 that is, very close to 4.00.

Overall analysis of Table 5A.5 brings out the following striking features of K.V. Kamath's style and behavior as a Change Maestro:

- Majority of the items are in the "Most Visible" category. Almost all the items in this category have extremely high mean values.
- Only two items are in the "Visible" category.
- In all the items (except humility), the standard deviation is less than 1.00 indicating tremendous experienced homogeneity (in the eyes of the top and senior team members) about the Change Maestro competencies of K.V. Kamath.

Notes

1. Authors' views.
2. Authors gratefully acknowledge and appreciate the intellectual contributions and emotional support they received from Mr Ram Kumar, Director, Human Resources, ICICI Bank, in the course of this work. He spent many hours with authors in conceptualizing the framework and providing focused directions to the case. However, for the conclusions and views expressed in this case study of the ICICI Bank and regarding Mr K.V. Kamath as a Change Maestro, the authors own entire responsibility.
3. Twenty-five top team members were interviewed by the authors. The number of respondents varies since the interviewing method was largely unstructured; we recorded what they said, giving greater priority to what came out of top-of-the-mind in response to our broad questions, rather than getting them to respond to a set of questions.

6

SUNIL BHARTI MITTAL: THE GAME CHANGER

6

During one of his visits to Lucknow, Gandhi addressed a large gathering where he spoke about achieving freedom from British rule through the power of non-violence and non-cooperation. At the end of his speech, a well-known figure, Professor Acharya Kripalani commented, "Mr Gandhi, you may be a great authority on the Bible, Quran, and Gita but you don't have a sense of history. In the annals of history, there is not a single example of nations getting freedom without bloodshed and violence and here you are talking about freedom through non-cooperation and non-violence!" Through this comment, virtually, Kripalani conveyed that Gandhi was being unrealistic and impractical. In reply, Gandhi said, "Mr Kripalani, you may be right that Gandhi does not have a sense of history but Gandhi believes in creating history rather than being trapped by history." Through this statement, he communicated that history makers invariably creatively reinvent the paradigm and, thereby, change the rules of the game, rather than being trapped by tradition.

It may be worthwhile to explore the likely underpinnings of Gandhi's thought process in the context of India's freedom struggle. Gandhi was painfully aware of the abject absence of military power and the scarcity of required resources to precipitate a head-on collision with the British Empire which stood like Goliath. Perhaps, this prompted Gandhi to fight the war with the British using a non-traditional mode—non-cooperation and non-violence, which was hitherto unheard of. After Gandhi's successful *experiment with non-cooperation, it became a potent weapon used by many nations to assert and fight for freedom, notable examples being the struggle by Martin Luther King and Nelson Mandela. This powerful example brings out the message that great Change Maestros fight wars with their mighty enemies by creatively shifting the paradigm.*

This is the story of Bharti Airtel and its architect, Sunil Bharti Mittal, who in many ways, made game-changing moves in the telecom sector, like Gandhi had done in India's fight for freedom against the British. The rise of Airtel is similar to the story of David fighting Goliath using unconventional approaches, not treading the beaten path, boldly questioning established business models of vertical integration and replacing it with the model of virtual integration. Today, Bharti Airtel is a Marketing Company, having outsourced most of the activities including technology, which was once considered the core of the telecom business model. His initial steps in this direction were viewed with skepticism by telecom titans globally, but today, this has become the model which is adopted by many giants in the telecom space.

Albert Einstein puts it beautifully when he says, "Any intelligent fool can make things bigger and more compound.... It takes a touch of genius and a lot of courage to move in the opposite direction." Sunil Bharti Mittal is one of the rare geniuses who had the courage to go against the tide and carve out a new path, blazing a trail for others to follow. The story of Sunil Bharti Mittal encourages the new generation of aspiring entrepreneurs to escape the conformist tendencies and re-imagine, re-think, and re-parametricize the very boundaries of the business or project they undertake. He exhorts that innovation is the best way to win in this world—arguably, the only way to grow and succeed on a sustained basis.

This case study "Sunil Bharti Mittal: The Game Changer"[1] has been organized into the following three parts: Part I provides a brief profile sketch of Bharti Airtel; Part II highlights the action architecture and culture landscape of Bharti Airtel; and Part III discusses Sunil Mittal's profile and persona.

Part I: Brief Profile Sketch of Bharti Airtel

Bharti Telecom was set up in 1985 to manufacture India's first push button phones in collaboration with Siemens under the brand name Beetel. In its search for the right business opportunity, Bharti literally stumbled upon the telecom sector where Sunil Mittal (for details of the Change Maestro's profile, see Appendix 6A.1) felt in 1994–1995 "that this was the business of the future filled with opportunity." From such small beginnings Bharti Airtel was born (for details of the organization's profile, see Appendix 6A.2) in 1995. Today, Bharti Airtel is looked up to by the world for its innovative business models, its steep growth from operation in two circles, Delhi and Himachal Pradesh, with 0.1 million customers in as recently as 1999 to twenty-two circles and a 121.8 million customer base in December–April 2010 (179 million customers post takeover of Zain), making it the world's 5th largest mobile phone operator. The story is particularly stunning on account of the fact that the other players (in the telecom industry), who began operation in India around the same time, have been left far behind in the race to be the Number 1 telecom company. Bharti Airtel has, through strategic and bold moves, transformed itself into a force to be reckoned with in the telecom sector. Bharti Airtel has, in the last five years, grown by 642 percent in its revenue and 1,246 percent (see *Bharti Airtel Annual Report*, 2009: 7) in its profit. By any stretch of imagination and criterion, this growth is stupendous speaking volumes about Sunil Mittal's game-changing capabilities.

Part II: Action Architecture and Culture Landscape

The interview data analysis has been presented ahead as the following eight dominant themes:

- Entrepreneurial architecture
- Entrepreneurial innovation
- Mega vision with winning streak
- Customer always

- People power
- Performance excellence
- Ethical governance
- Mosaic culture

Entrepreneurial Architecture

The ingenuity of Airtel lies in evolving an entrepreneurial architecture, which is unconventional, never thought of, tried, and tested—so said all the interviewees. This entrepreneurial architecture has been radically different from the prevailing industry norms and practices in the telecom sector globally, again affirmed by all the interviewees.[2] The uniqueness of Airtel lies in not accepting prevalent practices and in continuously questioning them, as fifteen interviewees confirmed. Twelve executives said that Airtel constantly re-defines the paradigm and invents and evolves new business models which are more efficient, cost effective, customer-centric, and provide cutting-edge advantage to Airtel to be the industry leader. People further mentioned that they have developed their own paradigm of doing business which is radically different from the existing ones. Nine interviewees said: "Our business model has challenged the global conventional wisdom in telecom sector." Twelve interviewees said that the Airtel business model is solidly grounded in thorough understanding of the Indian business environment, customer profile, their spending capability, and Airtel's own financial resources.

The business model includes, according to twelve interviewees, working through joint ventures, partnerships, mergers and acquisitions, and outsourcing of technology, network, call centers, and select back-office functions. Fifteen interviewees said that Airtel believes in focusing on what "we can do the best" and outsource the rest to those who can do better than "us." Sixteen people informed us that in identifying partners, Airtel tied-up with the best in the business globally—Ericsson, IBM, Nokia, and others. Twelve people emphasized the unique relationship cultivated by Airtel with their partners. They said that Airtel's business model does not differentiate between the company and the service providers. Nine interviewees mentioned: "We genuinely believe they are our co-partners. In every meeting, relevant partners are always invited for discussions."

Twelve interviewees said their business architecture ensures that both company and co-partners (service providers and vendors) feel they are on the same side and both work for the same goal. Twelve people said that there is a win-win approach where all partners gain. Nine of them said Airtel is sensitive about partners and ensures that they are respected, and, as said by fifteen respondents, they are treated with dignity. Even those partners who have moved on (for various reasons), continue to have excellent relations with Airtel.

As many as six interviewees recalled when they started telecom services, British Telecom and Telecom Italia were Airtel's partners. They narrated that at that time, the telecom industry was operating on a set of assumptions and business principles: the first principle was that of Average Revenue Per User (ARPU)—the higher the ARPU, the better the company performance; the other popular notion was that a post-paid customer is a good customer, while a pre-paid customer is no good; therefore, pre-paid should be discouraged and post-paid should be emphasized; the third notion was that any company where the minutes of usage per customer were too high is doomed because the cost would be too high; the fourth big belief was that capital productivity in this industry must be very high—this was right, but the measure of productivity was capital expenditure as a percentage of sales; and the fifth principle was that rate per minute or tariff has to be very high. They said that at Airtel, after a few years of experience in the telecom industry, the top team re-examined these principles in the Indian context. After in-depth discussions, deliberations, and examination, they realized that all these notions did not hold good in the Indian context and concluded that each of these business tenets needed to be changed. Three of them went on to say that "had we followed these five tenets, India would have had about 25 million customers at the most." Such a figure was not acceptable to Sunil and Airtel. They said further that the top team looked at the business as a factory which produces minutes. Different factories produce different things; here, Airtel produces minutes. Like a factory, the aim was to produce and sell maximum number of minutes (which were being produced every day) and keep a certain margin per unit. Viewing the business from this perspective helped the team realize that along with post-paid, pre-paid is also a good business proposition, especially because it is a cash transaction and there are virtually no overheads (like selling and collecting the money) in dealing with the pre-paid product. Further, they realized that the more minutes more people used, the better it was for the company. Such thinking completely changed the business model. Another reason to focus on pre-paid was the affordability factor along with potentially large volumes. Therefore, the tariff in the pre-paid segment was deliberately kept low to promote widespread usage. The huge success of this model can be gauged from the fact that today, pre-paid constitutes more than 90 percent of the mobile telephony, according to the managing director of the company.

Twenty interviewees said that Airtel outsourced technology, including IT and network management, billing, and customer care. They said that "we" were the first one worldwide to outsource the entire network management and maintenance; "we" were the first to outsource billing (considered to be the heart of the telecom network); and "we" were the first ones to outsource the entire hardware, software, and billing management to IBM. Customer care was outsourced to the world's leading agencies like Mphasis and IBM-Daksh. This entrepreneurial architecture immensely helped Airtel in expanding the business base, making them highly cost competitive. All interviewees said with a sense of pride that this model is now followed globally. One person said that in India, this model has not only transformed Airtel, it has transformed society by building connectivity in the most remote areas of the country.

The DNA of this entrepreneurial culture is to seize the opportunity and move speedily for growth, affirmed nine interviewees. Twelve interviewees said Airtel believes in speedy growth and adopts both organic and inorganic growth strategies.

In Airtel, eleven interviewees said that marketing is the core competency and there is focused strategy on marketing, branding, and positioning. Sunil and the entire top team spend a lot of time on marketing, confirmed eighteen interviewees. All interviewees said that Sunil takes personal interest even in the choice of the brand ambassador, design of advertisements, and messages. All interviewees also said that the quality of Airtel advertisements is world-class.

Entrepreneurial Innovation

While entrepreneurial architecture primarily dealt with business models which contributed to the rapid growth of Airtel, in this section, an effort is made to highlight the processes and mindsets which facilitate innovation and keep the entrepreneurial passion burning bright.

All the interviewees said that Airtel is a highly ambitious organization. Sixteen interviewees described this in the following ways: Airtel has a mega vision and mega dream to be the best company in the world; it is a highly aggressive company; it is a fast-moving company; it is one company where risk-taking is encouraged and mistakes are not punished; the culture here encourages people to "go-ahead and do it." All the interviewees said that the telecom business is very competitive and that it is a war-like situation, where only the fittest will survive. There is a constant effort to become the fittest; there is always the zest to move from the best to the next in this war-like situation.

According to as many as eighteen interviewees, this is one company which is a great symbiosis of professional passion along with entrepreneurial zest. "Intrapreneuring" is the managerial mantra here—how to do things better; differently; and faster. Over the years, Airtel has moved from "Entrepreneurial Entrepreneurs" to "Entrepreneurial Professionals" focus. Today, Sunil Mittal and Airtel are very clear not to move from the "Entrepreneurial Professional" to "Professional Professional" model. Fifteen interviewees said that they do not want to lose the entrepreneurial fervor which Sunil Mittal has built over the years (which has been the basic force driving innovation, growth and movement from one horizon to the next at Airtel).

Interviewees further described the culture which supports innovation in Airtel: eighteen people said this company hates bureaucratization; sixteen said Airtel is nimble-footed; nine interviewees said "'we' have a small company soul and 'we' move with lightening speed;" and nine people said Airtel has the zest to create the future. Eleven people also used phrases like "positive disquiet," "creative dissatisfaction," and "restlessness" to describe the culture at Airtel. One interviewee claimed: "We want to keep moving ahead toward new horizons, transforming our organization, and creating new offerings to our customers."

As many as eight interviewees said that the mantra of Sunil Mittal is to learn, un-learn, and re-learn; the process involves forgetting the old practices in order to create the best. Wherever needed, current practices, strategies, and processes are removed to make way for next practices. In this company, there is continuous creative destruction: Create–Destroy–Recreate is in the Airtel DNA. As one of the directors in Bharti Airtel said, "we never liked where we have reached regardless of the massive success and magnificent milestones. There have been instances when we have systematically and methodically dismantled our own success models to create fresh ones." Airtel has enormous opportunity-sensing capability, as pointed out by fifteen interviewees. Eighteen people stressed the point that this company continuously seeks business opportunities and quickly grabs them. All interviews agreed that many business innovations have taken place in this company.

Mega Vision with Winning Streak

Everyone proudly expressed that Airtel is a unique company with big dreams and great vision. "In such a short span, we have built the largest customer base with market capitalization of ₹ 1,25,808 crores [₹ 1,258.08 billion]," with highest brand value in the telecom sector. Yet, for Sunil Mittal, this is just the beginning of a new journey. The MD said: "Our aim now is to be number one and fly our flag globally in many countries." Twenty-one people said that it is a collective vision and it is appropriate to dream now. It is the vision which is moving the organization forward at such a great pace, mentioned fifteen interviewees. One person was heard saying we never look back and constantly work to increase the distance between us and the next competitor. Twenty-one respondents said that this company always looks to the future. This is the one company with continuously expanding vision and continuously moving targets, said sixteen interviewees. All the interviewed people said that the biggest source of energy is the vision set by Sunil Mittal and his passion for the same.

It is not only about mega vision; there is an equal passion to achieve it and win, as indicated by the following statements:

Twenty interviewees said that this company runs ahead of others.

There is high restlessness here, said eighteen interviewees.

Fifteen people said in Airtel, there is so much to achieve.

Nine people responded by saying this company likes to work fast because the vision is so big.

Eighteen interviewees claimed people here love to take on challenges.

Twenty-one interviewees said people have a "can do" attitude in Airtel.

One person remarked, "whatever our competitors do in a certain span of time, we do the same in half the time."

We are a very aggressive company, affirmed nineteen interviewees.

We never feel diffident in the face of difficulties, mentioned fifteen people.

Airtel has a great fighting spirit, as confirmed by fifteen interviewees.

In fact, said nine interviewees, Sunil has the spirit of taking on challenges.

"Sunil never gives up," said twelve people.

Seven interviewees mentioned Sunil has resilience, tenacity, and perseverance to face any challenge with the spirit to win.

Five people said the company seeks opportunities in the face of adversities.

The spirit to win continuously pushes all of us to take up challenges with great passion, five interviewees pointed put.

Two interviewees said "our winning spirit is behind our phenomenal growth and outstanding success in a short span of ten years."

It is no wonder, therefore, that Airtel has already achieved the vision set forth to be achieved by 2010 a year ahead of schedule.

Customer Always

Twenty-two interviewees said that Sunil Mittal strongly believes that the customer is at the heart of the business and also said that they subscribe to this. Fifteen interviewees claimed Bharti Airtel believes in doing business keeping the customer interest at the center. "Begin with the end in mind" is the motto here, confirmed nine respondents.

Nine among the total people interviewed also explained that Airtel believes in evolving its business model keeping the customers' needs in mind. "Airtel's move toward mass scale pre-paid customer acquisition was based on understanding the customer needs and affordability," said twelve people. Five members of the top team said, "we carry out extensive market research ourselves" which indicates the high focus of the company on understanding the customer. Eighteen people said: "We want to have a first hand feel of the customer issues and problems." According to five interviewees, Sunil Mittal believes in understanding the customer and himself goes and meets them. Likewise, other members of the top team also practice this, sometimes even going to remote villages to experience moments of truth. Airtel wants to build such a deep connect with the customers that they should view Airtel with the trust of LIC and the innovation of Apple, said the MD. Fifteen interviewees said that Airtel wants to continuously connect, trust, and strengthen "our" relationship with the customers. The brand "Airtel" has been built in a short period of just over a decade, a brand which touches the heart of everyone across 1.2 billion Indians, mentioned nine interviewees. We continuously launch new products and services, said Airtel's MD. He further said people love it even if they do not use the new features.

In Airtel, special attention is paid to the call centers dealing with customer issues, grievances, and problems. Nine interviewees said "we closely monitor their functioning and do extensive analysis of the data flowing from there to improve our customer-related processes."

According to three top leaders of Airtel, Sunil Mittal says:

> ... we must win the heart of both the Blackberry customer who gives us ₹ 50,000 a month as well as the humble villager who gives us ₹ 50 per month. We go all out to connect across the entire spectrum of customers, not just the Blackberry user.

As also said by Sunil Mittal:

> Airtel has very heavy customer orientation, we are very touchy when a customer comes back to us saying he is not satisfied with our services, it is like a crisis in the organization, right from the top to bottom every body's goal is to build businesses which are serving the customers.

People Power

Sunil Mittal has built a company where the slogan is "Employees First, Customer Always." As many as eighteen interviewees said that they are excited to work here because it is a caring, friendly, and helpful company. Twenty-one interviewees said the company provides immense space and freedom to experiment, take risks, try new methods, and innovate. Eighteen interviewees also said that they feel deeply connected to this company because of the way "we are valued, respected and made to feel special" by the Chairman and the MD. Sunil is accessible and humble, said twenty-one interviewees; eighteen interviewees said "he has tremendous listening ability." Sunil is very inspirational and we feel charged even if we meet him for a few minutes, remarked twenty interviewees. Nine people said Airtel has got a small company soul. There is a sense of community, connectedness, and bonding, said twenty-one interviewees. Eighteen people said Airtel grooms, builds, and mentors people to become better leaders.

All the interviewees highlighted that the greatest excitement to work in Airtel is the high level of empowerment and freedom the company provides. This company believes in delegation and empowerment, not close supervision, confirmed twelve interviewees. One person said this place gives people the opportunity to utilize their potential and provides them with a platform to prove their worth. Eleven interviewees said Airtel believes that innovation, thinking differently, out-of-box approach, and building a cutting-edge organization emanate from the quality of people.

The focus on empowerment in this organization emerges from the realization that the most potent resource which Airtel has is its people, as the MD affirmed. Many of the interviewees (twelve of them) said that the slogan "Employees First, Customer Always" is based on the belief that if employees are fully empowered, if employees are given freedom to experiment, if employees are highly motivated, and if employees are fully trained, they will serve the customer better and make them happy. One of the directors said, "Airtel believes that companies win the wars [of competition] not only through the power of weapons but through the passion, fervor, excitement, enthusiasm, and commitment of people." The faith in people power has led the company to hire the best quality people globally—those who have had global exposure and global outlook—to fulfill the dream to become a truly global MNC.

Performance Excellence

All the interviewees said that there was high focus on performance excellence in Airtel and described it as follows:

> In Airtel performance excellence is a moving target; it is a journey not a destination; it is always re-defined and the performance bar is continuously raised; result orientation is very high in this company; the entrepreneurial reward structure, promotions, recognition, and celebration are geared at promoting performance excellence and target achievement.

Along with delegation and empowerment, twelve persons said that there is a clear and sharp definition of accountability through key result areas; there are stretch targets, creation of challenges, excitement, and high energy, as eighteen interviewees confirmed. People do not get a chance to slide into the comfort zone in this company because according to eighteen interviewees, everyday brings new excitement, new demands, and new challenges. Twelve interviewees said that since Airtel is a highly entrepreneurial and innovative company, there is constant creation of new demands and new challenges for its employees. Along with the challenging work environment, six interviewees said Airtel has, for many years, also practiced the Balanced Score Card Systems focusing on topline growth, market share growth, Earnings before Interest, Taxes, Depriciation, and Amortization (EBITDA) growth, brand score, people motivation, etc. In this company, nine interviewees claimed performance is monitored monthly on these parameters and corrective actions are evolved.

Six interviewees clearly said that Sunil Mittal believes not only in the dream, he simultaneously emphasizes execution excellence—to be the best; the fastest; and the most competitive. Thus, speedy execution without losing focus on quality is the mantra of Airtel.

Fourteen executives cited that Airtel's shift in focus over the years from speed to quality to customer to employee has demanded new competencies, new mindsets, and new skills, thus, bringing new challenges and excitement and continuous renewal of employee capabilities.

Ethical Governance

The interviewees cited some notable awards won by Airtel between 2006 and 2008: In 2008, it won the World's 25 most valuable telecom brands award awarded by Brand Finance Plc; in 2007–2008, the Top telecom company of the year (2007) awarded by NDTV Profit; in 2006, it was among the top 10 best performing companies in the world. The company has received the highest Governance and Value Creation (GVC), namely, Level 1 rating by Credit Rating and Information Services of India Ltd (CRISIL) in 2004, 2006, and 2008. According to the interviewees, these awards are testimony to the confidence which Bharti Airtel enjoys in the public domain. This reiterates Bharti Airtel's capability in creating wealth for its stakeholders while adopting sound corporate governance practices.

All the twenty-one interviewees said that one thing that clearly distinguishes "us" from many other large companies is the culture of extreme transparency and ethical approach nine interviewees said they do not mind taking on any party on matters of principles; on matters of principle, Airtel does not compromise, said eighteen interviewees. Five people said we never give any incorrect (false) statement, while eight said we never promise anything that we cannot fulfill. We follow the law of the land, mentioned twelve respondents. Five interviewees said while fighting with competitors, we explore innovative solutions and building competitive edge rather than using unethical means and questionable practices. In fact ethical governance is the cornerstone of our group, said one respondent.

People cited Sunil Mittal's belief in this matter, saying, "adoption of unethical means can give only temporal edge but in the long run, only the right means will make us the leader and the winner."

Sunil Mittal believes in *Satyameva Jayate* as the winning philosophy, two interviewees noted. Airtel follows strict disclosure norms to all stakeholders, said nine interviewees. Five people said Airtel has a very distinguished board with many eminent members like Arun Bharat Ram, Ajay Lal, N. Kumar,

Pulak Chandan Prasad, and many others. They also said the company has many board-level committees like Audit Committee, HR and Remuneration Committee, and Investor Grievance Committee. The company has a formal code of conduct which, according to five interviewees, is signed by everybody who joins the company.

Five interviewees said while dealing with stakeholders, the company is extremely fair and transparent, and with a win-win spirit, ensures that everyone benefits and grows. As many as eight participants said that Bharti always demonstrates courage of conviction to stand up for what is right rather than only doing the right things. This stance makes it very clear to all employees what Airtel stands for and what is the right path to walk in this company. Nineteen people highlighted that Bharti Airtel also has a strong social conscience with spirit of giving back to the society through Bharti Foundation which provides schools and teachers in rural areas.

Mosaic Culture

As many as ffiteen interviewees talked of Bharti Airtel as a mosaic in a melting pot (like the USA). All the interviewees said that Airtel values diversity whether by gender, race, region, industry experience, or range of global exposure. According to the Head, HR, most of the people at senior and middle levels have come in from different companies—Pepsi, Coke, Unilever, IBM, etc.—based strictly on their merit; each one brings in something unique which is valued by Airtel.

Eighteen interviewees brought out that there is a strong belief in the company that diversity brings in new thinking, new approaches, and new innovations, which together create a cutting-edge organization. Some of the executives (six, in this case) said that there is a conscious effort to bring in diversity in Airtel, whether it is in vendor selection or hiring talent, without sacrificing excellence. Airtel is also trying to build a gender balance, according to the Head, HR. The great success of Airtel lies in creating convergence in the thinking and approach among diverse people so that all move toward the larger organizational goal, as mentioned by nine interviewees. Eighteen interviewees said that the company believes in, and consistently practices, a win-win approach, respect for people, establishing co-partners, and valuing good ideas, along with being upfront and adopting ethical practices. Summing this in Sunil Mittal's words, one can say Airtel comprises "a team of stars which is trying very hard to be a star team."

Action Architecture and Culture Landscape of Bharti Airtel: Salient Contours

A combined view of the responses from interviews and questionnaire (for details of questionnaire data of organizational culture of Bharti Airtel, see Appendix 6A.3) reveals the following striking picture of Bharti Airtel achievements, action architecture, and culture landscape:

- Airtel has demonstrated a truly unprecedented and mind-boggling growth both in its revenue as well as profits (for details of financial performance of Bharti Airtel from 2003–2009, see Appendix 6A.4). In the last six years (2003–2009), its income revenue has grown from ₹ 17 billion to approximately ₹ 374 billion, registering a growth of 1,511 percent. In 2003, the net profit was ₹ 0.002 billion which touched approximately ₹ 79 billion in 2009. The profits for this period have grown 39,294 percent. The expansion of customer base from 10,000 in a single circle in 1997 to 135 million in 2010 has been a true saga of the pioneering spirit of Airtel to become India's largest telecom giant. After the Zain takeover in 2010, Airtel has become the 5th largest telecom player globally. Airtel's stupendous achievements and contributions have been recognized through a galaxy of awards, notably, the following: it was ranked among the 50 best listed companies in Asia-Pacific region by Forbes, recalled eight interviewees; world's most valuable telecom brands, said eight interviewees; company of the year by *The Economic Times*, said seven interviewees; and Asia's best GSM Carrier awarded by Telecom Asia, as recalled by five interviewees.
- In Airtel, there is continued thrust on building competitive edge and making it a truly global organization.
- The company culture is entrepreneurial, outward focused with thrust on making the business rules rather than following the beaten track.

- Bharti Airtel is a company where there is a zest to win through out-of-the-box thinking and people power.
- Airtel believes in the dictum of "Begin with the end in mind" which has made it a truly customer-centric organization.
- Airtel emphasizes results along with vibrant zest for performance excellence.
- The most distinctive feature of Airtel has been it is highly transparent and ethical governance system.
- Airtel bets on its people and lays emphasis on taking care of them and grooming them.
- In Airtel, the response to external demands and challenges has been extremely speedy.

In sum, Airtel powerfully uses multiple drivers of competitiveness—ethical governance; people power; customerization; entrepreneurial innovation; performance excellence; and speedy response—for building competitive edge and creating a winning and game changing organization.

Part III: Sunil Mittal—His Profile and Persona

The following eleven themes emerged from the interview data:

- Visionary
- Entrepreneurial
- Empowering
- Inspirational
- Man of the people
- Learning and evolving
- Humility
- Ethical
- Global mindset
- Winning streak
- Balancing contradictions

Visionary

All the twenty-one interviewees unanimously said that Sunil is a highly visionary leader. Twelve interviewees said he is a man with a mega vision: he really thinks big and has faith in his vision and dream. Twelve people also said he has tremendous ability to dream big and also to realize them. He is not only visionary: he is extremely bold, courageous, and an ambitious leader, said fifteen people. Twenty interviewees said that even when he was not a big player, he still had faith in his vision and grand dream. All the interviewees spoke in awe of the fact that fifteen years ago, even though Sunil was a small player in telecom operating only in the Delhi circle, he was dreaming of making Airtel the world's best, largest, and most admired company.

Nineteen people said that Sunil's vision keeps expanding as the company reaches new milestones. Everyone cited the phenomenal growth of the company starting from a small single circle operating in Delhi in 1995 to the present day when Airtel has its presence in all the twenty-two circles covering every nook and corner of this country. It has approximately 120 thousand route km of optic fiber spread across the country (*Bharti Airtel Annual Report*, 2009) and over 100 thousand base stations across the country, covering 84 percent of the population. Their customer base has today touched a whopping 125 million from a mere 0.1 million in 1999 (Source: Company IPO document in http://airtel.in/wps/wcm/connect/about+bharti+airtel/Bharti+Airtel/Investor+Relations/Shares).

According to eighteen interviewees, this phenomenal growth has taken place because of Sunil's vision and leadership.

According to one of the executives in the top leadership team, in spite of the phenomenal growth experienced by Airtel, Sunil is that rare leader who is never satisfied with his achievements and looks ahead at the next curve of achievement. He sees every achievement as a part of the journey and with every step, his dream grows bigger.

According to seventeen interviewees, Sunil has a huge amount of self-propelling drive within and ability to continue pushing on. The most recent and stunning indicator of Sunil's bold vision is the intent to double customer base from 100 million to 200 million; eight people said that Sunil thinks ahead to the next two years, three years, or five years, and works out alternatives and options. His scenario-building is on a much bigger canvas than most leaders they have worked with. People think of the normal scenario, while Sunil thinks beyond the obvious, visible, and unpredictable scenarios.

Entrepreneurial

All the interviewees lauded Sunil Mittal as highly entrepreneurial. In fact, fourteen interviewees said that not only is he an entrepreneur par excellence, he converts possibilities into results; nine people said he makes the impossible possible; twenty-one said he is futuristic and is great at spotting opportunities, which is how he moved into telecom industry; and eighteen interviewees said he quickly converts the threat into opportunities, rather than cry over problems. According to fourteen interviewees, he has some sixth sense in sensing opportunities. Not only does Sunil have an opportunity-sensing mind, he is able to convert the same into strategic actions.

Fifteen people see him as decisive and firm and once his mind is made up, he pushes the idea through. All interviewees highlighted him as a bold and courageous decision-maker and said that he has strong risk-taking ability. Once he is convinced of an idea, he pursues it till the end, confirmed twelve respondents. Sunil believes in being the mover first in sensing and seizing the opportunity. As many as eighteen interviewees gave the example of his decision to be the first mover in the rural sector, while other players were awaiting government subsidy. When the government did not announce the expected subsidy, those directly dealing with this proposal felt low. Three interviewees mentioned when they discussed this matter with him he said, "lets move ahead anyway. While the other players wait for the subsidy, we will go rural and we will get the first mover advantage."

The story of Bharti Airtel's steep ascent is in fact the story of Sunil Mittal and his strong entrepreneurial spirit. The twists and turns which the company took since its early beginnings, the way the company got into the telecom business, and the strategic decisions Airtel made ahead of others, are all indicative of his highly opportunity-sensing, risk-taking, speedy, bold, and confident mindset, all of these being an integral part of the entrepreneurial fabric. As many as eighteen interviewees said that Sunil works on the concept of creating co-intrapreneurs. Nineteen interviewees mentioned in Airtel we have entrepreneurs at multiple levels and said that people here work in a non-bureaucratic manner.

Empowering

All interviewees highly appreciated Sunil's empowering and supportive style. Fifteen of them said that he delegates a lot, and according to nineteen others, he believes in empowering others. Eleven people said that they had never experienced so much of independence of authority and operation in any other organization. Once he has confidence and trust in you, he gives you full authority and delegation, said nine respondents.

Eighteen among the total number of interviewees said that Sunil is a supportive leader who wants the team to aim and think big. He wants "us" to do what is needed and efforts are made to help and support, remarked nine interviewees. Five interviewees said he has a highly enabling approach and does not believe in the commanding approach. He encourages people to take bold decisions, mentioned fifteen respondents. According to one of the top executives, Sunil says, "go ahead and take the decision. I will back you if something goes wrong. As long as your heart is in the right place when you took that decision, don't worry about the consequences." He is known to advice the CEO of every business to "take charge, do things which are right for the organization, if mistakes happen, we will back you up. Don't worry, nothing will happen go ahead."

Empowering people and backing them up, this is a part of the Airtel ethos, according to eighteen interviewees. Fifteen interviewees said this has inspired people in Bharti Airtel to innovate, take risks, and perform fearlessly. We have never seen him taking personal credit for Bharti's achievements, commented nine interviewees. Twelve people said when he talks of success he gives full credit to the team. Eight interviewees affirmed he believes in shared and collective leadership. "Through this style he has inspired all of us to give our best," said twelve people.

Inspirational

Sunil Mittal is a highly inspiring and motivating leader, said all the interviewees. Twenty people said he is a man of high energy. According to all the interviewees, he sets stretch goals for himself and works hard to meet them. When people see him like a commander in the field, the troops get energized automatically, commented nine interviewees. Eleven people said his enthusiasm and passion galvanizes and motivates people. One interviewee said Sunil is very inspiring; he encourages intense debates and discussions on issues and those who participate in them walk away feeling very excited, valued, and elated. Another interviewee said through his style, he brings out the best in the people around him. Five interviewees said even his presence in the room is stimulating and increases participation in discussions and a lot of people come up with creative ideas. A set of eleven people said when you meet Sunil, you feel charged and energized.

According to fifteen people, Sunil makes them feel they are valued and extremely important to the company. Nine interviewees mentioned he is authentic, straightforward, and value-based. He walks the talk and makes sure that the stated values are lived and practiced, said twelve interviewees. Whereas nine people said Sunil is decisive, bold, and courageous and always believes that action is better than inaction.

Sunil addresses the top 100 leaders formally twice a year. Nineteen people said that they eagerly await these events; listening to him is like taking a booster shot which pumps the adrenalin and makes us want to do more and more, said one interviewee. He is a passionate speaker, creating tremendous impact on the audience, according to nine interviewees. Twelve people said that he makes people feel that they are an integral part of the Airtel community. Airtel's vision is not only the vision of Sunil Bharti Mittal; it is also "our" vision, as per nine respondents. Through his empowering style, one person asserted that Airtel's vision became a shared vision and his values have become our shared values.

In addition to his impact on the audience as mentioned in the previous paragraphs, the interviewed people also highlighted his capability to connect with people one to one as mentioned ahead:

According to eighteen interviewees, he has great interpersonal skills in dealing with people and getting the best out of them.

He is an intense listener and gives full attention to what you have to say, making you feel that your ideas are valued, said twelve people.

Fifteen interviewees claimed he is a great communicator and speaks from the heart.

Sunil has a powerful engaging style, mentioned nine interviewees.

According to nine people, Sunil Mittal's greatest strength is that he is able to connect with as a human being rather than only as a leader. Any meeting with him is not merely transactional; it is inspirational.

In fact, as per five interviewees, he is highly charismatic and in his company, and people feel elated and charged around him.

Man of the People

All the interviewees said that Sunil's capability to connect with people, establish relationships, and nurture the same is phenomenal. Fifteen people said that he shares a strong bond with his own people. Twenty interviewees said he has an evolved sensitivity to people-related issues and concerns. He has a great memory and normally addresses people by their name, recalled eighteen respondents. In one to one meetings, eighteen people were heard to mention, Sunil is an intense listener paying full attention to what the person is saying. One person said, "it is like he has tuned into your frequency and is with you for the duration of the meeting." Nine respondents said he shows tremendous warmth and regard while communicating with people. Nine interviewees also said he always ensures that the other person is comfortable. Nine interviewees also observed that Sunil brings a strong personal touch while dealing with a person's problems and concerns. His sensitivity towards people is so high that he knows exactly how to deal with the person before him, as mentioned by one respondent.

According to six interviewees, he cherishes relationships with people and has nurtured them over the years; he has maintained such relations with those who knew him when he was an ordinary man. In every meeting that anyone has with Sunil, he leaves a positive and abiding impact, said nineteen respondents. Nine interviewees said people in Airtel look up to him; according to five, they see him as more than a business leader and value the opportunity to meet him and work with him. According to twelve interviewees, in Airtel, people can do anything for him and, thirteen people said that his people-centric style has created a community which has close ties and bonds. According to thirteen of them, he is great networker and has built abiding relationships at different levels—political executives; bureaucrats; business leaders; and others.

Sunil Mittal's people-centric style has created many friends and admirers. Sunil says: "My natural layer is compassion, I like to help people, I like to do things for them you know ... and that comes in the form of our Bharti foundation and other works."

Learning and Evolving

Fourteen interviewees who have worked closely with him for more than a decade said that Sunil Mittal is continuously evolving as a leader; he learns from moment to moment. All the interviewees said that Sunil Mittal has a hunger to learn and continuously improve himself and Airtel.

According to twelve team members who have seen him from the beginning, he is a man who continuously re-invents—Airtel has been re-invented many times in terms of strategy; structure; processes; focus; and culture in the short decade and a half of its existence. Fifteen interviewees gave the example of Airtel as an evolving organization. They said that initially Airtel was an entrepreneur–entrepreneur company, which it then re-invented into an entrepreneur–professional company, and now it is a professional–entrepreneur company, as also mentioned earlier in this chapter.

Interestingly, nine people said that Sunil is a leader who has no hesitation to accept his limitations and ask questions if he does not know something. Although he has strong views on issues, he is amenable to changing them. All interviewees said that he listens to contrarian views without rejecting them outright and is prepared to accept them depending on the logic. Fourteen interviewees said he has a reflecting temperament and he mulls over issues. Over the years, as ten people said, people have noticed his shift from being a typical entrepreneur to an entrepreneur manager to an entrepreneur mentor. Today, he has delegated organizational issues and spends a lot of time in building the leadership pipeline.

Again, nine interviewess said he constantly updates himself on new developments in a wide range of domains including the telecom sector. Eighteen interviewees said that Sunil's spirit of inquiry is very high; he is curious, experimenting, always exploring new business models, managerial practices, and processes.

All the interviewees confirmed that it is his vision and learning stance which are responsible for transformation of Airtel.

Humility

All the interviewees said that Sunil is a symbol of humility. Twenty people said that Sunil is a global business icon in terms of wealth creation, institution building, evolving new business models in creating the fastest growing company in telecom sector, etc. They said that given his global stature, phenomenal achievement, and numerous accolades, it is surprising that success has not affected him; it has not made him arrogant and self-opinionated. Twelve interviewees appreciated his large bandwidth in terms of his capability to connect with heads of state, global business icons as well as a humble rural customer. All interviewees unequivocally said that even today, he is approachable, accessible, and easy to communicate with—he is available over the phone and SMS anytime of the day or night.

The interviewees also expressed in different ways why they considered Sunil to be humble—he is down to earth; in touch with the ground reality; simple in his living and eating habits; he does not throw tantrums; he never throw his weight around; or he still does not mind going and meeting a clerk in any ministry of the government if the work requires it.

Some people (five among the total interviewed group) narrated that when he invites people to his house for dinner, he takes care to ensure that the menu is perfect, and even if there are a hundred guests, he will personally escort each person; he makes you feel that you are valued and special, said seven people in this context. Eight of them narrated the recent bi-annual address to the top 100 leaders. Sunil began his address by saying:

> Wherever I travel in the world, I have access to attend meetings with heads of state and highly accomplished business leaders, but let me tell you guys, that this has been possible because of the hard work that each one of you has put in and the kind of Airtel that you have created. If it was not for your efforts, I would not have for the opportunity to rub shoulders with the sort of people that I do....

Some interviewees mentioned noticing moistening of his eyes as he spoke and said one could make out from his voice that he was speaking from his heart and meant every word; we could see that he was genuine, authentic, and honest, said three interviewees.

Ethical

All the interviewees said that honesty, transparency, and ethical and value-centric approach lie at the core of Sunil's character and style. Nineteen of them said that Sunil is honest, whereas fifteen said he is highly transparent. Fifteen people mentioned he always says: "Do the right thing."

Eight interviewees said that Airtel has gone through some very trying moments sometimes because of the fierce competition and, sometimes, because of government policies. Even in the worst situations, Sunil's motto has been to do the right thing, not to cut corners, adopt the right means, and follow the ethical governance route.

Sunil is one person who is above divisions of caste, creed, community, and country: he values diversity. Fairness, equity, and justice are the cornerstones of Airtel's reward policy. He values people for their ideas and contributions and not because of other considerations.

Nine interviewees said when the competition in the telecom industry intensified and the undercutting war began, Sunil said, "we shall fight in the ring and we shall play by the rules." Further, as fifteen interviewees mentioned, he said that the market will decide who will be the winner, not the government or unscrupulous players. All the interviewees mentioned, in such times, he said, "be focused, keep the customers happy, and the rest will follow."

Global Mindset

All the interviewees highlighted that Sunil Bharti Mittal believes in creating an organization of global scale and global reach. He believes that Airtel should set global benchmarks, as twenty interviewees mentioned. Eleven of them said Sunil's vision is to make Airtel an Indian MNC operating in different parts of the world.

Toward this end, Sunil has made efforts to have strategic alliances and joint ventures with global giants to broaden their "presence," as twelve interviewees confirmed. Nine people said Sunil has constituted a truly global board bringing in the best persons from all over the world. He has hired global talent and his top team today has people with global experiences and exposure, mentioned eleven respondents. Today, six people said, Sunil has become a global ambassador for India. One person confirmed at the global level, he represents India as part of many business delegations.

Winning Streak

All the interviewees said that Sunil Mittal possesses a great winning streak; they said that he believes in fighting the war rather than getting obsessed with winning the battle. Fifteen interviewees also said that he is highly perseverant, tenacious, and an optimist who never gives up. He has a huge fund of self-belief, as well as being bold and courageous, said fourteen interviewees. Fourteen of them said that his relentless quest to be the best and to be on the top indicates his intense winning streak. Many interviewees (twelve of them) said that he loves to find ingenious and innovative solutions to problems rather than win by using any means. One person described his reaction saying, "His eyes gleam at the thought of competition."

Using the chess analogy, five respondents said he thinks many moves ahead as compared to the opponent. "He is a great business strategist," said fifteen respondents, and, as per nine respondents, they have not met someone of this caliber. In the face of competition, nine interviewees said he is quick to re-orient the business strategy, to seize the opportunity, and gain the first-mover advantage.

Balancing Contradictions

Eighteen people lauded Sunil Mittal for balancing a range of contradictions. Eleven of them talked of him being both a visionary and a practical person with his feet on the ground; he flies high, yet is able to connect to ground realities. Fourteen interviewees commented that he is a dreamer, yet has an intuitive sense of the moment and acts with speed. He is an inspirational leader and a people's person, yet is a private person, according to five respondents. Seven people said he has burning ambition, yet believes in treading the ethical path. Amazingly, as per twelve interviewees, he combines high self-confidence with humility.

SUNIL MITTAL AS A CHANGE MAESTRO: SALIENT CONTOURS

Interview and questionnaire findings (for details of questionnaire data of Sunil Mittal's Change Maestro style, see Appendix 6A.5) bring out the following major profile and style characteristics of Sunil Mittal as a Change Maestro and person:

- Sunil Mittal is an entrepreneurial game changer, a dreamer with global vision, and possesses mega ambition.
- He is a powerful strategic thinker and business strategist par excellence along with tremendous business sense.
- Sunil Mittal is outstanding in connecting with people, respecting their dignity, and enabling and supporting them.
- He is highly result-focused, with tremendous speed of decision-making.
- Sunil Mittal is a truly game changing giant, who beautifully integrates vision, passion, and action.
- He has created Bharti Airtel where entrepreneurial innovation, customer centricity, performance excellence, and ethical governance are ways of life.
- All these capabilities of Sunil Mittal indicate that his bandwidth as a Change Maestro is very large.
- He fires all the cylinders of leadership—task, people, innovation, ethical governance, speed, and performance excellence—for achieving competitive edge and building a global telecom giant.

- Sunil Mittal's landmark contributions in such a short span of time have won him many awards, notably, Padma Bhushan, as nine interviewees mentioned, the Global Economy Prize by KIEL Institute, Germany, as nine interviewees recalled; the JRD Corporate Leadership Award by All India Management Association (AIMA), recalled by seven interviewees and, as five interviewees mentioned, the Best Asian Telecom CEO.
- Sunil Mittal is a man passionately possessed by the Airtel dream, always thinking and strategizing to take the company to the next horizon. He is a highly value-based person.
- He uses his formidable oratorical skills to passionately inspire his people with the big dream. He is a man who continuously meditates and reflects on Airtel. He is courageous and takes bold challenges head on and winning in many difficult situations.

Sunil Bharti Mittal: Concluding Contours

Sunil Bharti Mittal is the highly respected and well-known game changer of the telecom sector at the global level. He is the entrepreneur par excellence who has taken his organization to undreamt of heights. He is a dreamer possessed by the passion to make Airtel a global Goliath.

His voracious appetite for growth has been expanding with each success, which is reflected in the unparalleled and unprecedented growth of the company by any standard. He has evolved a new business model of co-partnership and virtual integration—something unheard of in the telecom sector—and made a huge success of it. Today, this model has many admirers and imitators. Sunil's vision for Airtel is truly global and transnational, and he is making Airtel continuously strive to realize this vision.

Sunil is a person for whom work is the biggest passion; he is switched on 24/7. Like a deer in the jungle, his mind is constantly jumping to sense what is happening around him. He has a great opportunity-sensing mind which he powerfully uses to strategize business plans of Airtel. Sunil Mittal is highly value centric, believes in ethical governance, and in fighting from within the ring, rather than stooping to use unfair means.

His capability to connect and build relationships is extraordinary, enabling him to gather many giants as co-partners of Airtel. He is extremely positive and believes in playing a win-win game. He is a highly inspiring orator who can galvanize people through the power of his passionate sharing of the dream for Airtel. He leads from the front and stands like a rock in the face of calamities. He is a people's man, strongly compassionate, and highly empowering. He influences people through the power of his role modeling where he integrates precept with practice.

Sunil has built an amazing corporate culture where there is self-driven credo of performance excellence; where entrepreneurial innovation is a way of life; where people have high empowerment; where human dignity is respected; where there is a culture of customer centricity, global outlook, ethical governance, and performance-centric reward systems; and where there is tremendous sense of community and familial concern. It is no wonder, thus, that Airtel has scaled many new heights and Sunil Bharti Mittal is considered to be India's telecom czar.

APPENDICES

Appendix 6A.1: Brief Sketch of Sunil Bharti Mittal

Sunil Bharti Mittal is the icon of first generation entrepreneurs and the youngest transformational leader of India. As the founder Chairman and Group CEO of Bharti Enterprises Limited, he has defined the growth and development of telecommunication sector in India and with remarkable prescience and entrepreneurial zeal diversified to other sectors of the economy—financial services; retail; manufacturing; realty; and agri-business.

Mr Mittal serves on several distinguished boards and committees. Some of the prominent ones include Board of Trustees of Carnegie Endowment for International Peace, Leadership Council of The Climate Group, Telecom Board of the International Telecommunication Union, International Business Council of the World Economic Forum, International Advisory Committee to the Board of Directors of NYSE Euro-next, International Business Advisory Council of

London, and the Advisory Board of the Global Economic Symposium. Besides, he is also on the boards of reputed academic institutes helping them initiate the change process. Prominent among them are Harvard Business School India Advisory Board, Executive Board of the Indian School of Business, Cambridge India Partnership Advisory Board, and INSEAD Global India Council.

Mr Mittal is the recipient of numerous awards and accolades which have recognized his invaluable contribution to Indian business. He has been honored with the Padma Bhushan, one of India's highest civilian awards. He is a member of Indo-US CEOs Forum and is also a former president of the CII (2007–2008).

Table 6A.1: Accolades to Sunil Bharti Mittal over the Last Decade, 2000–2009

2009	• Lal Bahadur Shastri National Award for Excellence in Public Administration, Academics, and Management.
	• "Global Economy Prize 2009" awarded by Kiel Institute, Germany.
2008	• "Global Vision" Award 2008 awarded by US–India Business Council (USIBC).
	• "GSMA Chairman's Award, 2008" awarded by GSM Association.
	• "Business Leader Transforming India, 2008" by NDTV Profit.
	• "Telecom Person of the Year" by Tele.net Telecom Operator Awards, 2008.
2007	• "Lakshmipat Singhania—IIM Lucknow National Leadership Award, 2007."
	• "JRD Tata Corporate Leadership Award, 2007" by All India Management Association.
	• "Business Leader of the Year, 2007" awarded by NDTV Profit.
	• "CEO of the Year, 2007" awarded by *Business Standard*.
	• Featured among *Business Week*'s top 50 influential Indians, 2007.
	• Outstanding Business Leader Award 2007 by Society of Indian Law Firms and ASSOCHAM.
2006	• "Asia Pacific CEO of Year, 2006" by Frost & Sullivan ICT Awards.
	• "Asia Businessman of the Year, 2006" by *Fortune*.
	• "Telecom Man of the Year 2006" by Voice&Data Online.

(continued)

(continued)

	• "Top Executive of the Year" by *Asiamoney* Awards, 2006. • Corporate and Philanthropic Leadership Award 2006 by American India Foundation. • Special Recognition Award 2006 by UK Trade and Investment India Business Awards.
2005	• "Business Leader of the Year, 2005" by *The Economic Times*. • "Best Asian Telecom CEO, 2005" by Telecom Asia.
2004	• "Asia Pacific CEO of Year, 2004" by Frost & Sullivan Asia Pacific ICT Awards. • "Ernst & Young Entrepreneur of the Year, 2004." • "India's Best People CEO, 2004" awarded by Hewitt Associates.
2003	• "CEO of the Year" by World HRD Congress, 2003.
2002	• "Businessman of the Year, 2002" by *Business India*. • "IT Man of the Year 2002" by *Dataquest*.
2001	• "Distinguished Entrepreneurship Award, 2001" by PHD Chamber of Commerce and Industry (PHDCCI).
2000	• "Ernst & Young Entrepreneur of the Year" in the ICE category, 2000. • "The Star of Asia, 2000" by *Business Week*.

Source: Company data.

Appendix 6A.2: Bharti Airtel—Communicating with a Heart

A first generation telecommunication enterprise, Bharti Airtel Limited has scaled unbelievable heights to become one of the largest business houses in India and yet it retains its heart to serve the cause of society through education and empowerment of the rural youth.

A bicycle-parts maker with a modest US$ 1,000 investment in 1976, today is one of India's most respected global company with a customer base of approximately 125 million,[3] an annual turnover of a whopping ₹ 373,521 million in 2009 or ₹ 37,352 crore and a market capitalization of over US$ 25 billion employing over 18,000 people! It is modern India's gripping original tale of rags to riches by three enterprising brothers from Ludhiana, a trading town of Punjab who built the diversified group with interest in telecom, retail, financial services, manufacturing, realty, and agri-business. Bharti Airtel, the flagship company of the group, ranks amongst the top ten companies in India in terms of market capitalization and is the single largest player in the fiercely competitive telecom field with a revenue market share of more than 30 percent.

A combination of grit, enterprise, high business acumen, and propitious circumstances led to the phenomenal success story of Airtel. The absolute showpiece of the 21st century fast-track corporate India, Airtel has forged long-term strategic partnerships with global leaders like Ericsson, Nokia Siemens, and Huawei for aggressive network expansion; Alcatel Lucent for managing fixed line, broadband, and Internet Protocol Television (IPTV) service; IBM for Information Technology; IBM Daksh, Mphasis, FirstSource, Teleperformance, Aegis, and HTMT for excellent customer service through call center operations; On Mobile, Comviva, Yahoo, Google, and Cellbrum to provide a unique experience in value added services, etc. The Bharti Group also has joint ventures with several global leaders including Wal-Mart for cash and carry and wholesale operations, AXA for financial services, and Del Monte for its agri-business. The group has diversified into retail business with its "Easy day" brand of retail stores.

How did the Mittal brothers do it? "Brave actions leading to big transformations" is the answer they give. It has to be brave since the tiny plant Bharti Telecom set up the collaboration of Siemens in 1985 to make push-button telephones had to face tremendous competition from a mushrooming growth of telephone instrument providers. But the Beetel brand of the company survived and is still a strong name to reckon with beginning the first chapter in the fabulous story of Bharti Airtel. The branded company Airtel, Delhi's first mobile service operator, was launched in 1995 by the Mittal brothers.

It has been a quarter century of blazing growth, tremendous challenges, big disappointments, and even bigger gains, an era when India leapfrogged into the 21st century based almost entirely on a technology revolution centered around information communication and entertainment (ICE). Riding the wave of change and total transformation of the economy, Airtel continued to build on its businesses competing for rights to operate in different market segments called the telecom circle. In 2004, when the company was adding 1 million customers per quarter, it realized the need of an extremely innovative, highly reliable, and robust technology solutions which a company like IBM could only provide. As part of its first-of-a-kind IT outsourcing agreement, IBM helped Bharti Airtel create a highly flexible platform for integrating its customer-facing processes across all lines of business.

An IBM case study states:

> A key driver of Bharti Airtel's decision to outsource its IT activities to IBM was the desire to channel its internal energies and resources into capitalizing on a spectacular market opportunity rather than on the enabling platforms needed to do so. The scorching growth of Bharti Airtel's customer base, and the ability of its business processes to keep up with this growth, illustrates the success of this strategy.

High process efficiency and scalability are the big factors in Airtel's growth story. The company's ability to bring activation from four days to two hours and the billing cycles from fifteen days to two hours and its readiness in using IBM platform to process millions of customers on its roll are the secrets behind the Airtel success. The result is that the company operates in all twenty-two telecom circles in India, and became the first private operator to have an all India presence. It also provides telemedia services (fixed line and broadband services through digital subscriber line or DSL) in ninety-five cities in India.

The company also operates 2G and 3G services in Sri Lanka from January 2009, the first overseas venture in telecom services by the company. The company has expanded its footprint to Bangladesh in January 2010 by acquiring 70 percent stake in Warid Telecom. The company's national long distance infrastructure comprises of over 118,000 route km of optical fiber along with sufficient last mile connectivity, providing a pan India reach. The international infrastructure includes ownership of the i2i submarine cable system connecting Chennai to Singapore, consortium ownership of the SMW4 submarine cable system connecting Chennai and Mumbai to Europe and Singapore, and investment in capacities across a number of diverse submarine cable systems across transatlantic and transpacific routes including Asia America Gateway (AAG), India Middle East and Western Europe (IMEWE), Unity North, Europe India Gateway (EIG), and Eastern Africa Submarine Cable System (EASSY). The company has also built terrestrial express connectivity to neighboring countries such as Nepal and Bhutan.

Leadership Made all the Difference

Bharti's achievement is also the personal achievement of a graduate from Punjab University and an alumnus of a CEO's program of Harvard Business School, Sunil Bharti Mittal, the second eldest of the three brothers, barely into his early 50s, making him also one of the youngest first-generation business achievers of India. "Refine your processes, strive for dominance and build your brand," is the mantra by which the young founder chairman and MD of Bharti Airtel Ltd led his company. Dominance in all the businesses beginning with telecommunication is a personal quest for Sunil Mittal and he has always succeeded in winning global recognition including the conferment of the highest of Indian civilian honors, Padma Bhushan. Sunil has been conferred the degree of Doctor of Science (Honoris Causa) by the G.B. Pant University of Agriculture and Technology and the degree of Doctor of Laws (Honoris Causa) by the University of Leeds, UK. He is also an Honorary Fellow of the Institution of Electronics and Telecommunication Engineers (IETE) and is a member of the Academy of Distinguished Entrepreneurs, Babson College, Wellesley, Massachusetts. He was also chosen the Asia Businessman of the Year by *Fortune*, and Asia Pacific CEO of the Year by Frost & Sullivan in 2006. The personal accolades and global recognition have motivated Sunil to achieve more and reach out to the farthest corners of the world. The vision he has set for the group for 2020 is—We will build India's finest conglomerate by:

- Always empowering and backing our people.
- Being loved and admired by our consumers and respected by our partners.
- Transforming millions of lives and making a positive impact on society.
- Being brave and unbounded in realizing our dreams.

Four Pillars of Growth

To achieve these ambitious goals, the company is structured into four strategic business units—Mobile; Telemedia; Enterprise; and Digital TV. The mobile business offers services in India, Sri Lanka, and Bangladesh. The telemedia business provides broadband, IPTV, and telephone services in ninety-five Indian cities. The enterprise business provides end-to-end telecom solutions to corporate customers and national and international long distance services to telecom companies or Telcos. The Digital TV business provides direct-to-home (DTH) TV services across India. The company has gone in for the best possible collaborations from around the world and has left no stone unturned in finding the right managerial talent to lead the businesses and induct the best possible technologies from the most reliable high quality supplier in the world. Being a truly global enterprise, the group has the flexibility to operate and source technologies, people, and also strategic tie-ups from across the globe. The footprint of the group, as a result, is in every aspect of ICE business and beyond. The retail, insurance, educational services, agriculture business, and real estate businesses expand the basket and add new dimensions to the growth curve of the Bharti Group.

At the core of it all lies the ability of the Mittal brothers to manage people along with investments, something which has come natural to them as per their track record: Bharti attracted investment from the globally-renowned investment and banking companies, such as Warburg Pincus, AIF Funds, IFC, and New York Life, as far back as in 2001. In 2007, Temasek Holdings, The Investment Corporation of Dubai, Goldman Sachs, Macquarie, AIF Capital, Citigroup & India Equity Partners (IEP), and Kohlberg Kravis Roberts & Company. (KKR) invested in Bharti Infratel, a subsidiary company set up to provide telecom infrastructure services to all the leading telecom operators in the country.

Apart from sheer business growth, Sunil believes a responsible corporate has a duty to give back to the community in which it operates. This belief has resulted in Bharti Foundation which is committed to providing education to the underprivileged children in rural India. Bharti Foundation, the philanthropic arm of the Bharti Group was set up in 2000 to help India's large mass of underprivileged children and youth population to realize their potential. Over the years the Foundation has been creating and supporting programs that bring about sustainable improvement in the field of education.

Bharti Foundation implements education programs in the field of both primary and higher education. The Satya Bharti School program is its flagship program which aims to provide free quality education to underprivileged children, with a special focus on the girl child, in the deepest rural pockets of the country. The Foundation also plans to open senior secondary schools to provide both pedagogical and vocational training to children to equip them for future employment opportunities within their own villages and communities. Currently, 236 Satya Bharti Primary Schools are operational across the states of Punjab, Rajasthan, Haryana, Uttar Pradesh, and Tamil Nadu, reaching out to approximately 30,000 children and employing more than 1,100 teachers.

In order to provide education and training opportunities to bright young people and develop future leaders and entrepreneurs from amongst them, Bharti Foundation has set up the Bharti School of Telecommunication Technology and Management at IIT Delhi and partnered with IIT Bombay to set up the Bharti Centre for Communication. The Foundation has also instituted the Bharti Scholarship and Mentorship program to support academically brilliant students from financially weak backgrounds.

The Bharti Group has entered into general and life insurance business with AXA of France, one of the largest players worldwide in the field of financial protection with operations in fifty-five countries. The company's retail strategy is two-pronged, to bring the best retailer from the US, Wal-Mart and also to launch its own personalized brand of retail stores called "Easy Day" neighborhood stores and "Easy Day Market"™ medium format store. The company has planned US$ 2–2.5 billion investments in retail operations by 2015.

The foray into entertainment was also conscious with the launch of DTH operations and later IPTV. Being the largest telecom operator having connectivity to most individuals and homes, bringing digital entertainment was the natural choice for the group. The investment in digital entertainment media met with instant success launching the company into yet another orbit of opportunity and growth. Agriculture business investments of the group came natural for the group routed into the most fertile region of the country, Punjab, except that the group that has grown with technology has also brought a sensitivity and difference to the entire farming business through a series of tie-ups with the best in its class.

As the country moves on a scorching 7–8 percent growth path, the telecom industry would have a strong role to play and being the leader of the pack, Bharti Airtel has its future challenges truly laid out! The country's overall tele-density is 49.5 percent as on January 31, 2010 as against global tele-density of 78.11 percent on December 31, 2008, which means the industry can comfortably grow by 70–80 percent. In the other areas of investment too, Bharti Group expects manifold growth trends. For Sunil Bharti Mittal, the future is cut out. He is a man with a mission, one which will change the face of India through communication, agriculture, and security to people and their lives.

Table 6A.2: Recognition and Accolades to Bharti Airtel, 2003–2008

2009	• Bharti Airtel has been rated as "Strongest Brand" in *The Economic Times*—Brand Finance "Brand Power Rating 2009." • Amongst "Fabulous 50 Companies" by Forbes Asia. • "Best Global Wholesale Carrier" for 2009 by Telecoms World. • India's Best Enterprise Connectivity Provider, 2009 by PC Quest. • Ranked amongst "Six Best Performing Technology Companies" in the world by *Business Week*. • Most Preferred Cellular Service Provider Award 2009 awarded by CNBC Awaaz. • Top Telecom Service Provider of the Year 2009 by Voice & Data. • "Service Provider of the Year" and "Wireless Service Provider of the Year" 2009 by Frost & Sullivan.
2008	• "50 Best listed companies in Asia Pacific" by *Forbes*. • "World's 25 Most valuable Telecom Brands" by Brand Finance Plc. • "Best Billing/Customer Care Solution" by GSM Mobile World Congress. • "Ranked among 50 largest and most liquid companies in BRIC countries" by Dow Jones BRIC 50.

Year	Awards
2007	• "Company of the Year 2007" by *The Economic Times*. • "Top Telecom company of the year 2007" by NDTV Profit. • "Annual Outsourcing Excellence Award" by *Forbes*. • Most Preferred Cellular Service Provider by CNBC AWAAZ Consumer Awards. • "Ranked 3rd globally for best returns to shareholders" by *Business Week*'s Infotech 100 list.
2006	• "IT Innovation Award for Business Model Innovation" by NASSCOM. • "Top 10 best performing companies in the world" by *Business Week* IT 100. • India's Best-managed company (large cap) by *Asiamoney*.
2005	• Ranked 13th among Asia's 50 best performing companies by *Business Week*. • "Asia's Best GSM carrier" by Telecom Asia. • World Communications Best Brand of the Year Award by Emap communications group. • Amongst the top 3 companies by *The Economic Times* top 500. • "Indian Mobile Operator of the Year" by Asian MobileNews. • Featured among world's Top 20 IT companies by *Business Week* IT 100. • "India's Best Managed Company" by *Asiamoney*. • Featured in Global 1000 (most valuable companies) by *Business Week*.
2004	• "Most respected company in telecom sector" by *Business World*. • "India's second best employer" by Hewitt Associates. • Mobile Operator of the Year in India and subcontinent by Asian MobileNews. • "India's Best Managed Company" by *Asiamoney*. • "400 best big companies of the World" by Forbes.
2003	• Second Best Asian Cellular Company by Euromoney Survey.

Source: Company data.

Appendix 6A.3: Organizational Culture of Bharti Airtel—Analysis of Questionnaire Data

Table 6A.3: Perceived Organizational Culture of Bharti Airtel

N = 68

S. No.	Organizational Culture	Mean	SD	Rank
1.	Ethical governance	4.70	0.58	1
2.	Result orientation	4.67	0.54	2
3.	Focus on building competitiveness	4.61	0.52	3
4.	Performance excellence	4.56	0.59	4
5.	Speed of response to external demands and challenges	4.52	0.59	5
6.	Entrepreneurial	4.47	0.66	6
7.	Responsiveness to the customer	4.39	0.58	7
8.	Openness to new ideas	4.38	0.67	8
9.	Openness and transparency	4.30	0.66	9.5
10.	Outward looking	4.30	0.70	9.5
11.	Trust	4.29	0.89	11
12.	Communication and information flow: Horizontal (a) Within the department	4.26	0.62	12.5
13.	Teamwork	4.26	0.59	12.5
14.	Empowerment and delegation	4.24	0.84	14
15.	Role clarity	4.23	0.72	16.5
16.	Performance-based promotion	4.23	0.70	16.5
17.	Focus on continuous improvement	4.23	0.74	16.5
18.	Participative	4.23	0.63	16.5
19.	Culture of celebration of achievements and successes	4.17	0.78	19.5
20.	Support for risk-taking	4.17	0.81	19.5
21.	Nurturing talent	4.15	0.71	21
22.	Communication and information flow: Vertical (a) Top-down	4.14	0.65	22.5

S. No.	Organizational Culture	Mean	SD	Rank
23.	People orientation	4.14	0.70	22.5
24.	Global perspectives	4.11	0.91	24
25.	Speed of response to internal demands	4.03	0.66	25
26.	Nurturing innovation	3.97	0.89	26
27.	Community culture	3.92	0.90	27
28.	Tolerance of differences	3.88	0.83	28
29.	Cross-functional collaboration	3.82	0.78	29
30.	Process focused	3.73	0.94	30
31.	Communication and information flow: Horizontal (b) Across the departments	3.62	0.89	31
32.	Communication and information flow: Vertical (b) Bottom-up	3.55	0.90	32
33.	Centralized decision-making process	3.52	0.85	33

Source: Authors.

A study of Table 6A.3 indicates that the mean values across all the thirty-three work culture parameters range from 3.52 to 4.70.

There is significant perceptual homogeneity across all the work culture attributes, the SD being less than 1 in all the cases.

Further perusal of this table brings out the following salient features:

- All the mean values are above average toward the higher side, the lowest being 3.52.
- Of the thirty-three work culture attributes, twenty-five have a mean value greater than 4.00 indicating that they are in the "High" to "Very High" zone.
- The top five items—ethical governance; result-oriented; focus on building competitiveness; performance excellence; and speed of response to external demands and challenges—have mean values greater than 4.50 indicating that they are tending toward "Very High." Analysis of these five items indicates that Airtel heavily emphasizes achieving competitiveness through

ethical governance, result orientation, performance excellence, and speedy response to external demands and challenges.
- Scrutiny of items ranging from mean value 4.47 to 4.26 brings out that Airtel emphasizes entrepreneurial culture, openness to new ideas, and outward-looking orientation with strong emphasis on customerization. Airtel lays emphasis on seamless communication and information flow and teamwork as well as on trust, which are the key ingredients for building a collaborative culture.
- Some of the noteworthy culture attributes falling in the range of 4.24 to 4.03 are empowerment and delegation, role clarity, participative, and support for risk-taking. Other important attributes are performance-based promotion and focus on continuous improvement. The strong people focus in Airtel is indicated by the culture of celebrating achievements and success, nurturing talent, and people orientation.

Appendix 6A.4: Financial Performance of Bharti Airtel at a Glance

Table 6A.4: Revenue and Profit of Bharti Airtel from 2003 to 2009 (in ₹ billion)

Year	Income Revenue	Net Profit
2003	0.17	0.002
2004	50.36	5.84
2005	81.56	12.11
2006	116.64	20.28
2007	184.2	40.62
2008	270.12	63.95
2009	373.52	78.59
% Change over 2003	219,617.65	3,929,400

Source: Bharti Airtel Annual Report, 2009: 7; values for 2003 have been obtained from Prowess database.

Appendix 6A.5: Sunil Mittal as a Change Maestro—Analysis of Questionnaire Data

Table 6A.5: *Perceived Style of Sunil Mittal as a Change Maestro*

N = 68

S. No.	Change Maestro Attributes	Mean	SD	Ranks
1.	Is entrepreneurial	4.98	0.12	1
2.	Is a visionary	4.95	0.21	2
3.	Is an effective communicator	4.92	0.27	3.5
4.	Has ambitious plans for the organization	4.92	0.27	3.5
5.	Is a strategic thinker	4.91	0.29	5
6.	Radiates positive energy	4.86	0.39	6.5
7.	Is a role model	4.86	0.39	6.5
8.	Provides a sense of clear direction	4.85	0.40	8.5
9.	Has high credibility	4.85	0.36	8.5
10.	Fast in making critical decisions	4.80	0.44	10
11.	Stands like a rock in the face of calamities	4.72	0.55	11.5
12.	Is open to new ideas	4.72	0.55	11.5
13.	Respects the dignity of others	4.67	0.56	13.5
14.	Has empowering and supporting attitude	4.67	0.51	13.5
15.	Is reliable	4.65	0.69	16.5
16.	Is result focused	4.65	0.57	16.5
17.	Has a global mindset	4.65	0.64	16.5
18.	Business strategist	4.65	0.54	16.5
19.	Makes people feel that they are valued by the organization	4.59	0.68	19
20.	Is honest and transparent	4.58	0.70	21
21.	Leads by example	4.58	0.68	21
22.	Is a man of words	4.58	0.80	21
23.	Leads from the front	4.55	0.71	23
24.	Humility	4.53	0.73	24
25.	Is innovative and creative	4.52	0.61	25
26.	Pursues excellence in everything	4.50	0.69	26.5
27.	Is interested in growth of his people	4.50	0.66	26.5
28.	Makes people feel that they have great worth	4.45	0.64	28

(continued)

(continued)

S. No.	Change Maestro Attributes	Mean	SD	Ranks
29.	Is fair and impartial	4.41	0.72	29.5
30.	Has a helping attitude	4.41	0.82	29.5
31.	Grooms and develops people	4.38	0.72	31
32.	Is a team builder	4.33	0.75	32
33.	Recognizes and rewards performance	4.30	0.78	33
34.	Sensitivity	4.18	0.80	34
35.	Is demanding and performance centric	4.14	0.77	35

Source: Authors.

The edge of Sunil Mittal as a Change Maestro has been presented in Table 6A.5. For the purpose of analysis, mean values of the thirty-five leader attributes have been classified into three categories: "Most Visible" with mean values 4.5 and above; "Highly Visible with mean values 3.5 to 4.4; and "Visible" with mean values 3.5 and below.

Perusal of this table brings out the following salient features that qualify Sunil Mittal's profile to be a Change Maestro:

- The top twenty-seven attributes are in the "Most Visible" category, with the mean values ranging from 4.50 to 4.98.
- The remaining eight items are in the "Highly Visible" category. The mean values range from 4.14 to 4.45.
- It is interesting to note that none of the attributes feature in the third category, that is, the "Visible" category.
- There is significant perceptual homogeneity about the profile of Sunil Bharti Mittal as a Change Maestro, the SDs across all thirty-five items being below 1.
- It is noteworthy that there are as many as ten items with a mean score of 4.80 and above, that is, falling in the "Most Visible" category. In fact, of these ten items, five attributes have mean scores greater than 4.91. The number one perceived attribute is entrepreneurial.
- Although twenty-seven items are in the "Most Visible" category, here, an effort is made to closely analyze positioning of only the top eighteen items, that is, a little more than fifty percent of the items.

- Analysis of these items brings out that six attributes—visionary, ambitious, strategic thinking, sense of clear direction, global mindset, and business strategist—which focus on clarity of vision, direction, and ambitious building for the organization in a global context. These items also indicate Sunil Mittal's ability as a strategist and as a strategic thinker.
- Attributes like effective communicator, radiates positive energy, respects the dignity of others, empowering, and supportive attitude reveal Sunil Mittal's' capability to connect, reach out, help, respect, and support people.
- Sunil Mittal is also perceived as a Change Maestro who can stand like a rock in the face of calamities as well as emphasizing result-orientation.
- In addition to these qualities, people also see Sunil Mittal as a reliable leader, open to new ideas, and a role model. It is evident that the greatest strength in his leadership profile is his entrepreneurial passion, which has been the key driver behind his outstanding achievements in building Airtel into the telecom Goliath.

Notes

1. Authors gratefully acknowledge and appreciate the intellectual contributions and emotional support they received from Mr Manoj Kohli, Joint Managing Director, Bharti Airtel, in the course of this work. He spent many hours with authors in conceptualizing the framework and providing focused directions to the case. However, for the conclusions and views expressed in this case study of Bharti Airtel and Sunil Bharti Mittal's style as a Change Maestro, the authors own entire responsibility.
2. Twenty-one top team members have been interviewed by the authors. The number of respondents varies since the interviewing method was largely unstructured; we recorded what they said, giving greater priority to what came out of top-of-the-mind in response to our broad questions, rather than getting them to respond to a set of questions.
3. All the financials are as per IGAAP, Source *Bharti Airtel Annual Report*, various years. The number reported here was as per US GAAP.

7

7
ANIL MANIBHAI NAIK: TOWARD THE NEXT ORBIT

This is the story of a renowned Athenian sculptor who was known far and wide for his genius and creativity in sculpting majestic marble statues. His statues were the epitome of beauty and grace. People who saw these sculptures were spellbound. Not only did the people admire him, he was also considered the jewel in the King's crown. Such was his mastery that the people of the kingdom felt he was incomparable.

The sculptor felt fortunate for receiving such adulation. He only had one dream: to make his son an outstanding sculptor who would surpass his father's achievements. He always shared this dream with his wife who encouraged him to mentor his son.

As the son grew older, the father constantly instructed and mentored him to practice and improve his sculpting skills. All the son's creations were met with constructive criticism and suggestions for improvement. Although the son did not appreciate the father's constant urging for improvement, he nonetheless obeyed him and continuously strove to get better. In the process, the son learnt to excel in his creations. One day he created such a stunning statue of a beautiful girl, that his father could not help but exclaim, "Perfect, this is perfect, my son!" Years went by and the son came up with many pieces, but none of these surpassed this creation. The son became complacent and stopped striving to better his art. His journey toward excellence therefore ended the day he began to believe he was the best.

The profile of A.M. Naik who believes that excellence is a journey, not a destination, who believes in ceaselessly striving to do better than before, who relentlessly reaches out to become the best, and who constantly creates the next curve both in his life and in the organization and takes the organization to the next orbit, is just the opposite of the spirit of the young Athenian in the story. A.M. Naik is a dreamer, to quote Oscar Wilde, who can find his "way by moonlight, and see the dawn before the rest of the world." More importantly, he stands out as a Change Maestro who did not build a ship by herding people together to collect wood and assign them tasks; but rather, taught them to long for the endless immensity of the sea, in Antoine de Saint-Exupéry's words.

This case study "A.M. Naik: Toward the Next Orbit"[1] has been organized into the following three parts: Part I provides a brief profile sketch of Larsen & Toubro (L&T); Part II highlights the action architecture and culture landscape of L&T; and Part III discusses A.M. Naik's profile and persona.

Part I: Brief Profile Sketch of Larsen & Toubro

L&T (for details of the organization's profile, see Appendix 7A.1) is an integrated group, engaged in technology, engineering, construction, and manufacturing. Today, it is recognized across India and in large parts of the Middle East and South East Asia as a company that is constantly reinventing itself with a passion to surpass its own high achievements and push back the frontiers of its capabilities.

L&T has been a diversified conglomerate known for its professionalism, free and empowering culture, ethical governance, customer-friendliness, and collaborative approach with customers, and also as a caring organization with a commitment to nation building. However, L&T was also a Goliath characterized with inward looking, fairly complacent, non-responsive, and slow-moving characteristics.

A.M. Naik (for details of the Change Maestro's profile, see Appendix 7A.2) inherited a conglomerate where people had a sense of belonging, an organization which had great talent; it was well known for its great history, but it lacked adequate focus and direction. A.M. Naik sensed, for a while, the looming threats to the future of L&T since the mid-1990s. As he put it, there was the "roar of competition from across the globe;" the tsunami of competition "which was going to hit India." A.M. Naik's global travels and keen observation of global trends made him declare to the board, "our competition is going to be so tough ... it is not going to allow us to exist...." It took mass departure of a thousand employees for the company to sit up and take notice of the situation.

PART II: ACTION ARCHITECTURE AND CULTURE LANDSCAPE

Content analysis of the interviews brought out twelve themes which are presented here:

- Quest for excellence
- Thinking tomorrow today
- Global thrust
- Focused growth strategy and thrust on value creation
- Speed
- Empowerment
- Entrepreneurial innovation
- Ethical organization
- Customer focus
- Caring organization
- Contribution-centric meritocracy
- Nurturing talent

Quest for Excellence

The quest for excellence drives organizations to continuously strive to improve all the levers of competitiveness. Organizations that believe in excellence relentlessly move forward from one level to the next.

In their quest for excellence, L&T stops at nothing. The words used by all the twenty interviewed persons give a glimpse of the excellence focus of the top team. They have described L&T as "unstoppable," "continuously strives for excellence," "achieves excellence in every field," "'can-do' attitude at all levels," "capacity and capability to achieve the impossible," "strongly committed to excellence," "(we) set high benchmarks, do not rest on our laurels," "(we) pursue excellence," "(we) strive for the leadership position in every field," and "(we) excel in achieving quality in every field of engineering."

The approach of being constantly in the quest for excellence has been introduced through the questioning approach by Naik. "We questioned everything except ethics and values in L&T," said nineteen interviewees.[2] "We have constantly waged a war on substandard operations and prefer not to get into such operations," replied fifteen interviewees. Fifteen respondents also said: "Our motto [since 1999] has been to constantly excel in engineering to remain at the top." "We have realized that if we don't lead in engineering we will never be in a project business, cutting edge technology, engineering and design," remarked fourteen people. Nine people recalled the following process where Naik also participated:

> We began the process of examining strategic business plans like businessmen and asked—What is the scale? What is the value being created? How much it will grow? Can it become a thousand crores in five years? If it is to become (worth) thousand crores, what action should be taken...?

Eighteen people also said: "We ask what is our USP compared to global leaders in the business?" The initial approach of questioning lead by Naik "helped us realize that we have to traverse many miles to become a global giant. Needless to say, this helped L&T to see everything through a new lens. This approach enabled L&T to think of tomorrow today."

Thinking Tomorrow Today

Winners think of tomorrow today. They restlessly scan the emerging trends in order to map the future; they identify issues and challenges and prepare themselves in anticipation of the imminent changes. Since the future provides opportunities, those organizations that do not spot them, stand to miss out on them and become irrelevant no matter how well they are doing today. Therefore, winning organizations seek to enfold the future into the present and realign organizational strategies, processes, structure, and people accordingly.

Almost all the respondents, that is, nineteen respondents, mentioned that L&T focusses on tomorrow, spots emerging opportunities, and prepares to effectively respond to emerging issues and challenges. According to all the interviewees, *thinking of tomorrow today* has been the mindset and spirit of L&T since 1999. The future scenario was initially injected by inviting consultants to make presentations to the board of L&T. Nine interviewees said: "This strategy forced us to start thinking on a much bigger scale, keeping in view the future more often than we were used to." One of the greatest things Naik did when he took over was to launch "Lakshya" and "Project Blue Chip," said fifteen respondents. According to eighteen interviewees: "Project Blue Chip made us think a little bigger than what we have been doing. It foresaw a lot of things." Eleven people mentioned: "Across the company, he made thinking ahead a habit." Through this process of envisioning, Naik ensured clarity of the broad direction for the L&T Group. This enabled L&T to align with the emerging future scenario. It also generated a positive challenge and excitement among the employees. Since they were part of the vision-building process through the Boston Consulting Group (BCG) workout sessions, the level of involvement among the senior team (top 200) was very high. Eighteen interviewees said that clarity of vision and vision-building exercises took place involving large number of members at the top and senior management levels, enabling them to think of the future and accordingly prepare the business strategy and operational processes.

In anticipation of imminent challenges to their survival, new strategies and mindsets were molded. Key thrust was placed on going global, ring fencing L&T, and getting into futuristic businesses. The new mindset was created by generating dissonance and mild anxiety, emphasizing the high levels of global competition and contrasting the same with L&T's inadequacy on this front and also by sharing data regarding missed opportunities, past failures, and employee turnover.

Business portfolio restructuring was initiated keeping in view the emerging future, L&T's core competencies, and the fit between the two, as fifteen interviewees mentioned. L&T decided to exit from UltraTech Cement by selling it to the Birlas, since cement did not have a strategic fit with L&T's core business.

A win-win strategy was worked out with the Birlas where L&T sold UltraTech to the former in return for their 15 percent stake which was then used to create the L&T Employees' Welfare Foundation where employees became shareholders. This was also a ring-fencing strategy preempting all future takeover bids. Everyone in L&T acknowledges Mr Naik's role in protecting the company's identity and enhancing the employees' interests. In the past, L&T had suffered because of takeover bids by the Chabbrias and Ambanis, which were highly publicized by the media. As one person puts it: "Mr Naik converted a losing battle; he averted adversity. [In fact] we compare Mr Naik to Winston Churchill during World War II, when he snatched victory from the jaws of defeat. Mr Naik created a golden opportunity in the resolution of the cement deal."

Apart from ring fencing L&T, another important feature was the foray into businesses which had great scope for future growth. Ten interviewees said:

> … right now we are going into power in a big way; we are also entering ship building and railways. These are all businesses where we are investing thousands of crores, which will give returns may be a decade down the line. This is an investment into the future; none of us will see the returns.…

This discussion brings out the fact that ever since Naik took over, the thrust on futuristic orientation was given great emphasis in L&T. In fact, the question "How will the future unfold?" has become the core question aiding the strategic planning of the company. This approach has significantly helped L&T to align all its business levers with future business imperatives. Futuristic orientation and heightened thrust on the future also compelled L&T to create strategies which could protect it from likely takeovers and acquisitions. In the past, attempts of corporate raiders have created tremendous anxiety and fear bordering on paranoia among employees.

Global Thrust

In the current business scenario, the globe has become truly seamless and borderless. To compete, survive, and excel in such a scenario, every business has to think global—in terms of global scale, global strategies, global processes, and global managerial talent.

All the twenty interviewed executives highlighted that one of the key focus areas at L&T over the last decade has been to go global and to compete and excel globally. We concluded that unless it did things differently, L&T could be in trouble. The thrust for going global that emerged from such an analysis was an outcome of the analysis of emerging global trends, opportunities, issues, and challenges, as per twelve interviewees.

The following statements substantiate the accelerated thrust given to going global in L&T:

> In the early period, post-1999, twenty interviewees said: "We were compelled to view everything from a global perspective."
>
> "L&T's vision is to be a global player and not remain a domestic player," remarked eighteen respondents.
>
> Twenty-three interviewees said that Naik has been responsible for bringing global perspective into the thinking of L&T-ites. It is today part of the collective psyche of all the L&T-ites.
>
> Seven people recalled: "When he took over, he started talking about the need for global perspective, global attitude. He concentrated on expanding the Infotech business, which had languished so far. As he started spending more time on it, his mind became globally tuned and the learning he brought back to the company, forced us to change our mindsets [on many issues]."

Global Thrust has become one of our major mantras to de-risk the business, said the interviewees. Nineteen of them said: "We now talk about becoming globally competitive—to have the ability to face competition, the ability to work in different environments, network in different environments, and the ability to take risks in different environment." According to five interviewees, Naik's exhortations have been so powerful to the extent that "we now benchmark ourselves with the world and try to be the best in terms of quality, aesthetic, delivery, service. We know very well that if we fall short on any of these things, we will cease to exist...."

Going global and working with a global perspective thus became one of the important aspects of L&T's vision. The importance of going global was highlighted by asking people to benchmark globally; it was talked of as a means to long-term sustenance and survival of L&T even on home ground. Going global became a part of the collective vision and mindset of people. In the beginning, it was inculcated through benchmarking with the best in the world. A plea was made for globalization by saying that L&T was in danger of extinction if they did not go global and did not benchmark with global players. The next step was moving from creating global mindset by global benchmarking to becoming a global player.

Focused Growth Strategy and Thrust on Value Creation

Great organizations need to continuously align, re-align, and appropriately respond to the changing business context. Those organizations which do not quickly align and adapt become laggards and then sink into oblivion. Another characteristic of great organizations is the thrust on value creation through divestment, portfolio restructuring, building cost and quality competitiveness, along with customerization, innovation, speed of response, and people power. All the interviewees unequivocally shared their satisfaction with the excellent work done by L&T toward building focused growth strategy and assigning importance to value creation. L&T was earlier engaged in a large number of businesses, many of them, as eighteen interviewees informed us, were unrelated and some of the companies were so small that they added little value.

According to seventeen interviewees, each business had to assess the value it was adding to L&T. They said: "It was decided that unless a business was at least worth 100 crores it was better to exit it," and "a lot of emphasis was placed on the bottom line, return on investments, utilization of funds … all business groups had to run businesses with the mindset of value creation." The sole aim, as eighteen people mentioned, was to see that "no one would be able to take over L&T." According to ten interviewees, "Mr Naik is ruthless about exiting businesses … for example he sold shipping … some businesses were given some time to scale up and if they couldn't do so, they had to exit." This forced L&T

to focus on the construction business which had 51 percent share of the L&T business portfolio, said eighteen interviewees.

Thus, the spirit of L&T has been to think big and focus on value creation. Fourteen people mentioned their company now does business worth ₹ 30,000 crores. They also said that the focus now is to go up the value chain and at the same time do bigger jobs, undertake bigger projects, and make bigger investments. "We have inculcated the concept of size and value creation in our thinking," said twelve interviewees. Eleven of them said: "Value has been created through portfolio restructuring." Sixteen interviewees said: "After Mr Naik became Chairman, engineers began to talk the language of finance and economics, something unusual in L&T." The thrust on shareholder value creation was further accentuated through the Employee Stock Ownership Plan (ESOP) scheme. ESOPs helped increase sense of ownership in the organization and concern for value creation for shareholders, since employees became shareholders.

Speed

In a fast-paced world where everyone is running, walking is equivalent to moving backward. In fact, the business world is characterized by the rule of the jungle where everyday, both the Tiger and the Gazelle, as also mentioned in Chapter 5, the case study on K.V. Kamath, prepare to run fast and outdo each other for survival. Those organizations which adopt this strategy to run faster than the competitors are most likely to survive, thrive, grow, and excel and have sustainable competitive edge.

All the interviewees clearly stated that L&T was a "sleeping giant" until Naik added velocity and converted it into a "sprinting giant," as said by twelve interviewees. Nine interviewees said: "L&T was hierarchical and in the name of due process, many ... decisions were delayed, although we believed we were being very professional." "Many business opportunities were lost because of the slow decision making process. L&T culture has changed after Naik brought in speed, urgency and quick response," said fourteen interviewees. They also said: "Now there is a sense of urgency and speed. We run faster and there is sense of urgency and resolve to move faster than the competitors."

Empowerment

There has been a significant shift in the collective psyche and expectations of people (whether blue or white collar) from their place of work. They dislike autocracy and centralization and crave for a free and open culture which is low on hierarchy. Such preferences are heightened among Indians who are highly educated and exposed to global trends and practices. Those organizations which believe in the philosophy of empowerment are able to unleash creative potential and people power. Those organizations which fail to do this stifle the power of ideas and innovation which constitute the bedrock of competitive edge.

A high degree of empowerment has been experienced by as many as nineteen interviewed executives of the L&T top team. The following statements reflect the scale and type of empowerment indicating an open yet productive culture, which is quite rare in the Indian corporate sector:

Ten interviewees said: "L&T encourages a high level of initiative."

All interviewees mentioned: "There is empowerment at all levels here."

"There is freedom of speech here," as per twelve interviewees.

"There is freedom to express disagreement," mentioned eleven interviewees.

According to fourteen interviewees: "There is freedom to experiment along with accountability."

"We are largely given freedom," said nine respondents.

Two people said: "We are not told what to do."

Fourteen interviewees said "... we are allowed to explore new standards, new benchmarks...."

"People do take inputs and ideas from others who are one or two levels up or down and no one minds," said seventeen interviewees. According to thirteen interviewees: "Here you don't wait for instructions, you act...." Fourteen people said: "In L&T, top management gives the broad direction and beyond that it is like a blank cheque.... There are 100s of things done in this group which happened without anyone breathing down your neck." One person was heard saying: "Empowerment is high in this group and that's how we are able to manage highly specialized businesses ranging from construction to IT to nuclear."

According to three senior team members, Naik selectively involves himself; either when the field is new or where he feels concerned about progress; otherwise, he does not get into details. In fact seven senior team members narrated episodes where they were reprimanded by the chairman because they waited for instructions.

It is important to mention that although people are trusted and plenty of freedom and empowerment is given to people. This does not mean that misuse is tolerated. One executive said:

> At the slightest indication of somebody not remaining within the culture and discipline [of L&T] we have found ways to either remove him, or reduce him to a position where he cannot misuse power. In my life I have removed four or five individuals when it came to light that they cannot be trusted; otherwise we generally trust people.

This view has also been expressed by six other heads of divisions.

L&T has reaped the fruits of nurturing such a highly empowered work culture. Today, there is tremendous amount of togetherness among employees; there is loyalty and a sense of belonging. All the employees expressed that the spin-off of the empowerment philosophy has been greater identification, sense of ownership, collaborative spirit, and pride of being an L&T-ite.

Entrepreneurial Innovation

Business history demonstrates that most business empires begin to decay by the time they reach the 4th or 5th generation and then they die out. This is a global phenomenon and it affects most organizations. One of the most important contributory factors to this phenomenon has been the slow mortality of the entrepreneurial spirit. Non-entrepreneurial organizations are characterized by low risk-taking, low opportunity sensing, slow response to emerging business trends, and hierarchical orientation that focuses more on procedures and processes in the name of professionalism. Great organizations, therefore, make continuous efforts to avoid the trap of inertia by striving to promote a culture of risk taking, innovation, empowerment, and tolerance toward mistakes.

In Naik's era, L&T witnessed the flowering of an entrepreneurial and innovative culture. This view has been shared by all the interviewees. This was a big shift from the inward-looking, complacent, and bureaucratic culture which prevailed in the pre-Naik era. In the name of professionalism, there was low initiative and inadequate speed of response. The complacency and inertia for embracing change of the organization was shaken up by Naik's statements such as the following recorded by ten interviewees: "The attitude of non-aggression and low risk-taking will lead us nowhere. We will lose the game very fast;" "Mere professionalism is not going to succeed; we need entrepreneurship … we need many new initiatives to create shareholder value." Naik's efforts have yielded the L&T culture a sense of urgency, entrepreneurship, and innovation along with professionalism. Twelve people said: "We now believe that professionalism is good up to a point, but you need to marry entrepreneurship along with it; your ability to understand and take risks is important.…" Eleven interviewees mentioned the following:

> Entrepreneurship, risk-taking, and a sense of urgency were brought into L&T. It is not that you need to take hurried decisions but you need to understand risk quickly, because you don't have much time and therefore you have to sharpen your skill of taking risk and risk management. This spirit was brought into L&T by Naik.

"If you make mistakes in L&T you will not be penalised unless you repeat them, so it's a very good learning organization," said fourteen interviewees. Nine people said: "L&T's tremendously free and empowered culture creates immense opportunity for people to experiment, take risks, and learn from mistakes." Eleven others said: "Here mistakes are seen as learning opportunities." Eighteen interviewees shared the same view which is presented as follows:

> L&T gives a long rope to people and with this comes high tolerance for mistakes. I made lot of mistakes for some of which I could have been sacked in any other organization. I think the company tolerates mistakes like a member of the family.… I think it's the L&T culture. When you make mistakes as

long as you don't have any personal interest, the company allows you to learn [from them]; you are not punished unless you have made the blunder to defraud the company. This is a great culture in L&T.

According to fifteen people: "In L&T we are allowed to experiment." Eleven of the interviewed people said: "In L&T making mistakes does not come in the way of getting rewards so long as the intention is genuine." Ten interviewees were of the view that because of the prevalence of such a culture, nobody from the top to bottom will think too fearfully about jumping into something new. According to eight interviewees, Naik was known to say: "Mere professionalism is not going to succeed, add some entrepreneurship.... If you are just professional you are forgetting the business. Entrepreneurship is important ... we have to create shareholder value," and "L&T culture now has both entrepreneurship and professionalism."

Ethical Organization

Human history provides ample evidence that truth ultimately triumphs. Studies on nations and winning organizations bring out the power of ethics in excelling, growing, and winning. In this perspective, L&T is one of the shining beacons among Indian organizations.

All L&T-ites take great pride in the ethical orientation of their company. All top team members we met said, "We are an ethical organization" and cited examples illustrating this statement. Almost all of them stated that "our values are transparency, ethics, and integrity." L&T has a zero tolerance policy to any transgressions on ethics, mentioned by twenty interviewees. According to three divisional heads, any form of unethical behavior was not tolerated at L&T and those indulging in it were "simply dismissed". This has been echoed by as many as eighteen top team members.

Government officials dealing with L&T are most unhappy, according to five interviewed executives, who indicated this as proof of the low instances of bribery by the organization. Their (government officials') assignment—to look after L&T work (excise related and others)—is described by them as equivalent

Lunch and Tea (L&T) alluding to the lack of opportunity to get favors, mentioned five executives. Such above-the-board dealings are a unique feature of L&T unlike many other business organizations where government officials are able to get large favors, as some seven executives stated.

Ethical culture is strongly reinforced by valuing individual integrity. Ethical stance is so strongly ingrained in the organization that today, "any L&T-ite can refuse to do something if it is unethical even if his superior asks him to do it," said nine interviewees and according to eight others, "no action will be taken against him if he refuses."

Most L&T-ites we met were justifiably proud of the achievements L&T made through ethical means. Fourteen people said: "We play by the rules and succeed. We have achieved many firsts as an organization without breaking any rules." "All our contract dealings are straight," said eighteen people. Nineteen of them expressed that because of the ethical stance of L&T, "we feel very comfortable working here." "We don't feel any tension or stress," said fifteen people. Twelve people said "whoever we meet outside L&T, whether government officials, CM, PM, we are respected and get appointments very easily." Fourteen interviewees remarked "even vendors and customers feel proud to be associated with L&T." "L&T has reaped rich dividends over the long term because of this approach and this is reflected in its excellence in performance," affirmed nine interviewees.

It is possible to conclude from these testimonials, that L&T is an ethical organization. People evidently feel proud to belong to this company and feel good to succeed as an organization by using ethical means.

Customer Focus

The role and relevance of the customer for business excellence has nowhere been better articulated by none other than Gandhiji when he said that customer is god. In fact, it is not an exaggeration to say that organizations exist because of the customer; if organizations did not care about the customer, they would be out of business. It is not surprising, therefore, that globally all businesses have used the customer-centric approach for creating winning organizations. Some companies even went to the extent of saying that employees are paid by the customer and, therefore, "our" prime duty is to serve the customer.

L&T is a highly customer-focused organization and it has been their slogan in the past: "In service lies success." This motto has been the guiding principle for L&T-ites has since inception according to nineteen interviewees. This orientation of L&T has heightened in the last decade. Eighteen people we spoke to said that customer service has been strongly emphasized here. The quotes which follow indicate the depth of customer orientation which exists in L&T:

> "Take care of the customer and profit would rise," is the slogan of L&T, as thirteen people said.
>
> Fifteen people said: "In the L&T culture is ingrained the belief that customer satisfaction even at the risk of incurring minor losses is most important."
>
> "L&T is known for good customer relationships," claimed twelve people.
>
> "Strong customer focus exists in L&T.... If you have to argue with your boss in customer's interest and take care of the customer, it is accepted because customer orientation is highly valued," mentioned thirteen interviewees.
>
> Nine people said: "Since we are always with the customer, the customer is always with us."
>
> According to twelve interviewees: "In L&T there is a sense of partnership with the customer."

Caring Organization

Experiences and research seem to indicate that Westerners tend to have more transactional relationships at the workplace; in contrast, Indians tend to view the organization as an extended family and, even, community. They, therefore, feel the need to belong to and also be cared for by the organization. When organizations take care of people, they are better able to mobilize them; however, when this need is not adequately met with, it can lead to anxiety, a sense of distancing, and reduced organizational commitment.

Nineteen interviewed people emphasized that L&T is a caring organization. Fourteen of them said: "The Company takes very good care of its people;"

fourteen of them also said it is a "helpful organization." Fifteen interviewees said: "The company pays attention to employee needs and expectations and has tried to take care of them." "Although it is not an organization that pays the highest ... it looks after the needs of its employees and compensates by taking interest in the welfare of employees," fourteen interviewees pointed this out. Fourteen people also said: "If people have a personal problem, it is given highest priority and there is someone to listen to the problem." One person mentioned:

> When there are personal problems there is a kind of treatment like family. My mother had a heart attack in Jaipur.... I had difficulty getting an air ticket.... I got a call from Naik and he said, "Don't worry; if you are unable to get a commercial flight we will keep the company aircraft ready for you." This gesture is something one can't forget.... [I] respect the organization for what it does for its employees.

Concern for the well being of L&T-ites was shown by L&T when the decision was taken to make employees shareholders in L&T. Apart from preempting the likelihood of a takeover of the group, this move made people rich beyond their dreams, something which they could have never imagined possible on their relatively modest salaries.

From this discussion, it can be decisively concluded that L&T demonstrates a high degree of concern toward employee welfare; it spends time to understand the needs and expectations of employees through interactions and helping people when they have personal problems. Such a caring culture has led to employee dedication and attachment to the organization and created a tremendous sense of ownership.

Contribution-centric Meritocracy

According to all the individuals interviewed for the study, L&T is a highly professional company where performance is a key requirement. Performance has been strongly emphasized in this organization. They said "we have created an atmosphere where people believe that they are expected to perform." Seventeen people remarked: "Professionally it is possible to excel here." Fifteen interviewees said "… if you have a thirst to do something you will get a platform to do it here." All the interviewed executives highlighted that L&T is a meritocracy where people are rewarded for their work and contribution as indicated by the following quotes:

> Twenty interviewees said: "L&T is a meritocracy. There is no distinction made based on caste and community."
>
> Nineteen interviewees claimed "if you have merit you can grow here."
>
> Five interviewees talked of Naik in this strain: "[Naik] who joined here as a junior engineer, and has come up to reach this level … same is the case with the directors…. All this has been possible because the company believes in merit."
>
> Nine people believe L&T is a truly public organization, not owned by any business group…. This is a great motivator … because if you have mettle there is no limit to where you can reach in L&T.
>
> "At the end of the day, there are no godfathers in this company, merit matters here," said thirteen interviewees.

The connection between performance and reward has been strongly emphasized in L&T in the last decade, and this has further brought the thrust on contribution and merit in this organization. Naik started introducing measures (for quantification of person's contribution) rather than relying only on judgment and opinion of superiors. This helped in differentiating between high performers and average performers which enabled L&T to give differentiated rewards.

The performance-reward link is visible in the following statement made by eighteen interviewees: "Those who contribute and perform get due recognition and rewards." They also said:

> Now there is a structure in the reward system which forces you to actually densely populate the ends of the curve [a reference to the normal probability curve used for appraisal and rewards; normally HR departments insist that the ends should be thinly populated not exceeding 5 percent].

"There is performance based reward here," said twelve people. Eighteen interviewees said: "Promotion and reward are being given on the basis of performance." Sixteen people mentioned: "In L&T people have been by-passed if they were not doing well and, in some cases, people have been asked to leave; in fact we have had 2–3 rounds of VRS." "Identifying the performers, identifying those who have the potential to become future leaders has been given importance here in the Naik period," exclaimed nineteen interviewees.

During our work in training and consulting, we came across around 50,000 business managers. Most of them were cynical about performance appraisal and reward systems, citing favoritism and bias in rewarding people. In such a context, the L&T experience on this parameter seems quite heartening.

Nurturing Talent

Battles are not won with guns but through people—their collective endurance, zest, and will to win—behind the guns! This has been more relevant in the corporate world particularly in the context where all round, organizations are facing a paucity of talented manpower. When Naik took over as the CMD of L&T, he voiced two major concerns:

- Why are people exiting L&T and how to stem the flow? and
- How to attract talent from leading institutions—IITs and IIMs?

He wanted to raise the company profile to make it a preferred employer, "a place of employment for top notch people," as twelve interviewees claimed. In his view, the leadership issue became the most critical issue for heightening competitiveness in L&T. In fact, for a couple of years, he played the key role in HR policy formulation and monitoring implementation, said seventeen interviewees. He de-emphasized the role of seniority for promotion and heightened the thrust on merit, contribution, and potential. Under his guidance, the HR introduced management techniques like the 360 degree appraisal, assessment centers, mentoring, and counseling, for building the leadership bank in L&T. They also introduced the high potential fast track scheme which had its critics in the beginning, as fifteen employees told us. In L&T, now, there is emphasis on younger people holding higher positions: "We now have a career plan where people can become General Managers by 40, so that they have enough time to make their impact on the business divisions and the sectors they manage," remarked nine interviewees.

Action Architecture and Culture Landscape of L&T: Salient Contours

Viewing all the findings emerging from both the interview and questionnaire responses (for details of questionnaire data of organizational culture of L&T, see Appendix 7A.3), bring out the following landmark features of L&T achievements, action architecture and culture landscape:

- L&T has delivered stunning financial performance over the last six years (for details of financial performance of L&T from 2003 to 2009, see Appendix 7A.4). During this period, its revenue has grown from approximately ₹ 109 billion to ₹ 46,108 billion, registering a growth of 274 percent. The story of growth in profits has been even more incredible demonstrating a growth of 691 percent, increasing from approximately 4 billion to 30 billion. This outstanding performance has brought many laurels to L&T. In 2009, L&T had the distinction of being ranked as one of the top 50 of the world's most reputable firms; it received the Golden Peacock Award for its corporate social initiatives in 2009. L&T is the recipient of the prestigious NDTV Profit Business Leadership award from NDTV Profit (2008) and the best CSR Award was bestowed by the Bombay Stock Exchange in 2008.
- Ethical governance, the backbone of creation and sustenance of the competitive edge, is perceived to be the most important culture attribute in L&T.
- In L&T change is a way of life. The company believes in continuously sharpening its competitiveness through toning systems, processes, and strategy.
- The work culture of L&T is predominantly performance centric and contribution focused. L&T has high degree of customer centricity along with teamwork and empowerment.
- People in L&T are treated as the most valued assets and their talent effectively utilized.

- L&T has an outward-looking work culture indicating its quick response to external demands and challenges.
- Innovation, the greatest mantra of our time for building competitive edge, is an important culture marker of L&T.
- Overall, it can be concluded that while L&T has been using all the drivers of excellence, the most prominently used are ethical governance, people power, customer centricity, and entrepreneurial innovation.

Part III: A.M. Naik—His Profile and Persona

After having read of the monumental growth story as well as the unique cultural nuances of L&T, at this stage, readers may be curious to get an insight into the man behind this story—A.M. Naik. This part of the case study is designed to highlight the salient characteristics of Naik's profile as a leader and as an individual.

The following sixteen emergent themes have been identified through content analysis of the interview data. They have been presented in order of importance keeping in view the conviction which the respondents demonstrated while speaking about A.M. Naik:

- Unflagging passion for work
- Ambition
- Futuristic vision: Enfolding the future into the present
- Strategic thinker
- Connecting horizon with ground
- Relentless quest for excellence
- Performance-centric empowerment
- Entrepreneurial ownership
- Courageous and bold: Leads from the front
- Talent sculptor
- Care and concern for people
- Continued learnability
- Simplicity
- Elephantine memory

- Constituency management: Communicating with people inside and outside L&T
- Synthesizing diversity

Unflagging Passion for Work

Eighteen interviewed persons said that Naik has tremendous passion and commitment toward work. Work is worship for him; he is a workaholic working around fifteen hours a day. He has boundless fervor and devotion for L&T. The following quotes said by the interviewees substantiate his passion for work:

"He is a company man. He will do anything and everything for the company. We say his life is L&T," said twenty interviewees.

Twenty interviewees also said: "He is always trying to do what is the best for L&T...."

According to each of the nineteen interviewees: "His commitment to the organization is unmatched. I don't think anybody can do what he does...."

Nine people mentioned: "His passion, his commitment, I don't know what to call it.... He goes to the US and you suddenly get a call and you look at the watch and realize that it is probably 4:00 am there. He calls from there and starts discussing work."

To one interviewee, "this company and the affairs of this company continue to run in him. It's a phenomenon ... it's too much I tell you and it does take a toll on his health."

"Mr Naik hates to lose and so he works five times or as many times harder to ensure that he wins," according to nine interviewees.

Fourteen interviewees mentioned the following: "He is 67 years old and yet he is the first to come to office [apart from housekeeping personnel] and he is the last to leave. He works from 7:45 in the morning to 10:45 at night," and "In his dictionary there is no holiday ... he works on Saturdays and Sundays. He lives on the ground floor of his bungalow and has converted the guest room [upper floor] into an office."

> "There is a mini-board room with video conferencing at his house and he holds a lot of meetings there on holidays," said seventeen interviewees.
>
> Twenty interviewees affirmed: "He is addicted to work."

Sixteen interviewees said:

> He flies back from the US, touches down at 7:00 in the morning in Mumbai and comes directly to the office. He asks for the colleagues who have traveled along with him and gets to hear that they are late "because of jetlag." There is no jetlag for Naik. The moment he lands meetings begin. Even if the meetings extend till midnight, next morning he is the first person to reach the office by 8:00 am, while office timings are from 9:00 am.

"We are amazed at the kind of stamina he has shown despite his bad health," mentioned eighteen interviewees.

All these discussions powerfully reveal that Naik has only one grand obsession: to create an L&T which is global, world-class, winning, technologically strong, and excelling. His entire life work has been devoted to L&T. He has channeled his passion, energy, and devotion to building L&T. In fact, Naik lives, eats, breathes, and sleeps L&T. No wonder, therefore, his wife said (when we interviewed her), "I am the second wife; Naik's first wife is L&T."

Ambition

All the twenty interviewees said that Naik's ambition is boundless. Nineteen of them said, "he is always thinking about the next milestone," while fifteen of them said, "he is never satisfied with the achievements and restlessly looks to the next goal post."

In fact, it is this essential characteristic to compete with himself and to constantly better his previous performance records that often leads him to critically compare himself to the people he meets. He is known to rate himself vis-à-vis others (on capabilities) and use this information to improve himself, as said by eighteen executives. Nine of them said, "some people cited that after conducting important meetings, Naik evaluates the way he has conducted the meetings as well as the outcomes and grades himself from A+ to C!"

Four people said not only is Naik ambitious, he has also created the air of ambition among the top team and infused in them the desire to achieve and raise the bar continuously. It is this ambition which powerfully fuels his passion for work and it is no wonder that he is also a workaholic, obsessed with achievements, and continuously raising the bar of performance both for L&T and himself.

Futuristic Vision: Enfolding the Future into the Present

Those who think of tomorrow in the present day, create both a better today as well as a better tomorrow. However, to create a tomorrow, one must have futuristic orientation and envisioning power. The leader who is devoid of vision can hardly see the future, much less lead the organization into the future. While describing Naik's strengths, all the interviewees said that Naik is "futuristic", "he is a man with a clear vision," "he is concerned about the future of L&T in the emerging scenario," "he continuously scans the environment to see how the future is emerging," and "he used scenario analysis for preparing the business plans, repositioning, and restructuring the organization." They also said: "There was no clear vision statement for L&T but we developed our vision statement as soon after Naik took charge of L&T." Seven people said, "Mr Naik had a clear vision in the early 1990s [when the Indian economy was closed] that we should become a global player," and eighteen interviewees said, "he made people think from a global perspective." Fourteen people said, "he started spending more time abroad, his mind became globally attuned and the learning he brought back to the company, forced us to think globally, and change our mindset."

In most of the meetings with the top team, five members mentioned Naik is famous for saying the following: "Don't give me your market share in India; tell me what it is at the global level." After some time, the same top team members said "we came up with a figure—1.2 percent which suddenly made us feel small." Nineteen people said: "Our vision is not only to be a powerful national player, we should have significant global presence in all the businesses." "Mr Naik gave us a global vision," said eleven interviewees. "The vision for

L&T was of much faster growth compared to the past," according to thirteen interviewees. "Now vision has become clearly articulated unlike in the past," mentioned four interviewees. To three interviewees: "In terms of scale of vision and speed [to achieve it], Mr Naik thinks big like the Ambanis."

Strategic Thinker

Strategic thinking is the most critical requirement for growth-seeking organizations. This entails anticipating the future, creating likely scenarios, and preparing the blueprint for architecting organizational growth strategy. This has been the common mode in all competing, excelling, and winning organizations. CEOs play a key role in providing strategic architecture and direction to their organizations.

All the persons interviewed for this case study lauded Naik's strategic thinking capability and cited strategic moves made by him. According to them, the move to exit those businesses which added little value (less than ₹ 100 crores) to L&T, going into new lines of businesses, the decision to stick to core engineering and, therefore, exit cement and others, and the move to go into global markets not only to spread the risk, but also to prepare the company to face competition on home ground, indicate his strong strategic orientation. Eighteen interviewees said that the strategic thinking on Naik's part is normally two to three steps ahead of others which includes a series of contingency plans.

Although he was pushing for global spread of businesses, he wanted to retain the focus on the Indian market at the same time. He said:

> ... we want to restrict ourselves to 25 percent or 30 percent in the global market ... let's not forget that India is a growing country, domestic market is pretty strong; let us also not forget that the company has also contributed to the development and growth of the country and this fundamental thing should not go away.

Naik, thus, appropriately combined the growth focus of the company both on the Indian as well as the global domain.

Eighteen interviewees said that Naik has a razor-sharp strategic thinking substantiated by the following statements:

> "He has a natural gift of looking beyond the present and, as a result, he develops his own strategy and then just goes ahead with that strategy. He is not worried about who will say what. Once he is convinced, he takes things forward with speed, seven interviewees mentioned this point.
>
> Eleven interviewees mentioned: "He is able to collate all information on emerging trends and direct it towards what ever is pertinent to L&T and we think this makes him a strategist ... he thinks in the future."
>
> "He made us look at everything from global perspective," said twenty interviewees.
>
> According to twenty interviewees: "Mr Naik is extraordinarily good in strategic thinking with futuristic thrust—everything he does is strategic—managing the board, getting into new businesses, people management, etc., in all the areas the [his] thinking is strategic. Long term vision and strategic thinking are an integral part of his leadership style."
>
> To eleven respondents: "He is a strategic architect with financial acumen. His mathematical calculations are so quick and his memory is so sharp that no one can mislead him."

From this discussion, one can conclude that Naik is a strategic thinker par excellence. He has enormous capability to look ahead, look around, anticipate the future, and strategize business actions, to take advantage of emerging opportunity.

Connecting Horizon with Ground

The popular description "Head in the clouds with feet on the ground" is a metaphor for integrating thought with action. Vivekananda's view—"thought without action does not have any value and action without thought is a futile exercise"—elaborates on the importance of integrating both thought and action. In the organizational reality, vision without execution remains a dream and execution without vision is a directionless activity.

All the interviewees said that Naik not only operates strategically with the big picture perspective, he is equally capable of coming to the ground level and engaging in minute details: nineteen people have mentioned that he goes into micro details wherever needed. "Normally, as one goes higher up one doesn't look into operational details; Naik however has the ability to balance both," said fifteen interviewees. "He can get into operational details and can predict what is likely to go wrong," mentioned seventeen interviewees. Twelve people said: "He puts himself in the shoes of the lowest level executive. He will imagine from the other man's point of view; he can identify very quickly what could go wrong." Along with his huge sweep across sixty businesses, Naik also gets involved in the details, in those areas which he feels are important and his involvement can add value, as said by twenty interviewees.

Change Maestros are known to successfully synthesize both macro and micro aspects of management. They have the unique ability to connect horizon with the ground which Naik does through strong follow up. He has executive assistants assigned to each line of business; they participate in meetings relevant to the business and also do rigorous follow up on the progress report to Naik.

Naik involves himself when he believes that there is a large business opportunity which L&T can benefit from. For example, he felt that service business had the maximum potential and, therefore, he started spending time on the info-tech business; now he is doing the same thing in real estate development.

Naik wants to know details of everything, said seventeen interviewees. If you ring him up right now for example, he will tell you the cost of each turbine. There are more than sixty businesses and many products in each of line of business, but he remembers everything. Fifteen people remarked: "His bandwidth is very-very large." "He wants to go into details of everything. He will tell you how many investments we are going to make, how many people, how many strategic units are there under. He is a hands-on man," said eighteen interviewees. Fourteen interviewees said that Naik is an extraordinary three-dimensional chess player, visualizing the invisible and making his strategic moves.

This description shows that Naik has tremendous mastery over integrating strategic thinking with strategic action. He has a large bandwidth and can comfortably operate at both levels—macro and micro—and also quickly switch from one mode to another with ease.

Relentless Quest for Excellence

Dissatisfaction is a sign of the need to move ahead, do more, and do better than before, rather than resting on one's laurels. In fact, a perusal of the history of all great achievers brings out that their discontent with the present propels them to continuously shift the goal post of performance excellence.

As mentioned earlier, all interviewees said Naik is known to continuously raise the bar of performance excellence and relentlessly drive the organization toward this. He is demanding both of himself and others. Given the number of hours, Naik has been putting in at work every day of his working life, it can be said that he has worked for eighty years in this organization! In fact, at one of the recent events, as fifteen people recalled, the Home Minister Mr Chidambaram (then Union Finance Minister) went to the extent of publicly saying this. All the people whom we interviewed said that Naik has very high standards for excellence. Not only does he drive others to better their previous performance, he seeks to do the same himself.

Given ahead are some quotes which further illustrate Naik's relentless quest for excellence:

> "A.M. Naik is really demanding and ... drives you for performance excellence ... somebody you really can admire," said fifteen interviewees.
>
> Eight people said he expects the Group Presidents to show a high standard of performance. When it does not reach that level he tries to counsel them by posing questions to them: "If you were a global leader what you would have thought? Suppose this was your own business would you have taken such a decision?"
>
> Seventeen interviewees said: "Mr Naik appreciates [performance and results] but quickly follows it up with tips for improvement."
>
> "... I think he worries that too much appreciation and satisfaction, may create a sense of complacency," said one person.

We tried to find out how people felt about Naik's demanding nature. It appears that despite being so demanding, he commands the respect and admiration from all. Why? The answer solely lies in what he has done for the organization and also the fact that he has devoted himself 100 percent for the organization. His "high energy levels and selfless kind of devotion to the job at hand" has made people admire and respect him, said ten people. Naik's stamina is amazing and no one ever heard of him falling ill. Even though he is unwell, he will pop antibiotics, take pain killers, and still be in office. According to twenty persons, he has never ever missed office because of sickness or illness:

> His energy almost borders on the super human ... he is actually like a dynamo. Once he decides something has to be done, he wants it done not in double quick time; he is also a multi-tasker, so he can handle a number of diverse things simultaneously.

Performance-centric Empowerment

The core philosophy of empowerment hinges upon enabling people to perform and deliver results, using the power of creativity, risk-taking ability, and entrepreneurial talent. In the organizational context, empowerment has to be linked with performance else it may lead to a situation of laissez-faire, gradually resulting in organizational drift. While empowering people, seventeen executives mentioned "Mr Naik ensures that empowerment results in high quality performance for L&T." Fifteen people said the empowerment is selective and "only those who deliver results are given a free hand to experiment. They are fully empowered to take risks and make decisions." In fact, Naik goes to the extent of building new businesses around the talents of highly capable people, as nineteen interviewees asserted. This is because he strongly believes that without the right person at the right job results will suffer. Through this approach, he has built many performance-centric leaders, as noted by eighteen interviewees. Seven people said: "Mr Naik provides tremendous degree of freedom and in fact sometimes you get scared with the level of empowerment you have. Here you are the boss and you have to decide." "Along with giving such empowerment, Mr Naik is also highly demanding and lays a lot of emphasis on the bottom line," recorded thirteen interviewees. All the interviewees said: "He likes people who are absolutely passionate about their work and results."

Entrepreneurial Ownership

As mentioned earlier, one of the reasons for the decay of organizations continuing beyond three generations is the loss of entrepreneurial appetite and zeal. It is such a sense of ownership which triggers passion and fosters risk-taking for organizational growth. Change Maestros with entrepreneurial ownership ceaselessly seek out opportunities for growth of the organization, whether it means creating a new path or going into the blue ocean zones of business.

Eighteen interviewees said that Naik is a "perfect entrepreneur" in the entire L&T leadership team. Seven of them said that he continuously looks for new avenues to create growth and value-add. Seventeen senior executives said that "most of us are professionals, not entrepreneurs like Mr Naik." Twelve people also talked of his native sense of wisdom for wealth creation and adding value. Seventeen people said: "He has tremendous business sense, clearly he has the pulse to understand when and where money can be made, perhaps because of his extensive travels and meetings with large number of business leaders from across the world. He uses both intuition and his thinking." "He doesn't only operate at the knowledge level, but has the knack of converting everything in financial terms," all interviewees noted this. Because of this orientation, L&T has transformed from a monolithic, bureaucratic giant to a nimble-footed opportunity-seeking and value-adding organization for all the stakeholders.

Courageous and Bold: Leads from the Front

Courage of conviction is the essence of outstanding Change Maestros. It is the courage of conviction which enables the leader to be bold, brave, and lead from the front and stand like a rock in the face of calamities. Viewed in this perspective, all the interviewees said the following about their leader, Naik:

Nineteen people said: "He stands like a rock and he is able to face any adversities."

Ten people believe, "He is a fearless man."

Nine people said: "He is not even slightly uncomfortable with confrontation any time of the day or night."

"He is a fearless leader, and his convictions are very strong and he does not bother about consequences," mentioned eleven interviewees.

Eleven people were of the view that "Mr Naik is very gutsy and can go to any extent to confront."

Nine people said: "He is very straightforward."

Nine people also said: "He is very bold in his approach whether meeting a rough union leader in L&T or King Abdullah in Saudi Arabia" and that "he is very daring; not afraid of anything."

Thirteen people narrated the following episode:

Many years ago, he used to be the only manager who used to come on shop-floor rounds at 2 am and exhort people on the shop-floor to work rather than sleep. In retaliation, workers tampered with his scooter, something which could have resulted in an accident. However, this incident did not scare or stop him from making the late night surprise checks on the shop-floor. This single act made a legend out of him as a gutsy, fearless guy.

"He is rough and tough, does not mince his words, but he doesn't use bad words ... doesn't abuse," said seventeen interviewees. Another aspect of his boldness is his tendency to lead from the front. Fifteen interviewees mentioned: "When he feels convinced that something requires to be done, he will start doing it, others follow him." "He definitely leads from the front and in case of crisis he will not shy away," as noted by eighteen interviewees. Nine people were heard saying: "If there is a difficult thing to do he will never ever expect anyone to do anything that he himself is not willing to do." Eleven people said: "At the end of the day his balance tilts toward hands on mode" and "He is a leader in any situation." All interviewees mentioned: "He believes in leading from the front."

Eleven interviewees mentioned the following:

> He was very different from the beginning.... He used to manage his division "Group 2" in a different way. If necessary, he used to fight with the management and he used to make his own rules for "Group 2." When he was younger he was a fighter, kind of a rebel. During those days the only person whom workers were afraid of was Mr Naik."

His rural upbringing and his early successes in school and college (where he was an acknowledged leader) set the stage for the development of this quality. At work, his early wins vis-à-vis workers on the shop-floor gave a tremendous boost to his basic courage and established his public image as a bold person.

Talent Sculptor

In a knowledge-centric business world, talent is the biggest weapon for winning the corporate Olympiad, which Change Maestros like Jack Welch and others have used very effectively. As a Change Maestro, Naik values talent and is a firm believer that unless the right talent is available, businesses cannot thrive. Hence, he has laid high focus on nurturing and shaping talent wherever he has seen the spark in people. In fact, Naik has been a firm believer in talent building. All interviewees mentioned "he is a true believer in developing young talent in the company because he considers them to be the future of L&T."

The following quotes indicate his approach towards nurturing talent in L&T:

> Sixteen people said: "He used to travel all over the country to various locations and rather than allowing the senior most person to make the presentation, he would ask persons 2–3 layers down the line to do it. This was a way of getting to identify and assess leadership talent in the organization. He would give such persons challenging assignments giving them a chance to prove themselves."

Naik has emphasized on lateral recruitments so as to bring in the needed talent in L&T, as fourteen people said.

Fifteen people commented: "He has given value to the role of HR and paid a lot of attention to this aspect; he himself spends time to spot the talent from outside to join the company at senior level."

"He is always ready to see a good candidate," as said by twelve people.

Eleven respondents said "he is the biggest HR man in L&T."

Seventeen interviewees said "he has laid a lot of emphasis on training and leadership development of promising talent and sent them to the best centres worldwide for training. Naik's focus on grooming talent has immensely helped L&T to create a competitive and performance mindset."

Care and Concern for People

One essential capability which outstanding Change Maestros have demonstrated is the capability to connect with, energize, and mobilize people. In fact, the core of leadership influence lies in connecting with people, understanding their problems, and responding to their needs. All interviewed persons said that Naik's ability to connect with people is immense. The following quotes made by the interviewees illustrate Naik's penchant for relating with people and showing care and concern for them:

Fifteen interviewees said: "He knows about the families of his employees, he remembers things like someone's son or daughter studying in the US and so on."

All the interviewees mentioned: "He is a warm hearted person. When he hosts a get-together in his house, or a meeting, he makes it a point to ensure that everybody has their lunch; he always remembers and takes care of the most junior person during meal-times. He is extremely hospitable and he makes it a point, that no one misses his/her tea, coffee snacks and meals, etc., when he schedules meetings at his residence."

"He asks everyone, he doesn't stand on hierarchy…" said eighteen interviewees.

Eleven of them said: "He remembers people's preferences and ensures that they are taken care of."

"When he schedules meeting at Pali Hill or in his place, he first thinks of how people would come or go, what flights they would take. He accommodates meeting timings to suit the convenience of outstation executives," said ten executives.

Fourteen people remarked: "He is a caring person in emergencies and critical situations."

Twelve interviewees said "he is always there to help his people; he will go even out of the way to help them. Some of us have difficulty in keeping touch with our own relations and acquaintances. But Naik attends 90 percent invitations for weddings to which L&T-ites invite him."

Citing his humanness and simplicity, one senior executive communicated to us saying "he is the most humane of the 16 bosses I have had."

Because of this quality of Naik, all L&T-ites across the organizations, say "he is one of us."

According to thirteen interviewees: "He ensured that post retirement, seniors are also taken care of; they can continue with the company as consultant or half time or whatever. That really took care of people at a different level. People feel happy to remain associated with L&T."

Continued Learnability

Change begins from self. No one can change others or the environment unless they are themselves prepared to change. In fact, Gandhi once said, "be the change you wish to see." Naik has demonstrated this quality not only as a young junior engineer at L&T, but continues to do so even today. His most powerful strength is his high learning orientation. People give examples of his initial lack of command over English, his tendency to observe people and learn something from each one of them, asking for feedback, to benchmark himself and rate his own conduct of each important meeting, to learn about all the sixty businesses especially the info-tech business. The statements cited ahead indicate his high learning orientation which was first observed in the company when he was a young engineer:

> "He is a ceaseless learner; he has the mind of child ... very curious to learn," said all the interviewees.
>
> "Even now if he meets with someone new, he will learn a lot and will immediately put it into action," pointed out fourteen interviewees.
>
> Twelve respondents mentioned: "He continuously evaluates himself and his style in various situations."
>
> As one senior person who has seen him from the early days put it, "I have seen him when he was possibly 25–26 and I am seeing him today; in those days we used to make fun of his English and today he has an excellent command."

Such is his desire to learn and better himself. His learning journey has been such that today Naik is a powerful speaker who speaks in persuasive, impassioned English.

One of prominent examples of his learning orientation can be seen in the way Naik steered the info-tech business, mastering the intricacies of a new technology, a tough job at age fifty-nine years. Today, five interviewees said "he can discuss info-tech with the depth and ease of an expert." During interviews fifteen people said that he learns by taking feedback and reflecting upon it. "He used to tell people around him: 'If I make mistakes, please point it out to me,'" said four people.

Seventeen people said:

> Every area he worked as a leader he mastered that subject and accepted it as a challenge; he was very good manufacturing man when he started his career, then he understood he must know business, then he became a good marketing man; he understood all business, then he understood finance.

"It is very difficult for a person to understand 60-odd businesses but he worked hard and developed understanding of each of the L&T businesses," said nineteen respondents. Ten interviewees said that he also learns from those meets by closely observing them and continuously benchmarking himself against them. His continuous self-assessment is very much visible when he attends any presentation; for example, if there are ten persons coming to make a presentation, on a piece of paper, he would have assessed all of them and graded them A, B, or C, thus, he assesses himself as well as others. "One of the most amazing things is the amount of new knowledge and learning he has acquired and accordingly changed himself over the years," mentioned seven interviewees. Another important characteristic which he displays is open-mindedness, a lack of rigidly holding on to his own views and opinions. He listens to contrarian views. Thus, his high learning orientation is his greatest strength.

A.M. Naik describes his relentless quest to learn in the following words:

> I am a constant believer that you can always learn. Everyday I go to the office in the morning. I think what I will achieve today.... That's why I am constantly changing. I am constantly in touch with my feedback with everyone as on line with everybody. My learning is through interaction, introspection and practicing to improve for tomorrow. You make mistakes, you learn, you see the result.

Simplicity

A perusal of the life of all great Change Maestros brings out one striking quality—simplicity. Simplicity of lifestyle, personal needs, approachability, and touching the lives of people. As a quality, simplicity arouses admiration in the minds of the general public, especially in the Indian context. All the twenty interviewees in this case study highlighted the simplicity of Naik in the following words:

> Nineteen people said, "as a human he is simple and he leads a simple life without any extravagance; lifestyle is not flashy or showy."
>
> One interviewee remarked: "He is approachable ... even if my wife picks the phone, he does not announce that he is the Chairman of L&T, he speaks very informally and politely."

"As a person, he has his feet firmly on the ground," affirmed fifteen interviewees.

"His lifestyle is need based not want based," said seventeen interviewees.

Fifteen people mentioned: "He values interpersonal relationships. He is always available to us when we are in trouble."

Elephantine Memory

An elephantine memory enables a person to be fully connected with past events, learn from them, and prepare for the future. Vivekananda went to the extent of saying that history is repeated because people do not connect with the past and learn from it. In the organizational context, elephantine memory immensely facilitates monitoring and follow-up of decisions taken, both of which are critical components of effective management. Elephantine memory, that is, the ability to remember names, numbers, minute details of meetings, presentations, etc., help Naik in building relationships, keeping track of developments as well as in review meetings. Mr Naik has been variously described as a super computer, a hard disk, and a camera, said all the interviewed executives. In day-to-day life, this simply makes him faster than others. Some of the salient quotes in this respect are presented here:

> Eighteen people mentioned: "He has a fantastic memory.... Mr Naik remembers a large number of mobile numbers—numbers of administrative assistants, senior managers and deputy managers. He does not need to check the cell phone to get a number."

"He remembers minutest details of meetings," mentioned fifteen respondents.

A senior executive went to the extent of saying, "his superb memory helps him in good networking. He keeps relationship even after 30–40 years."

Fourteen people were of the opinion that he has a "fantastic memory; he will keep in touch with people on the phone what's going on, so every little thing he knows."

"Even socially, while entertaining he will remember exactly who asked for which drink and ensures that no mistakes are made," said ten interviewees.

Sixteen interviewees said the following: "He never forgets anything; he has a supercomputer memory for faces and names. Even if he goes on the shop floor there are 100s of workers who he knows by name. His memory is a matter of discussion at various parties within L&T and people speak about it with deep awe."

"If you have told him a number once he remembers it two years later so there is no way you can hoodwink him [on facts and data]," mentioned two interviewees.

"He has an amazingly strong memory. There is nothing that he will forget. He discusses all his data and budgets hands free; even without carrying any documents he gives full and accurate details," fifteen people pointed this out.

According to five interviewees: "In a presentation he can spot even if there is a small variation in the numbers."

One person related the following incident: "I remember having once showing him a presentation and he immediately responded, 'Mr XX, the last time we met, you told me that our project will be 1,000 crores but here it is only 900 crores now.' He has such a sharp memory, he will tell you what happened chronologically year by year not referring to any paper ... its really fantastic."

Eighteen interviewees were of the opinion that anything you have spoken to him is recorded and reproduced verbatim.

Constituency Management

The primary job of a leader, especially at the CEO level, is to engage in managing the constituency and nurturing the same. In the case of the CEO, the constituencies are both internal and external. External constituents consist of board, shareholders, media, government, suppliers, and customers, while internal constituents are employees. Great CEOs not only manage them effectively, but also nurture and promote their interest. Everyone overwhelmingly said that he is phenomenal in nurturing all stakeholders. Interviewed people also cited the example of his easy access to various ministers at both the state and central levels, even going to the extent of access to the Prime Minister of India: "Whenever Mr Naik wants to meet them he can get the appointment in no time," said twelve interviewees. According to fifteen interviewees, Naik also has strong networking with various influential Indian CEOs and, like the others, has easy access to them as well.

Naik's constituency management has succeeded in creating immense goodwill for L&T in the governmental corridors of power. All the interviewees said: "We got all the support from the government at the time of UltraTech Cement dispute between L&T and Aditya Birla Group." Naik has not only been adept at external constituency management, he has also been equally savvy at internal constituency management. Seventeen interviewees cited the example of the creation of the employee welfare fund in which 15 percent of L&T's shares were transferred. This both protected L&T from future takeover bids and also powerfully nurtured the internal constituency making them rich beyond their dreams. Besides this, Naik has also got a powerful style of addressing meetings of employees, connecting with them, and also going out of his way to help when they are in trouble. Naik also lays emphasis on being fair to customers in terms of quality, delivery, and speed. According to all the interviewed executives, this has been the L&T culture and Mr Naik has further heightened this.

Synthesizing Diversity

According to eighteen interviewees, Naik has the ability to operate at far higher levels than most people. This higher level was explained by them as his being: *(a)* tough on style but soft on concern for people; *(b)* strong on visualizing the macro picture of the emerging future as well as focusing on the details of the present; and *(c)* concern for and balancing multiple stakeholders including the government, unions, investors, and employees. Above all, fifteen persons highlighted his tireless passion not only for the business but also for society. Six people said that Naik spends large sums of his personal wealth for societal development. These highlight Naik's ability to seamlessly handle divergent forces.

A.M. Naik as a Change Maestro: Salient Contours

The following salient characteristics of Naik's style as a Change Maestro have emerged from the responses gathered from both the interview and questionnaire (for details of questionnaire data of A.M. Naik's Change Maestro style, see Appendix 7A.5):

- Mr A.M. Naik possesses and deploys a wide range of leadership competencies which are crucial for the growth of an organization like L&T.
- He is a man of great ambition for L&T.
- He is a visionary with a global mindset, a strategic thinker with entrepreneurial bent, and a leader who provides a clear sense of direction.
- Naik is highly result-focused performance-centric person and pursues excellence in everything.
- He is a person who leads from the front, radiates positive energy, stands like a rock in the face of calamity, leads by example, and is an outstanding communicator.
- His oceanic passion and commitment toward L&T are very well supported by his result orientation as well as care and concern for his people.
- He has a very futuristic and focused vision, an elephantine memory along with entrepreneurial streak of ownership.
- His concern and care (people focus) along with performance focus, excellence orientation, and future focus for the organization form a very blend making him a Change Maestro.
- His courageous and bold behavior is highly valued by people and, therefore, they look up to him as a role model.
- Naik has a reflective temperament. He has enormous learning orientation which makes him a continuously self-renewing leader.

- He has combined macro and micro management capabilities and this has significantly enabled him to connect horizon with ground.
- His reach, his power of networking, and managing of the constituency has given him a larger than life image.
- Naik uses the power of envisioning the future and preparing the organization for the same, and in this process he views the globe as the business arena for L&T.
- He uses the power of performance excellence and continuously raising the bar for pushing L&T into the next orbit.
- He also mobilizes people power through communication and role modeling and channelizes the power of the collective to achieve the organization's grand dream and vision.
- Naik is so totally wedded to L&T that he romances L&T and lives and breathes L&T.
- All these qualities together are driven forward by the sheer power of his passionate ambition and convictions and this helped propel L&T from one orbit to the next.
- Naik has become one of the legendary leadership icons in India and this has been recognized through many accolades and awards, some of them being the Padma Bhushan (in 2009), Business Leader of the Year Award by *The Economic Times* (in 2009), and featured among India's fifty most powerful people by *Business Week* (in 2008).

A.M. Naik: Concluding Contours

A.M. Naik, the passionately committed L&T-ite who continuously pushed the group to the next horizon, is a man who dreamt many dreams for L&T, and successfully actualized the same. He is a man with oceanic dreams to build India as a great nation and to this end he uses L&T as a platform. Thus, his ambition has always aligned with building the country.

Creating economic freedom for senior employees through ESOPs and bringing prosperity to all stakeholders, while continuing to build a powerful

India, is something which relentlessly drives Naik to give everything to build L&T. Ring-fencing L&T by creating an employee-owned organization has been his greatest contribution to secure the future of L&T from all takeover threats, a problem which L&T faced in the past.

He is a leader who is always dissatisfied with the present. He always strives to take L&T from good to great and keeps shifting the benchmarks to surpass previous performance like Jonathan Livingstone Seagull, a seagull in Richard Bach's 1970 novel of the same name.

Naik's USP lies in combining vision and execution. He firmly believes that it is only those people who can rapidly switch their perspective from a lofty 40,000 ft to look at the nitty-gritty ground level details that can convert the vision into reality. He is of the view that between a great vision and its realization, there are hundreds of small steps to be taken and that each step has to be planned, strategized, and executed. Thus, Naik's thought process indicates a high degree of capability to deal with complexity, to co-ordinate and integrate a whole lot of different data and events using both linear and non-linear routes, and, above all, evolve many multiple likely mental scenarios.

Naik is reputed as the man who has worked in L&T for eighty years—calculated in terms of the number of hours he has put in for the last forty years. Such is his obsession with L&T. He is the first person to enter the premises and the last to leave whenever he is in town. The secret of his energy lies in his devotion and passion for the cause of the company. He believes that achievement and success are about velocity of action and scale and that these together make a company win in the face of tough global competition.

Naik is legendary for his vibrant curiosity, logical mind, extra fast wit and responses, high learning orientation, and sharp memory for names and numbers. He has tremendous networking capability and establishes instantly connects with people. He is a negotiator par excellence whether in dealing with presidents, ministers, or sheikhs across the globe. People are in awe of his high energy levels, drive, winning attitude, his understanding and knowledge of each of his top team members (100 of them), and his speed of intellect. He is constantly taking feedback, assessing his own actions, and striving to continuously improve himself. He is a highly value-based leader with a steady focus on fair, equitable, and transparent means to get things done.

One of his biggest contributions to L&T has been the creation of the entrepreneurial spirit and encouraging entrepreneur leaders, believing that they multiply value for the organization. The excellence centric, action focused, entrepreneurial culture which Naik built has enabled L&T to continuously catapult from one orbit to the other.

Appendices

Appendix 7A.1: L&T—Where Engineering Answers the Call of the Imagination

L&T has demonstrated that imagination and engineering, if combined, could build the most amazing engineering and construction company. The word in the English lexicon, "Imagineering," denotes L&T's remarkable ability to imagine the future and then engineer it to reality.

• Oil drilling platforms	• Factories
• Gas and oil pipelines	• Railway construction
• Dams	• Huge electrical substations
• Airports	• Towers and transmission equipment
• Ports	• Boilers among myriad other things in India and many other international destinations as well
• Townships	

L&T, as a name, is renowned for setting up and managing large and complex projects in the arid deserts of the Gulf, South East Asia, Africa, Russia, and many other places around the world. The company has taken everything in its stride—be it the frenetic infrastructure development from the 1950s to the 1980s, the newly minted info-tech revolution which raged till the turn of the millennium, and the revival of the globalization thrust as also the core sector development of the current century—and has grown like a colossus. The story of US$ 8.5

billion diversified engineering conglomerate almost mirrors the way India itself had weathered the post-independence upheaval, balanced its developmental priorities, and emerged as financial superpower untouched by the global economic meltdown.

The Beginning

It is fascinating to know that this behemoth has grown from modest beginnings in the shape of a small engineering and trading company set up in 1938 by two Danish men—Henning Holck-Larsen and S.K. Toubro. The two friends arrived on Indian shores as representatives of the Danish engineering firm F.L. Smidth & Co. in connection with the merger of cement companies that later grouped into the Associated Cement Companies. The original partnership firm they founded to source plant and equipment from European markets in 1938 was converted into a public limited company in 1946. Beginning with the import of machinery from Europe, L&T rapidly took on engineering and construction assignments of increasing sophistication. Today, the company sets engineering benchmarks in terms of scale and complexity.

In the years that followed after independence, the company built its business spanning diverse areas such as:

- Engineering and construction projects
- Construction
- Electrical and electronics
- Machinery and industrial products
- High-tech manufacture
- Power
- Information technology

Unstoppable Growth

The L&T run is unstoppable. The company continues to pile up its order book with a vision firmly on retaining its position as a global heavy engineering, construction, and electrical industry giant.

The company signed a contract with the public sector Oil and Natural Gas Corporation (ONGC) for a US$ 1.8 billion or ₹ 5,800 crore contract at the start of August 2009 augmenting its prominent position as a big player in the Indian hydrocarbons business segment. The contract was won against some of the best known names in the business like Hyundai, Samsung, and National Projects Constructions Corporation.

ECC, the Engineering Construction & Contracts Division of L&T, which bagged the contract, has emerged as India's largest construction organization. The company has received an order valued over ₹ 2,000 crores in September from GMR Energy Limited, a GMR Group company, for setting up a 2 × 384 MW gas-based power plant at Vemagiri, near Rajamundry, Andhra Pradesh, on a lumpsum turnkey basis.

Many of the country's prized landmarks—its exquisite buildings; tallest structures; largest industrial projects; longest flyovers; and highest viaducts—have been built by ECC. Leading-edge capabilities of ECC cover every discipline of construction: civil; mechanical; electrical; and instrumentation engineering.

Leadership Engine

L&T owes its success to a team endowed with visionary leadership—starting with the original partners themselves. The company makes no bones about the way it goes about acquiring its manpower and puts them through the pace before assigning responsibility and leadership and leaves the rest of the decision-making being undertaken through a transparent and democratic process. This system ensures total freedom to the leadership to make their own decisions and also hold themselves accountable to the outcome, a strategy which most Fortune 500 companies follow, resulting in rapid growth of their fortunes.

The company does not forget its obligations to society and has been an active player in the social sector with a number of rural, healthcare, and educational projects being designed for the poor.

Table 7A.1a: *Projects Undertaken by L&T in Major Core and Infrastructure Sectors of the Indian Industry*

Sector	Projects
Engineering and Construction L&T Power Heavy Engineering	L&T's engineering and construction track record consists of successful implementation of turnkey projects in major core and infrastructure sectors of Indian industry. L&T has integrated its strengths in process technology, basic and detailed engineering, equipment fabrication, procurement, project management, erection and construction, and commissioning to offer single-point responsibility under stringent delivery schedules. Strategic alliances with world leaders enable L&T to access technical know-how and execute process-intensive large-scale turnkey projects to maintain its leadership position. Its core competencies in engineering include highly qualified and experienced personnel from various disciplines and state-of-the-art facilities. L&T is the only Indian EPC company pre-qualified for executing large, process-intensive projects for oil & gas, refinery, petrochemical and fertilizer sectors.
	L&T has taken initiatives in synergizing its internal strengths developed over decades in the areas of project management, engineering, manufacturing, and construction by setting up an organization focused on opportunities in coal-based, gas-based, and nuclear power projects. This business provides turnkey solutions for setting up utility power plants, co-generation, and captive power plants on EPC basis. It also provides power plant engineering services through L&T–Sargent & Lundy Limited, a joint venture of L&T and Sargent & Lundy, USA. L&T has formed two joint ventures with Mitsubishi Heavy Industries, Japan, to manufacture supercritical boilers and steam turbine generators. In 2008–2009, significant progress was made in setting up manufacturing facilities for supercritical boilers and turbines at Hazira.

(continued)

(continued)

Sector	Projects
	L&T is acknowledged as one of the top five fabrication companies in the world, with engineering and manufacturing capabilities that are among the most sought after in industry. Operating at the higher end of the technological spectrum, L&T has led the way in Indian industry in introducing new processes, products and materials in manufacturing. L&T also has the logistics capabilities of fabricating and supplying over-dimensional equipment to tight delivery schedules. L&T's globally-benchmarked workshops are located at Powai in Mumbai, Hazira and Baroda in Gujarat, and Vizag in Andhra Pradesh.
Shipbuilding	L&T's ship-building facility at Hazira is geared to construct specialized high-tech ocean-going vessels. The shipyard has fabrication facilities and a slipway to launch the vessels, along with jetties for outfitting the ships under construction. L&T is building an additional ship-building and repair yard on India's eastern coast at Kattupalli near Ennore.
Construction	ECC—the Engineering Construction & Contracts Division of L&T—is India's largest construction organization. Many of the country's prized landmarks—its exquisite buildings, tallest structures, largest industrial projects, longest flyovers, highest viaducts, longest pipelines ... have all been built by L&T. L&T's leading edge capabilities cover every discipline of construction—civil, mechanical, electrical, and instrumentation. L&T has also expanded its focus to the Middle East, South East Asia, Russia, CIS, Mauritius, African, and SAARC countries. L&T also has keen interest in the markets of Indian Ocean rim countries, Africa and Latin America.

Sector	Projects
Electrical & Electronics	L&T is a major international manufacturer of a wide range of electrical and electronic products and systems. In the electrical segment, the Company holds leadership position in low tension switchgear in India, and is rapidly establishing itself in international markets. L&T also manufactures custom-engineered switchboards for industrial sectors like power, refineries, petrochemical, cement.... In the electronic segment, L&T offers a wide range of meters and provides complete control and automation systems for industries. Medical equipment and systems manufactured by L&T include advanced ultrasound scanners and patient monitoring systems. Its products are widely sold in markets in Europe and Australia.
Information Technology	Larsen & Toubro Info-tech Limited, a 100 percent subsidiary of the L&T, offers comprehensive, end-to-end software solutions and services with a focus on Manufacturing, Banking, Financial Services, and Insurance (BFSI) and Communications & Embedded Systems. It provides a cost cutting partnership in the realm of offshore outsourcing, application integration and package implementation. Leveraging the heritage and domain expertise of the parent company, its services encompass a broad technology spectrum, catering to leading international companies across the globe. It leverages the L&T parentage to also provide services in the embedded intelligence and e-Engineering space.
Machinery & Industrial Products	L&T manufactures markets and provides service support for critical construction and mining machinery—surface miners, hydraulic excavators, aggregate crushers, loader backhoes, and vibratory compactors; supplies a wide range of rubber processing machinery and injection molding machines; and markets valves and allied products and a range of sophisticated application-engineered welding alloys.

Source: Company data.

Table 7A.1b: Recent Recognition and Accolades for L&T

2010	• The leading business magazine, *Business Today*, ranked L&T the "Best Company to Work For" in the manufacturing sector in its annual survey that covered 8,742 respondents in 1,000 organizations across 800 cities in India.
2009	• The successful $ 600 million QIP and Convertible Bonds issue by L&T has been selected for an achievement award by *FinanceAsia*, a leading Hong Kong-based publication for the investor and analyst community, citing it as "Best India Deal."
• L&T has been awarded the first EuroFinance Award for excellence in corporate treasury management on November 26, 2009.
• L&T's Sustainability Report 2008 was ranked among the top 4 in the country by Asian Sustainability Rating on November 10, 2009.
• *FinanceAsia* has rated L&T as one of India's best managed companies. L&T has also ranked 4th in the categories of corporate governance, investor relation, and most committed to a strong dividend policy. The poll ranked L&T's CFO, Mr Y.M. Deosthalee, as one of India's Best CFOs on November 3, 2009.
• L&T secured the International Golden Peacock Award for its Corporate Social initiatives on February 26, 2009.
2008	• In a study by Reputation Institute, a New York-based research and consultancy firm, L&T has been ranked in the top 50 of the world's 200 most reputable firms.
• The Confederation of Indian Industry (CII) conferred upon L&T the Corporate Wellness Award in appreciation of the employee welfare activities of the company.
• The Federation of Indian Chambers of Commerce & Industry (FICCI) honored L&T with its Annual Award 2007–2008 for "Outstanding Corporate Vision."
• The Nuclear Equipment Business (NEB) of L&T has won the Industrial Excellence Award instituted by the Indian Nuclear Society (INS) for the second time on November 24, 2008.
• A ₹ 5 postage stamp in honor of Henning Holck-Larsen, co-founder of L&T, was released by the Department of Posts on June 12, 2008 to recognize his contribution to nation-building.

	- A survey conducted by the country's leading business magazine *Business Today* and consultancy firm Ernst & Young has rated L&T as "The Best Managed Company in India." - The Indian Chemical Council (ICC) presented L&T its prestigious award for excellence in chemical plant design and engineering. The award recognizes L&T's signal contribution to technological advancement in this field. - NDTV Profit, one of the most respected TV channels in the country, awarded L&T the prestigious "NDTV Profit Business Leadership Award" in the infrastructure category twice. L&T was commended for playing a crucial role in the development of infrastructure in post-independent India. - The Bombay Stock Exchange awarded L&T the Best Corporate Social Responsibility Award. - The Engineering Export Promotion Council (EEPC), Kolkata, awarded L&T, the esteemed National Top Exporters Trophy.
2006	- The Mumbai based CHEMTECH Foundation bestowed on L&T its prestigious OCEANTEX 2006 "Emerging Global Company Award." - L&T won professional recognition for its unique culture and ethos by securing *The Economic Times*–India Group of Institutes Award for "Organizations that Create a Learning Culture."
2003	- Most Respected Company Award 2003 in the Infrastructure Sector from *Businessworld*, India's premier business weekly. - Ranked 6th in the "Top Companies for Leaders" study conducted by Hewitt Associates, the world's largest HR service provider. - The Jamnalal Bajaj Uchit Vyavahar Puraskar from the Council for Fair Business Practices. - Civic Award by the Bombay Chamber of Commerce and Industry for outstanding contribution to community service.

Source: Company data.

Appendix 7A.2: Brief Sketch of A.M. Naik

A.M. Naik has carved a unique niche amongst the pantheon of transformational leaders of corporate India. He is the finest example of someone who, through sheer tenacity and commitment, succeeded in transforming his company from one of the most successful engineering giants of India into a global colossus. A technocrat by training who joined his company as a junior engineer in 1965, Naik rose through the ranks to become the MD & CEO, and then the chairman on December 29, 2003. With an engaging mind, Naik embarked on a well-crafted strategy that involved aggressive market entry and diversification into new product market domains along with mergers and acquisitions and even takeovers. Simultaneously, he inaugurated and catalyzed the process of indigenizing the manufacture of critical equipment for process industries especially in the defense and nuclear energy sectors. Today, L&T is synonymous with brand India in carrying out complex engineering, electrical, project management, and consulting projects around the world. It is no surprise that he was decorated with the highest civilian honor, the Padma Bhushan in 2009 for his achievement in creating one of India's very own MNCs. The Queen of Denmark appointed Naik as the honorary consul for the country in India and also conferred the prestigious honor of Knight of the Order of the Dannenberg in the year 2008. Naik is also on the board of IIM Ahmedabad and CII National Committee on Defense.

Table 7A.2: Accolades to A.M. Naik, 2008–2009

2009	• Mr A.M. Naik, CMD, has been honored with the Qimpro Platinum Standard–National Statesman Award for Excellence in Business by the Qimpro Foundation in recognition of his sharp business acumen, strong leadership, and enduring vision. • In recognition of the extraordinary leadership and exemplary vision of Mr A.M. Naik, in transforming L&T into an engineering powerhouse, the Mumbai-based National Institute of Industrial Engineering (NITIE), honored him with its prestigious Lakshya Business Visionary Award On October 26, 2009.

	- L&T's CMD, A.M. Naik, was conferred the Bharat Shiromani Award for his outstanding contribution to Indian industry. - A.M. Naik was awarded the country's most coveted honors—the Padma Bhushan by the President of India, Mrs Pratibha Patil on March 31, 2009. - Naik was awarded the coveted Business Leader of the Year by *The Economic Times* in acknowledgement of his clarity of vision, entrepreneurial ability, business acumen, and integrity. - The Government of Gujarat conferred the Gujarat Garima (Pride of Gujarat) award on Naik.
2008	- Naik was honored with the E&Y Entrepreneur of the Year Award in the professional category by Ernst & Young on November 26, 2008. - The Indian Merchants' Chamber & the Asian Centre for Corporate Governance & Sustainability conferred him with the prestigious "Transformational Leader Award—2008." - Naik was awarded the prestigious V. Krishnamurthy Award for Excellence by the Centre for Organization Development, Hyderabad, for his visionary and transformational leadership. - Naik was honored with the E&Y Entrepreneur of the Year Award in the professional category by Ernst & Young. - Appreciating the contribution by Naik to the fields of engineering and technology, and to the country's growth, the Kolkata-based Institution of Engineers India (IEI), has honored him with IEI Engineering Personality trophy. - Naik was featured among "India's 50 Most Powerful People" by the prestigious international publication *Business Week*, which stated: "Thanks to Mr. Naik, Indian engineering giant L&T continues to be a blue chip stock, and the first-choice contractor to build new private and state-owned manufacturing and utilities projects. Naik is also aggressively pitching for business overseas" (Lakshman and Kripalani 2007).

(continued)

(continued)

- The Indian Institution of Industrial Engineering (IIIE), a professional body of industrial engineers in India, honored Naik with its highly acclaimed "Outstanding Chief Executive Award" for his professional eminence and inspiring leadership.
- Naik was conferred the prestigious "Management Man of the Year" Award by India's premier management institute, the Bombay Management Association (BMA).
- Sankara Nethralaya, India's foremost Medical Research Foundation in eye care services, honored Naik with the Sankara Ratna Award.
- New Delhi-based Foundation of Indian Industry and Economists (FIIE) conferred on Naik, its prestigious Lifetime Achievement Excellence Award for Best Corporate Man of the Decade.
- Naik was honored with the JRD Tata Corporate Leadership Award by India's premier management organization, AIMA, New Delhi.

Source: Company data.

L&T's co-founder, the late Mr Holck-Larsen had received several national and international encomiums including the Padma Bhushan, the Magsaysay Award for International Understanding, the Sir Jehangir Ghandy Medal for Industrial Peace, and the Chemical Industry Stalwart Award.

Appendix 7A.3: Organizational Culture of L&T—Analysis of Questionnaire Data

Table 7A.3: Perceived Organizational Culture of L&T

N = 98

S. No.	Organizational Culture	Mean	SD	Ranks
1.	Ethical governance	4.44	0.63	1
2.	Performance excellence	4.29	0.56	2
3.	Result orientation	4.28	0.56	3
4.	Performance-based promotion	4.24	0.61	4
5.	Responsiveness to the customer	4.23	0.70	5

S. No.	Organizational Culture	Mean	SD	Ranks
6.	Teamwork	4.15	0.58	6.5
7.	Focus on continuous improvement	4.15	0.72	6.5
8.	Trust	4.10	0.78	8
9.	Focus on building competitiveness	4.00	0.73	9
10.	Communication and information flow: Horizontal (a) Within the department	3.97	0.80	10
11.	Nurturing talent	3.95	0.70	11
12.	Communication and information flow: Vertical (a) Top-down	3.94	0.70	12
13.	Global perspectives	3.93	0.76	13
14.	Outward looking	3.91	0.69	14
15.	Openness to new ideas	3.90	0.84	15
16.	Participative	3.87	0.67	16
17.	Openness and transparency	3.86	0.84	17
18.	Role clarity	3.85	0.69	18
19.	Speed of response to external demands and challenges	3.84	0.67	19
20.	Empowerment and delegation	3.83	0.84	20
21.	People orientation	3.79	0.72	21
22.	Nurturing innovation	3.71	0.83	22
23.	Process focused	3.67	0.85	23
24.	Support for risk-taking	3.62	0.88	24
25.	Speed of response to internal demands	3.61	0.72	25
26.	Entrepreneurial	3.55	0.83	26
27.	Community culture	3.52	0.85	27
28.	Tolerance of differences	3.51	0.91	28
29.	Cross-functional collaboration	3.49	0.71	29
30.	Centralized decision-making process	3.45	0.91	30
31.	Culture of celebration of achievements and successes	3.32	0.88	31
32.	Communication and information flow: Vertical (b) Bottom-up	3.22	0.93	32
33.	Communication and information flow: Horizontal (b) Across the departments	3.19	0.91	33

Source: Authors.

An analysis of Table 7A.3 highlights the following prominent features of the L&T organizational culture:

- On a 5-point scale, the perceived culture attributes range from a minimum of 3.19 to a maximum of 4.40. This indicates that all work culture attributes are perceived to be in the range of "Most Visible" and "Highly Visible."
- The SDs across all the culture attributes range from a minimum of 0.63 to a maximum of 0.91, indicating significant homogeneity in the perception of work culture at L&T.
- Nine parameters have a mean value above 4.00 on a 5-point scale. These are: ethical governance; performance excellence; result oriented; performance-based promotion; responsiveness to customer; focus on continuous improvement; teamwork; trust; and focus on building competitiveness. Further perusal of this table makes it evident that five of the nine parameters—performance excellence; result oriented; performance-based promotion; focus on continuous improvement; and focus on building competitiveness—are associated with achievement and result orientation.
- The second category "Highly Visible" consists of nineteen items. Five of these are related to people power—nurturing talent; people participation; role clarity; empowerment and delegation; people orientation. All these items have a mean higher than 3.70 indicating a fairly high position in the cluster. This finding clearly indicates that people perceive themselves as valued, involved, empowered, nurtured, and cared for contributors of the organizations.
- A famous adage goes, "Begin with the end in mind." In the organizational context, this means integrating the organization with the outside world, since business opportunities lay there. Items like global perspective, outward looking, openness to new ideas, and speedy response to external demands and challenges as available on the questionnaire, clearly show that L&T has an outward-looking work culture indicating its quick response to external demands and challenges. Innovation, the greatest mantra of our time for competitive edge, is perceived as an important culture marker of L&T, as indicated by the high mean values on nurturing innovation, support for risk-taking, entrepreneurial culture, and tolerance of differences of ideas.

- Relatively speaking, the culture of celebration of achievements, bottom-up communication, and interdepartmental communication do not fall in the "Outstanding" and "Very Good" categories.

Appendix 7A.4: Financial Performance of L&T at a Glance

Table 7A.4: Revenue and Profit of Larsen & Toubro, 2003–2009 (in ₹ billion)

Year	Income Revenue	Net Profit
2003	108.57	3.8
2004	111.07	6
2005	145.99	6.97
2006	167.47	10.51
2007	207	18.1
2008	295.61	23.04
2009	406.08	30.07
% Change over 2003	274.03	691.32

Source: L&T's Consolidated Financial Highlights. Adapted from Annual Report, page 17 titled "Consolidated Financials Highlights." Available online at http://www.larsentoubro.com/lntcorporate/LnT_DWS/Downloads.aspx?res=P_CORP_CINV_AFNC_AANL_ALNT&year=2009.

Appendix 7A.5: A.M. Naik as a Change Maestro—Analysis of Questionnaire Data

Table 7A.5: Perceived Style of A.M. Naik as a Change Maestro

N = 98

S. No.	Change Maestro Attributes	Mean	SD	Ranks
1.	Has ambitious plans for the organization	4.95	0.22	1
2.	Is result-focused	4.86	0.38	2
3.	Leads from the front	4.85	0.41	3
4.	Is demanding and performance centric	4.82	0.39	4
5.	Radiates positive energy	4.81	0.45	5

(continued)

(continued)

S. No.	Change Maestro Attributes	Mean	SD	Ranks
6.	Is a visionary	4.80	0.45	6
7.	Is an effective communicator	4.78	0.44	7
8.	Stands like a rock in the face of calamities	4.74	0.52	8
9.	Has a global mindset	4.73	0.57	9
10.	Leads by example	4.69	0.53	10
11.	Is a strategic thinker	4.65	0.50	11
12.	Pursues excellence in everything	4.61	0.62	12
13.	Is entrepreneurial	4.59	0.64	13
14.	Provides a sense of clear direction	4.52	0.61	14
15.	Has high credibility	4.47	0.72	15
16.	Is reliable	4.44	0.70	16
17.	Is honest and transparent	4.42	0.70	17
18.	Fast in making critical decisions	4.41	0.74	18
19.	Is innovative and creative	4.40	0.78	19
20.	Recognizes and rewards performance	4.39	0.75	20
21.	Is a role model	4.37	0.9	21.5
22.	Business strategist	4.37	0.85	21.5
23.	Is a man of words	4.35	0.77	23
24.	Is interested in growth of his people	4.16	0.80	24
25.	Has helping attitude	4.15	0.96	25
26.	Is fair and impartial	4.06	0.82	26
27.	Is open to new ideas	4.02	0.90	27
28.	Is a team builder	3.87	0.95	28
29.	Sensitivity	3.84	0.89	29
30.	Grooms and develops people	3.83	0.91	30
31.	Makes people feel that they are valued by the organization	3.70	0.90	31
32.	Has empowering and supporting attitude	3.69	0.91	32
33.	Makes people feel that they have great worth	3.52	1.05	33
34.	Respects the dignity of others	3.32	1.04	34
35.	Humility	3.30	1.15	35

Source: Authors.

Table 7A.5 brings out the style and profile of A.M. Naik as a Change Maestro, as perceived and experienced by ninety-eight members belonging to the top and senior management team. The mean values of the thirty-five items have been broadly grouped into three categories for the purpose of analysis: "Most Visible" with mean value of 4.5 and above; "Highly Visible" with mean value ranging from 3.5 to 4.49; and "Visible" with mean value ranging from 3.30 to 3.49. Perusal of this table brings out the following salient points:

- On a 5-point scale all the leadership attributes are rated fairly high. The mean values range from 3.30 to 4.95 indicate that the rating of thirty-three attributes either fall in the "Most Visible" category as per data collected from fourteen interviewees or in the "Highly Visible" category as per data gathered from nineteen interviewees. The highest mean rating is in the case of ambitious plan for the organization and lowest is in the case of humility.
- In case of thirty-two items, the range of the SD is less than 1, indicating high degree of homogeneity of perception. Only in the case of three items, SDs are = > 1.00, indicating variation in perception on these three leadership style attributes—makes people feel they have great worth, respects the dignity of others; and humility.
- Fourteen items feature in the "Most Visible" category with mean values of 4.50 and above.

Notes

1. Authors gratefully acknowledge and appreciate the support they received from S.N. Roy, Executive Vice President and Head, Corporate Initiatives, L&T, in preparing this case study. The authors, however, own entire responsibility for the conclusions and views expressed in this case study of the work culture of L&T and the style of A.M. Naik as a Change Maestro.
2. Twenty top team members interviewed were by the authors. The number of respondent varies since the interviewing method was largely unstructured; we recorded what they said, giving greater priority to what came out of top-of-the-mind in response to our broad questions, rather than getting them to respond to a set of questions.

8

8
KIRAN MAZUMDAR SHAW: ENTREPRENEURIAL PATH BREAKER

This is the story of a King who ruled a mighty kingdom somewhere in south India. The King was known for his valor and loved for his magnanimity, large heartedness, and just rule. He built tree-lined avenues, dharamshalas (rest houses) for travelers, temples for worship, and also a few educational institutions. His contributions had far-reaching impact on the lives of people—both haves and have-nots.

One day he decided to give up the throne and install a worthy successor who could carry his mission further. The King had three children—two sons and one daughter—whom he dearly loved and yet wished to make a prudent choice; therefore, he sought the advice of his Guru. As per the Guru's advice, he gave each of the children 100 gold coins and asked them to create something which would profoundly impact society not only within the Kingdom but also far and wide across the land.

The eldest of the three children thought hard and decided that he needed a lot more money to do something worthwhile and match his father's expectations. He thought that the only way to quickly make a lot of money was to play a game of dice. Unfortunately for him, each time he played, he lost and finally was left with no money. His dreams of becoming King were razed to the ground and could not face his father. The second son also thought he needed more money to actualize his father's, the King's, grand dream. He tried hard to raise money from relatives and friends, but remained unsuccessful because people were not convinced by his plan of action and were unsure of his productive use of the money. He unsuccessfully kept trying to mobilize resources and finally gave up all hope of becoming his father's successor.

The third offspring was Akanksha, a spirited and independent young princess, popular among the people for her love, concern, and wisdom. Before formulating her plan, she traveled far and wide to understand the concerns and needs of the people in the region, both within her father's kingdom as well as in the neighboring kingdoms. She was happy to see that people in her father's kingdom had a reasonably good life compared to those in the surrounding kingdoms. However, what struck her was the absence of centers of higher learning and education in the entire region, which she felt was important to transform the lives of the people. People were traveling thousands of miles to Varanasi for higher learning in Vedas, Astronomy, Medicine, Arts, and Mathematics. She realized that only the wealthy could afford to go to such places and acquire knowledge. She also realized that to build a powerful kingdom, pursuit of knowledge was, among other things, the biggest prerequisite. She, therefore, took up the mission of building centers of higher learning which she felt could have far-reaching impact not only on people of this kingdom, but also those living in neighboring kingdoms.

She felt passionately for the cause, but was painfully aware of the paucity of resources. She struggled with ways and means to raise resources, but could not achieve enough to fulfill her grand vision. Yet she did not give up hope and finally came up with the idea of inviting large number of scholars, kings, and princes to a conclave. Many dignitaries arrived from far and wide and there she spoke passionately about her dream to build a university which would serve as a hub for scholarly pursuit for the region. Many kings and princes were captivated by her vision and plans and joined this laudable movement. In due course as the university got built, scholars from different parts gravitated toward this center. At the end of the two-year period, the King adjudged the work of the Princess as by far the most impactful and decided to appoint her as his worthy successor.

This story powerfully portrays the persona of Kiran Mazumdar Shaw, and the great organization Biocon, which she has successfully built. Kiran Mazumdar Shaw is the epitome of great vision with unbounded determination and zest to passionately pursue the same. Kiran's life is one of strong determination and endeavor to transcend limitations, finding innovative approaches and solutions, and relentlessly executing her dream. This is the story of Kiran who is, in a true sense, the entrepreneurial path breaker.

The story of Akanksha reflects, in many ways, the story of Kiran—a biotechnology pioneer and one of India's wealthiest women who is hailed as the "Mother of Invention" by *New York Times* and India's "Biotech Queen" by *The Economist*. She, like Akanksha, displayed unconventional thinking and boldness in starting a venture in Brewery which was traditionally seen as male monopoly. She is a true example of the one who actually dared to tread that "less traveled" path.

In the words of Goethe, "Boldness has genius, magic and power in it" and Kiran has amply displayed them all in her journey, characterized with grit and determination, as an entrepreneurial path breaker. Vincent Van Gogh says that great things are done by people who are not afraid to be great. Kiran dreamt of things that were never dreamt of and asked herself why she could not dream of them. She combined her vision with venture and brought into being the visible from the invisible.

This case study "Kiran Mazumdar Shaw: Entrepreneurial Path Breaker"[1] has been organized into the following three parts: Part I provides a brief profile sketch of Biocon; Part II highlights the action architecture and culture landscape of Biocon; and Part III discusses Kiran Mazumdar Shaw's profile and persona.

PART I: BRIEF PROFILE SKETCH OF BIOCON

Beginnings with a garage for an office and ₹ 10,000 as seed capital, Biocon India was born (for details of the organization's profile, see Appendix 8A.1). Thirty-two years hence, this pioneering company, today, is Asia's largest biotech company. It is is among the few Indian companies which is into discovery, ranked 20th among global biotech companies, and is richly awarded and recognized for its outstanding achievements. Biocon is known as an innovative company, which has successfully reinvented itself in response to business opportunities and challenges from a fermentation-based enzymes producer to a bio-pharma company.

Above all, the company is known for significantly bringing down the cost of some critical drugs in India. It is significant that worldwide, only bio-pharma companies like Biocon have been able to break the traditional monopoly of big pharma in drug discovery, by using the molecular biology route, thereby, aiding a significant drop in prices. Biocon stands out as a highly innovative company spending around 8 percent of revenue on research and development (R&D)—with a plan to rise in the next few years—as against 3 percent spent by other Indian pharma companies. Biocon is one of the few companies which, till date, has filed 950 patent applications, which is an indicator of its serious efforts to create and protect knowledge, rather than use shortcut techniques to do business. The company has been the preferred global supplier of statins and is set to become the largest producer of recombinant human insulin in Asia. In addition, Biocon has the distinction of being the first company to commercialize human insulin-Insugen, and the first to launch proprietary anti-cancer drug, a monoclonal antibody-based drug called BioMab EFR®.

In 2004, Biocon's first initial public offering (IPO) was oversubscribed by thirty-three times and on Day 1 the bourse closed with a market value of $ 1.11 billion. It also made Kiran Mazumdar Shaw, CMD of Biocon Ltd (for details of the Change Maestro's profile, see Appendix 8A.2), the richest woman in India.

Part II: Action Architecture and Culture Landscape

The emergent eleven patterns from content analyses of interview data are conceptualized and presented here:

- Strategy architecture
- Entrepreneurial passion
- Global vision
- Futuristic

- Creating the second curve
- Empowerment
- Non-hierarchical
- Happening place
- Quest for excellence
- Caring community
- Ethical governance

Strategy Architecture

In the lifespan of Biocon since its inception, Kiran has launched many initiatives to create robust strategy architecture. The key initiatives with far-reaching impact on Biocon are presented ahead. In order to provide a perspective on the initiatives, a brief historical sketch has also been provided so that the reader can appreciate the relevance of the bold initiatives.

From 1978 to 1988, the joint venture between Biocon Bio-chemicals, Ireland and Biocon India has operated smoothly. As early as 1982, Kiran, however, decided to go beyond meeting the requirements of the partner company, and set up an R&D center called Bio-Chemizyme India (BCZ) to develop novel enzymes. This was a key initiative in setting a strong foundation to create the spirit of science and scientific endeavor in Biocon. In 1989, Unilever Plc. acquired Biocon Bio-chemicals in Ireland and merged it with Quest International. Biocon continued a relationship with this entity over the next decade and supplied industrial enzymes to it. In 1995, Unilever acquired shares in Biocon from Biocon Bio-chemicals, Ireland. The year 1999 saw Glentech International acquiring the entire shareholding of Unilever in Biocon, Biocon Quest India Limited (BQIL) and BCZ.

In 2000, Kiran changed the game by acquiring the entire Biocon shareholding back from Glentech. This was a truly bold and courageous decision at that time, considering that Glentech was the customer for 75 percent of the production by the company. This move liberated Biocon, making it an independent organization, empowering it to shape its own destiny, and map its own path.

Although a pioneering Biotech company, for twenty years since its inception, Biocon remained a small and niche producer and exporter in the industrial enzymes segment. In 1998, Kiran Mazumdar Shaw realized that with the potential in enzymes being limited, growing exponentially from a turnover of ₹ 75 crore was next to impossible in that business segment. On hindsight, it is possible to say that this became a defining moment both for her and for Biocon as she asked herself the following question:

"Why are we only making enzymes? Why not look at some other products based on the technology we have developed for enzymes?" She replied: "I felt pharma biotech could give me a much bigger growth potential than enzymes, that's where we started our journey" in the bio-pharma segment.

This shift into the bio-pharma segment proved to be the key reinvention strategy for Biocon, which subsequently charged ahead on a high growth trajectory, growing exponentially for six years in a row to become a ₹ 500 crore company by 2004. Being the early movers into this space in India, Biocon had a head start which helped it immensely. Kiran had rightly spotted the opportunity which lay in one of India's biggest challenges—providing affordable healthcare to the vast masses of its population. Until then, many drugs, for example drugs for diabetes, cholesterol, and cancer, were expensive because they lay with a few global pharma giants and, thus, beyond the reach of the common man. India is on the threshold with the largest number of diabetes, heart disease as well as cancer patients in the world and desperately needs low-cost medicines. It is in this space that Biocon decided to develop new molecules and work to bring down costs of critical drugs. According to Kiran, their business model hinges on "developing affordable innovative solutions which have a lot of local relevance but a huge global impact." Initially, two programs were finalized: one was insulin:

> ... because I [Kiran] felt India had a very high diabetic burden and I felt that if we could develop a novel option for insulin, we could look at it as a global opportunity; and the other was statins, which were the cholesterol reducing agents, again produced by fermentation. I felt that that was also a global opportunity.

Biocon's first branded formulation, which came out in 2004, was insulin. It was the first company to produce insulin in pecchia fermentation mode.

By the time Biocon became a ₹ 500 crore company, Kiran realized that it needed scale and size to secure its position on the global map. With this in view, she went for an IPO in 2004, which made Biocon a billion dollar plus company, providing it needed muscle and funds to expand and grow. Today, it is close to being a 2,000 bio-pharma conglomerate.

Another stream of strategies is evident right from 1994 when Kiran brought a strategic shift in the Biocon focus from it being predominantly a producer of industrial enzymes to providing contract services to global pharmaceutical giants. It was a humongous task to persuade international giants to sub-contract research to a tiny company like Biocon. However, Kiran impressed upon them to buy her idea and, slowly, global giants began to outsource contract research work to Biocon. Such a strategic move enabled Biocon to build world-class R&D infrastructure through funded contract activities which otherwise would have been an extremely expensive proposition.

In 2000, another landmark strategy was to set up Clinigene—a contract trials subsidiary for conducting clinical trials. In 2002, Kiran ventured into drug development, thus, moving up the value chain from generic manufacturing to proprietary molecules. These strategies made Biocon a company with a foothold in three domains: manufacturing products; conducting research; and providing research services.

Post 2004, Biocon embarked on a new journey of going global by striking strategic alliances, acquisitions, and joint ventures for marketing and research. Through this strategy, Biocon has now made its presence felt in the Gulf region, Europe, along with a tie-up in Cuba. In 2007, the enzyme business was divested to Novozyme, thus, bringing complete focus onto bio-pharmaceuticals. Today, Biocon has end to end capability from drug discovery to clinical trials to manufacturing and marketing.

However, among all these strategic options, Biocon has laid emphasis on competitive co-partnership—while in research area, they co-partner with some companies, in the products and marketing space, they aggressively compete with them in some markets, thus following a robust strategy of competitive collaboration.

Entrepreneurial Passion

Kiran's entrepreneurial mind could sense that Biocon needed scale and entrepreneurial DNA for building competitive edge and unleashing the innovative power of its people. With this in view, she selected people with entrepreneurial fervor and then nurtured their entrepreneurial talent.

All the interviewees emphatically highlighted the entrepreneurial character of the Biocon team. According to the three heads interviewed by us,[2] not only is Kiran an entrepreneur, she has created an entrepreneurial spirit. Nine interviewees said: "The top team consists of very good entrepreneurs...." Twenty interviewees mentioned: "We have an entrepreneurial mindset." According to fifteen interviewees, Biocon is very entrepreneur-driven. And according to thirteen respondents, the company supports entrepreneurial ambition.

According to many of the top team members, they do not always have to look toward Kiran. If they feel something is important then, as per eighteen interviewees, "we do it"; "the top team has a strong belief in themselves and in their own teams," said twelve people. As one of the company advisors observed: "When faced with challenges Biocon's response is 'we can do it, there's no reason why we can't do it.'" Some interviewees said: "The move from statins to insulin, the monopoly of only two or three companies worldwide, was a phenomenally bold step for them to take." Some others said: "We never inherited anything, everything here is created by the employees; the whole of Biocon shares the strategic direction and leadership set by Kiran. Kiran acknowledges that Biocon is a company made by the people." Yet some others remarked: "Biotech was a completely new business; all of us have actually shaped the company, when we did not have the brand name, we did not have the money, and we did not have the experience...."

Risk-taking, which comprises the key aspect of entrepreneurial orientation, has been clearly brought out in the following quotes:

> Twenty-one interviewees said: "Biocon is a risk-taking organization."
>
> Fifteen people said: "We take big risks."
>
> Nineteen people were of the opinion that Biocon is "not a punitive culture."

"Mistakes are seen here as a part of the game," said fifteen interviewees.

One respondent said: "The bosses won't kill you if you make a mistake, because everybody here tries to do a better job. Mistakes do happen, but our bosses have never behaved in a way that, 'Okay, this guy has made this mistake, finish him.'"

These statements show that Kiran has created an organization where entrepreneurship is a way of life. In this company an entrepreneurial path breaker is backed by professional entrepreneurs, something quite uncommon in most organizations.

Global Vision

Nineteen interviewees said that Biocon is a truly global company. When we think about Biocon, we think of global scale, global processes, and global standards, said fifteen interviewees. Nine interviewees said that in Biocon, the focus is to beat global giants when it comes to cost competitiveness. "Our product Insugen has forced global giants to bring down costs of insulin in India by 30 percent. In this case we are the global leaders in cost competitiveness," said fifteen interviewees.

Fifteen interviewees said that many people joined Biocon after having left great global academic centers and lucrative options because they were attracted by Kiran's dream and vision to create Biocon as a great global institution. As many as nineteen respondents cited that Biocon, today, is ranked among the top twenty bio-pharma companies in the world. The growth strategy of Biocon is to have global alliances, acquisitions, and joint ventures as a route to actualize global vision.

Futuristic

Biocon is a highly opportunity-sensing organization and according to sixteen interviewees, it thinks of tomorrow today. In the last decade, it has been preparing itself to take on the challenge of providing affordable healthcare to ageing populations in the area of diabetes, cancer, and degenerative diseases. Today, Biocon has many products in the pipeline which will fructify in the coming five to seven years, which will thereby enable Biocon to produce affordable drugs, said fifteen interviewees; thus, giving the company a huge competitive advantage. According to fourteen interviewees, substantial progress has been made in creating the oral anti-diabetic drug, that is, oral insulin. In addition, they mentioned that Biocon is also developing the arthritis drug—T1H, a drug for multiple sclerosis and a whole range of bio-stimulants. Their novel cancer drug, BioMab, which has hit the market, is a better drug, in terms of lesser side effects, than the other similar available products.

Eighteen interviewees emphasized that Biocon has developed world-class R&D. Nine people said: "R&D is our future and we are securing it by funding R&D." According to ten interviewees: "We continuously upgrade our R&D facilities." Many interviewees (that is, eleven interviewees) said that in Biocon, there is a lot of cutting-edge futuristic research in anticipation of emerging healthcare issues and challenges.

From this discussion, it is clear that Biocon is preparing for the challenges of healthcare by developing drugs through the bio-pharma route. Many programs are on, they have a rich pipeline, and if the developments fructify, they will be able to provide affordable drugs to treat many diseases. Their thrust on R&D is, thus, a natural outcome of this futuristic orientation.

Creating the Second Curve

Over the years, Biocon has had a dynamic growth strategy constantly creating the second curve before the first curve declines, mentioned eighteen interviewees. Twenty-two interviewees explained that in the initial twenty years, Biocon was into enzymes, then they moved to statins (cholesterol-busting drugs), and later, in 1999, to bio-pharma and services thereby creating a new curve for the business. When the dream of becoming a "global bio-pharma company with global scale" crystallized, Kiran decided that they had to find ways and means to reach out globally, since the typical route of building up from the ground level would take too long. With this in mind, Biocon has adopted multiple routes for growth—competition; collaboration; alliances; joint ventures; and acquisitions.

Eighteen interviewees cited Biocon's thrust to create the second curve of excellence in the processes, speed of decision-making as well as converting ideas into action. Seventeen among these respondents said that Biocon is continuously endeavoring to bring down costs and provide affordable drugs which India is in desperate need of.

From this discussion, it can be concluded that Biocon continuously strives to create the second curve in all their activities with a view to create competitive edge.

Empowerment

All the persons we interviewed said there is independence and freedom to work in Biocon. Twenty interviewees said that leaders at various levels have full freedom and flexibility to do things. Fifteen respondents said that Biocon has a culture of freedom as well as support and encouragement. According to eighteen people, there is plenty of opportunity to experiment in the company. Twenty-two people remarked that there is very little interference in the work undertaken at Biocon. Fourteen people said that employees are encouraged to pick up new challenges and work on them. One of the business heads expressed the spirit of empowerment in Biocon very eloquently: "Basically all of us in the senior management team, are expected to develop our own teams. We try to be enablers [not controllers] who develop people, who can keep the growth happening, who can attract the right talent."

Interviewed people also highlighted that they experience a tremendous sense of ownership in Biocon. All interviewees said that "people think it is their own company." One person explained this very well by saying:

> We think Biocon belongs to us. I think this department belongs to me. That's the way I work, just like at home, whatever I do is mine. If there's a failure, it's my failure, if there's a success, it's my success. That's the freedom which Biocon has given all of us.

According to one of the top team members, "a lot of people hold very responsible positions at a young age here [Biocon]." Nineteen interviewees said that, in Biocon, people are given responsibilities based on their performance, irrespective of age. Eleven interviewees responded that here, people are valued for their ideas, not their position. One person said: "There is freedom. If you want to do something which is good, you have the freedom to do it. So I would say Biocon is far more horizontal, highly transparent, and interactive."

These statements indicate the high levels of empowerment experienced by people in Biocon. There is tremendous independence, freedom of decision-making, and action. As a result, people own the place psychologically, in terms of both successes and failures and give their best. One of the positive outcomes of such an environment has been that Biocon has successfully created many leaders across the organization.

Non-hierarchical

All the twenty-three interviewees mentioned that in Biocon, people are on a first name basis; all queue up for lunch in the canteen regardless of their position, including Kiran. They also said that Kiran has encouraged the creation of an organization which has no hierarchies, no bureaucracy; there are no level differences in anything. Fourteen people highlighted that the culture in the company is very transparent; people can walk into the rooms of the senior members in case of problems showing that they are accessible even to the junior-most employee. According to eighteen interviewees, there is no formal system of addressing people as "Sir" or "Ma'am." Twelve people said that the organization is flat, non-hierarchical; there is a very friendly atmosphere and, therefore, decision-making is very quick.

Nineteen interviewees also said that the culture is open and seamless. One of the interviewees explained further saying that "in fact if there is a problem faced by someone he can even go across groups directly and get help without having to go to the head of that group for permission." Eighteen people also said that they are all encouraged to communicate freely across the organization. Above all, it is noteworthy that Kiran has kept her doors open and if the matter is important, such that it does need her attention "many of us can walk across to her office," informed twenty interviewees.

Further proof of the non-hierarchical culture, according to seventeen interviewees, lies in the fact that there is a frank and open style of functioning in Biocon. Debates and discussions are held among colleagues regardless of the position they hold or their function in the organization.

All the interviewees feel that there is plenty of freedom for people to take initiative. As the head, R&D explained:

> ... in general, you can only be effective and use people's potential to the maximum when they have freedom to speak and science itself cannot flower without freedom. So in Biocon we strongly encourage people to question. There is a very debate-oriented and discussion-oriented culture here.

Thus, the environment is non-hierarchical, there is a strong networking culture. A multi-disciplinary approach to problem solving is encouraged, said five interviewees.

From the discussion in this section, one can say that in Biocon there is a culture of debate, discussion, and dialoging regardless of the positions they hold in the company. In Biocon, there is an open-door policy where people are accessible and have freedom to raise questions to anyone regardless of hierarchical positions.

Happening Place

All the people we met mentioned that Biocon is a "happening place," "invigorating," "challenging," and "exciting". As many as twenty interviewees said that Biocon is a happening place with new developments taking place everyday. According to twelve respondents, one does not feel like one is coming to a "workplace"; people interact continuously, going across, talking to each other, getting ideas and solving problems. Fifteen people were of the opinion that "everyday people are doing something new and that gives an excitement in life." Eighteen people said: "In Biocon work is fun, work is enjoyable. People look forward to come to work everyday!" Twenty-one interviewees remarked that Biocon is a "great place to work". Twelve people feel that it is a great opportunity to work here because of the quality of leadership and interactions. According to nine interviewees, challenging jobs are given to people from the day they join. Fourteen people emphatically said that the quality of work is most satisfying and there is constant excitement because everyday people are expected to do things differently, and they enjoy this freedom. As many as nine interviewees mentioned that Biocon is a growing company and people have the freedom to experiment, innovate, and do things differently.

All the interviewees highlighted that Biocon is a highly innovative company and it is this factor which contributes to the challenging and exciting work environment as indicated in the views shared ahead.

According to fifteen interviewees, Biocon has a culture of creativity and innovation. This has been further elaborated by one of the interviewees who said: "In Biocon, innovation is in our DNA, it is there in our spirit. We tend to ask: 'What new things are you doing? What is it that you are doing differently?'" One person recalled one of the earliest employees of Biocon saying:

> When you want to be a pioneer, when you want to make the first move, you have to do things that others have not done, this is the mantra of Biocon. For example, we were the first company to launch an indigenous monoclonal antibody in India. We had to do a lot of backend innovation work before the project could reach this stage.

One interviewee said: "There is something new happening here. Every year you add new capabilities, every year, the organization has to grow because for us, to not grow means to collapse." Seven interviewees asserted: "We do things differently, we take different opportunities and we approach opportunities differently, like we were the first one to launch this novel anti-cancer product in India." One person also said: "I think Biocon is a pioneering company, different and innovative, even from the time we did enzymes—how many enzymes companies were there in India at that time?" According to another executive we interviewed, "Biocon means cutting-edge innovation. We do innovation across the entire pipeline ranging from incremental to breakthrough."

As many as seventeen persons said that Biocon dreams of making oral insulin: "it has not been developed anywhere else in the world." One person said that "the underlying thread is that we want to do something different, we want to be innovative, we are willing to take the risks, that few other Indian companies are known for." Eleven interviewees said that in Biocon they want to be known as an Indian company that is doing something creative and innovative. Fourteen respondents were of the opinion that Biocon would like to be recognized as a company that has always brought innovative products, creating products out of India, from conceptualization to execution.

According to twenty interviewees, innovation is promoted in Biocon through various means—thirteen people said that there are plenty of discussions and debates and scope for expressing different viewpoints. Twelve interviewees suggested if there is a challenge in terms of work, five different groups will work on five different ideas or approaches to solve the same problem, and out of those ideas, the one most beneficial idea will be implemented first; thus, they said, nurturing innovation is a way of life in Biocon. Seven interviewees said: "Every quarter, generally, there is a review of the work done and we come to know the problems, and whoever has an idea is free to go and work on it." According to nine interviewees, innovation is promoted right from the induction stage in Biocon. As part of the induction program among other things, new employees are groomed to think innovatively.

Quest for Excellence

It is perhaps Kiran's passion for science, her high exposure to global best practices, and global ambitions which have ingrained a deep quest for excellence in Biocon. Early on in the organization, she ensured instilling an Intellectual Property (IP) consciousness (and patenting) through training, according to the Head, IP. According to eighteen interviewees, there is a strong focus on excellence in Biocon; there is no scope for being mediocre. According to the head of Marketing: "We are very protective about brand Biocon and this leads to excellence. We try to do everything in the best possible way. It is imbibed in us. We will see that nothing is compromised before products get to the market."

The quest for excellence is present in everything they do, whether it is product quality, best campus, best research, or best brains. Kiran's passion, "I want to build brand India, brand Biocon, brand Bio-tech.... I want to make sure that Biocon is something which India can be very proud of" is probably one of the driving forces behind this continued quest for excellence.

According to one of the Chief Operating Officers (COOs) "a lot of focus is given to quality of performance. Feedback is given round the year, not once in a year, so that people know our expectations."

Fourteen interviewees said that recognition and reward schemes are also used to further promote excellence, as evident in the views shared ahead. The general view shared by fifteen interviewees was that people can grow fast to any level here depending on excellence in performance at Biocon. Nine people mentioned that many young people hold senior positions here; and they have risen solely based on their excellence in contribution to Biocon. Some of the top level interviewees mentioned that although there are formal processes of performance review meetings, it goes beyond that. The high interaction culture ensures that everyone knows what is happening and who is doing what—innovation; innovative ideas; and new developments—and when someone is rewarded, others appreciate it.

All the twenty-three interviewees mentioned that there is high appreciation for excellent contribution. Five interviewees said: "Biocon's culture is a very appreciative culture." "Sometimes the company goes the extra mile to appreciate somebody for excellent contribution," said four interviewees. Three people remarked: "When we have a good sale, Kiran will come here and say 'Congratulations' informally; she'll shake a few hands and people feel very happy about it." Promotions are used to express appreciation, to the extent that Kiran personally makes announcements to the Biocon community. "Sometimes we have a gathering in the canteen and Kiran herself announced the promotions," said three respondents. Nine people remembered, last year (in 2009) Kiran did not have the time to announce the promotions, so she personally greeted the promoted lot over the phone.

ESOPs have also been used as a great instrument to promote excellence. In the first round, 300 excellent performers were given ESOPs and, now, 1,000 people are eligible for this scheme.

Fifteen interviewees mentioned that on Biocon Day, awards are given to those employees who have contributed significantly or made outstanding contribution in front of the entire Biocon community, which people regard as a great recognition. In addition to this, there are also financial rewards at the end of the year.

Caring Community

All the interviewees said that Biocon is a caring and humane company. Fifteen interviewees further said that in Biocon, a lot of importance is given to the employees. Nine of them said that "people are valued here." Twelve respondents said that "Biocon takes very good care of [its] employees." According to eleven interviewed people, "it's a very caring company especially when people are in difficulties." The company gives not just monetary support; it gives moral support and mental support, asserted five interviewees.

Along with being caring and humane, another important aspect is the emphasis given to teams and teamwork. As many as nineteen interviewees mentioned that teamwork is strongly emphasized in Biocon. People are encouraged to work in teams, said fourteen interviewees. Ten people were of the opinion that Biocon strongly believes that 70 percent of performance flows from the team and 30 percent from the individual level. Teamwork is very good in Biocon, remarked nineteen respondents. Nine people said there are inter-departmental teams and they have worked successfully. Inter-departmental conflicts are minimal and people get along well with each other, said nine people. According to six interviewees: "When we have a problem, we sit together and sort it out." One person said: "When sales and marketing team did well, the finance president took them out for dinner—such things are common here but rare in other organizations." There is very close coordination between the different functions. The interactions between the various departments, especially research and manufacturing, research and marketing, and marketing and manufacturing, are quite cohesive, they talk to each other quite often, mentioned seven interviewees. Eleven people said that once you work here, it is so difficult to work somewhere else because of the feeling of togetherness and of being wanted.

These statements provide insights into bonding at the emotional level in the Biocon community. Teams have been given a lot of emphasis and interviewees experience high degree of togetherness, a sense of being wanted and feeling valued, which also reflect the warmth and bonding among the teams. Further, interviewees experienced Biocon as caring, humane, understanding, and as a company that looks after the whole person rather than just the employee. People feel valued in this company as human beings apart from the rewards and focus on innovations and achievements. People talk to each other informally, although at the formal level the Chinese walls are maintained.

Another related aspect which has been brought out is regarding the low politics in the company. Most of the employees expressed that the organization is not political in its style of functioning. Nine people said: "People don't go to your boss to talk about mistakes made by you—they approach the person directly and tell them." "At meetings Kiran makes people feel so secure that there is no question of politics," mentioned five people. One person mentioned: "I think openness, communication which exists in Biocon helps to minimize politics." Twelve people remarked if there is a mistake made, there are no politics around it. One interviewee said, "it is hard to bring in nepotism or play favorites because everything is so transparent here." The apolitical nature of the organization indicated in these quotes further reinforces the positive community bonding which has been nurtured in Biocon.

There is a sense of being part of an extended family since everyone knows about his/her colleagues and their families. Kiran is known to simply drop at her colleagues' homes when they or their loved ones are unwell. The fact that Kiran got homes built for her top team members reflects her communitarian sense. The concern she shows for Biocon employees and the help she extends in times of need is, by now, legendary. At the workplace, the sense of easy informality, walking into each others offices, meeting, discussing, and resolving matters (as mentioned earlier) enhances the sense of connectedness. Kiran personally announcing the awards and the celebrations and recognition certificates contribute in a big way to building the sense of community. All the interviewees expressed a tremendous sense of pride in being a part of the Biocon community.

Ethical Governance

All the interviewees emphasized that Biocon is a highly ethical company. Seventeen people said that they "believe in doing things the right way." Eleven interviewees responded that they do not like to use unfair means. They are conscious of government rules and regulations and work within the regulatory framework, said nine people. Five people said whenever Biocon designs new facilities, they work for the optimum effluents treatment with focus on the local norms. Even in packaging they are conscious of how they use natural resources, mentioned one interviewee. According to nine of them, this company believes in openness, trust, and integrity and tries to tell people what they are doing within the company, through media and conferences. Biocon is open and honest in all business transactions, affirmed eleven interviewees. Contribution to nation building and bringing affordable healthcare are forms of giving back to society, reflecting the company's ethical behavior, according to all the interviewees. The strong belief in ethics, which is visible in all the practices and policies of Biocon, emanates from Kiran, who says: "I believe that achievement without a sense of honesty and a sense of integrity is worth nothing. That's what my father used to tell me and I used to really agree with him. This is what I have tried to instill in Biocon."

ACTION ARCHITECTURE AND CULTURE LANDSCAPE OF BIOCON: SALIENT CONTOURS

The interview and questionnaire responses (for details of questionnaire data of organizational culture of Biocon, see Appendix 8A.3) reveal the following unique features about Biocon's achievements, action architecture and culture DNA:

- The financial performance of Biocon in the last five years (for details of financial performance of Biocon from 2003 to 2009, see Appendix 8A.4) demonstrates mind-boggling achievement. During this period, its revenue has jumped from approximately ₹ 3 billion in 2003 to approximately ₹ 10 billion in 2009 showing a growth of 270 percent. Equally impressive has been the growth in profits which jumped from ₹ 36 million in 2003 to over ₹ 1 billion in 2009. There has been a 227 percent jump in revenue growth and a 1,108 percent jump in profit growth. Its multiple contributions and achievements have catapulted Biocon into the league of the global top twenty biotechnology companies (in 2008). This is a singularly magnificent achievement for a company which was started in the 1980s with a seed capital of only ₹ 10,000.

- This is a company where innovation and continuous improvement are the ways of life. The company has a deep appetite for innovation and, therefore, strives in endless pursuit of new ideas. This spirit has made Biocon a center for scientific endeavor and a hub for innovation and, in many ways, a true science campus.
- The company has a culture of openness, transparency, ethical governance, and high moral character.
- Biocon is highly outward-focused with global reach in mind. In Biocon, teamwork and trust are essential.
- Biocon is highly customer-focused and speedy in response.
- Biocon lays strong emphasis on performance excellence.

Part III: Kiran Mazumdar Shaw: Her Profile and Persona

From the interview data, the following fourteen themes emerged:

- Himalayan ambition
- Crystal gazer
- Connecting horizon with ground
- Entrepreneurial risk taker
- Excellence seeker
- Accessible and authentic
- Humility
- High learnability
- Innovative perspective
- Higher values
- Caring
- Empowering and trusting

- Inspirational
- Blending diversity

Himalayan Ambition

Dreams, ambition, and purpose are the basic fuel, which propels a human being to move, take risks, and surmount all difficulties. The bigger the dream and ambition, the greater the energy a human being is able to channelize toward its achievement. Great leaders besides having a Himalayan ambition also have mastery over excellent execution. The lives of great Change Maestros bring out the power of ambition, dreams, and larger purpose, and mastery over execution in their extraordinary achievements.

All the interviewees said that Kiran has a grand and bold ambition for Biocon. According to twelve interviewees, Kiran dreams big. Eleven people said she wants to create a global impact. Eight people were of the opinion that the sky is the limit for her ambition for Biocon. She is very keen on making a big mark globally, remarked eight interviewees. According to ten interviewees, she is absolutely clear about her ambition. She keeps telling people where Biocon should be and the ambition that she has for Biocon. Nine people mentioned that she is very ambitious and definitely wants to make this company a billion dollar company through the innovation route. Twenty interviewees said that she has very high aspirations for Biocon; her goal is to be the best. She always says "we have to be the best." According to nineteen interviewees she is aspiring to be the best globally; she wants to make her company at the top, Number 1, and the best biotech company in the world. And she is relentlessly working toward this goal.

The mentioned statements clearly reveal Kiran's high ambition for Biocon. The company already features in the world's top twenty biotech companies. It is evidently this ambition which has been fueling the relentless growth of Biocon over the decades. She is proving to the world that high quality pharma products can be manufactured in India, in an organization headed by a woman.

Crystal Gazer

Great leaders, by thinking ahead, come up with new strategies, approaches, and alternatives to ensure continued survival and growth of their institutions. Being rooted in the present and not developing crystal-gazing capability surely leads organizations toward extinction. Organizations, therefore, need crystal gazers who are futuristic and who can understand emerging trends, sense the opportunity, and capitalize on it.

All the interviewees spoke admiringly about Kiran's capability to see the future as evident from the following statements:

Twelve interviewees said that in every opportunity, Kiran sees new potential for Biocon: "She sees future much better than others. She started with enzymes and then she decided that the future will be very much cutting edge solutions to medical problems, so she reinvented herself into a new company altogether and most of her products are related to that."

One interviewee said that "she is a person with a very clear idea about what she would like Biocon to be."

According to eleven interviewees, she is a visionary who conceptualizes the way forward; who can see the distant future.

To nine people, she is a visionary; she started a small company and had the vision to make it a well-known global company.

"She probably has a third eye somewhere, when things are happening, she probably sees opportunities and grabs them, because I am sure opportunities pass by all of us," remarked one respondent.

She also has this innate gift of seeing an opportunity, according to twelve respondents.

Nine interviewees said that she is able to see trends beyond the obvious.

Five interviewees mentioned that she is very futuristic, she can see the emerging tomorrow very clearly. She sees Biocon in a global perspective, sees global challenges and prepares the company to respond to global trends not only in India but also globally. She has been so forward thinking that on bio-similar monoclonal antibodies, Biocon started work ten years ago, while in the US it started much later.

Connecting Horizon with Ground

Excellence is the mantra adopted by all winning organizations. Organizations with great ideas and poor execution remain dreamers and turn their dreams into dust. Great leaders like Gandhi, Martin Luther King, Jack Welch, Larry Bossidy, and Steve Jobs demonstrate the capability of flying in the sky and swooping to the ground level, thus connecting horizon with ground.

Like these great leaders, Kiran also demonstrates this quality of connecting horizon with the ground. She has tremendous business sense and, in fact, is an outstanding business strategist, who knows exactly when to make the right move and change the gears of business. As pointed out earlier, she is a crystal gazer: she has the capability of using both a binocular vision and that of a magnifying lens. She can comfortably operate both on ideas and action. She combines the big picture with details when needed. All these capabilities qualify Kiran as a hands-on leader.

Entrepreneurial Risk Taker

Change Maestros, who have made the difference and taken their organizations to new horizons, have been non-traditional and non-conformist: they have sought to create a new path. They have the zeal to work against all odds and are known to be risk takers, innovators, and entrepreneurial, with courage of conviction. They are the entrepreneurial risk takers. It is this spirit which enables them to create impact and make a mark. Kiran Mazumdar Shaw epitomizes entrepreneurial passion with zeal for winning against all odds by finding innovative solutions.

All the interviewees spoke about Kiran's entrepreneurial orientation along with her risk-taking capability. Seventeen of them said that she is very brave and courageous. Fifteen interviewees informed that she is an entrepreneur par excellence; she takes decisions based on her gut feel and intuitive power. She is entrepreneurial and a risk taker, confirmed ten interviewees. According to six respondents, when the pharma world had given up trying to manufacture oral insulin, Biocon carried on conducting research and is now in Phase III of clinical trials. This indicates her entrepreneurial ability to adopt unbeaten track and pursue it. In Kiran's words, "I am always looking at an innovation-led strategy that differentiates."

She has a tremendous risk appetite to the extent of selling her personal wealth and then reinvesting the money in Biocon. She has the knack of moving into new areas—to follow the unbeaten track. She was the first mover in the biotechnology sector in India as well the first mover in bio-pharma in India. Both of these are glaring examples of her entrepreneurial risk-taking. When she decided to buy out Unilever shares, there were venture capital companies ready to buy her out, in which situation, she could have easily become richer by a 100 crore of rupees. However, Kiran was not tempted to sell out, her focus being more on growing the company and instead, decided to buy out Unilever stakes.

Excellence Seeker

Great leaders always shift their goal posts; they raise the bar of performance and continuously try to move the organization to the next orbit. This passion keeps the organization charged-up and pushes it to the next horizon. Great leaders are restless, impatient with the status quo, and continuously endeavor to move things from the already best situation to next and even better option. They are like the Olympians ceaselessly seeking to create new records. Excellence-seeking is integral to Kiran's mindset and style.

According to nineteen interviewees, Kiran has the excellence mindset. Her favorite question, as per nine interviewees, is whether, "there is a better way to do this?" And as per nine interviewees, she asks if "there is a smarter way to do this? A more intelligent way to do this?" Twelve people recalled her asking: "Is there something that we have learnt along the way which enables further improvement?" Twelve interviewees said that she has very high expectations from her employees and she literally pulls them up to the standard where she wants to go. She has a very clear vision, which she articulates very well and is able to take people to that level, said nine respondents. One person said that she does not hesitate to blast you if you go wrong, but that comes from a deep sense of involvement with the organization. Fourteen people were of the opinion that because of her high expectations, she is able to extract the best from people. One person said:

> A person of her stature dealing with such serious things like biotechnology and science gets equally involved in making of the Biocon logo. She asks questions like "how can we make it better, what are the thoughts behind the logo?" indicating her capability to come down to ground level execution. She is very interested in knowing what's going on and the thinking behind it.

Accessible and Authentic

All the interviewees said that Kiran is highly approachable, accessible, open minded, empowering, and friendly. People walk into her cabin and have healthy debates about business-related matters. She is available for day-to-day problem-solving; she can be accessed for a quick chat on the mobile or a phone call or one can also send her an email, said eighteen interviewees. According to fifteen people, "she is an amiable person and there is no arrogance at all in her demeanor."

She has a large bandwidth and is able to interact with people across levels and issues as indicated by the following views shared by the interviewees:

> "She interacts at any level depending on the work," said fifteen people.
>
> Twelve interviewees mentioned that they have seen her going on the site and interacting even with people who are doing the hands-on job.
>
> Nine people mentioned that in R&D, she has been spotted speaking with bench-level scientists.
>
> Eight people said that she is equally comfortable interacting with the people at the shop-floor level or even with the gardener.
>
> All interviewees said that her doors are always open.
>
> She never says no to anyone, mentioned seventeen interviewees. "Whether it's a gardener or a COO, when they visit her, they are treated equally," remarked thirteen interviewees.

Twelve people said that Kiran is not only approachable, but she also listens to them. Nine people affirmed that she does not say that she has made up her mind and hence will do what she things is right. Fifteen people said that "she can talk to the President of the US, she can talk to the sweeper of Biocon, and she can talk to the patient." She is willing to listen to people, has a lot of respect for her employees, and treats people with a lot of openness and respect, remarked sixteen employees. Eleven interviewees also said that she never conveys, through her behavior, that she is the boss and, therefore, things should go the way she wants them to be done.

Even those at supervisory levels in the factory do not hesitate to openly talk about issues in departmental reviews, so said some eleven interviewees. Kiran accepts open criticism on business-related issues, mentioned eleven interviewees. According to nine interviewees, even if she takes a decision and somebody brings it to her notice that it is incorrect, she reflects upon it and does not hesitate to reverse that decision. She is not bullheaded; she is very receptive to feedback, said one person. All the interviewees said that communicating with Kiran has been extremely easy because of her accessibility and amiability.

Everyone was unanimous in saying that Kiran is frank, straightforward, forthright, and clear in her thinking and expression. Twelve people said that there is no ambiguity in her communication. What you see is what you get; she tells you what she thinks, said nine interviewees. "She can appreciate you, she can shout at you; she is genuine upfront ... straight from the heart," said six people. One interviewee said: "You don't have to sit and read her, she'll tell the concerned person exactly what she thinks." Eighteen people asserted that Kiran speaks her mind. Nine people said that if she does not like something, she is very prompt to inform the employees of the same, thereby maintaining a very open style of working in Biocon.

From this discussion, it can be concluded that Kiran is accessible and approachable. She listens to people, accepts views, is open to criticism and does not impose; there is no fear of reprimand or repercussions. She is genuine, straightforward and forthright, hence people know where they stand with her.

Humility

In his well-known book, *Good to Great*, Jim Collins highlighted the importance of humility in the profile of great leaders. He assigns the highest position (at level 5) to humility in his levels of leadership model (Collins, 2001). In the Ramayana, Tulsidas described the profile of great people and contrasted the same with the profile of less evolved people. He stated that humility is the hallmark of a great person while arrogance is the characteristic of less evolved people. As people become more accomplished, they demonstrate greater levels of humility.

In our consulting experiences, we have invariably seen that people in top leadership positions are respected neither for their position nor for their wealth, but for their humility (among other personal qualities). It is the sense of humility which evokes respect and love for the leaders. This has been the hallmark of leaders like Gandhi, Mandela, Martin Luther King, J.R.D. Tata, Jamsetji Tata, and G.D. Birla. Kiran Mazumdar Shaw profoundly embodies a sense of humility in her demeanor and conduct with people.

Most of the people we interviewed (eighteen among the total interviewees) said that when they meet Kiran, she gives them the feeling that they are valued, wanted, and respected for their views. She is an intense listener and appreciative of different views, said eleven people.

All the interviewees highlighted that Kiran is a humble person.

Fifteen of them said: "Success has not gone to her head."

Nine people said that "she is [a] down to earth" person.

According to eleven interviewees, she does not throw her weight around.

Six people feel that she is still very grounded.

Nine respondents said that she does not think "I am the boss."

Four people claim that she "does not say, 'I am the boss,' do as I say."

According to four interviewees, "she is still very human; money has not got to her."

"She doesn't want people to get up when she enters. If she comes into my room, I can sit and talk to her, she has absolutely no airs about that," recorded one interviewee.

One person further said: "She is extremely down to earth. Even today, if you bring her a *masala dosa* from a small shop, she will happily eat it."

She is not formidable at all, despite all her success, affirmed four interviewees.

High Learnability

Learnability enables business leaders to be open, highly receptive, and observant. They absorb information, facts, and changes taking place around them. This ability facilitates leaders to craft strategies, evolve processes, and structure to appropriately respond to events in and around the organization. Leaders with this ability are intense listeners, open to new ideas, prepared to be questioned, and change their stance depending on the situational requirement. These abilities make the Change Maestros constantly grow and evolve. It is the intense learnability of Kiran Mazumdar Shaw which has helped her to continuously re-invent herself and Biocon.

All the interviewees said that her learning orientation is extremely high. According to twenty interviewees, she is an avid reader, subjects ranging from art to current affairs to science. She has also been described as a very keen and alert listener by fifteen respondents. Eleven interviewees further said that she is very alert about her external environment; she knows everything that is happening not only within Biocon, but also in the industry, in the sector, and around the world. Nine people said that "if there is a policy decision happening in the US, she would be very much aware of it and get to know the content of those policy decisions." According to nineteen interviewees, within Biocon, Kiran knows everything that is happening in finance, production, marketing, and R&D.

She has a constant thirst for knowledge, said twenty respondents. In fact, nine people said that they were amazed at how much Kiran knows about R&D and what is happening at different levels in the company. She has a keen eye for detail as well as understanding of science. She is very smart and grasps things very fast, informed eleven interviewees.

According to six interviewees, who have known her for many years, Kiran has been evolving, learning, and growing. She sees something and immediately picks it up because she closely observes everything. She is a keen listener and ever ready to learn, said fifteen interviewees. One person said:

> She is not an R&D person but she knows much more than many R&D scientists. When they [the scientists in her lab] talk about the diseases, she sits

with these people and you should see the look in her eyes. She is like a sponge absorbing everything.

In addition, nineteen people mentioned that besides working tirelessly, Kiran entertains often and meets people. She is a frequent traveler; she goes everywhere and has a hang of everything. She networks a lot, meets people globally, and understands what is happening in different fields.

Innovative Perspective

An innovative mind is at the root of new ideas and new creation. This is so because the innovative mind is a curious and questioning mind which is dissatisfied with the status quo. Another hallmark of the innovative mind is the alertness and responsiveness to emerging opportunities and capability to appropriately change organizational strategies, structure, and processes. Such a mind is also flexible and can modify its own mode of functioning and suitably orient to shape the events. In the success story of Biocon, Kiran's innovative mind has played a key role.

All the twenty-three interviewees highlighted that Kiran is passionate about being innovative and creative; she has a basic urge to do things differently, said eighteen people. She always asks whether something can be done differently, as mentioned by twelve interviewees. Fifteen people mentioned that she comes up with very good ideas. For example, in the pharma sector, India was known more for reverse engineering than for innovative R&D. In the context where reverse engineering was a way of life, Kiran's focus on new discovery was a significant shift in indicating her zest for innovation. One person was heard saying: "When Kiran entered this sector, her eyes were always on new discovery so that shift to innovation was huge."

Kiran is extremely receptive to new ideas, highly innovation-oriented, very keen that we change the image of India from reverse engineers to exploration centric, doing something new and different, and willing to take the risk for it, mentioned eleven interviewees. Nine people said that they always found her coming up with very intelligent ways of doing things. Fifteen people recorded her constant question and quest as: "How can we do this differently?" Seventeen people said she answered this question in the following words: I want to do things differently, I don't believe the way that this is done is correct, I want to make diabetes treatment affordable for every Indian. Kiran has the knack of coming up with unique ideas which at first seem to be impossible, said six respondents.

Kiran's passions to do things differently, exploring different ways, and continuously questioning the way things are done reveal her innovative temperament and perspective. This indicates her quest to carve out a new trajectory, rather than following the beaten path. Such an approach further reflects her non-conformist and in many ways radical thinking.

Higher Values

Great leaders are above narrow self-interest. They are inspired by the grand dream and vision. They constantly work to make a difference in the lives of the common people. They are humanistic and believe in generously giving back to society. It is these qualities which make them admired, loved, and respected as leaders. Kiran Mazumdar Shaw also subscribes to higher level values and strives to make a difference. In her words: "I really think you cannot compromise on your principles, your values, and your ethics because that's what builds a company."

All the interviewees said that Kiran operates on higher values—for the nation; society; and people. She is highly ethical, said eighteen interviewees. Twelve people said she does not compromise on principles. According to nine respondents, she wants to show the world that it is possible to develop drugs in India rather than merely doing reverse engineering. Kiran takes a lot of pride and puts a lot of effort in bringing Indian biopharmaceutical center stage at the global level, said seventeen interviewees. Some people also said that she wishes to make a difference in various, be it policy, doing things right, or building pride in the "Made in India" label for pharmaceuticals. The eight people who have known her closely said that she is staunchly patriotic, that she will not give up her Indian passport for anything, that she is very proud to say "We are an Indian company with global aspirations." Fifteen people said that she shows a lot of interest in nation-building and has been involved at high levels in different committees. She is very passionate about healthcare and science in India. And she has her own charities that she runs through Biocon Foundation. She is involved in the Department of Biotechnology, Government of India and is trying to improve the status of biotechnology and education in this field.

She is also equally concerned about providing affordable healthcare to society. In discussions held with her, Kiran expresses this concern by constantly contributing to make India, and the world, a better place to live in.

Nineteen interviewees said that Kiran is not money-minded unlike many other industrialists. She has higher value systems like making significant contributions to science, society, and people, as has been mentioned earlier as well in this case study. She does not divert Biocon money and invest it elsewhere, which is a common practice in many family-owned organizations. The surpluses are re-invested in the company because her dream is to make Biocon a top global organization in the pharma sector, providing affordable drugs to help the common people. Through Biocon she would like to demonstrate to the world the power of India in developing drugs indigenously.

Caring

Great leaders create a sense of community in the organization through the care they provide. They go out of their way to be available to people in their hour of need, readily providing help and support. Through this process they move from transactional relationships to familial relationships. Such a relationship creates a deep bonding and a sense of connectedness among followers. Kiran is known as a generous person who has successfully created a close-knit Biocon community.

All the interviewees were really touched by Kiran's caring nature. Some recorded statements are provided ahead:

> All the twenty-three interviewees said that Kiran is a natural people's person.
>
> Eighteen people said "she rallies behind others and gives them whole-hearted support."
>
> Twelve people commented that she is a wonderful human being, wonderful friend, very compassionate, and always ready help people.

> According to five people, Kiran does a lot for people and that is why others do a lot for her without really asking any questions.
>
> Eleven interviewees talked about her empathy and her concern for people saying that she is a generous and large-hearted person.
>
> Nine people said that Kiran shows a lot of concern for her people right from the driver, gardener to the household staff and all the way up to her top team members.

Eleven interviewees said that Kiran knows a large number of people by their names, whether it is in the stores department or in the garden; she gives a lot of importance to everybody, she is very caring and affectionate, said five interviewees. She goes out of her way to understand people's problems, support them, and make them feel a part of Biocon family, said fourteen of the interviewed people. Eleven interviewees mentioned: "She treats everybody with love and respect regardless of what level they occupy. That is one of the great attributes that make people love her as a person." All the interviewees agreed that Kiran supports many good causes, for her relationships are sacrosanct, confirmed nine interviewees.

Kiran's care and concern for people has been expressed in the type of work environment and campus which has been created. Everyone spoke with a glow about the campus serenity and aesthetic environment. Kiran's philosophy also supports this. She says:

> I think it's important to give people an environment where they are very pleased and happy to be working there. And the only way you can do that is by creating a very aesthetic environment, by making sure that basic needs are met, and you give them also extra facilities which they will appreciate.

Empowering and Trusting

Leaders create multiple leaders at various levels in the organization. In fact they are known to build a community of enablers and, through them, they achieve their cherished goals. They normally adopt the mode of empowering, delegating, trusting, enabling, and mentoring their followers; Kiran is well known for possessing these capabilities. This provides ample opportunities to people to develop their leadership potential. Through these processes, they groom leaders at multiple levels. These approaches instill a sense of ownership among the followers. In fact these enablers become the foremost champions of the leaders' agenda and propagate the leader's mission with fervor and passion.

According to all the interviewees, Kiran is a highly empowering and trusting person; she gives power to people, assigns them responsibilities, and sets challenging targets. She inspires people to take challenges and encourages them to take decisions right or wrong and move ahead. According to twelve interviewees, she believes that making mistakes gives an opportunity to learn and take the risk. She is known to show a lot of faith in people; her trust is not blind, it is competency-based, said twelve people. Being a very good judge of people, she is able to assess whom to empower and to what extent. If she trusts people, she gives them complete and absolute authority to transact business, mentioned eleven interviewees. The interviewees said that she has given people so much empowerment that they feel they own the place.

In Kiran's words:

> I always tell people, we want you to own problems, not tasks. I don't want people to be told what to do. I want to throw a problem at them and say, "Solve it." Because that's what makes you a much better researcher, a much better manager, and a much better person in terms of productivity.... The moment you solve a problem, you get a great sense of confidence and achievement which spurs you on to doing much more.

Inspirational

The inspirational power of the leader galvanizes masses and channelizes their energies toward the common goal. Leaders wield inspirational power by focusing on the larger purpose, higher values, and agenda encompassing humanity. Through such focus and clear statement of a laudable goal, leaders create compelling meaning and urge among followers who own it and then go to any extent to pursue the same. Over a period of time, they become inspirational icons and role models. Kiran Mazumdar Shaw is a real inspiration not only in Biocon but also in the pharma sector.

She has struggled and built Biocon against all odds. She has been confronted with many difficulties, but has never succumbed to problems and pressures, as recorded by all the interviewees. She is a shining example of building a global institution from scratch, starting Biocon with a small amount of ₹ 10,000. All the interviewees said that such examples are very rare in this country. Fifteen interviewees said that Kiran is a real role model. They said that the success of Biocon has not gone into her head and that although she is such an accomplished person, she is extraordinarily humble. She is seen by each one of the interviewees as a person with higher values, who believes in working for the larger purpose and noble cause. All the interviewees said she is highly ethical, authentic, frank, and forthright; her capability to eloquently articulate her dreams, vision, and passion as well as actually contribute to society deeply touches people.

People highlighted her highly developed aesthetic sense. As many as twenty interviewees said that she is a great leader, a great human being, and, in many ways, comes across as a complete person. Fourteen interviewees said that they cite her as a living example of a leader who is making a difference in the lives of people and who is projecting India on the world stage in the bio-pharma sector. Fifteen people said that not only Bioconers feel inspired by her, all those who meet her feel the same. Seven persons who work with her very closely also said that the youth, especially young girls, are highly inspired by her and aspire to be like her.

Blending Diversity

Eighteen interviewees in Biocon have almost uniformly said that Kiran's personality beautifully combines a complex array of capabilities. Fourteen of these respondents said she combines quick intelligence with pragmatism and a sense of business. According to nine persons she is a pragmatic person, but is also authentic, humanistic, and sensitive to others. She tops this off with deep curiosity for science as well as passion for art, as recorded by twenty interviewees. She is a global citizen yet very Indian, according to eighteen people. Fifteen people said that she is equally at ease conversing with the humble gardener as well as with a nobel laureate.

Kiran Mazumdar Shaw as a Change Maestro: Salient Contours

The following noteworthy features about Kiran emerge from the interview and questionnaire responses (for details of questionnaire data of Kiran Mazumdar Shaw's style as a Change Maestro, see Appendix 8A.5):

- Kiran is an entrepreneurial strategist and a person with a grand global vision for biotechnology coupled with a Himalayan ambition.
- She is a highly transparent and honest person known for her integrity.
- She is an excellence seeker with powerful creative passion and openness to new ideas.
- She is a person who is reliable, leads from the front, stands like a rock in the face of calamities, and is, therefore, seen as a role model by others.
- She is a powerful communicator with tremendous capability to connect with people and mobilize and enthuse them.
- Her people connect is further enhanced because she is a humanist, takes care of her own people, and helps them when in need.
- She has a tremendous power to connect and display affection. She is empathetic, empowering, and enabling.
- She has great humanistic values and works for the larger cause encompassing society and humanity.
- She has a phenomenal memory for names, faces, and events.
- She has remarkable observational power; in fact, nothing misses her eye.
- Her ability to process information is at the speed of a super computer. She is usually ahead of others in her thinking.
- She has a highly discerning mind, which quickly grasps the heart of the matter, simplifies complex matters, and is able to conceptualize issues as well as solve problems. Thus, Kiran is highly decisive and action centric.

- She is capable of working with the nitty-gritty details without missing the big picture. She is both analytical as well as intuitive and also seamlessly combines emotions, thoughts, and actions.
- She is optimistic, psychologically tough, perseverant as well as courageous and bold.
- She relentlessly pursues performance excellence and catapults the organization into the next horizon.
- She is an independent thinker, a non-conformist, and an entrepreneurial risk taker who carves her own path and follows the unbeaten track.
- Kiran's greatest strength is her ability to powerfully synthesize cognitive, conative, and affective capabilities and utilize the same to propel Biocon to the next horizon.
- She has been honored with many awards and accolades, the most notable being the Padma Bhushan in 2005; Business Woman of the Year award in 2004, and the Veuve Clicquot Initiative for Economic Development for the Asia Award in 2007.

KIRAN MAZUMDAR SHAW: CONCLUDING CONTOURS

Kiran Mazumdar Shaw is the entrepreneurial path breaker who is probably doing for the bio-pharma sector in India, what Narayana Murthy and Azim Premji have done for the IT sector—putting it on the global map and being in the reckoning among global bio-pharma companies. She has a strong sense of national concern and pride which made her aim to build a respectable profile for India in the bio-pharma apace.

Kiran was driven more by a spirit of challenge and a sense of purpose to create an environment where scientists produce something really useful; and to create a very strong research engine as a core and integral part of the business. She, therefore, decided to build a business based on R&D because she felt if exciting opportunities are created in India, scientists will produce good results by staying back in India rather than witnessing a brain-drain. Her passion for the future is to build brand Biotech for India, something which will make India proud. She aims to do this by developing novel products which the world will take seriously.

Somewhere in her heart Kiran also wanted to demonstrate that women make just as good entrepreneurs, managers, or leaders as their male counterparts. This is something she has amply proved many times over. She networks a lot, meets different types of people, engages in civic issues, and supports art and culture as much as science because, in her judgment, both are creative pursuits.

She has a strong value system, believes in straight talk, and calls a spade a spade. She strongly believes that a company cannot compromise on principles, values, or ethics because these elements enable a company to build sustainable competitive edge. Today Biocon is highly respected for its quality, ethics, and principles.

She is highly demanding and excellence focused, someone who is never satisfied and continuously raising the bar of performance. Her passion has always been to move to the next best option. She combines this with generosity and large heartedness and a highly people-centric orientation.

Kiran has created an innovative informal culture in her company where people have so much freedom that they, psychologically speaking, own the place. Biocon has a very trusting, people friendly, open, and networked environment. All these culture factors have together made Biocon a true "science campus" where people love to discuss, debate, and brainstorm and come up with innovative ideas and solutions. It is no wonder, therefore, that this company has done exceptionally well to rank among the top 20 global biotech companies.

Appendices

Appendix 8A.1: Biocon—An Innovation-driven Company

History

From being a certified "Master Brewer" in 1974 to being India's richest first-generation woman entrepreneur, it has been a long and exciting journey for Kiran Mazumdar Shaw. A zoology graduate who ventured to become a beverages expert with a certificate in brewing from Australia's Ballarat Institute into the beverages domain, the powerful businesswoman chose to return to India and switch to becoming an entrepreneur after a brief stint with Carlton & United Beverages and Biocon Biochemicals Limited in Ireland. The field she chose was biotechnology, the then-fledging and almost-unheard-of field of business. Yet, with tenacity and sheer single-mindedness—for which she is well known and respected—she plowed on to create one of India's shining corporate examples in a modern scientific field. In the process, she also became a celebrity of sorts and a media cover girl.

Kiran Mazumdar Shaw started her company in 1978 with barely ₹ 10,000 as capital, separating enzymes from the papaya fruit abundantly available in Karnataka, for exporting to the USA. The venture was jointly created by her and her previous Irish employer, Biocon Biochemicals.

A rare winner of both the highest civilian honors of India, Padma Shri in 1989 and Padma Bhushan in 2005, the biotech entrepreneur—who is actively involved in the development of Bengaluru urban district, the location of her offices and plants—with a streak of civic activism, has taken the honors and accolades in her stride. Forever cheerful and energetic, Kiran has gone about her job without fatigue and any let-up in the past three decades and, in the process, has been able to build a highly technology-driven business conglomerate.

Even as a trainee manager with Biocon, Ireland, Kiran Mazumdar Shaw, was quite focused on her job and saw tremendous opportunity for the export of the enzymes she was handling in the Irish plant, from her native home in southern India. The first decade of her career as businesswoman was eventful, ending with the second highest civilian honor, the Padma Shri. The recognition was given to her owing to her achievement as a first-generation woman entrepreneur who was able to not only build her company from scratch, but also become an active voice for women entering business in India.

The year 1989 was a turning point in the corporate journey of Kiran Mazumdar Shaw. Unilever PLC took over the Irish company and merged it with one of its subsidiaries, Quest International. The move immediately opened the possibility of a much larger basket of opportunities and networks for the now fairly large business enterprise of Kiran Mazumdar Shaw. The move also, fortuitously, meant that the name Biocon became an exclusive identification for the Indian company. The brand equity and legacy of the Irish company, coupled with the massive brand-building exercise the Indian company had done, along with the personal charisma and recognition of its founder, Kiran

Mazumdar Shaw, made a heady mix and a fine amalgam of opportunity for the Indian company. In the same year, the company also became the first technology enterprise of India to receive funding from the US for a propriety technology which helped the company scale up its in-house research program, based on a proprietary solid substrate fermentation technology, from pilot to plant level. This put the company among the big league of technology- and knowledge-driven companies of the country. It also sowed the seeds for diversification into the pharmaceutical field which the company eventually entered.

The year 1994 marked yet another milestone when Biocon established Syngene International Pvt Ltd as a Custom Research Company (CRC) to address the growing need for outsourced R&D in the pharmaceutical sector. This made the company join the big league of pharmaceutical companies, from where there has been no looking back. The commercial success of Biocon's proprietary fermentation plant led to a three-fold expansion in the next two years and the company leveraged its technology platform to enter biopharmaceuticals and statins in the following years.

Even though the growth curve continued to rise, the genius in Kiran Mazumdar Shaw envisaged Biocon's future as a bio-pharma company. In the process she completely rewrote the future of the company. Being an enzymes producer, transcending to becoming a bio-pharma manufacturer was smooth as the company could leverage its microbial enzyme fermentation technology to develop lovastatin, a cholesterol-reducing small molecule that was due to lose patent protection. In a natural progression, the company, in 2001, entered the generic pharmaceutical molecules production which included immunosuppressant and insulin.

By the year 2000, Biocon had initiated an R&D program to develop the world's first pichia-derived recombinant human insulin and a year later, the company's dedicated lovastatin manufacturing facility received its first US FDA accreditation. The company could quickly build businesses across the entire drug value chain—from custom and clinical research (Syngene and Clinigene)—to manufacturing, development, and commercialization. On another front, Biocon entered into symbiotic partnerships with global pharma and biotech companies to rapidly co-develop proprietary products and enter high-growth markets.

By 2007, Biocon's historic enzymes business was accounting for less than 10 percent of the group's consolidated revenues. At the same time, the "greening" of corporate and political philosophy the world over was an encouraging sign for the future of enzymes. Opportunities were huge but so were the investments required to address them. Biocon was at a critical juncture of its growth. The management decided it prudent to unlock the value built over the years by a very successful and profitable enzymes business and deploy the same to move the biopharmaceuticals business up the value chain. In October 2007, Biocon divested its enzymes business to Novozymes A/S, a global enzymes major, for a consideration of $115 million. The resulting financial muscle strengthened the company's ability to expand its biopharmaceutical footprint.

Biocon continued to expand its presence in global markets and increase the visibility of its range of pharmaceuticals, among them, generics, bio-similars, and biologics, through aggressive marketing and branding. The company's strategic partnerships in developed markets are reaping rich rewards and setting the stage for sustained growth in the coming years.

In February 2008, Biocon made its first overseas foray by acquiring 70 percent stake in a specialty marketing and distribution company in Germany, AxiCorp GmbH. With the Europe, Middle East, and Africa (EMEA) region opening its doors to bio-similars, this timely and strategic acquisition allows the company to create a strong European presence to brand, market, and distribute its insulin as well as other products under development.

The Innovation Matrix: A Strategic Framework

Differentiation and a high degree of innovation distinguish all of Biocon's products and services. Combined with India's value advantage, they enable the company to develop and deliver novel and affordable therapeutics for global unmet medical needs.

Biocon's Innovation Matrix (see Figure 8A.1) is a four-dimensional endeavor which extends into the realms of the known and the unknown. Creativity in the known realm builds on existing knowledge and can result in two types of innovation: "Incremental" and "Evolutionary." Creativity that

Figure 8A.1: *The Innovation Matrix of Biocon*

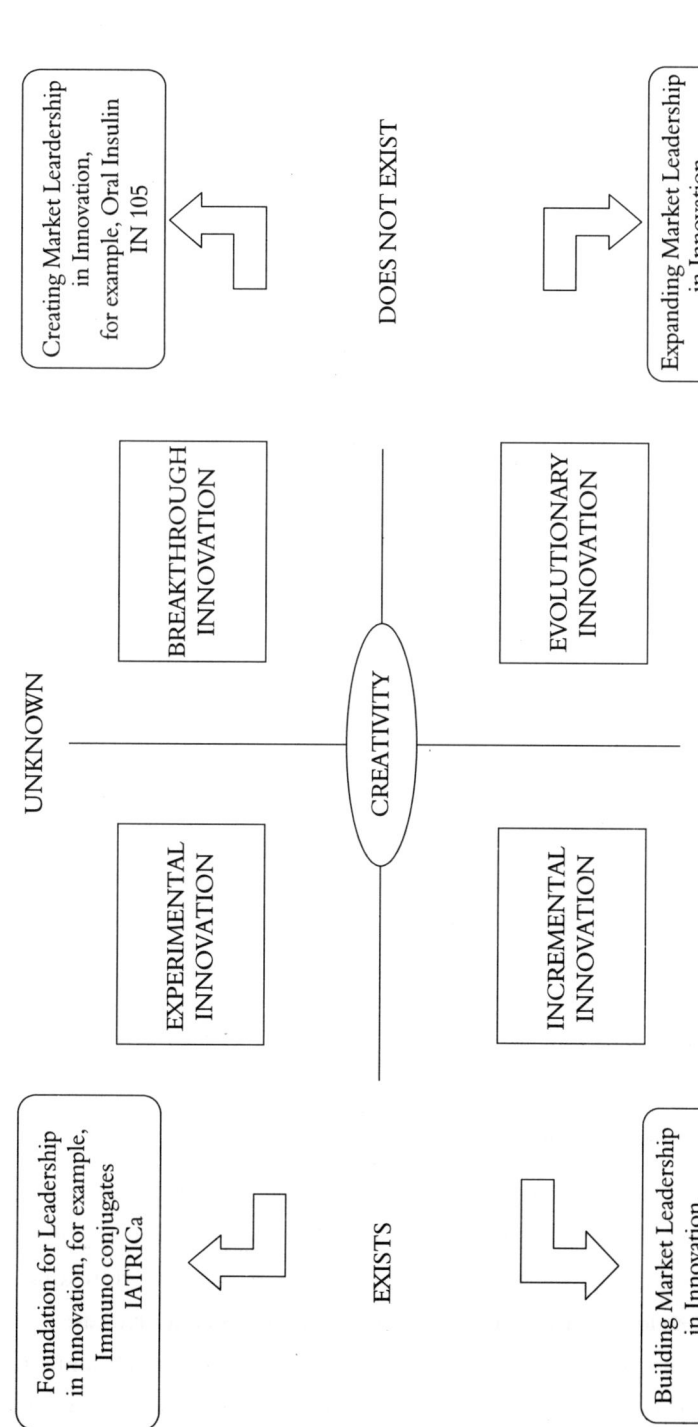

Source: http://www.biocon.com/biocon_aboutus.asp

challenges unknown boundaries and creates new knowledge is "Experimental" and "Transformational" in its impact. A portfolio that covers all four spheres enables Biocon to sustain innovation in the short, medium, and long term.

Their bio-similar insulin, an outcome of incremental innovation, is one of the world's most affordable therapies for insulin-dependent diabetes. Bio-generic monoclonal antibodies are forming the core of its evolutionary innovation strategy. In the more challenging area of experimental innovation, Biocon is at the cutting edge. It is developing conjugated antibodies with a US Biotech start-up, IATRICa, to potentially deliver therapeutic cancer vaccines. It is also pursuing a path of breakthrough innovation through Phase III human clinical trials to develop the world's first oral insulin. Biocon is thus rapidly moving towards commercializing novel biologics with a "Made in India" label.

Businesses

Biocon's fully integrated business model spans the entire drug value chain, from pre-clinical discovery to clinical development and through to commercialization. Biocon's businesses in custom research (Syngene), clinical development (Clinigene), and biopharmaceuticals (Biocon) provide multiple revenue streams to balance risk, drive innovation, deliver products, and accelerate growth. As it increases the complexity and scope of its own R&D and manufacturing operations, especially in new product discovery and development, it believes that custom and clinical research services will continue to offer important synergies (Figure 8A.2).

CSR: About Biocon Foundation

Biocon believes its CSR lies in bringing effective primary healthcare services to the doorsteps of the less privileged in rural and urban areas of India. It recognizes the need for a healthcare system that is participatory, addressing socio-economic development based on preventive rather than curative care.

To that end, Biocon established Biocon Foundation in December 2004, to conceptualize and implement its CSR mission of providing equal access to

Figure 8A.2: Businesses of Biocon

SYNGENE	CLINIGENE	BIOCON
PRE-CLINICAL DISCOVERY	CLINICAL DEVELOPMENT	COMMERCIALIZATION
• Chemistry • Medicinal chemistry • Library synthesis • Process R&D • Custom manufacturing • Analytical services • Polymer chemistry • Biology • Molecular biology • Protein sciences • Cell line services • Assay services • eADMET & PK services • Biologics	• Regulatory affairs • Clinical development • Human pharmacology • Clinical trial management • Bioanalytical research laboratory • Central laboratory • EDC, clinical data management & biostatics	• Research collaboration • Product development • Process development • Manufacturing • Regulatory filing • Marketing • Custom manufacturing • Licensing
➢ FTE-based programs ➢ Fee-for-service projects ➢ Risk-sharing projects	➢ BA/BE studies ➢ Phase I PK/PD ➢ Phase II–IV clinical trials	➢ Process scale UP ➢ Regulatory approvals ➢ Marketing & sales

Source: http://www.biocon.com/biocon_aboutus_business.asp

essential healthcare services, education, and economic opportunities, thereby accelerating social and economic inclusion. By establishing primary healthcare centers (PHCs), actively creating awareness about disease prevention, public health and sanitation, infrastructure building, and initiating programs in education, Biocon aims to empower under-served communities toward self-help, improved health, and, in good time, a better standard of living.

Health: The Biocon Foundation aims at providing essential primary healthcare services to individuals and families in target communities by means acceptable to them through their full participation and at costs that they can afford.

Education: To encourage talent and support academia, the Biocon Foundation has initiated a grant for talented and deserving students of the Guha Centre for Genetic Engineering and Biotechnology, University of Calcutta.

Infrastructure: The Biocon Foundation's sanitation initiative began in 2007 with the aim of offering poor rural communities access to safe and sustainable sanitation facilities. Through its programs, it endeavors to improve the health status of underprivileged village communities, decrease the environmental impact of inadequate sanitation practices, and, ultimately, generate economic benefits by increasing the number of workdays.

Table 8A.1: Recognition and Accolades to Biocon Ltd over the Last Decade, 2000–2009

Year	Awards
2009	• Biocon wins Bio-Excellence Award for Outstanding Achievement in the Healthcare Sector at Bangalore Bio. • Syngene wins Bio-Excellence Award for outstanding achievement in the Biotech Service Sector at Bangalore Bio. • Biocon's BIOMAb EGFR™ wins "Product of the Year," BioSpectrum Awards. • Biocon wins prestigious Bio-Singapore Asia Pacific Biotechnology Award for Best Listed Company. • Biocon bags IDMA "Best Patent of the Year" award.
2008	• Biocon is ranked among the top 20 global biotechnology companies (Source: *Med Ad News*, June 2008). • Biocon is the 7th largest biotech employer in the world (Source: *Med Ad News*, June 2008).
2007	• Syngene receives "BioServices Company of the Year," BioSpectrum Awards. • Biocon's BIOMAb EGFR™ wins "Product of the Year," BioSpectrum Awards.
2006	• Best IT User Award in the Pharmaceutical Sector, NASSCOM.

2004	• India's first and No. 1 biotech company with a global ranking of 16 (Source: *Biospectrum*, July 2004). • Biocon in India's top 5 life sciences companies (at close of trade as on July 30, 2004). • Best Reinvention of HR Function Award, Indira Group, Mumbai. • Best Employer of India Award, Hewitt.
2003	• Bio-Business Award for Bio-entrepreneurship, Rabo India. • Express Pharma Pulse Award for excellence in the pharmaceutical industry.
2001	• Biotech Product, Process Development and Commercialization Award, Department of Biotechnology, Ministry of Science and Technology, Government of India.
2000	• Technology Pioneer Recognition, World Economic Forum.

Source: http://www.biocon.com/biocon_aboutus_awards.asp

Appendix 8A.2: Brief Sketch of Kiran Mazumdar Shaw

The lone lodestar of success among the women corporate leaders and a powerful global brand in the emerging area of biotechnology, Kiran Mazumdar Shaw has a permanent place in the Indian hall of fame for transformational leaders. A successful technocrat of global standing, Ms Kiran Mazumdar Shaw is the CMD of Biocon Limited which she founded in 1978. Thus started the beginning of a revolution in the area of biotechnology in India. Under her stewardship, Biocon has evolved from an industrial enzymes company to a fully integrated bio-pharmaceutical enterprise encompassing a well-balanced business portfolio of products and services with a research focus on diabetes, oncology, and auto-immune disease. In recognition of her stellar achievements and contribution, she has been conferred by the Government of India its top civilian honors, the Padma Shri and Padma Bhushan.

Ms Shaw is highly respected in the corporate world and has been recently voted by *Nature Biotechnology* as "The Most Influential in Bio-business Person" outside Europe and the USA. She chairs Karnataka's Vision Group on Biotechnology and also served on the Board of Science Foundation, Ireland. She presently serves on the Advisory Council of the Government's Department of

Biotechnology, on the Board of Trade, Ministry of Commerce & Industry, Governing Body of the Indian Pharmacopoeia Commission, an Autonomous Body of the Government of India, and is part of the Prime Minister's Council on Trade & Industry in India and the US–India CEO Forum.

Table 8A.2: *Accolades to Kiran Mazumdar Shaw over the Last Decade, 1999–2009*

2009	• Honored with "Nikkei Asia Prize" for Regional Growth.
	• Honored with "Express Pharmaceutical Leadership Summit Award" for Dynamic Entrepreneur.
2007	• Honored with the "Veuve Clicquot Initiative for Economic Development for Asia" award.
2005	• Padma Bhushan Award, one of India's highest civilian honors, from the President of India, Dr A.P.J. Abdul Kalam.
	• The Indian Chamber of Commerce Lifetime Achievement Award.
	• Rotary Award for Corporate Citizenship.
	• Business Leader of the Year Award—Biotechnology, Chemtech—by Pharma Bio Awards.
2004	• Business Woman of the Year Award, *The Economic Times*.
2003	• Alumni High Achiever Award, Australian Alumni Association.
2002	• Karnataka Rajyotsava Award for pioneering biotechnology in India, the Government of Karnataka.
	• Best Entrepreneur: Healthcare & Life Sciences Award, Ernst & Young.
	• Sir M. Visvesvaraya Memorial Award for contribution to biotechnology, Federation of Karnataka Chambers of Commerce & Industry (FKCCI).
1999	• Woman of the Year Award, International Women's Association, Chennai.

Source: http://www.biocon.com/biocon_aboutus_awards.asp
Note: Kiran Mazumdar Shaw has also received several notable awards before 1999, such as the Padma Shri for Pioneering Biotechnology in India, Government of India in 1989, Best Woman Entrepreneur Award, National Institute of Marketing Management, India in 1982.

Appendix 8A.3: Organizational Culture of Biocon—Analysis of Questionnaire Data

Table 8A.3: Perceived Organizational Culture of Biocon

N = 38

S. No.	Organizational Culture	Mean	SD	Ranks
1.	Result orientation	4.29	0.80	1
2.	Teamwork	4.11	0.65	2.5
3.	Performance excellence	4.11	0.86	2.5
4.	Trust	4.08	0.92	4.5
5.	Responsiveness to the customer	4.08	0.76	4.5
6.	Openness and transparency	3.97	0.88	7
7.	Ethical governance	3.97	0.94	7
8.	Outward looking	3.97	0.80	7
9.	Global perspectives	3.95	0.80	9.5
10.	Focus on building competitiveness	3.95	0.80	9.5
11.	Nurturing innovation	3.92	0.85	12
12.	Focus on continuous improvement	3.92	0.80	12
13.	Openness to new ideas	3.92	0.91	12
14.	Communication and information flow: Horizontal (a) Within the department	3.89	0.92	14
15.	Performance-based promotion	3.79	0.78	15.5
16.	People orientation	3.79	0.84	15.5
17.	Role clarity	3.76	0.94	17.5
18.	Entrepreneurial	3.76	0.80	17.5
19.	Speed of response to external demands and challenges	3.73	0.87	19
20.	Empowerment and delegation	3.66	0.94	21
21.	Process focused	3.66	0.97	21
22.	Nurturing talent	3.66	0.88	21
23.	Cross-functional collaboration	3.59	0.80	23.5
24.	Participative	3.59	0.86	23.5
25.	Culture of celebration of achievements and successes	3.55	0.83	25.5

(continued)

(continued)

S. No.	Organizational Culture	Mean	SD	Ranks
26.	Support for risk-taking	3.55	0.95	25.5
27.	Communication and information flow: Vertical (b) Bottom-up	3.53	0.86	27.5
28.	Centralized decision-making process	3.53	0.83	27.5
29.	Speed of response to internal demands	3.49	0.96	29
30.	Communication and information flow: Vertical (a) Top-down	3.45	0.86	30.5
31.	Tolerance of differences	3.45	0.83	30.5
32.	Community culture	3.42	0.98	32
33.	Communication and information flow: Horizontal (b) Across the departments	3.37	0.91	33

Source: Author.

Perusal of Table 8A.3 brings out the following salient work culture attributes:

- The mean values across all the work culture parameters are above average ranging from 3.37 to 4.29.
- The SDs range from 0.65 to 0.98. All of them are below 1 SD indicating consistency of response and significant perceptual homogeneity.
- Approximately 85 percent of the work culture items have a mean value above 3.5 on a 5-point scale.
- There are five items which have mean values above 4.

Further analysis of this table shows that in Biocon, result orientation and performance execution are highly valued. Along with this is the high responsiveness to customer need indicating that Biocon values customerization and customer centricity. Another important characteristic of the Biocon work culture is the high degree of teamwork and trust.

Further perusal of the items ranked 6–20 in the table brings out that Biocon strongly believes in ethical governance and transparency. Biocon is an outward-looking company with global perspective. This is the company where innovation, continuous improvement, and openness to new ideas are strongly embedded in the culture DNA. There is a culture of meritocracy with high accent on performance–reward linkage. Another salient feature of Biocon culture is its entrepreneurial orientation with speedy response to external demands and challenges. This company also believes in empowerment and delegation is the backbone for creating a sense of ownership among the employees.

Appendix 8A.4: Financial Performance of Biocon at a Glance

Table 8A.4: Sales and Profit of Biocon Ltd, 2003–2009 (in ₹ billion)

Year	Income Revenue	Net Profit
2003	2.77	0.36
2004	5.36	1.25
2005	6.88	1.74
2006	7.26	1.33
2007	8.89	1.58
2008	9.05	4.35
2009	10.25	1.12
% Change over 2003	270.04	211.11

Source: Prowess website.

Appendix 8A.5: Kiran Mazumdar Shaw as a Change Maestro—Analysis of Questionnaire Data

Table 8A.5: Perceived Style of Kiran Mazumdar Shaw as a Change Maestro

N = 38

S. No.	Change Maestro Attributes	Mean	SD	Rank
1.	Is entrepreneurial	4.89	0.31	1
2.	Has ambitious plans for the organization	4.82	0.39	2
3.	Is an effective communicator	4.66	0.58	3.5
4.	Radiates positive energy	4.66	0.53	3.5

(continued)

(continued)

S. No.	Change Maestro Attributes	Mean	SD	Rank
5.	Is a role model	4.63	0.59	5
6.	Is result focused	4.61	0.55	6.5
7.	Is a visionary	4.61	0.79	6.5
8.	Has high credibility	4.57	0.65	8
9.	Leads from the front	4.55	0.60	9.5
10.	Has a global mindset	4.55	0.55	9.5
11.	Is open to new ideas	4.50	0.65	11
12.	Is demanding and performance centric	4.47	0.65	12.5
13.	Is innovative and creative	4.47	0.65	12.5
14.	Is a strategic thinker	4.42	0.72	15
15.	Has empowering and supporting attitude	4.42	0.72	15
16.	Stands like a rock in the face of calamities	4.42	0.83	15
17.	Fast in making critical decisions	4.37	0.67	17
18.	Is honest and transparent	4.34	0.71	19
19.	Is reliable	4.34	0.67	19
20.	Leads by example	4.34	0.85	19
21.	Pursues excellence in everything	4.32	0.62	21.5
22.	Business strategist	4.32	0.74	21.5
23.	Provides a sense of clear direction	4.29	0.77	23
24.	Is a team builder	4.26	0.72	24
25.	Recognizes and rewards performance	4.16	0.82	25.5
26.	Humility	4.16	0.93	25.5
27.	Respects the dignity of others	4.14	0.86	27
28.	Has helping attitude	4.13	0.81	28
29.	Is fair and impartial	4.08	0.85	29.5
30.	Sensitivity	4.08	0.75	29.5
31.	Is a person of words	4.00	0.75	31
32.	Makes people feel that they are valued by the organization	3.97	0.97	32.5

S. No.	Change Maestro Attributes	Mean	SD	Rank
33.	Makes people feel that they have great worth	3.97	0.85	32.5
34.	Is interested in growth of his people	3.95	0.96	34
35.	Grooms and develops people	3.92	0.88	35

Source: Author.

Table 8A.5 depicts the profile of Kiran Mazumdar Shaw as a Change Maestro, as perceived by thirty-eight senior executives working closely with Kiran. For the purpose of analysis, the mean values of the thirty-five items have been broadly categorized into three groups: "Most Visible" with mean of 4.5 and above; "Highly Visible" with a mean ranging from 3.5 to 4.4; and "Visible" with mean value less than 3.5.

Perusal of this table brings out the following key findings:

- All the thirty-five attributes describing Kiran as a Change Maestro have mean values in the range of 3.92 to 4.89, that is, they are either in the "Most Visible" or "Highly Visible" categories. Interestingly there is no leadership attribute falling in the "Visible" (less than 3.5) category.
- The top eleven items have mean values 4.5 and above (on a 5-point scale); 62 percent items (the items numbered from 12 to 35) are in the "Highly Visible" category with a mean range of 3.9 to 4.47.
- The SDs across all thirty-five items are less than 1 indicating significant perceptual homogeneity regarding Kiran's leadership style.
- Analysis items in the "Most Visible" category show that Kiran is highly ambitious with a strong entrepreneurial streak. She is also highly visionary viewing the globe as the business arena. Kiran is a great communicator, which indicates her enormous capability to connect with people. People see her as a person who radiates a lot of positive energy, enabling Kiran to draw people toward her. She is a person who has high credibility and leads from the front. At the same time she is seen as a person with tremendous result orientation and one who is always open to new ideas. All these qualities have helped Kiran to be viewed as a role model by others.

Examination of the items in the "Highly Visible" cluster shows that Kiran is highly demanding and performance centric and pursues excellence in everything. Kiran is a strategic thinker as well as a great business strategist. Qualities like standing like a rock in the face of calamities, being honest and transparent, and leading by example contributes to her image as a reliable person. Kiran is a person with significant innovative and creative capabilities.

In addition to these qualities, Kiran is perceived as a person who respects the dignity of others, has a helping attitude with tremendous sensitivity toward others. Kiran is also seen as a leader who is full of humility while dealing with others.

Notes

1. Authors gratefully acknowledge and appreciate the intellectual contributions and emotional support they received from Ms Paula Sengupta, Head, Corporate Communications, Biocon, in the course of this work. She spent many hours with the authors in conceptualizing the framework and providing focused directions to the case study. However, for the conclusions and views expressed in this case study about Biocon and Kiran Mazumdar Shaw as a Change Maestro, the authors own entire responsibility.
2. Twenty-three top team members were interviewed by the authors. The number of respondents varies since the interviewing method was largely unstructured; we recorded what they said, giving greater priority to what came out of top-of-the-mind in response to our broad questions, rather than getting them to respond to a set of questions.

9

9

CHANGE MAESTROS: ACTION ARCHITECTURE AND PERSONA

Chapters 2–8 provide the readers a fairly good idea about each Change Maestro's profile, persona, and action architecture. After perusing these details, the reader may be eager to know the similarities and differences among the Change Maestros: Do they fall in the same mold or are they different? Have they followed the same path or have they used a different trajectory for building their organizations? This chapter tries to address these questions. It has been organized in the following three parts: Part I presents the organizational culture and action architecture built by the Change Maestros to create winning organizations; Part II portrays the Change Maestros' profile and persona; and Part III examines the impact of Change Maestros on organizational culture and financial architecture.

PART I: ORGANIZATIONAL CULTURE AND ACTION ARCHITECTURE

Findings on organizational culture, one of the key vehicles for a Change Maestro to convert his dreams into reality, are examined in this part under four sections: overall pattern of the organizational culture[1]; comparison of the action architecture and organizational culture patterns across the seven organizations[2]; comparative picture of the organizational culture across the seven organizations; and identification of the underlying organizational culture factors.

Overall Mean Values of Organizational Culture

Table 9.1: Means, Standard Deviations, and Ranks

S. No.	Organizational Culture Attributes	Mean	SD	Ranks
1.	Ethical governance	4.41	0.70	1
2.	Result oriented	4.40	0.66	2
3.	Performance excellence	4.30	0.69	3
4.	Focus on building competitiveness	4.19	0.76	4
5.	Focus on continuous improvement	4.16	0.76	6
6.	Teamwork	4.16	0.65	6
7.	Openness to new ideas	4.16	0.79	6
8.	Responsiveness to the customer	4.15	0.77	8
9.	Performance-based promotion	4.13	0.73	9.5
10.	Global perspectives	4.13	0.82	9.5
11.	Trust	4.12	0.81	11
12.	Outward looking	4.08	0.75	12
13.	Speed of response to external demands and challenges	4.07	0.80	13
14.	Entrepreneurial	4.04	0.88	14
15.	Openness and transparency	4.03	0.78	15
16.	Nurturing talent	4.02	0.78	16
17.	Empowerment and delegation	4.00	0.84	17.5
18.	Role clarity	4.00	0.74	17.5
19.	Communication and information flow: Horizontal (a) Within the department	3.98	0.77	19.5
20.	People orientation	3.98	0.76	19.5
21.	Participative	3.96	0.71	21
22.	Nurturing innovation	3.91	0.88	22
23.	Support for risk-taking	3.87	0.87	23
24.	Communication and information flow: Vertical (a) Top-down	3.81	0.797	24.5
25.	Process focused	3.81	0.86	24.5
26.	Speed of response to internal demands	3.78	0.82	26
27.	Community culture	3.77	0.89	27

S. No.	Organizational Culture Attributes	Mean	SD	Ranks
28.	Culture of celebration of achievements and successes	3.71	0.92	28
29.	Tolerance of differences	3.63	0.84	29
30.	Cross-functional collaboration	3.60	0.80	30
31.	Communication and information flow: Vertical (b) Bottom-up	3.47	0.91	31
32.	Communication and information flow: Horizontal (b) Across the departments	3.41	0.88	32
33.	Centralized decision-making process	3.34	0.89	33

Notes: $N = 525$ (all data on a 5-point scale).
Ranks derived from the mean values, the highest mean being assigned Rank 1 and lowest being 33.

Table 9.1 presents the overall mean values of the organizational culture. Perusal of this table brings out the following salient features:

- The mean values across the enlisted thirty-three organizational culture attributes range from 3.34 to 4.41. This pattern indicates that all the mean values are on fairly higher side.
- There is significant homogeneity of responses across all the culture items as indicated by the low SDs (<1.00).
- It is noteworthy that half of the organizational culture items have a mean value above 4 which indicates very high prevalence of these work culture characteristics.
- The top five culture items from this list are ethical governance, result orientation, performance excellence, building competitive edge, and focus on continuous improvement.

Based on these findings it is possible to conclude that all the seven Change Maestros have been using the prominent levers like ethical governance, result orientation, performance excellence, and continuous improvement for building competitive edge.

Comparative Picture of Action Architecture and Organizational Culture Built by the CEOs

Table 9.2: *Comparative Picture of Organizational Culture*

Birla = 25	L&T = 20	ICICI = 25	JSW = 18	UTI/IDBI = 21	Biocon = 23	Airtel = 21
Value-driven governance	Quest for excellence	Continued growth velocity	Mega growth vision	Seamless communication	Strategy architecture	Entrepreneurial Architecture
Global: Taking India to the world	Thinking tomorrow today	Reinventing the financial sector landscape	Entrepreneurial DNA	Scripting a new vision	Entrepreneurial passion	Entrepreneurial innovation
Futuristic and forward looking group	Global thrust	Entrepreneurial innovation	Toward the next milestone	Openness	Global vision	Mega vision with winning streak
People centricity	Focused growth strategy and thrust on value creation	Thinking big	Empowerment with accountability	Empowerment	Futuristic	Customer always
Robust growth strategy	Speed	Execution centric	Quest for excellence	Talent management	Creating second curve	People power
Toward meritocracy with personal touch	Empowerment	Seamless organization	High performance recognition	Recognition	Empowerment	Performance excellence
Managing change with continuity	Entrepreneurial Innovation	Empowerment with accountability	People focus	Ethical governance	Non-hierarchical	Ethical governance
	Ethical organization	Techno-centric work culture	Ethical governance	Promoting innovation	Happening place	Mosaic culture
	Customer focus	Contribution-centric meritocracy	Beyond profit: social concerns	Speedy decision-making	Quest for excellence	
	Caring organization	Shaping talent/building leaders	Shaping talent	Performance orientation	Caring community	
	Contribution-centric meritocracy			Restructuring and role clarification	Ethical governance	
	Nurturing talent					

Table 9.2 presents the dominant picture of the action architecture and organizational culture built by the Change Maestros based on the analysis of interview data from their organizations. Analysis of this table shows that all the seven Change Maestros by and large lay heavy emphasis on building an ethical governance, a global vision, an entrepreneurial innovation, a customer centricity, have a quest for continued growth and performance excellence, have a performance-centric reward system, adopt a futuristic and forward-looking orientation, have a corporate citizenship, and a caring and empowering culture. These nine elements of organizational culture have been strongly developed by all the Change Maestros irrespective of industry sector and the growth stage of the organization.

Comparative Picture of Organizational Culture: Company-wise

Table 9.3 brings out the comparative analysis of each organization paired with the other six. The significant correlation values indicate that organizational cultures (across the seven companies) are significantly similar to each other. In

Table 9.3: Rank Order Coefficients of Correlation across Twenty-one Company Pairs

Company Pairs	Spearman Rank-Order Correlation: ρ
Birla Group–L&T	0.78
Birla Group–ICICI	0.56
Birla Group–JSW	0.73
Birla Group–UTI/IDBI	0.59
Birla Group–Airtel	0.60
Birla Group–Biocon	0.64
L&T–ICICI	0.61
L&T–JSW	0.68
L&T–UTI/IDBI	0.73
L&T–Airtel	0.72
L&T–Biocon	0.79
ICICI–JSW	0.72

(continued)

(continued)

Company Pairs	Spearman Rank-Order Correlation: ρ
ICICI–UTI/IDBI	0.48
ICICI–Airtel	0.75
ICICI–Biocon	0.62
JSW–UTI/IDBI	0.60
JSW–Airtel	0.76
JSW–Biocon	0.80
UTI/IDBI–Airtel	0.71
UTI/IDBI–Biocon	0.81
Airtel–Biocon	0.75

Note: All ρ significant at $p = >0.05$ at table value $= 0.34$.

other words, all the seven Change Maestros have nurtured more or less a similar work culture to build winning organizations. If we juxtapose findings on organizational culture and action architecture from Tables 9.1 to 9.3 (considering both questionnaire and interview data) it can be reiterated that Change Maestros have built significantly similar organizational culture.

Identification of the Underlying Organizational Culture Factors

In order to identify the broad constructs underlying the thirty-three organizational culture items, Exploratory Factor Analysis (EFA)[3] has been conducted. Table 9.4 presents the factors, eigenvalues, percentages of variance explained and scale reliability indicators (see Appendix 9A.1 for statistical details).

The six factors which emerged from the principal component analysis are: excellence centric (16.65); stakeholders' focus (13.16); experimenting (11.65); goal and role clarity (8.26); boundary-less communication (7.75); and centralization (4.17) which has been illustrated in Figure 9.1.

Further analysis of all the six factors together indicates that all the Change Maestros practice the mantra of excellence—excellence is a journey not a destination. They give high importance to stakeholders' interests and are responsive to their needs. They also have a strong fervor to experiment,

Table 9.4: *Factors, Eigenvalues, Explained Variance, and Scale Reliability of Organizational Culture Items*

Variables	Factors	% of Variance	No. of Items	Eigenvalue[a]	Cronbach's Alpha[b]
Organizational Culture	Excellence centric	16.653	9	5.496	0.90
	Stakeholders' focus	13.161	10	4.343	0.90
	Experimenting	11.653	5	3.846	0.81
	Goal and role clarity	8.262	4	2.727	0.70
	Boundary-less communication	7.746	4	2.556	0.76
	Centralization	4.170	1	1.376	*

Notes: Total % of variance = 61.646.
*Cronbach alpha not conducted because of single item.
[a]Factors with Eigenvalue 1 and above retained.
[b]Cronbach's alpha values ranged from 0.69–0.90 which is close to or above 0.70, the accepted norm (Nunnally, 1978) indicating statistical adequacy and scale reliability.

Figure 9.1: *Factors of Organizational Culture**

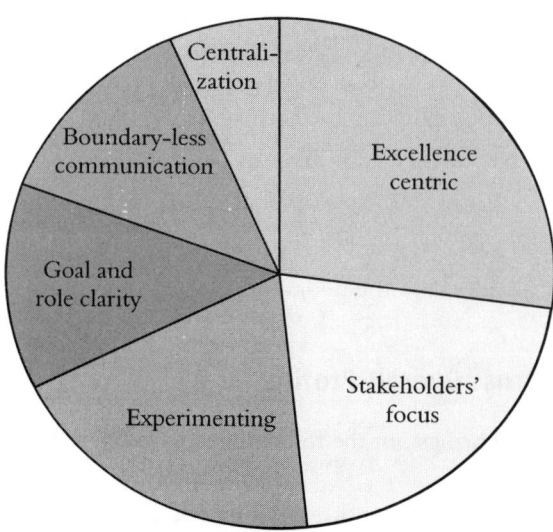

Note: *Percentage values in the figure are that of variance of each factor.

explore, and take risks. They are open to new ideas and significantly empower their people indicating the entrepreneurial character of these organizations. Change Maestros also set clarity of direction and role, link reward to performance, along with emphasis on teamwork. Further, they promote seamless communication and information flow. In these companies, cross-functional collaboration and decentralization are encouraged and there is virtually no silo culture.

Weaving the findings across Tables 9.1 to 9.3 the following salient features are seen:

- All the organizational culture attributes are highly prevalent to a "High" or "Very High" extent.
- There is significant homogeneity of organizational culture across the seven organizations under study.
- Change Maestros built work cultures characterized by ethical governance, excellence centricity, stakeholders' focus, experimenting through entrepreneurial innovation, promoting boundary-less communication, and goal and role clarity. In other words, these drivers have been used in all the seven organizations for building competitive edge.

Part II: Change Maestros' Profile and Persona

This part of the chapter portrays the comparative picture on the Change Maestros' profile and persona. Data in this part have been examined and presented in five sections: Change Maestros' overall profile[4]; the dominant patterns of their profile[5]; their self-perceived vs. top team perceptions; the extent of similarity among their profiles; and the underlying factors of their profiles.

Change Maestros: Overall Profile

Perusal of Table 9.5 brings out the following key findings:

- Mean values across all the Change Maestros' competencies range from 4.1 to 4.89. In fact two-thirds of these items are in the range of 4.52 to 4.89.

Table 9.5: Overall Mean Values of Change Maestros' Profile

S. No.	Change Maestros' Attributes	Mean	SD	Rank
1.	Has ambitious plans for the organization	4.89	0.34	1
2.	Is a visionary	4.80	0.49	2
3.	Radiates positive energy	4.77	0.48	3
4.	Has a global mindset	4.76	0.53	4
5.	Has high credibility	4.74	0.53	5.5
6.	Is a strategic thinker	4.74	0.51	5.5
7.	Is entrepreneurial	4.72	0.58	7
8.	Is result focused	4.67	0.59	8
9.	Stands like a rock in the face of calamities	4.65	0.63	9
10.	Is a role model	4.64	0.64	10
11.	Is an effective communicator	4.62	0.64	11.5
12.	Is reliable	4.62	0.62	11.5
13.	Pursues excellence in everything	4.59	0.61	13.5
14.	Is honest and transparent	4.59	0.67	13.5
15.	Provides a sense of clear direction	4.58	0.63	15
16.	Business strategist	4.55	0.69	16
17.	Fast in making critical decisions	4.54	0.68	17
18.	Leads by example	4.53	0.69	18
19.	Is open to new ideas	4.52	0.69	19.5
20.	Leads from the front	4.52	0.75	19.5
21.	Is innovative and creative	4.50	0.69	21
22.	Is a man of words	4.47	0.77	22
23.	Has an empowering and supporting attitude	4.44	0.74	23.5
24.	Recognizes and rewards performance	4.44	0.72	23.5
25.	Is demanding and performance centric	4.41	0.76	25
26.	Is interested in growth of his people	4.39	0.73	26
27.	Is fair and impartial	4.32	0.78	27.5
28.	Has helping attitude	4.32	0.82	27.5

(continued)

(continued)

S. No.	Change Maestros' Attributes	Mean	SD	Rank
29.	Makes people feel that they are valued by the organization	4.30	0.83	29
30.	Respects the dignity of others	4.29	0.90	30
31.	Is a team builder	4.27	0.82	31
32.	Grooms and develops people	4.22	0.83	32
33.	Makes people feel that they have great worth	4.19	0.88	33
34.	Humility	4.16	1.03	34
35.	Sensitivity	4.12	0.84	35

Notes: N = 525.
Ranks derived from the mean values, the highest mean has been assigned Rank 1 and lowest Rank 35.

- There is significant homogeneity across the items, the SDs being less than 1 ($p \leq 1$).

Viewing these findings together it can be concluded that Change Maestros' profiles are clearly visible and known to people. Further perusal of the Top 15 attributes of the Change Maestros leads us to the following conclusions:

- Change Maestros are highly ambitious and are visionary strategists with global perspective.
- They are entrepreneurial path breakers and demonstrate endless appetite for growth and experimentation.
- They are also obsessed with performance excellence and keep raising the bar of performance.
- They connect with people through the power of positive energy and communication.
- They are perceived as role models and as persons of credibility and courage who stand rock like in the face of calamities.

Dominant Patterns

Table 9.6 shows the salient attributes and behavior of the Change Maestros which have emerged from content analysis of the interview data. Analysis of this table indicates that Change Maestros are highly ethical, they have Himalayan ambition with a futuristic vision, and are strategy architects with global perspective and deep appetite for growth as well as quest for excellence. They are also highly entrepreneurial with passion for risk-taking and experimentation. They are highly people-centric with talent-building abilities and an empowering attitude. They are extremely bold and courageous with high learnability and credibility. Above all they are holistic in terms of their focus both on the big picture as well as the details, present as well as the future, strategy as well as implementation and idea as well as action.

Table 9.6: Change Maestros' Dominant Profile

• Ethical	• Entrepreneurial
• High ambition	• Performance centricity
• Visionary	• Empowering
• Strategic architect	• Talent shaper
• Quest for excellence	• Credibility
• Deep appetite for growth	• Bold and courageous
• Global perspective	• Learnability: Evolving
• Crystal gazer: Futuristic	• Holistic

Putting together the results of Tables 9.5 and 9.6 brings out powerful similarity in the findings about Change Maestros profile and persona. Such findings show that irrespective of the mode of inquiry used for data gathering, whether questionnaire or interview, there is a high degree of similarity in the pattern of findings. In other words, there is congruity between the responses of the group on the structured questionnaire and in the interviews.

Self Perceived vs. Top Team Perceptions

Table 9.7 shows the extent of similarity between the leaders' self-assessment vs. that of his top team. Analysis of this table brings out an extremely important and striking finding: there is a significant congruity between Change Maestros' self-assessment and perceptions of the top team as indicated by the rank order correlation values (ranging from 0.77 to 0.86, all of them being significant at $p = > 0.05$ level). Findings such as these indicate that all the Change Maestros in this study are open and transparent, they practice what they preach, and people can read their minds. Needless to say these qualities heighten Change Maestros' credibility.

Table 9.7: Change Maestros' Self-assessment vs. Perceived Profile

Leader–Top Team's Perception	Spearman Rank-Order Correlation Coefficient: ρ
K.M. Birla	0.86
M. Damodaran	0.77
Sajjan Jindal	0.78
K.V. Kamath	0.86
Sunil Bharti Mittal	0.83
A.M. Naik	0.85
Kiran Mazumdar Shaw	0.82

Note: All ρ significant at $p \geq 0.05$ at table value $= 0.34$.

Extent of Similarity between the Change Maestros

Table 9.8 shows the extent of similarity between the profiles of the seven Change Maestros. Analysis of these rank coefficients shows that out of the seven Change Maestros, six have significantly similar profiles (indicated by ρ values greater than 0.34). Though the profile of K.M. Birla is positively correlated with that of K.V. Kamath, Sajjan Jindal, M. Damodaran, and Sunil Bharti Mittal, the correlation values are not significant. However, his profile is different when compared with A.M. Naik and Kiran Mazumdar Shaw as indicated by the negative, though insignificant, correlation value.

Table 9.8: Rank Order Coefficients of Correlation across Twenty-one Change Maestros' Pairs

Combinations	Spearman Rank-Order Correlation: ρ
K.M. Birla–A.M. Naik	-0.28
K.M. Birla–K.V. Kamath	-0.00
K.M. Birla–Sajjan Jindal	0.04
K.M. Birla–M. Damodaran	0.10
K.M. Birla–Sunil Bharti Mittal	0.29
K.M. Birla–Kiran Mazumdar Shaw	-0.02
A.M. Naik–K.V. Kamath	0.67
A.M. Naik–Sajjan Jindal	0.67
A.M. Naik–M. Damodaran	0.47
A.M. Naik–Sunil Bharti Mittal	0.42
A.M. Naik–Kiran Mazumdar Shaw	0.73
K.V. Kamath–Sajjan Jindal	0.63
K.V. Kamath–M. Damodaran	0.42
K.V. Kamath–Sunil Bharti Mittal	0.55
K.V. Kamath–Kiran Mazumdar Shaw	0.69
Sajjan Jindal–M. Damodaran	0.38
Sajjan Jindal–Sunil Bharti Mittal	0.62
Sajjan Jindal–Kiran Mazumdar Shaw	0.73
M. Damodaran–Sunil Bharti Mittal	0.65
M. Damodaran–Kiran Mazumdar Shaw	0.46
Sunil Bharti Mittal–Kiran Mazumdar Shaw	0.70

Note: ρ values to be significant at $p \geq 0.05$ which should reach or exceed table value = 0.34.

Change Maestros Profile: Underlying Factors

In order to identify the broad Change Maestro constructs underlying the thirty-five items, EFA[6] has been conducted. Table 9.9 presents the factors, eigenvalues, percentage of variance explained, and scale reliability indicators. Based on the item loadings, these factors have been labeled as follows: enabler (24.93); excellence seeker (8.98); direction setter (8.050); visionary strategist (7.81); role

Table 9.9: *Factors, Eigenvalues, Explained Variance, and Scale Reliability of Change Maestros' Profile Items*

Variables	Factors	% of Variance	No. of Items	Eigen-value[a]	Cronbach's Alpha[b]
Change Maestros' Behavior	Enabler	24.929	16	8.725	0.95
	Excellence seeker	8.978	5	3.142	0.74
	Direction setter	8.047	5	2.817	0.75
	Visionary strategist	7.814	5	2.735	0.76
	Role model	6.763	2	2.367	0.69
	Credibility	4.208	1	1.473	*

Notes: Total % of Variance = 60.741.
*Cronbach Alpha not calculated because of single item.
[a] Factors with Eigenvalue 1 and above retained.
[b] Cronbach's alpha values ranged from 0.69 to 0.95 which is close to or above 0.70, the accepted norm (Nunnally, 1978) indicating statistical adequacy and scale reliability.

model (6.76); and credibility (4.21). It is thus clear that Change Maestros assign greatest importance to being an enabler, as indicated by the highest percentage of variance explained by this factor.

These factors have been diagrammatically represented in Figure 9.2.

The study of all these six factors highlights the following dominant modes used by Change Maestros:

- These Change Maestros follow the enabling style and strongly believe in people power. Through this approach they inspire people, galvanize them, and channelize their energies toward organizational goals. They are humble; they respect people and make them feel valued. They are helpful, sensitive, and empowering. They are talent builders who believe in grooming and developing people. They are persons of high credibility which has been built on their fairness, honesty, transparency, and reliability.
- These Change Maestros are unrelenting in their quest for excellence. They keep raising the bar of performance and nudge the organization members toward the next level of performance. They have Himalayan ambition with a global mindset. Such a quest for excellence reflects their positive disquiet and restlessness, continuously seeking to better their own performance.

Figure 9.2: *Factors of Change Maestros' Behavior**

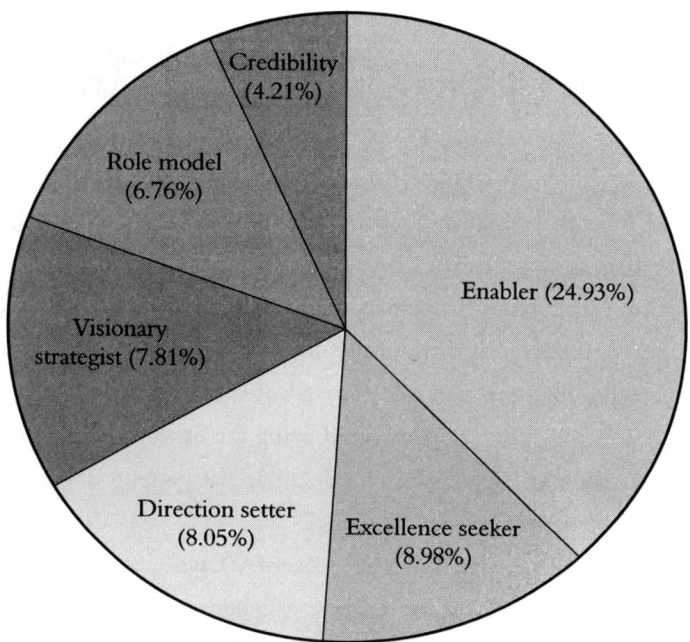

Note: *Percentage values in the figure are that of variance of each factor.

- All Change Maestros are clear about their vision for the organization and as are clear about the path to tread on to actualize the vision. They communicate this effectively to the role holders. They inspire confidence through their positivity and their rock-like support along with speedy decision-making which unleash the entrepreneurial spirit in the organization.
- All the Change Maestros are visionary strategists as well as entrepreneurial innovators. They are role models because of their ability to integrate practice with precept. They are also seen to stand by their words.

These findings lead to the conclusion that Change Maestros have developed mastery over integrating a range of leadership competencies—business strategy; people; processes; innovation; and ethical orientation—building forward momentum and constantly achieving excellence, and using them appropriately for creating cutting-edge organizations.

Part III: Change Maestros' Impact: Organizational Culture and Financial Performance

The authors of this book are of the view that organizational culture is an expression of Change Maestros' beliefs, mindsets, and styles. Therefore, the basic assumption of this book has been that Change Maestros build organizational culture and nurture the same for creating winning organizations. It is in this perspective that this part of the chapter examines the impact of Change Maestros' style on organization culture as well as financial performance. Impact of the Change Maestros on organization culture (excellence centric, stakeholders' focus, experimenting, goal and role clarity, boundary-less communication, and centralization factors[7]) has been analyzed using the Structural Equation Modeling (see Appendix 9A.2, Table 9A.2a for details). The path model used to test the relationship is given in Figure 9.3.

Figure 9.3 indicates that Change Maestros have a significant impact on all the five organizational culture factors: excellence centric; stakeholders' focus; experimenting; goal and role clarity; and boundary-less communication (see Appendix 9A.2, Table 9A.2b for details of statistical analysis and significance levels).

It can thus be seen that Change Maestros have the strongest impact on building excellence-centric workplace, while focusing on stakeholders' interests, and creating an experimenting and entrepreneurial organization. Thus, they primarily operate through the mantras of excellence, stakeholders' centricity, and entrepreneurial innovation, followed by creating seamless organization along with goal and role clarity.

Table 9.10 presents the financial performance of the seven companies under study in terms of revenue and profits during 2003–2008. This table highlights that in revenue terms, the Aditya Birla Group has grown 2.42 times, JSW 3.53 times, ICICI 2.24 times, Airtel 1,511 times, L&T 1.72 times, and Biocon 2.27 times over the mentioned period. However, performance growth in net profit term has been much superior. The Aditya Birla Group has grown in this respect more or less five times, JSW 16 times, ICICI 2.45 times, Airtel 39,294 times,

Figure 9.3: *Change Maestros' Impact on Organizational Culture*

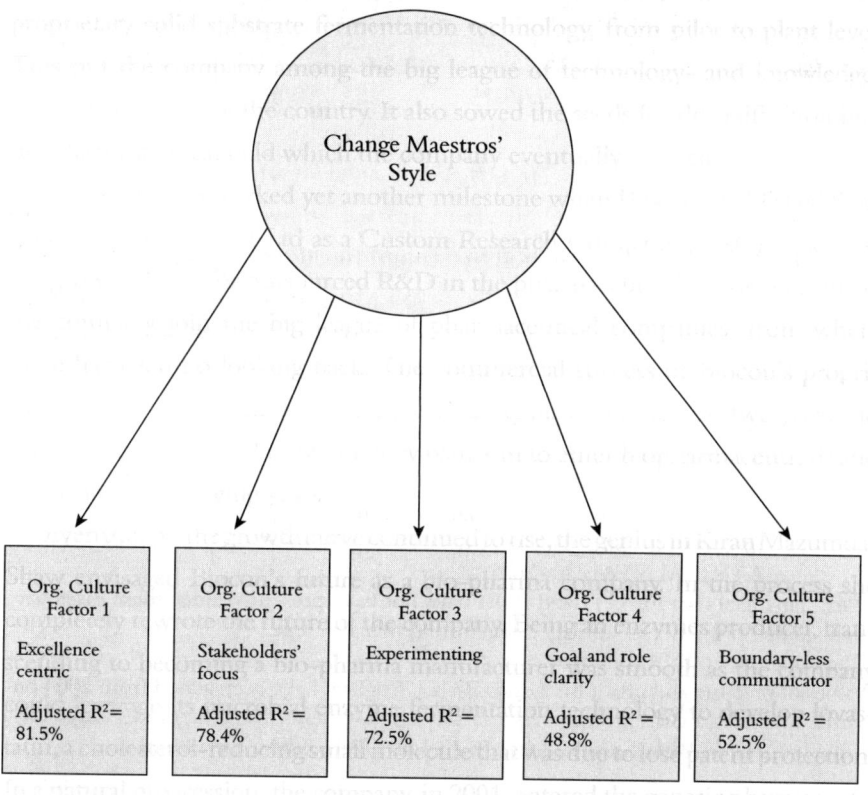

Path Model—Single Leadership IV (Independent Variable) to Multiple Culture Dependent Variables

Org. Culture Factor 1	Org. Culture Factor 2	Org. Culture Factor 3	Org. Culture Factor 4	Org. Culture Factor 5
Excellence centric	Stakeholders' focus	Experimenting	Goal and role clarity	Boundary-less communicator
Adjusted R^2 = 81.5%	Adjusted R^2 = 78.4%	Adjusted R^2 = 72.5%	Adjusted R^2 = 48.8%	Adjusted R^2 = 52.5%

Note: Adjusted R^2 is squared multiple correlations.

L&T 5 times, and Biocon 11 times. The financial performance, thus, in all the companies has been very impressive and mind-boggling by any standard. Such exemplary performance justifies labeling these CEOs as Change Maestros.

The following broad conclusions can be drawn by viewing all the findings together in a holistic sense:

- All the organizational culture attributes have high visibility and dominant presence and there is a significant perceptual homogeneity about them.

*Table 9.10: Comparison of Percentage Change in Revenue and Profit across the Seven Organizations Over Time**

S. No.	Organization	Revenue			Net Profit		
		2003	2009	% Change	2003	2009	% Change
1.	Aditya Birla Group§	126.23	455.73	261	10.63	50.39	374
2.	JSW Steel Ltd	27.86	140.01	403	−1.11	4.59	514
3.	ICICI Bank	125.33	399.75	219	12.06	37.58	212
4.	Airtel	0.17	373.52	219,618	0.002	78.59	3,929,400
5.	L&T	108.57	406.08	274	3.8	30.07	691
6.	Biocon Ltd	2.77	10.25	270	0.36	1.12	211

Sources: a. Prowess. 2003. Aditya Birla Group, ICICI, Airtel, Biocon.
  b. Bharti Airtel Annual Report, 2009, p. 7.
  c. JSW Annual Report 2009–2010, p. 8.
  d. Annual Report of L&T is available online at http://www.larsentoubro.com/lntcorporate/LnT_DWS/Downloads.aspx?res=P_CORP_CINV_AFNC_AANL_ALNT&year=2009

Notes: Financial data for UTI and IDBI have not been presented since these cases have been studied primarily as stories of turnaround management.
*The values are in INR (billions).
§Values of revenue and profit for Aditya Birla UltraTech have been added from 2004 onwards. The Aditya Birla group includes Aditya Birla Chemicals (India) Ltd, Aditya Birla Nuvo Ltd, Aditya Birla Grasim, Aditya Birla UltraTech, Aditya Birla Hindalco.

- Combining findings from both questionnaire and interview data reveals that all the companies have built organizational culture with strong focus on ethical orientation, performance excellence, global vision, customer centricity, quest for continued growth, entrepreneurial innovation and corporate citizenship, building competitive edge, teamwork, openness to new ideas, focus on continuous improvement, and trust. They have also nurtured organizational culture which has been futuristic and forward-looking which in turn has been empowering and open to new ideas for continuous improvement.

ACTION ARCHITECTURE AND PERSONA 429

- Six broad organizational culture constructs which emerged from the factor analysis are: excellence centric; stakeholder focus; experimenting; goal and role clarity; boundary-less communication; and decentralization.
- All the seven organizations have significantly similar organizational cultures.
- Change Maestros' competencies are highly visible to their organizational members and there is a significant perceptual homogeneity about their profile and persona.
- There is significant match between Change Maestros' perception of their styles and the perception held by their team members about them.
- All the Change Maestros have more or less similar profiles and persona.
- The Change Maestros are strongly characterized by the following attributes: Himalayan ambition; global vision; role models; and credibility. They are strategists and entrepreneurial innovators, strive for excellence and always aim for growth. They look ahead and are empowering and focus on shaping talent. They are bold and courageous and their desire to learn more and more renders them into evolving human beings.
- The five broad Change Maestros constructs which emerged from factor analysis conducted as shown in this chapter are Change Maestro as an enabler, excellence seeker, a direction setter, visionary, role model, and as a credible figure.

From this analysis it can be concluded that the seven Change Maestros are highly holistic and operate on multiple gears for building competitive edge and creating successful organizations. Clearly, their competency bandwidth is large and they switch from one to the other as per contextual demand.

Intensive analysis about the persona, profile, and styles of these seven Change Maestros and their organizations show that they followed the mantras practiced by other Change Maestros as mentioned in Chapter 1. These mantras are himalayan vision, customer centric, people engagement, building organizational culture, winning streak, creative destruction, and evolving self.

APPENDICES

Appendix 9A.1: Exploratory Factor Analysis

Table 9A.1a: Rotated Component Matrix of Organizational Culture

Rotated Component Matrix

	Component					
	1	2	3	4	5	6
Eigenvalue	5.496	4.343	3.846	2.727	2.556	1.376
% variance	16.653	13.161	11.653	8.262	7.746	4.170
Cumulative % variance	16.653	29.815	41.468	49.731	57.477	61.646
Number of items	9	10	5	4	4	1
Reliability (Cronbach's Alpha)	.90	.90	.81	.70	.76	
Factor Names	Excellence Centric	Stakeholders' Focus	Experimenting	Goal and Role Clarity	Boundary-less Communication	Centralization
Result oriented	.764	–	–	–	–	–
Performance excellence	.729	–	–	–	–	–
Speed of response to external demands and challenges	.600	–	–	–	–	–
Nurturing innovation	.592	–	–	–	–	–
Focus on building competitiveness	.584	–	–	–	–	–

Focus on continuous improvement	.553	–	–	–	–	–
Openness to new ideas	.528	–	–	–	–	–
Entrepreneurial	.524	–	–	–	–	–
Speed of response to internal demands	.513	–	–	–	–	–
Nurturing talent	–	.463	–	–	–	–
People orientation	–	.694	–	–	–	–
Community culture	–	.591	–	–	–	–
Responsiveness to the customer	–	.561	–	–	–	–
Participative	–	.559	–	–	–	–
Process focused	–	.544	–	–	–	–
Global perspectives	–	.524	–	–	–	–
Ethical governance	–	.519	–	–	–	–
Outward looking	–	.490	–	–	–	–
Trust	–	.489	–	–	–	–
Tolerance of differences	–	–	.700	–	–	–
Support for risk-taking	–	–	.612	–	–	–

(continued)

(continued)

Factor Names	Excellence Centric	Stakeholders' Focus	Experimenting	Goal and Role Clarity	Boundary-less Communication	Centralization
Empowerment and delegation	–	–	.609	–	–	–
Openness and transparency	–	–	.464	–	–	–
Culture of celebration of achievements and successes	–	–	.444	–	–	–
Communication and information flow: Vertical (a) Top-down	–	–	–	.642	–	–
Role clarity	–	–	–	.620	–	–
Performance-based promotion	–	–	–	.532	–	–
Teamwork (within the department)	–	–	–	.525	–	–
Communication and information flow: Vertical (b) Bottom-up	–	–	–	–	.739	–

Communication and information flow: Horizontal (b) Across the departments	–	–	–	–	.652	–
Communication and information flow: Horizontal (a) Within the department	–	–	–	–	.612	–
Cross-functional collaboration	–	–	–	–	.435	–
Centralized decision-making process	–	–	–	–	–	.736

Source: Authors.

Notes: Extraction Method: Principal Component Analysis.
Rotation Method: Varimax with Kaiser Normalization.
Rotation converged in 23 iterations; items with .40 and above loadings retained; item cross loading on more than one factor (with difference of .9 and below with each other) were dropped as per convention.

Table 9A.1b: Rotated Component Matrix of Change Maestro Behavior

	Rotated Component Matrix					
	Component					
	1	2	3	4	5	6
Eigenvalue	8.725	3.142	2.817	2.735	2.367	1.473
% variance	24.929	8.978	8.047	7.814	6.763	4.208
Cumulative % variance	24.929	33.907	41.955	49.769	56.532	60.741
Number of items	16	5	5	5	2	1
Reliability (Cronbach's Alpha)	.95	.74	.75	.76	.69	–
Respects the dignity of others	.839	–	–	–	–	–
Makes people feel that they have great worth	.822	–	–	–	–	–
Has empowering and supporting attitude	.803	–	–	–	–	–
Makes people feel that they are valued by the organization	.795	–	–	–	–	–
Humility	.762	–	–	–	–	–
Has helping attitude	.699	–	–	–	–	–

Sensitivity	.696	–	–	–	–
Is fair and impartial	.680	–	–	–	–
Is interested in growth of his people	.680	–	–	–	–
Grooms and develops people	.664	–	–	–	–
Is a team builder	.655	–	–	–	–
Is open to new ideas	.648	–	–	–	–
Is a role model	.586	–	–	–	–
Has high credibility	.585	–	–	–	–
Is honest and transparent	.583	–	–	–	–
Is reliable	.556	–	–	–	–
Is result focused	.809	–	–	–	–
Is demanding and performance centric	.723	–	–	–	–
Pursues excellence in everything	.612	–	–	–	–

(continued)

(continued)

Factor Names	Enabler	Excellence Seeker	Direction Setter	Visionary Strategist	Role Model	Credibility
Has ambitious plans for the organization	–	.557	–	–	–	–
Has a global mindset	–	.448	–	–	–	–
Provides a sense of clear direction	–	–	.607	–	–	–
Is an effective communicator	–	–	.589	–	–	–
Radiates positive energy	–	–	.521	–	–	–
Stands like a rock in the face of calamities	–	–	.483	–	–	–
Fast in making critical decisions	–	–	.474	–	–	–
Recognizes and rewards performance	–	–	–	–	–	–
Is a strategic thinker	–	–	–	.694	–	–
Business strategist	–	–	–	.627	–	–

Is a visionary	—	—	.567	—	—
Is innovative and creative	—	—	.537	—	—
Is entrepreneurial	—	—	.511	—	—
Leads from the front	—	—	—	.784	—
Leads by example	—	—	—	.664	—
Is a man of words	—	—	—	—	.582

Source: Authors.

Notes: Extraction Method: Principal Component Analysis.
Rotation Method: Varimax with Kaiser Normalization.
Rotation converged in 16 iterations; items with .40 and above loadings retained; item cross loading on more than one factor (with difference of .9 and below with each other) were dropped as per convention.

Table 9A.1c: Means, SDs, Inter-correlations among the Sub-scales of Change Maestro Behavior Inventory and Organizational Culture Inventory

	1	2	3	4	5	6	7	8	9	10	11	12	Mean	SD
Enabler	1.000												4.382	.5766
Excellence Seeker	.268**	1.000											4.664	.4048
Direction Setter	.513**	.482**	1.000										4.632	.4334
Visionary Strategist	.500**	.569**	.577**	1.000									4.661	.4292
Role Model	.406**	.360**	.549**	.431**	1.000								4.525	.6292
Credibility	.560**	.312**	.394**	.381**	.263**	1.000							4.471	.7674
Excellence Centric	.504**	.535**	.478**	.592**	.327**	.341**	1.000						4.110	.5969
Stakeholders' Focus	.582**	.427**	.436**	.534**	.367**	.391**	.833**	1.000					4.042	.5704
Experimenting	.534**	.341**	.396**	.451**	.256**	.326**	.767**	.762**	1.000				3.848	.6409
Goal and Role Clarity	.360**	.354**	.399**	.419**	.313**	.276**	.635**	.621**	.606**	1.000			4.024	.5276
Boundary-less Communication	.394**	.343**	.347**	.374**	.252**	.262**	.661**	.650**	.616**	.585**	1.000		3.613	.6432
Centralization	.152**	.079	.108*	.117**	.014	.097*	.205**	.245**	.246**	.162**	.229**	1.000	3.342	.8927

Source: Authors.
Notes: N = 525.
*Significant at .05 level.
**Significant at .01 level.

Appendix 9A.2: Structural Equation Modeling

Measurement models for the factors of Change Maestro's style and Culture were tested. Since the last two factors of Change Maestro's style construct—role model and credibility—and the last factor of culture construct—decentralization—had less than three items or factors, they were dropped from SEM analysis. Both the models proved to be a good fit as indicated by the values in Table 9A.2a.

Table 9A.2a: Fit Measures of the Measurement Model

Fit Indices of Default Model	Measurement Model 2: Culture Factors to Culture
CMIN/df	2.52
GFI	1
RMSEA	0.00

Source: Authors.

Further, to examine the link between the variables of Change Maestro's style and work culture, we used the following path model.

To calculate the fit indices that explain the relationships between the hypothesized paths among the latent constructs, we used the AMOS 4.0 SEM procedures (Arbuckle and Wothke 1999).

We utilized the Maximum Likelihood Estimation (MLE) algorithm in order to determine the fit indices. Accordingly, we report the Goodness-of-Fit Index (GFI) and the Root Mean Square Error of Approximation (RMSEA) as the absolute fit measures. According to Byrne (2001), absolute fit measures should be used for comparison between the hypothesized model and an absence of any other model.

According to Hair et al. (1998), the recommended fit values for CMIN/df (Normed chi-square/standardized form) are ≤ 3, and that for GFI are > 0.90. Likewise, while an RMSEA of 0 indicates perfect fit, values that are less than 0.07 are considered as good fits.

Table 9A.2b shows the fit measures of the proposed model.

Table 9A.2b: *Fit Measures of the Path Model*

Fit Indices of Default Model (the hypothesized model)	Path Model
CMIN/df	2.97
GFI	0.98
RMSEA	0.04

Source: Authors.

Implications

- This path model has been built to understand the contribution of Change Maestros' style to the respective factors of work culture. Thus, it is important to check the Adjusted R^2 (Squared Multiple Correlation) of each of these factors to understand their contribution respectively. As can be seen from Figure 9.2, it can be inferred that leadership contributes significantly to all the culture factors—excellence centric; stakeholders' focus; experimenting; goal and role clarity; and boundary-less communication. However, based on the amount of variance explained through leadership in each of the culture factors separately, it can be concluded that leadership has maximum variance (81.5 percent) in excellence-centric culture factor, followed by stakeholders' focus (78.4 percent), experimenting (72.5 percent), boundary-less communication (52.5 percent), and last, goal clarity (48.8 percent).

NOTES

1. This section is based on the questionnaire filled up by top, senior, and senior middle level executives.
2. This section is based on the interviews held with the top and senior level executives.
3. SPSS package has been used to conduct principle component analysis; varimax rotation converged in six iterations. The factors cumulatively explained 61.65 of the variance (see Appendix 9A.1, Table 9A.1a for details on items in each factor).
4. This section is based on the questionnaire distributed to the top, senior, and senior middle executives.
5. This section is interview-based.

6. SPSS package has been used to conduct principle component analysis; varimax rotation converged in six iterations. The factors cumulatively explained 60.74 of the variance (see Appendix 9A.1, Table 9A.1b for further details on items in each factor).
7. Factors arrived at based on the Principle Component Analysis (PCA) discussed earlier, four of the six factors, namely, enabler, excellence seeker, direction setter, and visionary strategist have been used. The remaining factors are role model and credibility and have been dropped since they had two items and one item, respectively, and hence did not meet the conditions for conducting SEM. SEM, and not Multiple Regression Analysis (MRA), has been used because we were interested to assess the impact on the single Change Maestros' score on multiple work culture factors. MRA analysis on single independent and single dependent variables was conducted. See Appendix 9A.2, Table 9A.2a for details and Appendix 9A.1, Table 9A.1c for mean, SD, and correlation matrix.

10

Figure 5A.1 Operations of ICICI Bank

CHANGE MAESTROS' GESTALT

10

The conductor's hand rises and falls, a thousand violins resonate and the opera house reverberates with mellifluous music, with every player, playing her best music, mesmerized by the maestro's moving magic wand—it is the music that enchants and binds both the creator and the audience in one surreal experience! Shift to the real world, it is only the Change Maestro who, like the music conductor, integrates his vision and actions with that of the people and together they co-create powerful organizations and great institutions.

The purpose of writing this book is both to celebrate the Change Maestros and to show how they created great institutions and built the sense of pride in their team members. A leader is known by his deeds, but a Change Maestro touches people's lives in such a way that the impact is indelibly and positively palpable, even after he is gone. They change the people, their way of life, and the nations they reside in, and impact humanity by putting an indelible mark on the company's history synonymous with their own life journey.

The book unfolds the stories of seven Change Maestros who, on their unending quest for change, impact increasingly large numbers of people. They can be considered icons or role models for leadership. The book, as is expected, will, in some measure, fill the vacuum that exists in this literature and in the process of celebrating our kaleidoscopic Change Maestros, offer fresh insights to the readers. Gurus of wisdom also exist in the hardcore business arena affecting myriad lives—this is hoped to be conveyed effectively by the research carried out as part of this book.

The quest for capable leaders and Change Maestros exists in all spheres of organized society as well as in various aspects of human life. As mentioned in Chapter 1, the key elements that characterize great leaders and Change Maestros are: contextual sensitivity; compelling vision and purpose; winning streak; people connect and engagement; meaningful contribution with speed; creative destruction; culture architecture; and evolving self. It is a refreshing reassurance that in the contemporary society that is experiencing a serious crisis of leadership in all walks of life—be it political; social; economic; religious; or academic—such Change Maestros, in the process of building greater institutions, revive faith in the power of leadership.

How are these Maestros shaped then? Is it the exclusive domain of a few or does it take an accelerated evolution process that transcends space and time to become a Change Maestro? Unlike the leadership of a king or a political leader, Change Maestros somehow are not distant icons; they live under our own skin and their lives, worldview, and belief systems become a part of the lives of those who closely associate with them. This is the beauty of change that these Maestros evoke in the lives of those they touch, blending the manifold efforts of the multitude, energizing and inspiring each to give his/her best.

In fact throughout the research and writing phases of this book, the impact of interacting with these leaders lingered on, making us wonder at the scarcity of such leaders in society. Also as teachers of management and trainers of minds, it made us wonder whether the changes preached by these leaders can be taught to our students. Can they be made to appreciate the real import of the experiments being carried out by the Maestros in their fullest degree? Can the life events of these Change Maestros be translated into textbooks that could inspire aspiring managers to prepare their paths? We are confident that the format of this book and the case studies that are part of the offering and the extensive reference material provided would serve the purpose of not only bringing the Change Maestros alive to our readers, but also help in raising the bar on the debate regarding impact of business leadership on society and institutions.

In order to gain a holistic perspective and deeper understanding of leadership and Change Maestro phenomena, we followed an eclectic approach—gathering data using structured questionnaire; in-depth interviews; anthropological

CHANGE MAESTROS' GESTALT 447

inquiry as well as secondary data. We used this method despite it being highly tedious and time consuming, not to mention the challenges of getting access to the thinking of the Change Maestros, their families and the top teams, to overcome the limitations of using any single data gathering mode. Needless to say, such an approach enabled us to develop holistic insight into the Change Maestros' profile, persona, and action architecture.

SALIENT FINDINGS

Before dwelling on the Change Maestros' profile and their DNA, it would be fitting to present the actions and their impact on organizational performance, organizational culture, and business architecture. This will set the tone and provide the background for the reader to appreciate and develop insight into the Change Maestros' role, action strategy, and persona.

Viewing together the organizational culture and action architecture findings bring out the following organizational culture gestalt which the Change Maestros have used to create successful and competing organizations:

- While building organizational architecture and organizational culture, Change Maestros put a heavy accent on ethical governance, global vision, entrepreneurial innovation, customer centricity, quest for continued growth, performance excellence and performance-centric reward system, futuristic and forward-looking approach, good corporate citizenship, and providing a caring and empowering workplace. It would be noteworthy to highlight that such a pattern has emerged more or less, both through structured questionnaire and interview data gathered from the top team members and the Change Maestros. This has been further corroborated by the significant congruity which emerged through comparative analysis in the pattern of organizational culture across the seven organizations. In other words, irrespective of corporate ownership and business sector, there is an overarching pattern of organizational culture built by these Change Maestros to create great organizations.

- All the Change Maestros have had significant impact on the following five broad organizational culture constructs[1]: excellence centric; stakeholders' focus; experimenting; goal and role clarity; and boundary-less communication. This indicates that in all their respective companies, the Change Maestros have significantly impacted organizational culture through their strategies, mindsets, actions, and styles. In fact it appears that organizational culture is an expression of the Change Maestros' persona, their value systems, and their thought processes.
- They significantly contributed to raising financial performance of their organizations which has been mind-boggling by any standard.

The findings of the Change Maestros' profile and their persona are now presented:

- All the Change Maestros have been found to be highly ethical, ambitious with a global perspective along with an innovative thinking. They demonstrate futuristic orientation, a deep appetite for growth and a perennial quest for excellence in performance. They believe in the principle of customer centricity. They are extremely entrepreneurial in their approach and continuously carve out new trajectories for business growth. All Change Maestros have been found to be talent shapers, empowering, and highly credible. They are known to take up challenges and when need be, lead from the front. They demonstrate thirst for new learning and a constant desire to evolve. They have mastered the art of balancing and harmonizing contradictions, opposing forces and divergent views, enabling them to move effortlessly from one mode of functioning to another.
- Comparison of each Change Maestros' self-assessment about his own profile vis-à-vis the assessment by his top team, reveals a significant congruity between the two assessments. Such a powerful match indicates that the Change Maestros "walk-the-talk"—they mean what they say; there is consistency and predictability about their actions. This leads to establishing high levels of trust and confidence about the Change Maestros in the eyes of their followers and which tremendously strengthens their credibility.

- All the Change Maestros have more or less identical leadership competency frameworks.
- In-depth interviews with the Change Maestros revealed that all of them are big dreamers with a Himalayan ambition and global vision; all of them convey a sense of positive disquiet; they are highly ethical and value driven; they are bold, courageous, and passionate with a powerful streak of being entrepreneurial. They are talent architects; they are patriotic and demonstrate sensitivity toward social issues. They are open and observant with an alert antenna; they scan the context, sense opportunity, and convert the same into business strategy. They are able to view reality using both the magnifying lens as well as binoculars, alternating between the two as required. They are highly learning and evolving people. They are all Karma Yogis putting tremendous emphasis on action and execution.
- All of them expressed a great admiration for their parents as role models who shaped their life vision, values, and thoughts. Many of them also passionately mentioned Gandhi as their role models.
- Tremendous similarity has been found between the Change Maestros' attributes which emerged from the literature survey and present research.

During the process of our research, one of the things which fascinated us was the deep aesthetic sense that was evident in the lives of these businessmen and institution builders. These Change Maestros appear to be aesthetically tuned in and particular about the spaces that they create in the organization, not only for themselves but for all their employees. Above all they are the philosopher–kings who combine the power of the ruler and the consciousness of an evolved thinker philosopher.

Weaving these findings, it may be concluded that no matter what lens is used to view the Change Maestros, there is tremendous consistency in the findings about their profile and persona. While the questionnaire data gave us the broad-based perceived picture about them, the in-depth and open ended interviews enabled us to identify some new elements of the profile which escaped the questionnaire mode of data collection. We were able to triangulate the findings from these two sources with the Change Maestros' perception about themselves, which overlapped the views shared by their followers. Incidentally a significant overlap is also visible between the Change Maestros' DNA which emerged from this research and that which we found through literature survey. On the basis of such findings we can conclude that the cited attributes constitute the required DNA to be a Change Maestro in the Indian context.

At this stage we would like to reiterate the genesis of this work: leadership crisis and the relevance of the emergent model from this work to help address the prevalent leadership crisis in the contemporary corporate world. Before proposing the model, it would be desirable to examine the critical reasons for the leadership crisis in the corporate world. The following story (Osho, 2010) illustrates the core of the crisis:

> The Greek philosopher Pythagoras,[2] once upon a time decided to enter an Egyptian school—a secret and esoteric school of mysticism. To his dismay and surprise he was refused entry. He could not understand the reason why and being a tenacious and curious person, he applied again and again only to find that each time he was rejected. On inquiry it was conveyed that the prerequisite to enter this school was a special training that involved fasting and breathing. Pythagoras is reported to have said, "I have come for knowledge not for any sort of discipline." The school authorities insisted that he undergo the training should he decide to join the school saying, "We are not interested in mere knowledge; we are interested in actual experience." They said, "we believe that no knowledge is knowledge unless it is lived and experienced. So you will have to go on a forty day fast accompanied by breathing exercises along with a focused awareness on certain points."
>
> Since there was no way out, Pythagoras underwent the training. After forty days, Pythagoras reportedly told the school, "Today, the man before you is not the old Pythagoras. This man is a different man. I am reborn ... you were right and I was wrong. Earlier, my whole standpoint was wholly intellectual. After this 40 days experience, my centre of being has shifted. Now I am able to integrate both mind and heart. Now I can not only think but also feel. Before this training, I understood the world through the intellect alone. Now I can understand and experience reality both through the head and heart. Now truth is not a concept, to me it is life. It is not going to be a

philosophy, rather it is an experience." Incidentally, Indian tradition—unlike Greek tradition, where philosophy means love for knowledge—also defines philosophy as "Darshana" that is realization through seeing, not just through intellectual analysis. In other words, Darshana reflects emphasis on both knowledge and experience. Pythagoras[3] went with this insight to Greece and he became famous as the fountainhead of wisdom in the western world, because of his capability to integrate both head and heart and get in touch with reality in a gestalt sense rather than viewing it in an isolated, disintegrated and limited sense.

Unfortunately most of the scientists, philosophers, and thinkers tend to view world phenomena in terms of Gestalt duality and Newtonian reductionism. In Gestalt duality there is a split between the body and the soul, between the body and the mind, between the inner world and the outer world, between thought and action, between self and others, between person and environment, etc. In such Gestalt duality, therefore, one is incapable of seeing phenomena in totality—selecting one facet is at the expense of ignoring the other, like a coin with two sides which co-exist yet can never see each other. Newtonian reductionism splits matter into yet smaller parts for examining phenomena, the basic assumption being that the whole is equal to the sum of parts and nothing more. This view completely ignores the synergistic effects of elements interacting together and affecting each other, which creates something more than the sum of the parts, which of late is being strongly propounded by the quantum physicists, holistic theorists, and complexity theorists. The Newtonian mechanistic worldview negated the view propounded by classical Greeks and the Indian Vedantists both of whom emphasized "a cosmos filled with purpose and intelligence driven by the love of God for the benefit of man" (Zohar, 1990: 18). Both classical Greek and the Vedantist philosophy emphasize principles of interconnectedness, holism, and synergy.

Bertrand Russell highlighted the impact of the Newtonian worldview and its effect on the collective human psyche whereby viewing self only as an accidental entity, the sense of meaning, and purpose is completely lost (Zohar, 1990: 18). Russell laments the state of the human being:

> The world which science presents for our belief that man is the product of causes which had no prevision of the end they were achieving; that his origin, his growth, his hopes and fears, his loves and his beliefs, are but the outcome of accidental collocation of atoms; that no fire, no heroism, no intensity of thought and feeling, can preserve the individual beyond the grave; that all the labours of the ages, all the devotion, all the inspiration, all the noonday brightness of human genius, are destined to extinction in the vast death of the solar system, and that the whole temple of Man's achievement must inevitably be buried beneath the debris of a universe in ruins.... (Zohar, 1990: 19)

Similarly, Zohar asks:

> If we are nothing but accidental by products of creation and pawns in the play of larger forces wholly beyond our control, how can we exercise much meaningful responsibility, either for ourselves or towards others? On every side, morally, spiritually and aesthetically our culture seems to be under stress. Many of the old values and generally held beliefs have ceased to be unquestionable. We find ourselves grounded in nothing larger than ourselves and the great mass of people have been forced willy nilly, to live in the age of the existential hero—defiantly indifferent to the dead God, becoming makers of their own values and guardians of their own consciousness. (Zohar, 1990: 20)

Extending the concept of duality into religion, one can see that in most of the religions there is denigration of the body in favor of the soul. Societies of the East have tended to dwell more on the soul, while Western societies have dwelt more on mind and matter. Both perspectives are incomplete—we can discern in the world today that while the East is hungry for wealth, the West is hungry for soul and perhaps to be complete there is need for holistic integration of both. Holistic integration and balance are emphasized both by Chinese philosophy depicted in the principle of Yin and Yang—integration of masculine and feminine energies—and by Hindu philosophy symbolized in *Ardha-Nareeshwara*—union of masculine and feminine energies. In fact in Hindu philosophy, *Ardha-Nareeshwara* is the physical depiction of the highest form of evolution and actualization of human consciousness.

From this discussion it is clear that the dominant view about the world and the human being are characterized by Gestalt duality which has led to a sense of alienation, isolation among human beings, and a sense of disconnect from self, others, society, and universe. Therefore, there is a strong need to reorient the notions about the world and human beings moving from the Newtonian framework to quantum mechanical theory of consciousness and theory of holism, which say that everything is related, interdependent, and mutually influencing each other, where the whole is greater than the sum of the parts. Incidentally this integrational view has been emphasized both in classical Greek thought and in the Indian Vedantic system.

Applying this concept to the domain of leadership and Change Maestros' phenomenon, examining the findings of the study using a holistic lens would thus be very useful. An analysis of leadership in a Newtonian, non-holistic, and Gestalt duality framework would provide partial and limited understanding. It establishes that a leader and Change Maestro should be integrated at all the three levels: the self; business; and ecological levels.

At the level of the self there must be coherence and congruity among purpose, philosophy, values, attitudes, and styles (see Figure 10.1).

Similarly, at the organizational level there is a need for holistic integration of different aspects of business as well as the levers the Change Maestro normally uses to create winning organization—cost leadership; quality; customer centricity; people power; innovation leadership; speed and ethical governance (see Figure 10.2).

In addition, the Change Maestro must continuously align and realign business strategies with environmental demands and challenges. In other words, the business must be connected with emerging environmental issues and challenges.

In order to become a true Change Maestro there is a need for holistic integration of all three levels: self; organization; and business (see Figure 10.3).

Viewing the seven leaders in the study using the paradigm of Gestalt holism propounded earlier in this chapter shows the following:

454 IN SEARCH OF CHANGE MAESTROS

Figure 10.1 Integration at the Self Level

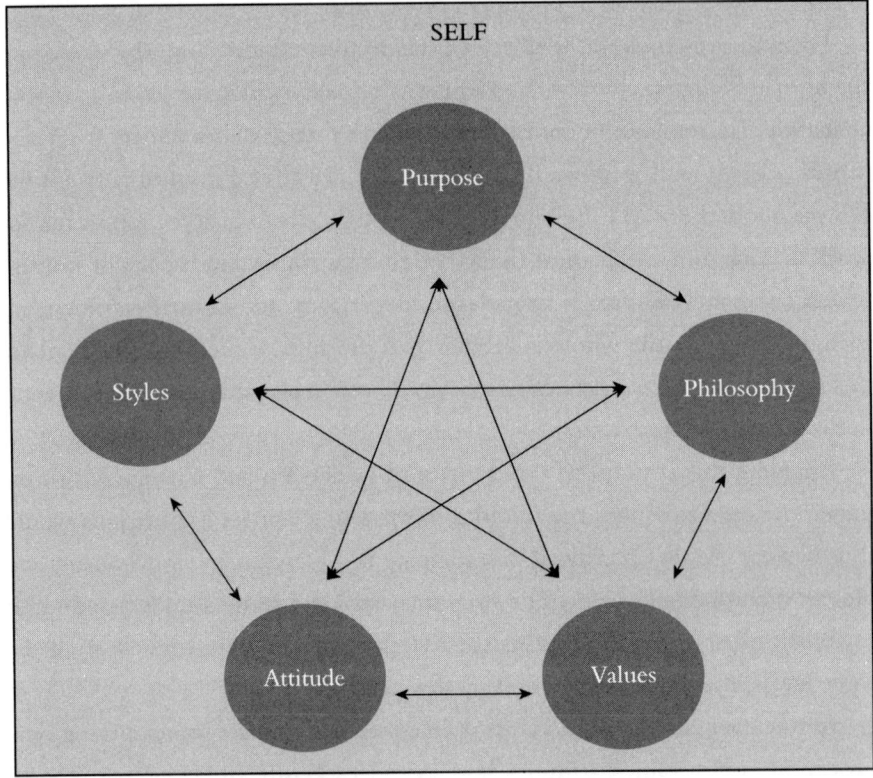

Source: Authors.

- There is consistency and coherence at the self level in all the seven Change Maestros. The philosophy, values, attitudes, and actions are synchronous with each other. There is alignment among these aspects of self leading to channeling of self-level energies in a concentrated fashion—like a laser beam—rather than being dissipated like searchlight. Needless to say, without such alignment, there would be contradictions and disconnectedness, which would dissipate self-level energies. It may bring inconsistency between the espoused and actual behaviors, negatively affecting credibility.
- This book reveals among other things, that Change Maestros leave a distinct impact on the organizational culture, action architecture, and business processes. Change Maestros powerfully connect with the organization

CHANGE MAESTROS' GESTALT   455

Figure 10.2 Integration at the Organizational Level

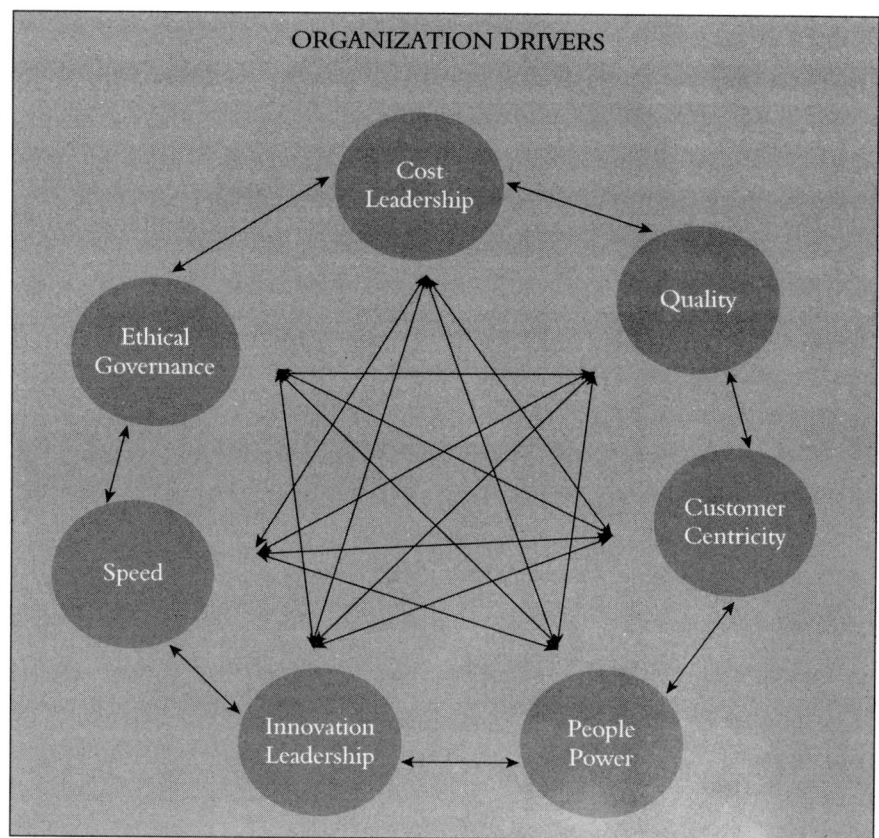

Source: Authors.

which becomes, in many ways, an extension of the leaders' persona—vision; values; styles; attitudes; and behavior. Thus, there is integration of the self level with the organizational level.

All Change Maestros have powerfully integrated all the facets of business. They have coherently used all the competitive levers and effortlessly moved from one to the other for building winning organizations. Their competency bandwidth is very large and they quickly and easily move across the range of competencies. This ease of movement reflects agility, flexibility, and adaptability, the touchstone of holistic leaders and Change Maestros.

Figure 10.3 *Change Maestros—Holistic Integration at all Three Levels*

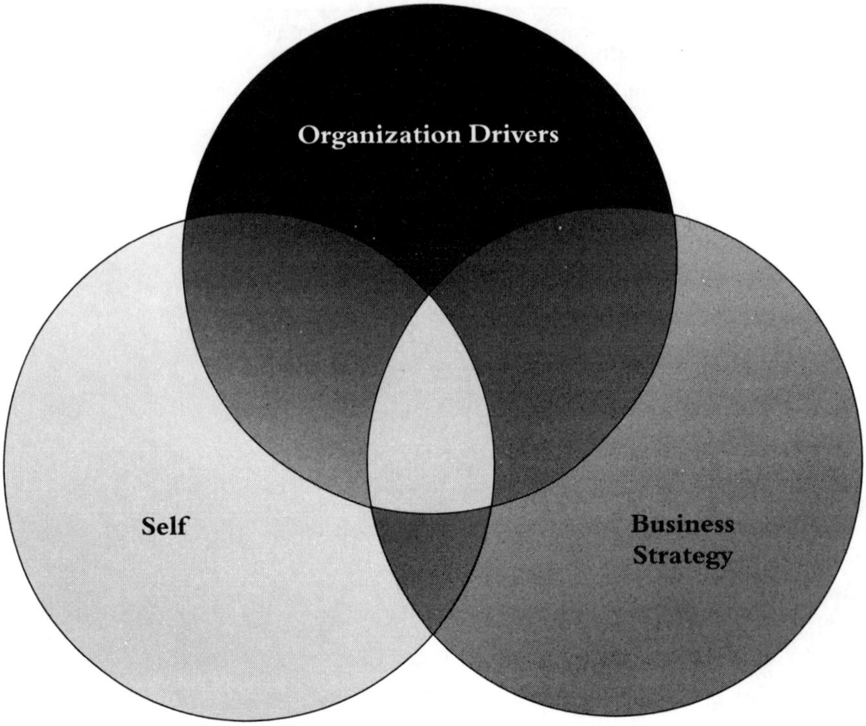

Organization Drivers

Self

Business Strategy

Source: Authors.

- All the seven Change Maestros have succeeded in powerfully aligning with the changing business environment and, when required, even changing the direction of the organization. The Change Maestros in our study emerged as the great captains of the ship, navigating in the high seas and aligning according to direction and velocity of wind, turbulence of the waves, and the destination to be reached. In many ways, these Change Maestros navigate their ships sometimes even without maps of the territory ahead, without stars to guide their direction, relying instead, on mental maps which they construct as well as thumb-rules and indicators which they have created from their experience. They have mastery over the pulse of the organization, from which they gauge the problems and build organizational fitness to cope with the environmental demands and challenges. They look within, around and beyond; they enfold the future into the present; they connect horizon with ground; they are excited by endless possibilities; they seek to take their organization to the next orbit, by being game changers and entrepreneurial path breakers. Through these processes, all the seven Change Maestros under study in this book have successfully integrated the organization with the business ecology and environment.

The extracted essence and distilled wisdom of this work powerfully brings out that "holism" and Gestalt integration at the self, business, and organizational ecology levels is the essence of becoming a Change Maestro. In fact, holism is the bedrock for building enduring Change Maestros. How can such a holistic approach be built among people at the self, family, academic, and organizational levels is the seminal question arising from these findings. In the subsequent paragraphs, we briefly outline suggestions regarding the role which can be played by the individual, family, academic institutions, and organizations, in order to groom and develop Change Maestros with holistic perspective and mindsets.

Bhagavad Gita,[4] the tome of Vedantic wisdom brings out the importance of self in enabling the person to blossom to the fullest potential. It says (Singh and Bhandarker, 2002: 169):

> Let a man raise his self by his self;
> Let him not debase his self,
> He alone indeed is his own friend
> He alone his own enemy

This quote conveys the central role played by a person in self-evolution. In fact the active role which a person has in tuning the mindset is brought out in the following quote (Singh and Bhandarker, 1989: 166):

> Let a man strive to purify his thoughts;
> What a man thinketh that is he;
> This is the eternal mystery...
> Man becomes that which he thinks

In fact leading thinkers like Carl Rogers (1989) and Nathaniel Branden (1989) also emphasized the role of self in "becoming" what one is capable of and evolving to one's potential. To actualize one's potential and become a fully evolved human being, the roles of reflection and meditation have been heavily emphasized by Patanjali, the father of Yoga, as well as by modern-day psychologists and therapists.

Self Level

The following list of questions, though not exhaustive, will enable the reader to commence on the journey of self-transformation:

- What is the purpose of my life?
- What have I done to actualize my life purpose?
- Is there connectedness and coherence among purpose, philosophy, values, attitudes, and styles?
- Do I seek feedback from persons around me about my styles and actions?
- Do I take time off and unwind through hobbies and then reflect?
- Am I able to switch off now and then from work and refresh myself?
- What is my level of awareness about self and others?
- Do I accept myself the way I am?
- Do I feel the urge to change some aspects of myself?
- Do I have high self-esteem?

Such questioning at the self level, opens up the seeker's mind to explore and come to grips with both strengths and weaknesses.

Family Level

According to the timeless wisdom of the Gita, in every human being there exists, to a greater or lesser extent, *gunas* like *sattvic* (state of harmony, balance, joy, and intelligence), *rajasic* (state of energy, action, change, and movement), and *tamasic* (state of darkness, inertia, inactivity, and materiality), which can be modified or altered through grooming and socialization. Indian scriptures expand the seminal concept of the human potential for self transformation from a lower state of consciousness—character; knowledge; behavior; moral standards; and personality—to a higher level through *samskaras*. In terms of the symbolic classification of the human personality, every human being is born a Shudhra who is then reborn through the process of socialization. He then becomes a wise man (*vipra*) through the mastery of scriptures and attains the status of a Brahmin through the understanding of cosmic reality. Such a view reveals the critical role played by family in socializing and grooming the individual and helping the person blossom to the fullest.

While playing the role as counselors and therapists we have invariably found that Indian families tend to emphasize scholastic achievement and career to such an extent that development of the person as well as a well-rounded human being suffers. People are rarely groomed to be leaders and the purpose, philosophy, and vision of life are not adequately emphasized. In contrast the Change Maestros in this study imbibed these from their parents indicating that parents can play an important role in the process of grooming.

Academic Institutions

The well-known Confucian quote reads:

> When I read I forget;
> When I see I remember;
> When I do I understand

This quote provides insight about the type of educational pedagogy which can best help in shaping and developing young minds to imbibe the needed values and develop a holistic mind to become future Change Maestros.

We now state some pertinent suggestions on this theme which would be most relevant for management schools. Bhandarker (2008) says that business schools (or B-schools) play a key role in heightening analytical power, self-confidence, communication and presentation skills, and capability at quick thinking. However, B-schools do not adequately groom team workers with high performance focus or inculcate capability to lead, mobilize, and inspire people, nor do they help them enhance capabilities like change management, entrepreneurial abilities, global mindsets, high ambiguity tolerance, and holistic business perspectives. In order to develop capabilities which they lack, B-schools will have to reorient their focus, evolve suitable teaching pedagogy, and sharply define the business they are in. They need to move from the preponderant:

From ⟶	To
Concept focus	Issue focus
Idea focus	Action focus
Cognitive focus	Emotive focus
Analytical focus	Holistic worldview
Grooming careerists	Grooming entrepreneurs and wealth creators
Status quo-ists	Change Maestros

The need is to move from the preponderant lecture-and-case method to experiential outbound, theater, films, and other such modes, which help bring a person in touch with his own values, styles, and mindsets. In fact B-schools need to inculcate a holistic vision of life. For this purpose, they should use classical works by social thinkers, philosophers, poets, artists, and writers to educate students. Autobiographies and biographies of great people can also help in this endeavor. They must seek to provide an integrated business perspective rather than just specialist and functionalist perspectives. They must also provide opportunities for holistic grooming of the students—being leaders; Change Maestros; working for the larger cause; building sensitivity to broader societal issues; and making a difference in whatever they do.

ORGANIZATIONAL LEVEL

Individuals spend most of their working life in organizations. Hence, organizations have the power to significantly influence their perspective, mindsets, styles, emotional states, and actions. They can bring a holistic perspective by building cross-functional teams, membership in various committees, giving them roles which can be the crucibles of transformation, job rotation, mentoring, coaching, providing global exposure, etc. Such strategies will help in developing integrated business perspectives, besides building insights about competencies which they have to inculcate to be leaders and Change Maestros. In addition, organizations can also evolve mechanisms and processes like 360-degree appraisal, assessment centers, mentoring through corporate priest and gurus, and to provide the mirror view about their persona, styles, and competencies.

Organizations must build awareness among employees about the competency sets relevant at different levels—at the levels of the manager; leader; and Change Maestro. They must also mentor them on ways to integrate the various competencies and effortlessly move from the manager level to the Change Maestro level.

The musical symphony, as mentioned in the beginning of the chapter, is an apt metaphor to describe the quintessential quality of the seven Change Maestros. In an epiphanic moment, we saw them as great conductors of symphonies—exciting and inspiring people through the power of collective vision and creating melodious harmony out of the confluence of myriad voices and multifarious instruments.

Notes

1. Findings from the factor analysis of work culture items as reported in Chapter 9.
2. One of the best minds Greece has ever produced.
3. This technique of meditation consists of focusing attention on the third eye, *Shivanetra* of Indian mythology, biologically known as the pineal gland, which is located between the two eyes. By focusing on the third eye, the higher consciousness (about the self, cosmos, and integration of self with cosmos) gets activated and developed creating the path toward holistic integration.
4. Bhagavad Gita is the sacred Hindu scripture that contains the divine discourse taught by Lord Krishna, considered to be the manifestation of God.

REFERENCES

Airtel. Various years. *Annual Report*. Available online at http://airtel.in/wps/wcm/connect/about%20bharti%20airtel/Bharti%20Airtel/Investor%20Relations/Results/Quarterly%20Results/2009-2010/PG_IR_RS_QuarterlyResults_2009_10

Allio, R.J. (2009). "Leadership—The Five Big Ideas," *Strategy and Leadership*, 37(2): 4–12.

Amabile, T.M., A. Schatzel, G.B. Moneta, and S.J. Kramer. (2004). "Leader Behaviors and the Work Environment for Creativity: Perceived Leader Support," *The Leadership Quarterly*, 15(1, February): 5–32.

Arbuckle, J.L. and W. Wothke. (1999). *AMOS 4.0 User's Guide*. Chicago, IL: Smallwaters Corporation.

Arnold, Sir Edwin. (2007). *Bhagavad Gita: Song Celestial*. London: Watkins Publishing.

Avolio, B.J. and F. Yammarino. (2002). *Transformational and Charismatic Leadership: The Road Ahead*. New York: Jai Press.

Barney, J.B. (1986). "Organizational Culture: Can It be a Source of Sustained Competitive Advantage?" *Academy of Management Review*, 11(3): 656–65.

Bass, B.M. (1985). *Leadership and Performance beyond Expectation*. New York: The Free Press.

Bennis, W.G. and R.J. Thomas. (2002), "Crucibles of Leadership," *Harvard Business Review*, 80(9): 39–45.

Berson, Y., S. Oreg, and T. Dvir. (2008). "CEO Values, Organizational Culture and Firm Outcomes," *Journal of Organizational Behavior*, 29(5): 615–33.

Bhandarker, A. (2008). *Shaping Business Leaders: What B-Schools Don't Do*. New Delhi: Response Books.

Birla, A.V. (1994). Speech given by A.V. Birla on Corporate Philosophy and Perspective.

Branden, Nathaniel. (1989). *Honoring the Self: Self-Esteem and Personal Transformation*. New York: Random House Publishing Group.

Burns, J.M. (1978). *Leadership*. New York: HarperCollins.

Byrne, B.M. (2001). *Structural Equation Modeling with AMOS: Basic Concepts, Applications, and Programming*. Mahwah, NJ: Lawrence Erlbaum Associates.

Carlzon, J. (1989). *Moments of Truth*. New York: HarperCollins.

Chan Teng, H. (2000). *Access the Minds of CEOs*. London: Marshall Cavendish Business.

Chun-Hsi Vivian Chen, Hung-Hui Li, and Ya-Yun. (2009). "Transformational Leadership and Creativity: Exploring the Mediating Effects of Creative Thinking and Intrinsic Motivation," *International Journal of Management and Enterprise Development*, 6(2): 198–211.

Collier, Peter with David Horowoa. (1994). *The Roosevelt—An American Saga*. New York: Simon & Schuster.

Collins, Jim. 2001. *Good to Great: Why Some Companies Make the Leap... and Others Don't*. HarperBusiness.

Connolly, J. (2009). "Positioning for the Future," *Business Strategy Review*, 20(3, September): 30–34.

Corelli, R. and V. Dwyer. (1991). "Welch Jack Reinvents GE Again," *The Economist*, March 30, p. 59.

Coutu, Diane (2009). "Leadership Lessons from Abraham Lincoln—A Conversation with Historian Goodwin D.K.," *Harvard Business Review South Asia*, April.

Dauphinais, G.W. (2000). *Wisdom of the CEO: 29 Global Leaders Tackle Today's Most Pressing Business Challenges*. New York: John Wiley.

Denison, D.R. (1990). *Corporate Culture and Organizational Effectiveness*. New York: Wiley.

Drucker, P.F. (2006). "What Executives Should Remember," *Harvard Business Review*, 84(2, February): 144–52.

Dyer, Jeffrey H., Hal B. Gregersen, and Clayton M. Christensen. (2009). "The Innovator's DNA: Five 'Discovery Skills' Separate True Innovators from the Rest of Us," *Harvard Business Review South Asia*, 87(12, December): 60–67.

Fernandez, J.A. (2004). "The Gentleman's Code of Confucius: Leadership by Values," *Organizational Dynamics*, 33(1): 21–31.

Fischer, Louis. (1997). *The Life of Mohandas Gandhi*. London: HarperCollins.

Fitzgerald, T.H. (1988). "Can Change in Organizational Culture Really Be Managed?" *Organizational Dynamics*, 17(2): 4–15.

Gardner, H. (1996). *Leading Minds: An Anatomy of Leadership*. London: HarperCollins.

Green, Stephen, F. Hassan, J. Immelt, M. Marks, and D. Meiland. (2003). "In Search of Global Leaders," *Harvard Business Review*, 81(8, August): 38–49.

Gross, Daniel and the Editors of *Forbes* Magazine. (1996). *Forbes—Greatest Business Stories of all Time*. New York: John Wiley and Sons.

Hair, J.F., R.E. Anderson, R.L. Tatham, and W.C. Black. (1998). *Multivariate Data Analysis*. 5th ed. Englewood Cliffs, NJ: Prentice-Hall.

Hambrick, D.C., D. Nadler, and M. Tushman. (1998). *Navigating Change: How CEOs, Top Teams, and Boards Steer Transformation*. Boston: Harvard Business School Press.

Hennessey, J.T. (1998). "'Reinventing' Government: Does Leadership Make the Difference?" *Public Administration Review*, 58(6): 522–32.

Hofstede, G. (1986). "The Usefulness of the Organizational Culture Concept," *Journal of Management Studies*, 23(3): 253–58.

Hotheinz, Paul. (1993). "Europe's Tough New Managers," *Fortune*, September 6, p. 114.

House, R.J., P.J. Hanges, M. Javidan, P. Dorfman, and V. Gupta. (2004). *Culture, Leadership and Organizations: The GLOBE Study of 62 Societies*. Thousand Oaks: Sage Publications.

Iacocca, Lee with William Novak. (1985). *Iacocca: An Autobiography*. New York: Bantam Books.

Jeffery, K.A. (2003). *What the Best CEOs Know: 7 Exceptional Leaders and their Lessons for Transforming any Business*. New York: McGraw-Hill.

Jo Hatch, M., M. Kostera, and A.K. Kosminski. (2005). *The Three Faces of Leadership: Manager, Artist, Priest*. London: Blackwell Publishers.

Judge, W.Q. (1999). *The Leader's Shadow: Exploring and Developing Executive Character*. Thousand Oaks: Sage Publications.

Kalam, A.P.J. (2003). "From Rameshwaram to Rashtrapati Bhawan," *Business Line*, August 25.

Kalam, A.P.J. with Y.S. Rajan. (1998). *India 2020—A Vision for the New Millennium*. New Delhi: Viking.

Kanter, R. (1983). *The Change Masters*. New York: Simon & Schuster.

Kase, K., F. Sáez, and H. Riquelme. (2005). *Transformational CEOs: Leadership and Management Success in Japan*. Cheltenham: Edward Elgar Publishing Ltd.

Khurana, Rakesh. (2002). *Searching for a Corporate Savior: The Irrational Quest for Charismatic CEOs*. Princeton, NJ: Princeton University Press.

Kirkpatrick, David. (1997). "Intel's Amazing Profit Making Machine," *Fortune*, India, February 17, p. 62.

Kotter, John P. (1997). *Matsushita Leadership: Lessons from the 20th Century's Most Remarkable Entrepreneur*. New York: The Free Press.

Krefting, L.A. and P.J. Frost. (1985). "Untangling Webs, Surfing Waves, and Wildcatting: A Multiple-Metaphor Perspective on Managing Culture," in P.J. Frost, L.F. Moore, Reis L. Meryl, C.C. Lundberg, and J. Martin (eds), *Reframing Organizational Culture*, pp. 155–68. Newbury Park, CA: Sage Publications.

Lafley, A.G. (2009). "What Only the CEO Can Do," *Harvard Business Review*, 87(5, May): 55–59.

Lala, R.M. (1992). *Beyond the Last Blue Mountain: The Life of J.R.D. Tata*. Delhi: Penguin Books.

Lakshman, Nandini and Manjeet Kripalani. 2007. "India's 50 Most Powerful People: The Politicians, Business Leaders, Film Stars, Athletes, and Designers behind India's Growing International Presence in the World," *Business Week*, August 13.

Lashinsky, Adam. (2009). "The Decade of Steve," *Fortune*, Asia Pacific Edition, November 23, No. 21, pp. 62–81.

Libert, B. and R. Faulk. (2009). *Winning Business Lessons of the Obama Campaign*. New York: Pearson Education Inc.

Mandela, Nelson. (1994). *Long Walk to Freedom—The Autobiography of Nelson Mandela*. Boston and New York: Little Brown and Company.

Marcoulides, George A. and Ronald H. Heck. (1993). "Organizational Culture and Performance: Proposing and Testing a Model," *Organizational Science*, 4(2, May): 209–25.

Mayo, A.J. and N. Nohria. (2005). "Zeitgeist Leadership," *Harvard Business Review*, 83(10, October): 45–60.

McClenahen, John S. (1994). "An Interview with Percy Barnevik, President and CEO of Zurich-based Asea Brown Boveri (ABB)—Forecasts Business Activities in Eastern and Central Europe," *Industry Week*, 243, June 6, p. 115.

Mintzberg, H. (2007). *Mintzberg on Management: Inside our Strange World of Organizations*. US: Hungry Minds Inc.

Mirvis, P.H., K. Avas, and G. Roth. (2003). *To the Desert and Back: The Story of the Most Dramatic Business Transformation on Record*. New York: John Wiley.

Mirvis, P.H. and L.T. Gunning. (2006). "Creating a Community of Leaders," *Organizational Dynamics*, 35(1): 69–82.

Mito, Setsuo. (1990). "Leadership Philosophy for High Industrial Success," *Honda Book of Management*. London: Kogan Page.

Moos, R. (1979). *Evaluating Educational Environments*. Palo Alto, CA: Consulting Psychologists Press.

Morita, Akio with E.M. Reingold and Mitsuko Shimomura. (1990). *Made in Japan: Akio Morita and Sony*. New York: Fontana Press.

Mumford, M.D. and B. Licuanan. (2004). "Leading for Innovation: Conclusions, Issues and Directions," *The Leadership Quarterly*, 15(1): 163–71.

Nanda, H.P. (1992). *The Days of My Years*. New Delhi: Penguin Books.

Nilekani, N. (2008). *Imagining India: Ideas for the New Century*. New Delhi: Penguin Books.

Nunnally, J.C. (1978). *Psychometric Theory*. 2nd ed. New York: McGraw-Hill.

Ogbonna, E. and L.C. Harris. (2000). "Leadership Style, Organizational Culture and Performance: Empirical Evidence from UK Companies," *International Journal of Human Resource Management*, 11(4): 766–88.

Osho. 2010. "The Magnetic Third Eye that Attracts Attention." Available online at http://timesofindia.indiatimes.com/life-style/spirituality/speaking-tree/The-magnetic-third-eye-that-attracts-attention/articleshow/5473163.cms

Ouchi, W.G. (1980). "Markets, Bureaucracies and Clans," *Administrative Science Quarterly*, 25(1): 129–41.

Pamela, T., Steven M. Farmer, and George B. Graen. (1999). "An Examination of Leadership and Employee Creativity: The Relevance of Traits and Relationships," *Personnel Psychology*, 52(3): 591–620.

Pandit, S. (2005). *Exemplary CEOs: Insights on Organizational Transformation*. New Delhi: Tata McGraw-Hill Publication Ltd.

Peters, T. and R. Waterman. (1982). *In Search of Excellence*. New York: Random House.

Philips, Donald T. (1992). *Lincoln on Leadership—Executive Strategies for Tough Times*. New York: Warner Books.

Piramal, Gita. (1996). *Business Maharajas*. New Delhi: Penguin Books.

Piramal, Gita and J. Netarwala. (2005). *Smart Leadership: Insights for CEOs*. New Delhi: Portfolio Penguin.

Price, B. and G. Ritcheske. (2001). *True Leaders: How Exceptional CEOs and Presidents Make a Difference by Building People and Profits*. Chicago: Dearborn Trade Publication.

Ramanujan, K.S. (1993). *Glimpses of a Prince among Patriots*. Madras: Sundara Pachuralayarn.

Robert, S. (1999). *Jack Welch and the GE Way: Management Insights and Leadership Secrets of the Legendary CEO*. New York: McGraw-Hill.

Rogers, Carl. (1989). *On Becoming a Person*. London: Constable.

Rosen, R. (2000). *Global Literacies: Lessons on Business Leadership and National Cultures*. New York: Simon & Schuster.

Schares, Gail E. (1993). "Percy Barnevik's Global Crusade," *Business Week*, December 6, pp. 56–59.

Schein, E.H. (1981). *Organizational Culture and Leadership*. San Francisco: Jossey-Bass.

———. (1992). *Organizational Culture and Leadership*. 2nd ed. San Francisco: Jossey-Bass.

Schlender, Brenton. (1992). "How Sony Keeps the Magic Going," *Fortune*, India, February 24, p. 77.

Schuman, Michael (2009). "Global Business: Storm Riders (Strategy)," *Time International Asia*, 173(24): 41–43.

Sheehy, G. (1990). *The Man Who Changed the World: The Life of Mikhail Gorbachev*. New York: HarperCollins.

Sherman, Stratford (1993). "Andy Grove: How Intel Makes Spending Pay Off," *Fortune*, February 22, p. 57.
Singh, P. and A. Bhandarker. (1989). *Corporate Success and Transformational Leadership*. New Delhi: Wiley Eastern.
———. (1994). *IAS Profile: Myths and Realities*. New Delhi: Wiley Eastern.
———. (2002). *Winning the Corporate Olympiad*. New Delhi: Vikas Publishing House Pvt Ltd.
Singh, P. and S. Verma. (2010). *Organizing and Managing in the Era of Globalization*. New Delhi: Response Books.
Sosik, J.J. and L.E. Megerian. (1999). "Understanding Leader Emotional Intelligence and Performance: The Role of Self-other Agreement on Transformational Leadership Perceptions," *Group & Organization Management*, 24(3): 367–90.
Spencer, S.M., Tharuma Rajah, Shyamala A. Narayan, Seetharaman Mohan, and Gaurav Lahiri. (2007). *The Indian CEO: A Portrait of Excellence*. New Delhi: Response Books.
Spreitzer, Gretchen M. (2006). "Leading to Grow and Growing to Lead: Leadership Development Lessons from Positive Organizational Studies," *Organizational Dynamics*, 35(4): 305–15.
Srinivas, S. (2009). "Bringing about Change, Smartly," *Business World*, December 28.
Srivastava, M.K. (2003). *Transformational Leadership*. Delhi: MacMillan Publication.
Stemler, S. (2001). "An Overview of Content Analysis," *Practical Assessment, Research and Evaluation*, 7(17): 1–8.
Stewart, T.A and A.P. Raman. (2007). "Lessons from Toyota's Long Drive," *Harvard Business Review*, 85(7/8, July/August): 74–83.
Strauss, A. and J. Corbin. (1990). *Basics of Qualitative Research: Grounded Theory Procedures and Techniques*. Newbury Park: Sage Publications.
Tichy, N.M. (2002). *The Cycle of Leadership*. New York: HarperCollins.
Tichy, N.M. and Stratford Sherman (1993). *Control Your Destiny or Someone Else Will: How Jack Welch is Making General Electric the World's Most Competitive Company*. New York: Double Day Currency.
Thomas, Edmund. (2007). *World's Greatest Speeches*. New Delhi: Pentagon Press.
Thomas, Prince Mathew. (2009). "The Lakshmi Mittal Interview—Of Strikes, Job Cuts, the Recession and His Vision," *Forbes*, India, May 18. Available online at http://business.in.com/interview/magazine-extra/the-lakshmi-mittal-interview/502/1 (downloaded on October 19, 2009).
Ulrich, D. and N. Smallwood. (2007). "Building a Leadership Brand," *Harvard Business Review*, 85(7/8, July–August): 92–100.
Walton, Sam. (1993). *Made in America—My Story*. New York: Bantam Books.

Watson, Lillian Eichler. (1988). *Light from Many Lamps*. New York: Fireside Book, Simon & Schuster.

Zacarro, S.J. (1996). *Models and Theories of Executive Leadership: A Conceptual/ Empirical Review and Integration*. Alexandria, VA: US Army Research Institute for the Behavioral and Social Sciences.

Zakaria, Rafiq (ed.). (1989). *A Study of Nehru*. New Delhi: Rupa and Co.

Zhihong, W. (2010). "Few Words but Many Seeds' Councels Chemchina President," *China Business Weekly*, January 9–10, p. 8.

Zohar, Danah. (1990). *The Quantum Self: Human Nature and Consciousness Defined by the New Physics*. New York: Quill/William Morrow.

INDEX

Here "f" with page reference refers to figure and "t" with page reference refers to table.

ABB, 19, 22
Action architecture
    Bharti Airtel, 253–266
    Biocon, 358–374
    comparative picture, 412t, 413
    ICICI Bank, 200–215
    IDBI, 122–123
    JSW Group, 155–167
    Larsen & Toubro (L&T), 299–316
    patterns, Change Maestros and, 445–446
    Sajjan Jindal, 175–176
    UTI, 104–105, 106, 121–122
Aditya Birla Group, 47–94
    accolades to, 84t–87t
    achievements, 61
    corporate social responsibility and, 53–54
    culture landscape of, 61
    employee retention and, 56–57
    financial performance of, 90, 90t
    futuristic orientation of, 55–56
    Gandhian idea of trusteeship and, 51
    global perspective of, 54–55, 61
    history, 79–80
    HR policy of, 57
    inheritors of, 80–82
    organizational culture of, 88t–89t, 89–90
    overview of, 49–50
    performance standards and, 58–59
    robust growth strategy of, 57–58
    robust processes of, 53
    transformation of, 59–61, 78
    Triple Bottom Line and, 54
    value-based indian multinational, 78–87
    value-driven governance, 50–54
ADR. *See* American Depositary Receipt (ADR)
Aggarwal, Askaran, 60
Airtel. *See* Bharti Airtel
Ambani, Dhirubhai, 14, 16, 20
American Constitutional System, 23
American Depositary Receipt (ADR), 232
ARPU. *See* Average Revenue Per User (ARPU)
Average Revenue Per User (ARPU), 255

Balanced Score Card Systems, 262
Barnevik, Percy, 9, 19, 24–25
Bharti Airtel, 280–286
    action architecture of, 253–266
    brief profile of, 253
    business innovations in, 257–258
    culture landscape of, 253–266
    customer centric, 259–260
    employee retention and, 261–262
    entrepreneurial architecture, 254–256
    ethical governance, 263–264
    financial performance of, 290t
    growth of, 284–286
    IBM and, 282
    mega vision of, 258–259
    mosaic culture, 264–265

organizational culture of, 288t–289t, 289–290
performance excellence, 262–263
recognition and accolades to, 286t–287t
uniqueness of, 254
Bhatt, O.P., 19
Biocon
　action architecture of, 359–375
　brief profile, 359–360
　business model, 398, 399f
　corporate social responsibility, 398–400
　culture landscape of, 359–376
　empowerment, 367–368
　entrepreneurial orientation, 364–365
　ethical governance in, 375
　financial performance of, 405t
　futuristic approach, 365–366
　global vision, 365
　growth strategy, 365–366
　happening place, 369–371
　history, 393–396
　Innovation Matrix, 396–398, 397f
　non-hierarchical culture, 368–369
　organizational culture of, 403t–404t, 404–405
　quest for excellence, 371–373
　recognition and accolades to, 400t–401t
　strategy, 361–363
"Biotech Queen," 359
Birla, Aditya Vikram, 9, 20, 79
Birla, Ghanshyam Das, 9, 20, 27, 79
Birla, Kumar Mangalam, xxx, 48–49, 74–78, 82–84. *See also* Aditya Birla Group
　accolades to, 76, 77t–78t
　as Change Maestro, 73–74, 91–93, 91t–92t
　empowering style, 68–70
　ethical orientation of, 65–67
　intellectual power, 70
　interpersonal skills, 64–65
　personality traits of, 62–75
　positions held by, 76
　principle of, 52
　as "silent contributor," 63
　as strategic thinker, 67–68

Birla, Shiv Narayan Seth, 80
Birla Institute of Technology and Science (BITS), 80
BITS. *See* Birla Institute of Technology and Science (BITS)
Boldness, A.M. Naik, 326–327
Branden, Nathaniel, 29, 456
Bureaucrats, 4
Business architecture
　of Bharti Airtel, 254–256

Carlson, Jan, 7
CDR. *See* Corporate debt restructuring (CDR)
Change Maestro
　A.M. Naik as, 334–335, 350t–351t, 352
　behavior, factors of, 421–423, 422t, 423f
　behavior, rotated component matrix of, 432t–435t
　dominant profile, 419, 419t
　holistic integration and, 450, 454f
　impact on financial performance, 424–427, 426t
　Kiran Mazumdar Shaw as, 389–390, 403t–405t, 405–406
　Kumar Mangalam Birla as, 73–74, 91–93, 91t–92t
　K.V. Kamath as, 228–229, 244t–245t, 245–247
　M. Damodaran as, 135–136, 147–149, 147t–148t
　organizational culture and, 409–416, 424–427, 425f
　organizational level integration and, 451, 453f, 458–459
　profile, 416–418, 417t–418t, 446–447
　role of academic institutions, 457–458
　role of family, 456–457
　Sajjan Jindal as, 182–183, 192t–193t, 193–194
　self-assessment vs. perceptions, 420, 420t
　self-level integration and, 451, 452f, 456
　similarities between, 420, 421t
　style and culture of, measurement models for, 437–438, 437t, 438t

INDEX   473

Sunil Bharti Mittal as, 276–277,
    291t–292t, 292–293
Change Maestros, 3–44
    conceptualization, 32
    contextual sensitivity, 6–8
    creative destruction, 21–25
    goals, 18–21
    identification, 33–34
    inventroy, 36–38
    organizational culture. *See*
        Organizational culture
    people connect and engagement,
        16–18
    self evolution, 25–29
    vision and purpose, 8–12
    winning streak, 12–16
Collins, Jim, 74
Communication strategy
    for IDBI, 109–110
    for UTI, 107–109
Connolly, John, 10
Content analysis method, 43
Contextual sensitivity, 6–8
Corporate debt restructuring (CDR), 172
Corporate social responsibility (CSR)
    Aditya Birla Group and, 53–54
    Biocon, 396–399
Creative destruction, 21–25
    deterrents to, 22
Credibility, of M. Damodaran, 132–133
Croc, Ray, 23
CSR. *See* Corporate social responsibility
    (CSR)

Damodaran, M., xxx–xxxi, 98–99,
    136–139. *See also* IDBI; UTI
    accolades to, 138t
    as Change Maestro, 135–136, 147–149,
        147t–148t
    credibility, 132–133
    empowerment by, 112–115
    enabler par excellence, 131
    ethical governance by, 117–118
    favorite mantra, 134
    humane orientation, 128–130
    interpersonal skill, 130–131
    personality traits of, 122–135

positivity, 132
    powerful communicator, 125–127
    renaissance artiste, 98–149
    strategic initiatives by, 107–121
    as talent shaper, 133–134
    and timely decision-making, 119
    as visionary strategist, 123–124
Development Financial Institution (DFI),
    102, 143, 199
DFI. *See* Development Financial
    Institution (DFI)
Dhawan, Satish, 17

"Easy Day," 285
EDs. *See* Executive Directors (EDs)
EFA. *See* Exploratory Factor Analysis
    (EFA)
"Emerging Corporate Olympiad: Mantras
    to Lead," xxviii
Employee Stock Ownership Plans
    (ESOPs), 161, 305
Empowerment, 112–115, 306–307, 365–368
    with accountability, 159–160, 210
Enabler
    M. Damodaran as, 131
Entrepreneurial innovation
    Larsen & Toubro, 307–309
Entrepreneurial ownership, ICICI Bank,
    204–206
Escorts Ltd, 11
ESOPs. *See* Employee Stock Ownership
    Plans (ESOPs)
Ethical governance
    Bharti Airtel, 263–264
    Biocon, 375
    JSW Group, 162–163
    by M. Damodaran, 117–118
Evolution, of self. *See* self evolution
Executive Directors (EDs), 100
Exploratory Factor Analysis (EFA), 416,
    424t

Fielmann, Gunther, 10
Financial performance
    of Aditya Birla Group, 90, 90t
    of Bharti Airtel, 290t
    of Biocon, 405t

Change Maestros' impact on, 426–429, 428t
  of ICICI Bank, 238, 243, 243t
  of JSW Group, 191t
  of Larsen & Toubro, 351t

Gandhi, xxvii
Gandhi, Mohandas Karamchand, 8, 13, 26
  leadership qualities, global impacts of, xxvi–xxviii
Gates, Bill, 11
GE, 22–23, 24
Gestalt duality, 451–454
GFI. *See* Goodness-of-Fit Index (GFI)
Global perspective
  of Aditya Birla Group, 54–55, 61
  Biocon, 365
  ICICI Bank, 206–207
Goals, 18–21
Goodness-of-Fit Index (GFI), 437
Gorbachev, M., 8, 21, 27
Governance and Value Creation (GVC), 263
Green, Stephen, 12–13
Grounded Theory Method, 42–43
Grove, Andy, 11, 14, 23–24
GVC. *See* Governance and Value Creation (GVC)

Holck-Larsen, Henning, 339
Honda, Soichiro, 18–19
Humane orientation
  M. Damodaran, 128–130
Humility
  Sunil Bharti Mittal, 273–274

IBM, and Bharti Airtel, 282
ICICI Bank, 231–238
  achievements, 215
  action architecture of, 200–215
  brief profile of, 199–200
  contribution-centric meritocracy, 211–212
  culture landscape of, 200–215
  empowerment with accountability, 210
  entrepreneurial ownership, 204–206, 215
  financial performance of, 238, 243, 243t
  global perspective, 206–207
  growth strategy, 200–202
  Indian financial sector and, 202–203
  milestones achieved by, 237
  operations, 233–234, 234f
  organizational culture of, 240t–241t, 241–243
  recognitions and accolades to, 238t
  role of technology in, 210–211
  as seamless organization, 209–210
  speedy execution, 207–209
  stretched goals setting, 206–207
  as talent shapers, 213–214
  work culture, 215
IDBI
  action architecture of, 122–123
  brief overview of, 102–103
  brief profile of, 143–145
  communication strategy for, 109–110
  empowerment in, 112–115
  ethical governance, 117–118
  organizational culture of, 145–147, 145t–146t
  performance orientation in, 120
  role clarifcation, 121
  strategic initiatives for, 107–121
  transformation of, 106
  Vision/Mission statement for, 111
  VRS in, 106
Idea Cellular, 55
Indian financial sector
  ICICI Bank and, 202–203
Indian Rayon and Industries Limited (IRIL), 81
Indo-Thai Synthetics Company Ltd, 81
Innovation Matrix, of Biocon, 396–398, 397f
Interpersonal skill
  M. Damodaran, 130–131
Interpersonal skills
  Kiran Mazumdar Shaw, 371–382
  Kumar Mangalam Birla, 64–65
  Sunil Bharti Mittal, 271–272
Interviews
  Change Maestro, 42

technique analysis, 42–43
top management team, 41–42
Inventories, 36–41
    Change Maestro, 36–38
    organizational culture, 39–41
IRIL. *See* Indian Rayon and Industries Limited (IRIL)

Jindal, Om Prakash, 185
Jindal, Sajjan, xxxi, 153–194. *See also* JSW Group
    accolades to, 188t
    action architecture, 175–176
    as Change Maestro, 182–183, 192t–193t, 193–194
    courageous and optimistic, 170–173
    optimism, 170–173
    people centricity and, 177–179
    personality traits of, 167–182
    resilience, 169–170
    social concerns, 179–181
    wealth-creating capability of, 173–175
Jindal Iron and Steel Company Ltd (JISCO), 155
JISCO. *See* Jindal Iron and Steel Company Ltd (JISCO)
Joint Parliamentary Committee (JPC), 101
Joint Plan Committee (JPC), 127
JPC. *See* Joint Parliamentary Committee (JPC); Joint Plan Committee (JPC)
JSW Group
    action architecture of, 155–167
    bar of excellence, 160
    brief profile of, 155, 184–186
    culture landscape of, 155–167
    employee centricity, 161–162
    empowerment with accountability, 159–160
    entrepreneurial style of functioning, 156–158
    ethical governance, 162–163
    financial performance of, 191t
    growth, 158–159
    mega growth vision of, 156
    organizational culture of, 189t–190t, 190–191
    performance management system, 161
    recognition and accolades to, 187t–188t
    social concerns, 163–165
    talent shaper, 165–166

Kalam, A.P.J. Abdul, 9, 17
Kamath, K.V., xxxi, 197–247. *See also* ICICI Bank
    accolades to, 239t–240t
    ambition, 217–218
    as Change Maestro, 228–229, 244t–245t, 245–247
    as entrepreneurial strategist, 218–220
    futuristic vision of, 216–217
    goal of excellence, 224–225
    learning orientation of, 226–227
    personality traits of, 216–228
    as statesman, 227–228
    strong memory, 225–226
    as talent shaper, 220–222
Kelleher, Herb, 16
King, Martin Luther, 8
Kochhar, Chanda, 235
Kume, Tadashi, 19

Lafley, A.G., 13
Lao Tzu, 16–17
Larsen & Toubro (L&T), 56, 339–346
    action architecture of, 299–316
    brief profile of, 298–299
    as caring organization, 311–312
    contribution-centric meritocracy, 312–314
    culture landscape of, 299–316
    customer centric, 310–311
    empowerment, 306–307
    entrepreneurial innovation, 307–309
    as ethical organization, 309–310
    financial performance of, 351t
    futuristic approach, 300–302
    global thrust, 302–304
    growth strategy, 304–305
    history, 339
    organizational culture of, 348t–349t, 350–351
    projects undertaken by, 341t–343t
    quest for excellence, 299–300

recognition and accolades to, 344t–345t
Leadership
  crisis, causes for, 450–453
Leadership, 3–4, 5. *See also* Change Maestros
  political, 4
Lincoln, Abraham, 8, 14, 20–21, 27
L&T. *See* Larsen & Toubro (L&T)

Mahindra, Keshub, 25
Malhotra, Naresh, 11
Malka, Puran, 60
Mandela, Nelson, 13
Mangalore Refineries and Petroleum Chemicals Ltd (MRPL), 52
Matsushita, 10, 27–28
Matsushita Electric Industrial Co. (MEI), 10
Maximum Likelihood Estimation (MLE) algorithm, 439
McDonald, 23
MEI. *See* Matsushita Electric Industrial Co. (MEI)
Meritocracy, contribution-centric
  ICICI Bank, 211–212
  Larsen & Toubro, 312–314
Mittal, L.N., 11, 20
Mittal, Sunil Bharti, xxxi–xxxii, 250–293. *See also* Bharti Airtel
  accolades to, 279t–280t
  achievement, 283
  as Change Maestro, 276–277, 291t–292t, 292–293
  empowering style of, 269
  ethical nature, 274
  global vision, 275
  as great learner, 272–273
  humility, 273–274
  inspiring and motivating leader, 270–271
  interpersonal skills, 271–272
  personality traits of, 266–276
  profile of, 278–279
  strong entrepreneurial spirit of, 268–269
  visionary, 267–268
  winning philosophy of, 263
  winning streak, 275
MLE algorithm. *See* Maximum Likelihood Estimation (MLE) algorithm
Moments of Truth, 7
Mosaic culture, Bharti Airtel, 264–265
"Mother of Invention," 359
MRPL. *See* Mangalore Refineries and Petroleum Chemicals Ltd (MRPL)
My Experiments with Truth, 26

Naik, A.M., xxxii, 297–353. *See also* Larsen & Toubro (L&T)
  accolades to, 346t–347t
  ambition, 318–319
  boldness, 326–328
  as Change Maestro, 335–336, 351t–352t, 353
  elephantine memory, 332–333
  employee centricity, 328–329
  futuristic vision of, 319–320
  learning orientation, 329–331
  passion for work, 317–318
  as perfect entrepreneur, 325
  personality traits of, 316–334
  simplicity, 331
  strategic thinking capability, 321–322
Nanda, H.P., 11
Nano, 19
NAV. *See* Net Asset Value (NAV)
Net Asset Value (NAV), 99
Newtonian reductionism, 451–453
Nilekani, Nandan, 9
Non-performing Assets (NPAs), 103
Novak, David, 17
NPAs. *See* Non-performing Assets (NPAs)

Openness, organizational, 111–112
Optimism, Sajjan Jindal, 170–173
Organizational culture, 29–31
  Aditya Birla Group, 88t–89t, 89–90
  Bharti Airtel, 288t–289t, 289–290
  Biocon, 403t–404t, 404–405
  Change Maestro and, 411–418
  comparative picture of, 414t, 415–416, 415t–416t

conceptualization, 32
defined, 29–30
factors of, 416–418, 417f, 417t
ICICI Bank, 240t–241t, 241–243
inventory, 39–41
JSW Group, 189t–190t, 190–191
Larsen & Toubro, 348t–349t, 350–351
overall mean values of, 412t–413t, 413
patterns, Change Maestros and, 447–449
rotated component matrix of, 430t–433t
UTI/IDBI, 145–147, 145t–146t

People connect and engagement, 16–18
Personality traits
A.M. Naik, 316–334
Kiran Mazumdar Shaw, 376–391
Kumar Mangalam Birla, 62–75
K.V. Kamath, 216–228
M. Damodaran, 122–135
Sajjan Jindal, 167–182
Sunil Bharti Mittal, 266–276
Political leaders, 4
Positivity, of M. Damodaran, 132
Pythagoras, 450–451

Ren Jian Xin, 10
Research methodology, 31–36
RMSEA. *See* Root Mean Square Error of Approximation (RMSEA)
Rogers, Carl, 28–29, 456
Root Mean Square Error of Approximation (RMSEA), 437
Russell, Bertrand, 491

SARFAESI Act. *See* Securitization and Reconstruction of Financial Assets and Enforcement of Security Interests (SARFAESI) Act
SASF. *See* Stressed Asset Stabilization Fund (SASF)
Satya Bharti School program, 285
SBI. *See* State Bank of India (SBI)
SBUs. *See* Strategic business units (SBUs)

Securitization and Reconstruction of Financial Assets and Enforcement of Security Interests (SARFAESI) Act, 202
Self-awareness, 28
Self evolution, 25–29
Shaw, Kiran Mazumdar, xxxii, 357–408. *See also* Biocon
accolades to, 400t–401t
caring nature of, 387–388
as Change Maestro, 391–392, 405t–407t, 407–408
empowering and trusting person, 388–389
entrepreneurial risk takers, 378–379
excellence seeker, 380–381
futuristic approach, 378
highly ambitious, 377
high moral values, 388–387
humility in, 382–383
innovative person, 385–386
inspirational power of, 389–390
interpersonal skills, 381–383
learnability, 384–385
outstanding business strategist, 379
personality traits of, 376–391
profile, 401–402
Smith, D., 28
Smith, Lou, 17
Smith, Stan, 17
Sony Corporation, 11
South West Airlines, 16
Specified Undertaking of UTI (SUUTI), 104
State Bank of India (SBI), 19
Statesman
K.V. Kamath as, 227–228
Strategic business units (SBUs), 58
Strategic initiatives
for UTI/IDBI, by M. Damodaran, 107–121
Stressed Asset Stabilization Fund (SASF), 106, xxxi
Stretched goals
setting of, ICICI Bank, 206–207
SUUTI. *See* Specified Undertaking of UTI (SUUTI)

Talent management, 115–116
Tata, J.R.D., 10–11, 14, 16
Tata, Ratan, 19–20
Tichy, Noel, 28
Toubro, S.K., 338
Transformation
 of Aditya Birla Group, 59–61, 78
 of IDBI, 106
Transparency International Survey, 2008, 51
Triple Bottom Line principle
 Aditya Birla Group and, 54
Trusteeship, Gandhian idea of
 Aditya Birla Group and, 51

UCE. See Unique competitive edge (UCE)
Unique competitive edge (UCE), 213
Unit Scheme-64 (US-64), UTI, 99, 101–102, 139
US-64, UTI. See Unit Scheme-64 (US-64), UTI
UTI
 action architecture of, 104–105, 106, 121–122
 brief overview of, 99–102
 brief profle of, 139–143
 communication strategy for, 107–109
 empowerment in, 112–115
 ethical governance, 117–118
 organizational culture of, 145–147, 145t–146t
 performance orientation in, 120
 recognition and accolades to, 140t–143t
 role clarifcation, 121
 strategic initiatives for, 107–121
 Vision/Mission statement for, 110
 VRS in, 105, 117

Vagul, N., 235
Value-driven governance, Aditya Birla Group, 50–54
Vision, 8–12
Visionary, Sunil Bharti Mittal, 267–268
Voluntary Retirement Scheme (VRS)
 in IDBI, 106
 in UTI, 105, 117
VRS. see Voluntary Retirement Scheme (VRS)

Watanabe, Katsuake, 9–10
Wealth-creating strategy
 Sajjan Jindal, 173–175
Welch, Jack, 9, 22–23, 24, 28
Weldon, William C., 10
Wilson, Joseph, 11
Winning streak
 Sunil Bharti Mittal, 275

Yamashita, 23

ABOUT THE AUTHORS AND RESEARCH TEAM

THE AUTHORS

An inspiring role model, **Pritam Singh** has spent his entire life tirelessly doing what he does best: awakening students, academia, corporate heads, and policy makers to raise their excellence to the next level. As the Chairman and Member of several policy-making committees and bodies of Government of India (GOI), he has stamped his perspective on policy issues that surround both management education and corporate management in India. As a consultant, he has worked with more than 200 CEOs in India and abroad.

Dr Pritam Singh has been one of the main architects for the Central Ministers' and Secretaries' Retreats in the Administrative Staff College of India, Hyderabad, to actualize the vision of Late Shri Rajiv Gandhi for developing the Central Ministers and Secretaries, Government of India, as transformational leaders and Change Masters.

As an academic administrator, Dr Pritam Singh has an unparalleled record of making significant differences in his roles as Director at Indian Institute of Management (IIM) Lucknow and Management Development Institute (MDI), Gurgaon and as Dean at the Administrative Staff College of India, Hyderabad, and IIM Bangalore. In the contemporary management world, he is, therefore, known as a Midas-touch leader.

A thought leader with extraordinary insight, Dr Pritam Singh is the author of seven academically reputed books, three of which are award winners. He has also published over sixty research papers in various national and international journals. He is a globally sought-after speaker and has addressed audiences in various countries.

His distinguished services were acknowledged by the country when the President of India conferred on him the prestigious "Padma Shri" award. MIRBIS, the leading global, management school in Moscow, honored him as the "Global Thought Leader" in 2006–2007. He was not just the first Indian, but the first Asian to have walked into this global hall of fame. He has also been the recipient of several prestigious awards, such as: the "Sarvapalli Radhakrishnan Memorial Award: Teacher of Teachers"; the "Lifetime Achievement Award by Vivekananda Foundation"; the TIE-UP California USA Outstanding Entrepreneur Award; Outstanding CEO, NHRD Award; Best Director Award of Indian Management Schools; and the First AIMA–Kewal Nohria Award for Academic Leadership in Management Education.

Asha Bhandarker is Raman Munjal Hero Honda Chair Professor of Leadership Studies at MDI, Gurgaon. She is a distinguished psychologist and a management thinker. She has been awarded the best teacher award at MDI and has received the best book award for her book titled *Winning the Corporate Olympiad: Renaissance Paradigm*. Her recent publication is titled *Shaping Business Leaders: What B Schools Don't Do*. She also has five published books and many articles in various national and international journals. Dr Bhandarker has been a Senior Fulbrighter and a Visiting Professor at Darden School of Business, University of Virginia and at George Mason University. She has been a visiting fellow at the London Business School.

The Research Team

Ajay Jain is Associate Professor in Organizational Behavior at MDI, Gurgaon. He has done his PhD from Indian Institute of Technology (IIT), Kanpur and a post-doctoral fellowship at Indian School of Business, Hyderabad. He has more than ten years of work experience. Dr Jain's research interests are Emotional Intelligence, Organizational Citizenship Behavior, and Leadership.

ABOUT THE AUTHORS AND RESEARCH TEAM

Sumita Rai is Associate Professor in Organizational Behavior at MDI, Gurgaon. She has done her PhD from IIT, Kanpur. She has more than ten years of work experience. Before joining MDI, she has been Faculty at IIM Lucknow and IIM Indore. Dr Rai's areas of interests are Leadership, Employee Motivation, Values, and Organizational Culture.